THE ART HERITAGE OF INDIA

Ladies in a Pleasure Garden. Last quarter of the 17th century. Sporting in a garden is an important feature of Sanskrit and Braja Bhasha poetry. The composition here is simple yet most effective. The colouring, with its massed greens relieved by spots of white and red flowers, is very effective. The colours of the costumes blend perfectly with the rest of the picture so that the general effect is extraordinarily rich yet without spoiling the harmony of the colour scheme.

(Courtesy, Prince of Wales Museum of Western India, Bombay)

THE
ART HERITAGE
OF INDIA

Comprising

INDIAN SCULPTURE AND PAINTING

AND

IDEALS OF INDIAN ART

by

E. B. HAVELL

Formerly Principal of the Government School of Art
and Keeper of the Art Gallery, Calcutta

Revised Edition with Notes

by

PRAMOD CHANDRA

Curator, Art Section, Prince of Wales Museum of Western India, Bombay

With 18 plates in colour and 207 monochrome illustrations

D. B. TARAPOREVALA SONS & CO. PRIVATE LTD.

TREASURE HOUSE OF BOOKS

210, Dr. D. Naoroji Road, Bombay 1

Published by Jal H. Taraporevala, for Messrs. D. B. Taraporevala Sons & Co. Private Ltd.,
Taj Building, 210, Dr. Dadabhai Naoroji Road, Fort, Bombay, and Printed by D. D. Karkaria
at Leaders Press Private Ltd., 108, Love Lane, Mazagaon, Bombay-10.

PREFACE TO NEW EDITION

WITH the end of the Pahari schools of painting in the nineteenth century the last vestiges of traditional art can be said to have disappeared from this country, and strange to say even its memory was all but lost within the passing of a few generations. The great artistic creations of ancient India had been lost and forgotten much earlier and reacquaintance with this aspect of our heritage really began with the researches of British and other European scholars into the antiquity of India. In the course of their labours they discovered once again the fallen monuments of the past, but by temperament and training they were unable to assess their true significance. Their reaction was a mixture of astonishment and revulsion, couched often in extreme language, which sought to deny the very existence of anything like Indian art, so that one is often led to wonder what it was that drove them to their labours, the fruits of which were so bitter.

It is also surprising to note the rapidity with which the Indian brought into association with Western culture began to loose his taste for Indian art, an aspect of his character that was the first to give way before alien pressures. Patronage shifted from traditional objects of art to tawdry works of European manufacture or its feeble native imitations. His religious instincts, however, were stronger and more deeply entrenched and this would account for the extra-ordinary popularity for the output of an artist like Ravi Varma which combined an academic realism of the most debased kind with an outward religiosity that still evoked spontaneous response.

It was against this arid and desert background that E. B. Havell, a remarkable Englishman by any standards, began his work the aim of which was to awaken a new love for the rich and forgotten heritage of our art through a proper understanding of its ideals, his words being directed not only to the Indians of his generation who needed to be reminded of their heritage, but all lovers of art. Displaying rare sensitiveness, he sought to grasp its message with a fine artistic perception. To him there existed a close connection between the forms of Indian art and the thought of which they are an expression, any true understanding and appreciation being impossible if Indian art was divorced from its religious, philosophical and symbolical aspects. If this was done, all that would be achieved, at the very best, would be an appreciation of mere surfaces, quite insufficient and inadequate for any real understanding.

Havell put forth these revolutionary ideas in *Indian Sculpture and Painting*, first published in 1908, and so electrifying was its impact that the work will count as a classic among the books on Indian art for a long time. In it he expounded his views with much persuasiveness and what we may now regard as missionary zeal, but there are passages full of eloquence and flashes of insight. He had his predilections too, and it is difficult for us to understand his under-estimation of the brilliant, nervous art of Amaravati, his evaluation of Indian influences on Chinese art which are sometimes far-fetched, or even his excessive praise for the phases of Indian art from the seventh-eighth century to the fourteenth century. One can understand the scorn he lavished upon the archaeologists and art historians of his time as he felt that it was their dead weight that was stifling true appreciation ; but it is now becoming clear that their pedestrian researches as well as those of their successors have resulted today in the proper classification of styles and the fixation of a broad chronological development that is as necessary to a complete and integrated understanding of art as are the efforts of the brilliant scholars and interpreters who expound its inner nature and lay bare the hidden sources of inspiration.

There was hostile reaction to his work also, and it is interesting in this connection to

v

recall the outburst of Sir George Birdwood, otherwise a sensitive and sympathetic observer of other expressions of Indian culture. At the close of a lecture by Havell arranged at the Royal Society of Arts in 1910, he was provoked to deliver an invective which was amongst the last of its kind : "Of 'fine art', the unfettered and impassioned realisation of the ideals kindled within us, by the things without us, I have upto the present, and through an experience of seventy-eight years, found no examples in India," and regarding the image of the Buddha, illustrated here as Plate 2A, he was equally caustic. "This senseless similitude in its immemorial fixed pose is nothing more than an uninspired brazen image, vacuously squinting down its nose to its thumbs and knees and toes. A boiled suet pudding would serve equally well as a symbol of passionless purity and serenity of soul." But the tide had begun to turn and the years that have passed since have witnessed the recognition of Indian art as an outstanding contribution to the sum of our artistic heritages.

A larger part of this success is no doubt due to his great successor Ananda Coomaraswamy who continued to interpret the message of Indian art with masterly erudition, unrivalled knowledge, and a sweeping breadth of vision, in a written style which is a model of precision, clarity and beauty. The present position of Indian art is largely due to the efforts of these two scholars whose work is so alike and at the same time so different from each other's.

Havell's other great service to Indian art was the inspiration he provided to Abanindra Nath Tagore which ultimately led to the creation of the modern Bengal School. Apart from its merits as an artistic style (Coomaraswamy was to comment that the artists of the Bengal School knew what they had to feel but there was no evidence, in their art, to show that they had actually felt), the School was primarily responsible for a deeper awareness amongst practicing artists of the mainsprings of their own art, and of the rich sources to which they were the real inheritors.

When Havell passed away in 1934 there was great sorrow amongst his numerous friends as well as admirers of Indian art. One can do no better than quote the words of Rabindranath Tagore : "E. B. Havell has passed away. The guiding spirit that led the revival of true Indian art ceases to be. This great Englishman came to show us the right path with his lamp of sympathy and understanding when we had lost confidence in our power to create and cherished a pathetic faith in the imitation of the West. With infinite patience he taught us to bring our offerings to the altar of our own gods. His efforts are richly rewarded by the inspiration to such masters as Abanindra Nath Tagore, Nandalal Bose and many others. No elaborate monument is required to perpetuate his name, for the work of Abanindra Nath Tagore and his school will be a living tribute to Mr. Havell's memory for all times to come."

This edition of Havell's *Indian Sculpture and Painting*, and *Ideals of Indian Art*, is a reprint of the editions of these books issued in 1928 and 1920 respectively, together with additional information about certain aspects of which he was either unaware or which require revision in the light of recent researches. These are given in the form of footnotes distinguished from the author's original notes by the appended initials, "P.C." Where the matter is of some length it has been put as an Appendix. Besides the original illustrations, several new ones have been incorporated and captioned by the Publishers to illustrate Havell's text as well as the editorial notes and appendices.

—P.C.

CONTENTS

PART I: INDIAN SCULPTURE AND PAINTING

SCULPTURE

Page

CHAPTER I: INTRODUCTORY 5-9

The change of attitude towards Indian art in Europe and in India—The ideals and characteristics of Indian art—Yoga and the Divine Ideal—The Himalayas in Indian art—The Indian Order of Architecture.

CHAPTER II: THE EVOLUTION OF THE DIVINE IDEAL 10-15

The mystery of the Divine Form—Yantras, or geometric symbols—Early Buddhism and Yoga— Kailāsa, the nave of the universal wheel—Mahāyāna Buddhism and image-worship—The great epoch of Indian sculpture and painting—The Images of the Divine Thinker—Mathematics and aesthetics—A symbol of the Creator's Mind—Indian and Chinese images—Indian artistic anatomy— The place of the Gandhāran school in Indian art.

CHAPTER III: THE EVOLUTION OF THE DIVINE IDEAL (*Continued*) .. 16-19

The symbolism of the triangle—The Image of the Divine Mother—Yantra and Mantra—A Sanskrit treatise on aesthetics—Images of Tārā, the Saviouress—The Divine Power as god and goddess— The androgynous image—The Divine Embrace—The conflict between good and evil—Shākta philosophy and art—Kāli.

CHAPTER IV: MYTHOLOGY AND METAPHYSICS 20-26

Sukrachārya on image-making—The keynote of Indian art—Anthropomorphism in images—The Divine Form in the Bhagavad Gītā—Multiple arms and heads—Images of Dharmapāla, Manjusri, and the Buddhist Trimūrti—Durgā slaying Mahisha—Sculpture at Elephanta and Ellora—Art in India a living force.

CHAPTER V: THE DANCE OF SIVA 27-30

The symbolism of the Dance—Ganesha.

CHAPTER VI: SCHOOLS OF SCULPTURE AND PAINTING 31-35

Brahmanical influence on Buddhist art—India's unbroken tradition—The Chola School of sculpture surviving in the present day—The renaissance of art in India—The modern Orissa School—A survey of Indian art and craft—A Tibetan writer on the Indian schools of sculpture and painting.

CHAPTER VII: THE HUMAN IDEAL AND THE SCULPTURES OF BHĀRHUT, SĀNCHĪ, AND AMARĀVATĪ 36-45

Indian idealism in relation to the art of everyday life—Art and education in ancient India—Art and Nature—The inspiration of Indian art—The technical characteristics of the sculptures of Bhārhut, Sānchī, and Amarāvatī—Their place in the evolution of the Indian ideal—The Amarāvatī sculptures and the influence of Gandhāran art—The ancient Indian universities the art centres of Asia.

vii

Page

CHAPTER VIII: BOROBUDUR—THE KAILĀSA OF JAVA 46-54

The old chronicles of Java and modern archaeological research—The design of Borobudur derived from the Indian stūpa—The symbolism of the stūpa—The builders' reminiscences of the pilgrimage to Kailāsa—Borobudur as the cosmic Yantra—The Dhyāni-Buddhas—The skyline of Borobudur—The sculptures of the procession path, eleven panels described and illustrated—The ethical value of Indian art.

CHAPTER IX: HINDU ART IN JAVA AND CAMBODIA—PORTRAITURE 55-61

The sculptures of Prambānam—Nakhon Vat—Portraiture in Indian sculpture—Ethnical types in uncanonical religious art—Two heads of Bhima—A head of the Buddha—A horse and charioteer from Kanārak in Orissa—Image of Kuvera—A Tibetan nun—National tradition and individualism in art.

PAINTING

CHAPTER X: INDIAN MURAL PAINTING 65-76

The great schools of mural painting—The *chitra-sālas*—Indian fresco—References to picture painting in Sanskrit literature—The Ajantā paintings, not merely an art of line—The great painting in Cave XVII—Head of Bodhisattva—The technical process of the Ajantā paintings—Modern Indian *fresco-buono*—The Sittannavāsal paintings—The Sigiri paintings—The Bagh paintings—The Ajantā tradition in modern times—Vaishnava icons—The Tibetan school—Colour symbolism—Popular pictorial art in the present day.

CHAPTER XI: PAINTING IN MOGUL TIMES 77-86

The Mongolian invasion and its effect on art—Oriental craftsmen as missionaries of civilisation—Their influence in Byzantine and Gothic art—Indian artist-missionaries in China—The rise of the Mogul school of painting—A picture by Shapur of Khurasan—Indian miniature painting in the reigns of Akbar and Jahāngīr—Rembrandt's use of Indian drawings—Shah Jahān and Aurangzīb.

CHAPTER XII: TYPICAL INDIAN MINIATURE PAINTINGS 87-96

Calligraphy and brush-drawing—Two brush-line drawings of Shah Jahān's school—A drawing by Ghulām—Portrait of Shah Jahān's Poet Laureate, by Bichitr—Portrait of Sultan Muhammad Kutb Shah of Golconda, by Mir Hashim—Portrait of Dara Shikoh—Ustād Mansūr and his work—Manohar—Genre painting by Bichitr—The Hindu schools of painting—Landscape—Indian impressionism—Night and effects of artificial light—The eighteenth century and after—Portraits of Europeans by an Indian artist—The modern tradition.

CHAPTER XIII: THE FUTURE OF INDIAN ART 97-109

Summary of historical development—Indian art in the nineteenth century—Art and the universities—The Victoria Memorial and New Delhi—The social position of Indian artists, past and present—Art administration and its effect—Public opinion and modern artistic taste—A renaissance of Indian painting—The Bombay and the New Calcutta Schools—The significance of the revival.

APPENDIX 110-118

The Indian process of Fresco Buono—An outline of Rajasthani painting.

CONTENTS ix

PART II : THE IDEALS OF INDIAN ART

Page

INTRODUCTION 122-124

CHAPTER I : THE ORIGIN OF INDIAN ART—THE VEDIC PERIOD .. 125-128
Art and philosophy—The Vedas and Upanishads—The keynote of Asiatic art—Brahmanical ritual in Vedic times.

CHAPTER II : THE ECLECTIC, OR TRANSITION PERIOD 129-133
Prejudice against anthropomorphic images—The subjectivity of art—Asokan art—The Gandharan school.

CHAPTER III : THE UNIVERSITIES OF NORTHERN INDIA AND THEIR INFLUENCE ON ASIATIC ART 134-142
Western art-teaching and Indian thought—The Indian physical ideal, or superman—The Buddhist divine ideal—Indian art and Yoga—A yogin's ritual—Mnemonic and psychic training—Chinese and Indian art.

CHAPTER IV : THE DEVELOPMENT OF THE DIVINE IDEAL 143-149
The common basis in Indian art and religion—The aura and *ûrnâ*—The *âsanas* and *mûdrâs*—The Dhyâni-Buddhas and Bodhisattvas—The Hindu divine ideal—Early Indian symbolism—The Churning of the Ocean.

CHAPTER V : THE TRIMÛRTI 150-158
The philosophic concept of the evolution of the Universe—Nârâyana absorbed in Yoga—The cosmic cross—The Swastika and Sauwastika—The *gunas* and classification of Hindu images—Brahmâ—Vishnu—Siva—The Vaishnavaites and Saivaites—Vishnu and his *avataras*—Siva's dance—Karttikeya—Siva and Daksha—Ganesha—Geometric symbolism and the *lingam*.

CHAPTER VI : THE FEMININE IDEAL 159-164
Sakti—Saraswati, Lakshmi, Durgâ, and Kâli—A legend of creation—The Indian woman—The divine ideal in woman—Parvati in sculpture—The marks of feminine beauty—An allegory of spring—Indian symbolism and its interpretation.

CHAPTER VII : THE THREE PATHS 165-171
Karma-marga, *bhakti-marga*, and *gnana-marga*, distinguishing three different temperaments—The Indian outlook upon nature—The unity of creation—The European critic—*Bhakti* in art—South Indian bronzes — India and Islam—The revival of Indian art.

CHAPTER VIII : THE HISTORICAL DEVELOPMENT OF INDIAN ART 172-179
The basis of Indian history—Buddhist and Jain art—The zenith of Indian art—Indian painting—Saivaite art —The epics—The Vaishnavaites and Sauras—The Moguls—Anglo-India and the future of Indian art.

DESCRIPTION OF PLATES 183-196
The great bas-reliefs at Mâmallapuram, Madras—The elephants at Kanârak—Ajantâ sculpture—Sculpture from the Baro temple—Head of a Bodhisattva—Sculpture at Elephanta and Ellora—Monolithic temple at Kalugumalai—Temple of Râjârânî at Bhuvaneshwar—Sculpture in the Vellore temple, Madras.

INDEX 197

ILLUSTRATIONS

COLOUR PLATES

Plate

	Ladies in a Pleasure Garden	*Frontispiece*
A.	An Apsara. Fresco from Sittanavasal	*Facing page* 68
B.	Bharata Requesting Rama to Return to Ayodhya	,, ,, 70
C.	Camel-fight	,, ,, 74
D.	Meeting of Rama and Parasurama	,, ,, 78
E.	Snake-charmer	,, ,, 82
F.	The Heroine Garlanding the Hero	,, ,, 84
G.	Study of a Woman by Govardhana	,, ,, 86
H.	An European Embassy	,, ,, 90
I.	A Pious Conclave	,, ,, 94
J.	Sultan Bayezid as a Prisoner before Taimur Shah	,, ,, 96
K.	The Village Beauty	,, ,, 98
L.	A Mughal Beauty	,, ,, 102
M.	Krishna Meeting Radha in the Forest	,, ,, 106
N.	Hero and Heroine in a Pavilion	,, ,, 108
O.	Giri Govardhan	,, ,, 110
P.	Lady Surprised at the Bath	,, ,, 112
Q.	Ragini Vasanta	,, ,, 116

MONOCHROME PLATES

			Facing page				*Facing page*
1.	A.	Buddha preaching at Benaras	8	11.	A.	A Nāga and Nāgini	20
	B.	Kanishka's relic casket	8		B.	Hammered copper image of Manjusri ..	20
	C.	Statute of emperor Kanishka	8	12.		Siva as Bhairava from Elephanta ..	21
2.	A.	Image of the Dhyāni-Buddha, from Borobudur	9	13.		Narasingha and Hiranya-Kācipu from Ellora	24
	B.	Image of Gautama Buddha from Anuradhapura, Ceylon	9	14.	A.	Alto-relievo or Durgā slaying Mahisha ..	25
3.	A.	Alto-relievo of Buddha	8		B.	Bodhisattva	25
	B.	Copper-gilt image of the Bodhisattva Padmapāni	8	15.	A.	Statue of a lady	24
					B.	The Bodhisattva Maitreya	24
4.		Copper-gilt image of Vajrapāni	9	16.	A.	Bronze image of Dharmapāla	25
5.	A.	Copper-gilt image of a Bodhisattva ..	12		B.	Siva as Natārāja	25
	B.	Katra Buddha from Mathura	12	17.	A.	Cast copper image of the Buddhist Trimūrti	34
6.	A.	Stone image of a Bodhisattva from Sarnath	13		B.	Ganesha dancing	34
	B.	Stone image of Siva as Dakshinamurti ..	13	18.		Ravana under Kailāsa from Ellora ..	35
7.	A.	Image in copper of Avalokiteshvara ..	12	19.		Siva as Natārāja	34
	B.	The Sudarsana-Chakra	12	20.		Dance scenes from Chindambaram temple	35
8.	A.	Stone image of Avalokiteshvara	13	21.	A.	Image of Ganesha from Indonesia ..	40
	B.	Stone image of Tārā	13		B.	The Gardner's Daughter by Shidhartha Mahāpatra	40
9.		Stone image of Prajnāpāramita from Indonesia	20	22.	A.	The Buddha in preaching attitude ..	41
10.	A.	Hammered copper image of Tārā from Tibet or Nepal	21		B.	Nāga couple	41
					C.	"White Tārā"	41
	B.	Siva-Ardhanāriswar from Elephanta ..	21		D.	Vajra-Tārā	41

Plate			Facing page
23.	A.	Relief from Bharhut: The Sundarsanā-Yakshini	40
	B.	Lion Capital, Sārnāth	40
	C.	Sculpture from Bharhut	40
24.		The Eastern Gateway of the Sānchī Stūpa	41
25.	A.	Dryad from the Eastern Gateway, Sānchī Stūpa	56
	B.	Detail from pillar of Eastern Gateway, Sānchī Stūpa	56
26.		Sculptures from the Eastern Gateway, Sānchī Stūpa:	57
	A.	Adoration of the symbol of the Dharma	57
	B.	Buddhist miracle of walking on the water	57
27.	A.	Sculptured slab from the base of the Great Stūpa, Amarāvatī	56
	B.	Pillared slab from Amarāvatī	56
28.	A.	Sculptured slab from Amarāvatī	57
	B.	Carving on coping of rail, Amarāvatī	57
29-34.		Reliefs from the procession path, Borobudur, Indonesia	60-61, 64-65
35-36.		Ramayana reliefs, Prambānam, Indonesia	64-65
37.	A, B.	Two heads of Bhima from the Dieng Plateau, Indonesia	64
	C.	Portrait of Chandragupta II on a coin	64
	D.	Portrait of Vasisthiputra Śatakarni on a coin	64
38.	A.	Head of the Buddha	65
	B.	Head of a Buddha in bronze	65
39.		Horse and Charioteer, Kanārak, Orissa	64
40.	A.	Gilt-copper image of Kuvera	65
	B.	Gilt-copper image of a Tibetan nun	65
41.	A.	Sketch showing the design and proportions of	66
	B.	The Buddha's return to his, painting in antechamber, Cave XVII, Ajantā	66
42.		Yashodharā and Rāhula. Detail from the painting of the Buddha's Return	67
43.		Head of Bodhisattva. Painting in Cave I, Ajantā	66
44.	A.	Modern mural decoration in Indian fresco buono	67
	B.	Fresco at Sittannavasal	67
45.	A.	Two paintings from Sigiri, Ceylon	72
	B.	Fresco from Sigiri, Ceylon	72
46.	A.	Wall painting from Sittannavasal	73
	B.	Wall painting from Badami	73
47.		Group from the great fresco of the Rang Mahall, Bagh	72
48.		Birth ceremony of the infant Krishna. Kangra School brush drawing	73
49.	A.	The Coronation of Rāma and Sitā	76
	B.	Camels fighting. Mughal School	76
50.		A nautch party at the court of Muhammad Tuglak, by Shapur of Khurasan	77
51.	A.	Detail from a palmleaf folio of a Ms. of Prajnaparamita	76
	B.	Portrait of Abdur-Rahim Khankhanan	76
	C.	Portrait of a divine, by Farrukh Beg, the Kalmuck	76
52.	A.	A duck. Mughal School	77
	B.	A lily, by Muhammad Nazar Samarkani	77
53.	A.	Unfinished painting showing the initial stages of a painter's work	80
	B.	Meeting between Rāma and Bharata. Page from a Ms. of the Rāmāyana	80
54.		Two brush-line portraits. School of Shah Jahān	81
55.	A.	Prince Muhammad Murad on the elephant Iqbal. From a drawing by Ghulam	80
	B.	Folio from a Ms. of Iyar-i-Danish. Mughal School	80
56.	A.	Portrait of Sultan Muhammad Kutb Shah of Golconda, by Mir Hashim	81
	B.	Muhammad Jam Qudsi, by Bichitr	81
57.		Prince Dārā Shikoh	88
58.	A.	A turkey-cock, by Ustād Mansūr	89
	B.	A pair of cranes. Mughal School	89
59.		Two Sāras, by Ustād Mansūr	88
60.	A.	A black buck, by Manohar	89
	B.	Portrait of Babar. Mughal School	89
61.	A.	The tambura player, by Bichitr	92
	B.	Worshipping Siva at night. Mughal School	92
62.		Bāz Bahādur and Rūp Mati	93
63.		Deer-hunting by night	92
64.	A.	Travellers round a camp fire	93
	B.	An illustration from a Ms. of Tawarikh-i-Khandan-i-Taimuriya. Mughal School	93
65.		In a Zanana Garden	100
66.		A music party	101
67.		Portraits of Anglo-Indians of the Georgian period. From drawings by a native artist	100
68.		Illustration to the Rubaiyat of Omar Khayyam, by Abanindra Nath Tagore	101
69.	A.	Kācha and Devājāni. A fresco painting by Abanindra Nath Tagore	104
	B.	A Sacrifice. Folio from a Ms. of Razmnamah. Mughal School	104
70.	A.	Portrait of an Anglo-Indian of the Georgian period	105
	B.	The end of the journey, by Abanindra Nath Tagore	105
71.		Siva-Sīmantinī, by Abanindra Nath Tagore	104

Plate   *Facing page*

72. A. The trial of the Princes, by Nanda Lal Bose 105
     B. Sati, by Nanda Lal Bose 105

73.   Rāsa Līla, by Asit Kumar Haldar   .. 114

74.   The flight of Lakshman Sen, by Surendra
         Nath Ganguly   115

75. A. Painted book cover. Western Indian style 114
     B. Folio from a *Kalpasutra* 114
     C,D. Illustrations from a Ms. of *Kalpasutra*
         painted at Jaunpur   114

76. A. Folio from a Ms. of *Sangrahani Sutra* .. 115
     B. Illustration from a Ms. of *Balagopala Stuti* 115

77. A. Great Feast. Illustration from a Ms.
         of the *Rāmāyana*. Scene from the
         Rāmāyana. Rajasthani School 118

78. A. Raga Malakosa. Painted at Chawand,
         Mewar   119
     B. Watching the crescent moon. Bundi School 119

79. A,B. Paintings from a Ragamala set, Malwa .. 118

80. A. Women bunting. Bikaner   119
     B. Krishna conversing with Gopis. Bikaner 119
     C. Woman feeding birds. From a set of
         Amarusataka, Malwa   119

81. A. Lovers' quarrel. Kishangarh 128
     B. Radha and Krishna in woodland scenery.
         Kangra 128

82. A,B. Seals from Mohenjodaro 129
     C. Seal with Univorn and Indus Valley script
         from Lothal   129
     D. Figure of bearded priest, from Mohenjodaro 129

83. A. The Bharhut Rail. Inner view of the
         East Gateway 128
     B. Yakshi from Didarganj, Patna 128

84. A. Avalokiteshvara 129
     B. Vishnu on Sesha. Ceiling slab from a
         temple at Aihole 129

85. A. The Churning of the Ocean. Part of a
         relief from the temple of Angkor, Cambodia 136
     B. The Trimūrti, Elephanta 136

86. A. Vishnu   137
     B. Vishnu-Varaha-Narasimha from Kashmir 137
     C. Brahma   137

87. A. Brahma. Ceiling slab from a temple at
         Aihole   136
     B. Nāgarāja from Nalanda 136
     C. Nāgarāja from Mathura 136

88.   Siva as Natārāja. A bronze in the
         Government Museum, Madras 137

89. A. Kartikeya in his war-chariot. Portion of a
         Kambodian relief 148
     B. Ganesha   148

90. A. Dancing Ganesha from Halebid   .. 149
     B. Ganesha from Idar   149

Plate   *Facing page*

91. A. Parvati dancing. Sculpture from the
         Kuruvatti Temple near Harpanahalli .. 148
     B. Parvati   148

92. A. Yakshi from Bharhut   149
     B. Chanda Yakshi from Bharhut depicting
         "Woman and Tree" motif   149
     C. Sundarsanā Yakshi from Bharhut   .. 149

93. A. A young woman pressing the Asoka-tree
         with her foot 152
     B. Two women from Mathura 152

94. A. Woman with parrot cage, from Mathura 153
     B. Yakshi from Mathura 153
     C. A sculpture of a young woman from the
         Tadpatri Temple, Madras 153

95. A. Bronze statuette of Apparswami   .. 152
     B. Bronze statuette of Sundaramurti Swami 152

96. A. Ibrahim-ka Rauza, Bijapur 153
     B. The Rauza of Rani Sipri, Ahmedabad .. 153

97.   The immortal Taj Mahal, Agra 160

98. A. Colossal statue of Gomatesvara, Sravan
         Belgola 161
     B. The Tower of Victory, Chitor 161

99. A. Interior of Dilwara Temple, Mount Abū 160
     B. Carved ceiling in Dilwara Temple, Mount
         Abū   160

100. A. Bird's-eye view of Girnār   161
     B. Pālitānā Temple 161

101. A. General view of Kailāsa temple, Ellora 168
     B. Temple of Sūrya at Mudherā, Gujerat .. 168

102. A. The Temple of the Sun, Kanārak, Orissa .. 169
     B. The great bas-relief at Māmallapuram,
         central part 169

103. A. The great bas-relief at Māmallapuram,
         right half 168
     B. Vishnu supporting the universe. Bas-relief
         at Māmallapuram 168

104. A. Lakshmi arising from the Sea of Milk.
         Bas-relief from Māmallapuram 169
     B. Sculpture of a bull at Māmallapuram .. 169

105. A. Elephant sculpture at Kanārak   184
     B. Nāgarāja. Bas-relief from the entrance
         to Cave XIX at Ajantā   184

106. A. Queen Māyā and the infant Prince
         Siddhartha sleeping. Bas-relief at Baro .. 185
     B. The "Linga" shrine, Elephanta 185

107. A. Head of a Bodhisattva, from Indonesia .. 184
     B. Siva dancing the Tāndavan, Ellora   .. 184

108. A. Siva dancing the Tāndavan, Elephanta .. 105
     B. Roof of monolithic temple at Kalugu-
         malai, Tinnevelly. 105

109. A. Temple of Rājarāni at Bhuvaneshwar, part
         of the western façade 192
     B. Pillar in the Siva Temple, Vellore .. 192

PART I

INDIAN SCULPTURE
AND PAINTING

PREFACE TO SECOND EDITION

THE circumstances under which this book was written twenty years ago have, in some respects, undergone a complete change. There has been a remarkable growth of interest in Indian art, both in Europe and in India, and appreciation has grown with better knowledge. Many writers besides myself have explored further the wonderful field of artistic research which India offers and have added greatly to its literature. Public and private collections of Indian sculpture and painting have been enriched, so that the material available for study in Europe is very much larger, and in India works of art which were commonly regarded as worthless are now valued as they should be. The new school of painting led by Dr. Abanindranath Tagore, C.I.E., has developed its influence vastly and helped to form a new school of criticism with the aim of representing the Indian point of view in the theory and practice of the fine arts.

These changes have necessitated a thorough revision of this pioneer work, both in the illustrations and the text. The latter has been to a great extent rewritten, and the wealth of new material provided by the Archæological Survey of India, the Archæological Survey of Hyderabad, the Victoria and Albert Museum, the British Museum, and by private enterprise, generously placed at my disposal, has enabled me to improve very much the quality of many of the illustrations.

On the vital question of the preservation and regeneration of Indian art the situation has changed very little. Indians who have thrown themselves with the enthusiasm of converts into the study of their own art have shown great ability in academic criticism and historical investigation, but, following too closely the lead of the European connoisseur, they have done very little constructive work to prevent the extinction of the living traditional art of India. From this point of view the building of New Delhi, the greatest opportunity of a century, has been a complete fiasco, and things remain as they were when this book was first written. On this subject, therefore, the views formerly expressed have required very little expansion or amendment.

I must acknowledge very warmly the kind help I have received in providing illustrations from Dr. F. D. K. Bosch, Director of the Archæological Survey of Netherlands India ; Sir John Marshall, Director-General of the Archæological Survey of India ; Mr. G. Yazdani, Director of the Archæological Survey of Hyderabad ; the Director and Secretary, Victoria and Albert Museum and Mr. C. Stanley Clarke, Curator of the Indian Section ; Mr. Laurence Binyon ; Mr. O. C. Gangoly, Editor of "Rupam" ; Mr. Asit Kumar Haldar, Principal, Government School of Arts and Crafts, Lucknow ; Mr. C. C. Holme, Editor of "The Studio" ; Lady M. D. Scott-Moncrieff ; and Dr. Abanindranath Tagore. I am under a special obligation to Mr. S. V. Ramasami Mdr. of Madras for the trouble he has taken in getting photographs of the important frescoes of Sittannavāsal.

OXFORD, *October* 1927.   E.B.H.

PREFACE TO FIRST EDITION

THE purpose of this book is artistic, not archæological; but I have ventured to differ entirely from archæological ideas of Indian fine art, which seem to me to give a completely distorted view of the intentions of Indian artists. It is not extraordinary that these archæological conclusions have hitherto been tacitly accepted by the few European experts who have worked for art in India; for those who are preoccupied with their own work and own ideas of art, and prejudiced by their education in Western academies, are naturally inclined to regard with complacency the influence and affluence which the present popular opinion of Indian fine art brings to them.

I do not anticipate that all my fellow-artists in Europe will at once accept the views which have forced themselves upon me gradually, and after long years of study. Having entered upon my study of Indian art with a full equipment of European academic prejudices, I know that they are not easily shaken off. No European can appreciate Indian art who does not divest himself of his Western prepossessions, endeavour to understand Indian thought, and place himself at the Indian point of view. I am convinced that those who do so will find my artistic conclusions inevitable; but there will always be many who believe it more interesting to use the wrong end of the telescope.

For historical and archæological facts I have consulted the best authorities, and endeavoured to avail myself of the latest researches. I have not attempted anything like a history, in the ordinary sense of the word, but an explanation. In the first attempt to deal with a subject covering so wide a field, and artistically almost unexplored, there are many difficulties. I have been obliged to leave untouched much that is necessary for a full treatment of it, but I hope I have succeeded in showing that the Indian ideal is not, as archæologists call it, a decadent and degenerate copy of a Græco-Roman prototype; that Indian fine art is not, as an Anglo-Indian critic puts it, a form of artistic cretinism, but an opening into a new world of æsthetic thought, full of the deepest interest, and worthy of the study of all Western artists.

I hope, also, that this book may save from oblivion and from the tender mercies of the ignorant Philistine the unique collection of the Calcutta Art Gallery. I still look forward to the time when our whole administrative policy in India will be guided by intelligent and consistent views of art; though, as the principal artistic errors in it were pointed out by Fergusson more than fifty years ago, the hope may seem to be a vain one. The ruthless vandalism which prevailed in his time has been checked. We no longer desecrate and detroy the masterpieces of the Moguls and the great monuments of ancient India: we patch them up and try to admire them. But there is still that insidious form of vandalism in our departmental system—much more cruel and deadly than active iconoclasm, because it acts through mind instead of matter—which continues blindly to crush out the means by which India might yet surpass the greatness of her ancient art.

When Great Britain's responsibility in this matter is recognised, the grievous wrong we unthinkingly do to Indian art and craft will command the attention it deserves. But my main object is to help educated Indians to a better understanding of their own national art, and to give them that faith and pride in it without which the wisest measures that any Government could devise will always be thrown away. After all, the future of Indian art is in their keeping, and they have dealt with it more cruelly than any Europeans have ever done.

Even if, for Europeans who think like Macaulay, all Indian art should be worthless, it will always remain a priceless boon for Indians, offering them something which the best

European art can never give them. Let Indians of the present generation, who through Macaulay's narrow and short-sighted policy have never enjoyed this precious heritage, see that their children are put in possession of it.

I am deeply indebted to His Honour Sir Andrew Fraser, Lieutenant-Governor of Bengal, and to Mr. A. Earle, I.C.S., Director of Public Instruction, Bengal, for their sympathy and support in the publication of this book. My friend and colleague, Mr. Abanindranath Tagore, whose artistic work is reviewed in the last chapter, has given me valuable help by his knowledge of Sanskrit literature. I owe also acknowledgments for courteous assistance to Dr. J. D. E. Schmeltz, Director of the Ethnographic Museum, Leyden ; Mr. G. P. Rouffær, of The Hague ; Mr. E. A. Von Saher, Director of the Colonial Museum, Haarlem ; Dr. A. K. Coomaraswamy ; Mr. Stanley Clarke, Director of the Indian Section, Victoria and Albert Museum, South Kensington ; Dr. Müller and Dr. A. von Lecoq, of the Royal Ethnographic Museum, Berlin ; Mr. F. W. Thomas, Librarian, and Mr. T. W. Arnold, Assistant Librarian, India Office ; and to Mr. E. Thurston, Superintendent, Central Museum, Madras. I must also thank Mr. W. Griggs, who has spared no efforts in the extremely difficult task of reproducing in colours the minute and delicate work of the Mogul miniature painters, and Mr. Imre G. Schwaiger, of Delhi and Simla, to whose exertions the Calcutta Art Gallery owes some of its choicest treasures.

January 1908.

CHAPTER I

INTRODUCTORY

*"Quand on veut comprendre un art, il faut regarder l'âme du
public auquel il s'adressait."*—H. TAINE, "Voyage en Italie."

IT is *prima facie* incredible that a highly developed civilisation, spreading over thousands
of years and over a vast area like India, which has produced a splendid literature and
expressed lofty ideals in building materials, should have lacked the capacity, or found
no occasion, for giving them expression in sculpture and painting.   Nevertheless, when
this book was first published, twenty years ago,[1] such was the general opinion of European
savants and art critics.   It was an hypothesis which had governed our whole educational
policy in India since universities, museums, art galleries, and schools of art were established under British rule.

Quotations from many eminent European writers illustrating this point of view were
given in the first edition of this book, but it is unnecessary to reprint them now or to
recall the contemptuous phrases with which an ardent admirer of Indian craftsmanship,
Sir George Birdwood, author of the official handbook to the Indian section of the Victoria
and Albert Museum, ridiculed the Indian artist's divine ideal. He, like Ruskin and other
Victorian critics, held that "the unfettered and impassioned realisation of the ideals
kindled within us by the things without us" was beyond the capacity of the Indian
craftsman.   Indian art to him meant no more than a pretty chintz, a rich brocade,
or gorgeous carpet, fantastic carving, or curious inlay ; and an ancient architecture
fascinating to the archæologist and tourist with its reminiscences of bygone pomp and
splendour, but an extinct art useless for the needs and ideals of our prosaic and practical
times.

The years which have passed since this controversy began have seen a remarkable
change in the attitude of European critics towards Indian art generally, though to
India's grievous injury her mistress art still remains under the blighting influence of
Victorian prejudice. The capacity of Indian builders for creative work is still belittled
and derided, but it is no longer necessary to urge the claims of Indian sculptors and
painters of bygone days to be regarded as artists rather than as purveyors of ethnological curiosities.   Judging by commercial values Indian sculpture and painting appear
to have an insignificant importance compared with the works of European masters,
but it is a healthy sign that a new school of artistic criticism has arisen in India which
seeks to appraise Indian art by its own standards rather than by the opinions
of the market-place or by the verdict of European assessors, not often entirely
disinterested.

Yet it must be borne in mind that the careful classification of Indian art into schools
and ritualistic categories, a work which is now pursued with so much interest by Indian
and European scholars, is likely to lead no further than the former attitude of indifference
or contempt, unless it is realised that Indian art is the true expression of Indian life and
of religion as the interpretation of life, not merely an æsthetic formula which the student
can learn by heart. To connect it with its own natural environment, to follow its actual
practice in the present day, will bring us nearer to its inspirational sources than the study
of its ritualistic canons, or the search for its æsthetic prescriptions in Sanskrit texts.

[1] in 1908.

5

For, as Mr. Laurence Binyon has well said, the supreme æsthetic quality of the great religious art of India lies in the fact that it is not self-conscious. "Design, colour composition, all the purely artistic elements of their work, were left to the more intuitive activities of the mind . . . it solves difficult problems not by scientifically working out a theory but simply—*ambulando*. Our most modern art tortures itself in its austere quest of a purely æsthetic aim. But it is a perplexing paradox of human nature that to choose a certain aim and to consciously pursue it rarely ends in perfect accomplishment of that aim : if the aim is reached it is at the cost of impoverishment."

Until the nineteenth century India has solved all her artistic problems in her own simple way—*ambulando*. Her ancient Aryan culture, a great philosophic synthesis covering the whole field of human endeavour, went on century after century enriching itself and all the races entering the Aryan pale with new experiences of life. The fury of iconoclasts who sought to destroy it by violence only gave new impulses to artistic creation, so that at the beginning of the nineteenth century Indian art was more varied in its local developments than the whole art of Europe, though in all this variety of formal expression it preserved its essential spiritual unity, the religious instinct which is ever its vital force.

It is true, as Mr. Binyon has said, that in the great art of India the religious import was everything to the artists ; they generally consecrated their lives to religion as many great European artists have done. But this does not imply that they turned away their eyes from the facts and phenomena of nature and made themselves incapable of rendering them truthfully, as Ruskin and many lesser critics have asserted. Indian artists were not ascetics who shut themselves out of the world, but mystics who communed with Nature to find the secret of the universal life.

The common philosophic basis of art in all countries assumes that art is not merely an imitation or record of facts and phenomena in Nature, but an interpretation—the effort of the human mind to grasp the inner beauty and meaning of the external facts of Nature. To the European Nature is always an obvious reality which must be studied, exploited, and analysed, so that the exact composition of every organic and inorganic element in it may be ascertained and explained.

"The modern citizen," as Taine says, "is constrained to confine himself to the little province of a specialist. One development excludes the others : he must be a professional man, politician, or savant, a man of business or a family man—he must shut himself up in one occupation and cut himself off from the others : he would be insufficient if he were not mutilated. For this reason he has lost his tranquillity, and art is deprived of its harmony. Moreover, the sculptor speaks no more to a religious city, but to a crowd of inquisitive individuals ; he ceases to be, for his part, citizen and priest—he is only a man and artist. He insists upon the anatomical detail which will attract the connoisseur and on the striking expression which will be understood by the ignorant. He is a superior kind of shopkeeper, who wishes to compel public attention and to keep it. He makes a simple work of art, and not a work of national art. The spectator pays him in praise and he pays the spectator in pleasure."[1]

Viewed from this secularist and pseudo-scientific angle, Indian art will always be unattractive and incomprehensible. But the Indian artist is not really blind to the beauties of Nature. He can be realistic in the European sense, though realism for him has a different meaning to that which we attach to it, for the philosophy which inspires him regards all that we see in nature as transitory, illusive phenomena, and declares that the only Reality is the Divine Essence or Spirit. Thus while modern European art hardly concerns itself with the Unseen, but limits its mental range to the realm of Nature and thus retains, even in its highest flights, the sense and form of its earthly environment,

[1] "Voyage en Italie," vol. ii, p. 165.

Indian art (like the Egyptian, of which it is the living representative) is always striving to realise something of the universal, the eternal, and the infinite.

European art, since the so-called Renaissance, has, as it were, its wings clipped: it knows only the beauty of earthly things. Indian art, soaring into the highest empyrean, is ever trying to bring down to earth something of the beauty of the things above.

The Greeks and the artists of the Renaissance who followed in their footsteps attempted to arrive at a scientific standard of beauty by a selection of what appeared to them most admirable in various types of humanity and in natural forms and appearances. Physical beauty attained by martial exercises was to the Greeks a divine characteristic : the perfect human animal received divine honours both before and after death. The Indian artist had an entirely different starting-point. He considered that the perfect human animal was an inadequate symbol for the beauty of the divine nature which comprehended all human qualities and transcended them all. It was only by meditating on the Ultimate Perfection that the artist's mind could perceive some glimmer of the beauty of the Godhead.

Mere bodily strength and mundane perfections of form are never glorified in Indian art. When the Indian artist models a representation of the Deity with an attenuated waist and suppresses all the smaller anatomical details so as to obtain an extreme simplicity of contour, the European draws a mental comparison with the ideas of Phidias or Michelangelo and declares that the Indian is sadly ignorant of anatomy and incapable of imitating the higher forms of nature.

But the Indian artist in the best period of Indian sculpture and painting was no more ignorant of anatomy than Phidias or Praxiteles. He would create a higher and more etherealised type than a Grecian athlete or a Roman senator, and suggest that spiritual beauty which according to his philosophy can only be reached by the surrender of worldly attachments and the suppression of worldly desires.

Indian art is essentially idealistic, mystic, symbolic, and transcendental. The artist is both priest and poet. In this respect Indian art is closely allied to the Gothic art of Europe—indeed, Gothic art is only the Eastern consciousness manifesting itself in a Western environment. But while the Christian art of the Middle Ages is always emotional, rendering literally the pain of the mortification of the flesh, the bodily sufferings of the Man of Sorrows, Indian art appeals more to the imagination and strives to realise the spirituality and abstraction of a supra-terrestrial sphere.

Indian mysticism has its philosophic system, the Yoga-śāstra ; Yoga was not and is not practised merely as a spiritual exercise leading to the beatific vision. It claims to be a psychological process of drawing into oneself the dynamis or the logos which controls the universe and to be adaptable for all kinds of mental and physical activity. It inspired the artist, poet, and musician as well as the mystic who sought spiritual enlightenment. It gave the craftsman his creative skill and the soldier perfect control over his weapons, the statesman his far-seeing vision, the seer and inspired thinker his super-natural powers.

Indian art thus deifies the power of mind over matter in the figure of the Perfect Yogi, the Divine Thinker, one which is commonly associated with Buddhism only, but is really a concept common to all schools of Indian theism. The attempt to trace the source of its inspiration exclusively from the artistic rendering of Buddhist legends, more especially from the efforts of the Græco-Baktrian school which was more or less foreign to India, has led to hopeless confusion and misconception of the motives of Indian artists. For the indigenous art of India is a great synthesis embracing many different theological and mythological elements, but inspired by a common ideal.

The historical Buddha was an adept in Yoga and through Yoga attained enlightenment. But when he was deified in Mahāyāna Buddhism, he was transfigured in Indian eyes as the Divine Yogi of the Himalayas, who in the form of a white elephant, the genius loci of the mountains, had entered the womb of Māyā and had been born on earth as the Prince Siddhartha. At the moment when as a sannyasin practising Yoga he attained enlightenment his divine nature was manifested in an apparition shining like gold purified of its earthly dross, with limbs rounded and smooth-skinned like a woman's, but with the massive neck and shoulders and narrow waist of an Indian hero—an abstract of Universal Form and a symbol of spiritual strength transcending human thought.

This was the common ideal for all images of the Divine Thinker whatever their special sectarian connotation might be. It appears under the names of different Buddhas and Bodhisattvas, of Brahmā, Vishnu, or Siva, of Mahāvīra and other Jain Tirthankaras. The Græco-Baktrian artists of Gandhāra caught a faint glimmer of the idea, but generally represented the divine Buddha as an Indo-Grecian Apollo or as a monk practising his daily *sādhana* within the walls of a Gandhāran monastery (Plate 1A). European critics poring over museum specimens and convinced that Indian artists, as Ruskin said, wilfully sealed up for themselves the book of life, have seized upon this commonplace academic prescription as the inspiring motive of the Indian divine ideal, to worship which pilgrims of all sects still climb the long and perilous ascent to the innermost recesses of the Himalayas.

In all Indian poetry, art, and mythology, the sublime nature of the Himalayas has always been regarded as a special revelation of divine beauty and as a fitting shrine for all the gods. On Mt. Kailāsa, the temple's glorious pinnacle, sits the Divine Thinker in His icy cell, controlling the Universe by the power of Yoga. Here Vyāsa, says the Mahābhārata, taught the Vedas to his disciples. Here is the heavenly staircase by which the Lord Buddha and many other Avatars descended to be born on earth, and here the heavenly Ganges falls in seven torrents over the mountain's crest. The sacred lake, Mānasarovara, fed by Kailāsa's snows, is the legendary source of the four world-rivers which water the four great continents, or the four petals of the World Lotus, another pregnant symbol in Indian art. The wild geese (*hamsas*) which drift thither with the monsoon winds, are to the pious Hindu symbols of the human soul winging its way to its heavenly resting-place.

The lake itself, "the most excellent Lake of the Mind," was physically the symbol of fertility, the Creator's Well whose perennial overflow was the world's life-stream. In Indian art, as in the classical art of Europe, mountains, rivers, and lakes were personified into deities, but the essential difference between the Indian and the Western outlook is that the Indian artistic symbol is not merely an æsthetic formula. The physical appearance, Nature herself, is always charged with spiritual significance; the idealism of the Vedas is the life and soul of Indian art. Thus the Creator's Himalayan well, the natural symbol, becomes the divine receptacle of the universal mind-force, *manas*, the lotus-jar holding the essence of purity, the nectar of immortality, *amrita*, which Vishnu churned from the Cosmic Ocean. The four world-rivers became the four Vedas, revealed to Indian seers on that holy spot.

In the classical Western orders of architecture, which official city builders regard as the most appropriate symbols of British achievements in India, the Corinthian capital —apart from its architectonic purpose—is merely a pleasing composition of acanthus leaves and volutes; the Tuscan, Doric, and Ionic only harmonious arrangements of mouldings and ornaments. If they meant more to the Greeks and Romans we have lost their feeling. The Indian builder in creating his symbolic order struck a deeper and more spiritual note; a suggestion of the glorious Himalayan vision which was ever present in his mind. The Himalayas formed the resplendent pillar of the heavenly vault, holding aloft as its capital the precious lotus-jar of immortality guarded by the lions of the four quarters and by the Dewas who won it in conflict with the powers of evil. This was the motif, drawn from India's own fount of inspiration, which the Indian craftsman with inexhaustible fantasy and power of adaptation has used for palace and mansion, temple and mosque, reception hall and council chamber from before the time

A. Buddha preaching at Benaras. A relief from Loriyan Tangai. Gandharan School. (*From a photograph in the India Office Library*).

B. Kanishka's relic casket from stupa at Peshawar. (*Photo Copyright by Dept. of Archaeology, Government of India*).

C. Statue of emperor Kanishka, 1st century A.D. (*Mathura Museum*).

PLATE I

B. Colossal image of Gautama Buddha, from Anuradhapura, Ceylon.

A. Image of the Dhyāni-Buddha, Amogha Siddha, from the north side of Borobudur.

PLATE 2

B. Copper-gilt image of the Bodhisattva Padmapāni, or Avalokiteshvara. Old Nepalese. Height, 22¼ in. (*Calcutta Art Gallery*).

PLATE 3

A. Alto-rilievo of the Buddha preaching, from Sarnāth.

Copper-gilt image of Vajrapāni, or Dorje Chang. Old Nepalese. Height, 19 in. (*Calcutta Art Gallery*).

PLATE 4

of Asoka down to the present day. Whatever may be the æsthetic value of the Western formula which modern departmentalism forces on the Indian craftsman, it can never be worth the loss to the world's art implied in the drying up of India's own inspirational sources, and the extinction of the great living tradition in which she expresses her spiritual ideals. The stagnant pool of a dead classicism from which even Christian churches in India seek to draw their æsthetic inspiration will not bring about a renaissance of art or a reawakening of India's spiritual life.

CHAPTER II

THE EVOLUTION OF THE DIVINE IDEAL

INDIAN artists for many centuries shrank from the thought of depicting for the common crowd the Yogi's vision of the Divine Form : like the secret lore of the Vedas it was a sacred mystery revealed to none but the elect. Even the Brahman versed in the philosophy of the Upanishads looked upon the Yogi's vision as an imperfect revelation of the Godhead which embraced all forms and transcended them all. The geometric forms used in Vedic ritual seemed to him more appropriate symbols of universal powers than any icons suggestive of human limitations, and to this day *yantras,* or geometric symbols, are used in higher Brahmanical ritual in preference to images of the Hindu pantheon (Figs. 2 and 3).

The primitive Buddhist Church did not hold with the practice of Yoga as a means of divine revelation. Meditation (*dhyāna*), which was the Buddhist equivalent of Yoga, was not for absorbing the nature of the Godhead but for instilling in the mind of the faithful the principles of the moral law which ruled the universe. The great Teacher of the Law had returned to his Himalayan abode whence he came and was now invisible. Early Buddhist artists were realists like the great Flemish masters, representing the miraculous as events of ordinary life, but following the Master's teaching they made no attempt to penetrate behind the veil. The mystical element characteristic of Indian iconography in its full artistic maturity does not on this account become prominent in the early Buddhist monuments, though the symbolical method of representing the Himalayas as the World Pillar supporting the Wheel of the Law appears as the principal motive of architectural structure. Fragmentary as the records of early Indian art are, they show that Buddhists did not cease to regard the Himalayas as the holiest of holy ground. Kapilavastu, Bodh-Gāyā, Sarnāth, and Kuçināgara were sanctified by the Master's footsteps in his final incarnation. But the end of the great northern pilgrimage was still Kailāsa, as it had been for the seers of Vedic times and for the heroes of the Mahābhārata. Kailāsa was the nave of the universal wheel, the focus of world forces, and even now the Buddhist pilgrim worships the mountain as the heavenly mansion of Buddhas and Bodhisattvas, while the Hindu sees in it the hermitage of the Divine Yogi, Siva.

When Buddhism in its Mahāyāna development became a definite theology, image-worship was not only tolerated but became an essential part of its *sādhana.* At the same time the philosophy of Buddhism adapted itself to the Brahmanical theory of Yoga and the natural desire of the devout Buddhist to worship the image of the Divine Yogi without the perilous climb to the heights of Kailāsa was gratified, for the temple artist was assumed to be able to transport himself by Yoga to the Tusita heavens and bring back a faithful portrait of the Blessed One.

Thus India's dream of the Universal Form which she had so long kept secret gradually materialised as the great epoch of Indian sculpture and painting began to dawn. At the beginning of the Christian Era and for some centuries previously, when the classic art of Europe had already passed its zenith, India was drawing in towards herself a great flood of artistic culture from Western Asia, derived originally from the far-distant sources of Babylonia and Assyria, but strongly tinged with the subsidiary stream which was then flowing into it from Greece and Rome. Out of these eclectic influences, joined with the old indigenous traditions, Indian religious thought quickly formulated a new synthesis of art, which in its turn became the source from which other currents flowed north, south, east, and west.

In the early centuries of the Christian era and from this Indian source came the inspiration of the great schools of Chinese painting which from the seventh to the thirteenth centuries stood first in the whole world. Successive hordes of Asiatic invaders, beginning with those which flocked like vultures to gather the spoil of the decaying Roman empire, kept open the highways between East and West and brought a reflex of the same traditions into Europe.

From the seaports of her eastern and western coasts streams of Indian colonists, missionaries, and craftsmen poured all over Southern Asia, Ceylon, Burma, Siam, Sumatra, Java, and far-distant Cambodia. Through China and Korea, Indian art entered Japan about the middle of the sixth century.

The Indian ideal came to fruition in the great religious sagas, the Mahābhārata and Rāmāyana, in Sakuntala and other masterpieces of the Sanskrit drama, in colossal schemes of temple sculpture, inspired by the work of the divine craftsman, Vishvakarma, who built the heavenly temple of the snows, and in many a frescoed court and hall the splendour of which can only be dimly realised in the fragments of Ajantā, Bagh, and Sigiri. And just as the many vernacular versions of the Sanskrit epics made the story of the Pāndava heroes and Rāma's romance as familiar to the common folk in India's eastern colonies as they were to the court bards of Indraprashta and Ayodhyā, so the image of the Divine Thinker of Kailāsa took a local shape and significance nearer to or farther from the original Himalayan concept, according to the cult which used it and its particular environment. The Buddhist sculptors of Gandhāra Hellenised it for their royal Kushān patrons, just as Christian artists gave Biblical scenes a local colour. China, Japan, Siam, Java, and Cambodia made it their own. Yet in each local re-shaping of the image some memory, faint or vivid, of the Indian ideal archetype lingers. Gandhāra knew the Divine Buddha's Himalayan shrine, for the famous relic casket of Kanishka's great stūpa at Peshawar (Plate 1B) shows the Buddha enthroned on the "seed-vessel of the World-Lotus" and the sacred geese flying round it. Java gave her mountains Himalayan names, and her greatest monument, Borobudur, is her Kailāsa.

Though the concept of the Divine Thinker must be said to be Indian, or Hindu, rather than Buddhist, by far the greatest number of classical examples of the image belong to Buddhism. The illustrations, Plates 2 to 5A show fine Buddhist examples dating from about the fourth century A.D., when the image assumed its most perfect Indian form, down to modern times. To find its proper place in Indian artistic thought one must look beyond its incidental legendary, mythological, or ritualistic associations and connect it with the primeval Indian ideal, the gigantic figure of the Deity enthroned on the world's highest snow-peak and revealing Himself in the glory of a Himalayan sunrise or sunset. This was the divine image which the Indian artist brought down to earth and used as a standard of physical perfection to which men as well as gods could attain by mental rather than by physical effort.

The wonderful Buddha of Anuradhapura, Plate 2B, is one of the few colossal images of early Gupta times which escaped the Muhammadan iconoclast. It was probably executed in the first half of the fourth century A.D., in the reign of King Meghadarma of Ceylon, by a sculptor from northern India. It represents the Buddha just emerging from the Yoga trance, the left leg being released from the "adamantine" pose of profound meditation, when both legs are firmly locked together. In modern times a false note of naturalism has been given to it by placing it under a real bodhi-tree, but originally it must have formed part of a great architectural scheme, like that of Borobudur, more in keeping with the idealism of the image. For the artist had no intention of showing the emaciated body of the Sakyan monk reduced to a living skeleton by a prolonged fast, as the Gandhāran sculptors sometimes vulgarly portrayed it—but the tremendous apparition of the Divine Yogi of the Himalayas which flashed upon the world when the Enlightened One attained Nirvana.

The worshipper saw also a symbolic meaning in the design of the image, regarded as pure form.   In Plate 2A it will be seen that the contours of the front view of the Dhyāni[1]-Buddha fit as closely as possible into a triangle ; the whole figure approximates to a pyramidal shape.   In the great temple of Borobudur where this Dhyāni-Buddha was placed, the builders elaborated the geometric symbolism by enclosing the image in a hollow, bell-shaped stone cupola, or dagoba, pierced by lattice-work formed by a row of intersecting triangles through the interstices of which the pilgrims viewed the image of the Dhyāni-Buddha, as the personification of the cosmic pyramid.   The Hindu, accustomed to the geometric symbolism of the *yantra* in his religious ritual, would perceive at once the sculptor's meaning.   The dagoba (Fig. 1) was the *yantra* of three dimensions representing the universe of pure form out of which the world-lotus evolved.   Within sat the Divine Inventor of the cosmic machine blessing His worshippers.

Hindu iconographic art, like modern cubism, joins mathematics with æsthetics.   In the *yantra* (Figs. 2 and 3) it shows the impersonal form of the Godhead developing mathematically from a central point (Bindu).   In the corresponding icon it reveals the personal aspect of the deity, or *devata*, evolving from the impersonal.   Modern Hindu ritual gives an interesting analogy with the geometric symbolism of the Borobudur Dhyāni-Buddha.   The principal object of worship in Vaishnava temples in Southern India is the Sudarśana Chakra, Vishnu's discus, which symbolises the Creator's mind, or the first thought of the Supreme Being when the desire of Creation moved Him to manifest Himself.   It is represented as a circle of fire (Plate 7B) with four projecting points of flame.   On one face of the chakra sits the Lion incarnation of Vishnu in Yogi pose enclosed in an equilateral triangle.   On the other face are two similar triangles, one standing on its apex and the other on its base, symbolising respectively the evolutionary and involutionary cosmic powers.   This is the mystic symbol of the universe known as King Solomon's Seal.   Within it stands the figure of Vishnu in his Boar incarnation—the one in which he raised the earth from the Flood.   He is armed at all points with his spiritual weapons with which he destroys *avidya*, or ignorance regarded as the source of all evil.

When the figure of the Divine Yogi is thus seen with its Himalayan background and placed in its proper metaphysical or religious environment the austerity and formality of design characteristic of Indian classical types seem to be not only appropriate but inevitable, even if the suavity and charm of Chinese and Japanese images may be more attractive to the Western mind.   The Buddha image came to China and Japan through Gandhāra, and in this new environment the austere Yogi of Kailāsa was transformed into the benignant guardian spirit of a delightful monastic garden.   Thus the aloofness and mystery of the Indian pilgrim's ideal were generally foreign to the art of China and Japan.

Chinese and Indian influences are blended in the fine gilt copper image of the Bodhisattva Padmapāni, or Avalokiteshvara, "the Lord who looks down with pity," who is the

---

[1] "The term Dhyāna (Jñāna) is a general expression for the four gradations of mystic meditation which have ethereal spaces or worlds corresponding to them, and a Dhyāni-Buddha is a Buddha who is supposed to exist as a kind of spiritual essence in those higher regions of abstract thought.   That is to say, every Buddha who appears on earth in a temporal body—with the object of teaching men how to gain Nirvana—exists also in an ideal counterpart, or ethereal representation of himself in these formless worlds of meditation.   These ideal Buddhas are as numerous as the human Buddhas, but as there are only five chief human Buddhas in the presentage—Kraka-chandra, Kanika-muni, Kāsyapa, Gautama, and the future Buddha, Maitreya, so there are only five corresponding Dhyāni-Buddhas—Vairocana, Akshobhya, Ratnasambhava, Amitabha, and Amogha-siddha (sometimes represented in images as possessing a third eye).   But this is not all.   Each of them produces, by a process of evolution, a kind of emanation from himself called a Dhyāni-Bodhisattva, to act as the practical head and guardian of the Buddhist community between the death of each human Buddha and the advent of his successor.   Hence there are five Bodhisattvas—Samanta-bhadra, Vajrapāni, Ratnapāni, Padmapāni (Avalokiteshvara), and Vīsvapāni—corresponding to the five Dhyāni-Buddhas, and to the five earthly Buddhas respectively.   In Nepal five corresponding female Shaktis or Tārā-devīs are named."—Sir M. Monier-Williams, "Buddhism," pp. 202-3.

A. Copper-gilt image of a Bodhisattva. Modern Nepalese. (*Calcutta Art Gallery*).

B. Katra Buddha from Mathura.

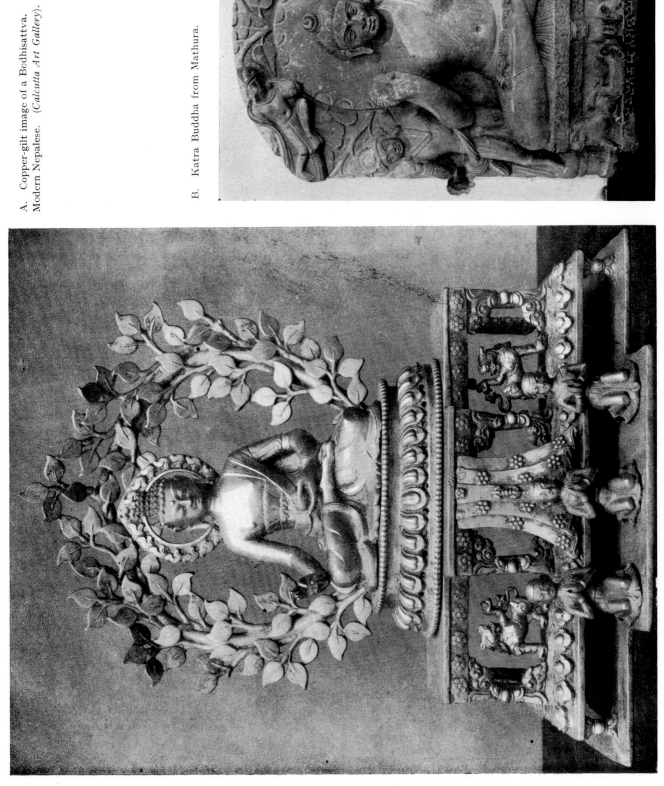

PLATE 5

B. Stone image of Siva as Dakshinamurti, Southern India.
(From a photograph by the Archaeological Survey of India).

A. Stone image of a Bodhisattva from Sarnath. 8th-9th century.
(From a photograph by the Archaeological Survey of India).

PLATE 6

A. Image in copper (cast) of Avalokiteshvara.
*(Boston Museum of Fine Arts. Photograph
by Dr. A. K. Coomaraswamy).*

B. The Sudarsana-Chakra, or Symbol of the Creator's Mind.
(From a photograph by the Archaeological Survey of India).

PLATE 7

B. Stone image of Tārā. Medieval. (*Indian Museum, Calcutta*).

A. Stone image of Avalokiteshvara. (*Indian Museum, Calcutta*).

PLATE 8

FIG. I.—Hollow yantra at Borobudur containing
an image of a Dhyāni-Buddha.

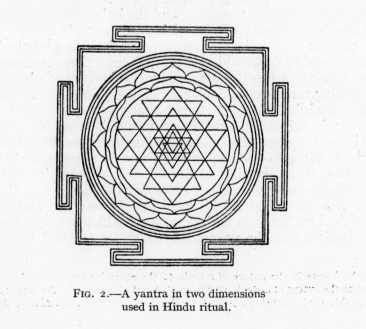

FIG. 2.—A yantra in two dimensions
used in Hindu ritual.

Bindu.

FIG. 3.—A yantra in three
dimensions cut in crystal
(Bindu on the top), used
in Hindu ritual. From
the original in the collection of Sir John Wood-
roffe.

guardian deity of Tibet (Plate 3B).   The image is entirely built up of hammered copper ; the tiara and other ornaments are set with rubies, turquoise, lapis, and crystal.   The beautiful modelling of the hands is especially noticeable.   It is probably of Nepalese workmanship, date uncertain.   More typically Indian is the very exquisite Nepalese image of Dorje Chang, or the Bodhisattva Vajrapāni, "the Wielder of the Thunderbolt," seated on his lotus-throne.   This is also of hammered copper-gilt, perhaps seventeenth-century work.   The tradition of the Divine Yogi survives in the modern art of Nepal, of which the cast copper-gilt image of a Bodhisattva, Plate 5A, is a good example.   Though inferior in execution it has the same fine feeling as the earlier art.   It is distinguished by the graceful conventionalisation of the bodhi-tree, disposed as a wreath round the Bodhi-sattva, who holds in his hand the jar of amrita, the nectar of immortality.   At the foot of the pedestal are the figures of the three devotees who have dedicated the image to some Nepalese or Tibetan shrine.

Many European critics, applying the academic prescriptions of Europe to Indian art without recognising its intentions and ideals, have attributed to the imagers of the divine form a deplorable lack of anatomical knowledge.   They have assumed that Indian artists, with the best opportunities in the world of studying the nude, were too ignorant and uncultured to draw or model the human form as it appears to the eye, and were content to make themselves feeble copyists of the models provided for them by the Gandhāran school.   The criticism is quite pointless when the finest examples of Indian sculpture and painting are considered.   The best Indian sculptors and painters did not fail in technical accomplishment, even in comparison with European standards.   In the idealised image of the divine form the bony structure of the body and limbs and the mechanism of the joints are perfectly understood, even though the muscular system is purposely simplified to express the artist's ideal.   Neither was the Indian artist tied down to one rigid formula of the divine ideal, though the static pose of the Yogi wholly absorbed in meditation gave the keynote of his symbolism.   The ritualistic poses prescribed for the Mahāyānist and Brahmanical pantheons became so numerous and varied that the temple artist would have had ample scope for his creative powers, as well as for his technical skill in rendering the form and action of the human body, even if a rich mythology had not provided him with other subjects.   The two Bodhisattvas, Plates 6A and 8A, and the monumental image of Siva, Plate 6B, in which the human side of the divine ideal is more prominent, are as perfect in the pure technique of contour and surface modelling as they are great in the rhythmic design of the figure and the balanced harmony of the decorative setting.   The Dancing Siva, Plate 19, is a well-known example of a very difficult movement rendered with perfect anatomical accuracy.   Such high technical accomplishment is by no means exceptional in Indian hieratic art, though there is sometimes a tendency to render the ideal beauty of the Perfect Yogi with poverty of plastic technique, flabbiness of surface modelling, and bad articulation of the joints.   Some of this weakness is shown in the Sarnāth Buddha, Plate 3A, found near the spot where the Buddha preached his first sermon.   It is evidently a Gupta craftsman's copy of some famous imager's masterpiece.   Such copies, good, bad, and indifferent, were doubtless made in prodigious numbers, and the tendency of a copyist is always to exaggerate the defects of the master's qualities.   The discriminating critic will not discern in such defects the essential characteristic of the Indian divine ideal.   Nor will he fail to place the Gandhāran School in its true place as a somewhat trivial local development in Indian art, a side current originating in political rather than artistic sources which was quickly absorbed into the main stream of Indian thought proceeding from its original Vedic ideal.

NOTE : Havell's remarks on the Gandhara school were in the nature of a reply to the excessive importance being given to it by the earlier archæologists who went to the extent of assigning it the credit for the invention of the Buddha image.   There has been much controversy on this topic, it being asserted by Foucher (*Art Graeco-Buddhique du*

Gandhara) and others that the Buddha image was conceived and executed by a Gandhara artist, the proposition being strongly denied by Coomaraswamy, "Origin of the Buddha Image," *Art Bulletin*, 1927, and other authors following him, of whom among the most important are Goloubew, Codrington and Mus.   According to Coomaraswamy, "While the Gandharan Buddha is stylistically Hellenistic, it follows the Indian tradition, verbal or plastic in every essential of its iconography.   The whole conception of the seated *yogi* and teacher is Indian, and foreign to Western psychology while the Indian *Yakshas* afford a prototype for the standing figures . . . . . .All that is really Hellenistic is the plasticity; the Gandharan sculptor, even supposing his priority in time, did not so much make an Apollo into a Buddha as a Buddha into an Apollo.   He may not have copied any Indian sculpture but his Buddha type and that of Mathura are equally based on a common literary and oral tradition." *History*, p. 52.   The dust of controversy has not yet settled but it is now the accepted view that the conception of the image is purely Indian and owes nothing to a school as mediocre as that of Gandhara, though there is a possibility that the actual image may have been born simultaneously in India and Gandhara.   For an excellent summary of the literature on the subject as well as a bibliography see Henri Deydier, *Contribution a l'etude de l'art du Gandhara*, Paris 1950, pp. 46-64.—P.C.

CHAPTER III

THE EVOLUTION OF THE DIVINE IDEAL—(*Continued*)

PERFECT knowledge, or abstract thought, regarded as the male principle and imaged in Indian art in the figure of the Divine Yogi, though it contains within Itself the germ of all things, remains inert without the will and power to create, which imply a cosmic energy, or *Shakti*. An equilateral triangle is the geometric symbol of the three co-ordinated cosmic powers, Will (Ichchā), Knowledge (Jñāna), and Action (Kriya), or the Three Aspects of the One, embodied in the Divine Form. When standing on its base the triangle symbolises the male principle; on its apex the female principle.[1] The two triangles intersecting each other make the six-petalled lotus symbol of the mystic Divine Embrace which completed the first act of creation.

The metaphysical concept is also personified in the image of the Divine Mother, who assumes many different names and forms, for every one of the divine beings, Devas or Devatās, projected from the One Supreme and acting as controlling intelligences of different parts of the universal machine, has his Shakti, or female energy. Every personified icon has also its corresponding *yantra* and *mantra*, the *yantra* being the symbol of pure form and the *mantra* the symbol of pure sound emanating from the Divine Word which set the universe in motion.

Brahmā, the Creator, as Artist gives the divine Idea, setting out the limits of the universal plan; Sarasvati, his Shakti, shapes it into things of beauty. As Musician He gives the time-beat of the universal rhythm; Sarasvati sings the divine song, the Song of Life. The distinction is observed in Indian musical practice: the drummer who beats the time (*tāla*) is always a man. In the *rāgas* and *rāginis*, the melodic root-forms which are the terrestrial counterparts of the divine *mantras*, the difference of functions or qualities is also expressed in terms of sex.

One of the few references to æsthetics so far discovered in Sanskrit literature—a dialogue between a king and his guru, or court chaplain, in the Vishnudharmottaram—emphasises the correspondence between music, dancing, and the art of the imager as different expressions of the universal rhythm. The student of the imager's art, which is closely connected with dancing (says the guru), should commence with learning the laws of singing, for all art is contained in the art of song. The same thought is to be found in the imager's own motifs and technical rules. Siva, as Mahādeva the Supreme Being, dances the Dance of the Cosmic rhythm, beating the time-beat with his drum. Krishna, the divine flute-player, teaches the eternal law of pulsation in dancing with the Gopis. The *mudrās* and *hastas*, finger-play and arm movement, and the *vangus*, or bodily inflexions of Indian iconography, reproduce the gestures and movements of the devadāsi, the temple dancer. The Indian musician and the artist use the same word *tāla*, the former to indicate the time-beat, the latter for his unit of proportion, the length of the face, which is divided into twelve *angulas* and more minute fractions suggestive of the microtones of the musical scale. The musical *rāgas* and *rāginis* have their graphic and plastic counterparts in the imager's *dhyānas* and *lakhanas*, Sanskrit formularies laying down for his guidance firstly the spiritual meaning and secondly the physical attributes of the deity represented.

Ethics and æsthetics are thus perfectly synthesised in Indian art. The artist regards humanity, with all its spiritual, intellectual, and physical attributes, as the microcosm

[1] Or, in a different connotation, fire and water respectively.

of the macrocosm. The Divine Pair, Man and Woman, representing the twin aspects of the Godhead, Purusha and Prakriti, Mind and Matter, symbolise the working of the universal æsthetic law, as it is imaged in the artist's mind. It is not the physical charms of the female form divine which are to captivate the worshipper—Indian art knows no Aphrodite or Diana—but the majesty and mystery of divine motherhood, expressed with wonderful sincerity of feeling and splendid craftsmanship in the image of Tārā, the Saviouress, one of the conceptions of Mahāyāna Buddhism (Plate 8B). The commanding pose, the jewelled tiara, and the right foot resting on the world-lotus proclaim her a queen of heaven. With the open right hand she bestows a gift upon the worshipper. In her left she holds a lotus flower : the colour of the flower signifies the special aspect of divinity displayed in the image. If it is white—without colour yet containing all colours—pure spirit is indicated. If it is red, the creative energy. Blue, the benign static power of the Maintainer of life, Vishnu, or his Mahāyānist counterpart, Avalokiteshvara. In this case the shape of the flower suggests the blue lotus.

In its austerity of outlook, simplicity of rhythm, and robust technique this image is typically Indian, of the classical school which had its great flowering time under the Gupta emperors, though this is several centuries later. We may compare with it a very graceful Tārā, Plate 10A, of the still later Nepāli-Tibetan school, in hammered copper, gilt and elaborately jewelled, which shows how Chinese influence transformed the Indian ideal. It is probably by the same hand as the image of Avalokiteshvara. (Plate 3B).

A beautiful image from Java, Plate 9, later than the Indian Tārā described above, and more ornate and florid in its technique, shows the Divine Mother in her gracious aspect as Prajñāpáramitā, the Spirit of Divine Wisdom, regarded as the Shakti of the Ādi-Buddha, the supreme deity of the Mahāyāna school. The body and the lower limbs have the rigid pose of the yogic trance, but the hands make the symbolic gestures (*mudrās*) of a spiritual teacher, and a book of the Law rests upon the lotus flower twined round her left arm.

It has been conjectured, says Dr. Vogel, that this image, while rendering the Buddhist ideal of Supreme Wisdom, is also intended as the posthumous statue of a Javanese queen, the consort of Rājasa, the first king of Singhasāri, *circa* A.D. 1222. In Java it was customary to raise temples over the ashes of deceased kings and queens, and to enshrine in them cult images bearing their likeness.[1]

All Indian images, Buddhist as well as Hindu, are given the attributes and insignia of royalty when they are meant to express the power of the Godhead in which the divine law, *dharma*, is embodied. God, as Power, is King or Queen—for the imager is allowed a certain latitude with regard to sex. God, as pure spirit, is the celibate monk or *muni*. The earthly monarch, who by virtue of his office is the defender of *dharma*, has always by his side his guru, or *purohita*, a disinterested spiritual adviser who is assumed to be an infallible interpreter of the Law and an expert in divine science.[2] The Javanese temple builders were therefore only expressing the Indian sentiment that a dutiful king or queen was an incarnation of divinity and as such entitled to divine honours. An Indian king often took the name of his *Ishta-devata*, his patron deity.

The duality of the Godhead as Being and Power is not always imaged as two distinct persons, the god and goddess. Brahmanical philosophy insisted that, as these concepts were only the two aspects of the One, they must be combined in one icon. The Ardha-nāri image of Siva (Plate 10B), in the great temple of Elephanta, an androgynous figure, half-male and half-female, in which the sculptor attempted to render the metaphysical idea realistically, is an artistic fiasco, although the three-headed bust of the Trimūrti

---

[1] "The Influences of Indian Art" (India Society's publication), pp. 84-5.

[2] For a further elaboration of the intimate relationship between *Sacerdotium* and *Regnum* see Ananda Coomaraswamy, *Spiritual Authority and Temporal Power in the Indian Theory of Government*, New Haven, Conn., 1942.—P.C.

in the same temple is wonderfully impressive (Plate 85B). The artistic difficulty is met quite simply and satisfactorily in the image of the Dancing Siva, Plate 19, by putting a man's ornament in one ear and a woman's ornament in the other.

The Indian imager deals with abstruse metaphysical ideas, which in the West are generally held to be beyond the limitations of art, and approaches them with so much reverence and sincerity that he rarely falls into banality or coarseness.

In the exquisite bas-relief of the two divinities of the underworld, Plate 11A, the sculptor, inspired by the romantic legends of the Indian water-sprites, has succeeded in rendering the mystic union of the Divine Pair with unaffected poetic feeling and masterly design. Joined together under the canopy of their extended serpent-hoods, making a glory round their heads, the goddess clings round the neck of her lord with her right arm, holding a lotus flower to his breast with her left, while he with both hands encircles their two bodies with a wedding garland, the sweeping curve of which makes rhythmic play with the jewelled collars and the movement of the arms. The subtle gradations of surface modelling, carried out to a delicate but not redundant finish, enhance the striking beauty of the linear design.

The Divine Power as god and goddess has another form of activity besides the creative one, exercised in the eternal conflict between good and evil, the Devas and Asuras. This is the constant theme of the Indian imager—Siva crushing a dwarf demon under his foot (Plates 16B and 19), or fighting the enemies of the gods (Plate 12) ; Vishnu in his Lion incarnation slaying the impious king Hiranya-kāçipu (Plate 13) ; Durgā destroying the buffalo-demon Mahisha (Plate 14A) ; Manjusri armed with the sword of knowledge to destroy ignorance (Plate 11B).

One of the many schools of Indian religious thought, the Shāktas, worship the divine Mother-Power as the supreme deity, under the name of Kālī, Devi, Mahā-Shaktī, and others. "She is the Great Queen (Mahārājnī) of Heaven and of yet higher worlds, of earth, and of the underworlds. To Her both Devas, Devis, and men give worship. Her feet are adored by even Brahmā, Vishnu, and Rudra."[1]

Shākta philosophy, says Sir John Woodroffe, in several respects gives an original presentment, both as regards doctrine and practice, of the great Vedantic theme of the One and Many. Shākta worship is perhaps the oldest of the many primitive cults which Vedantic philosophy assimilated and transformed, for in the remotest antiquity the goddess seems always to have taken precedence over the god, but its contributions to Indian art have not been great. Shākta ritual uses the symbolism of the yantra in preference to that of the icon, and most of the artistic conceptions of the Divine Mother have been appropriated by the other sects in which the Supreme Divinity is always God.

Kālī, as described in Shākta literature, is the personification of the Supreme Power which withdraws everything into Herself at the dissolution of the Universe. She stands naked in the dread cremation ground of space, where all worldly desires are burned away, dark as the Void in which the germ of all things reposed before the world began, dancing the Dance of universal destruction with dishevelled hair, lolling tongue, and with blood trickling from the corners of her mouth. A long string of skulls hangs round her neck, "the garland of letters", symbolising the universe of names and forms now being drawn into Her undivided Consciousness. Under her feet lies the prostrate corpse-like body of her husband, Siva. "He is white, because He is the illuminating (Prakēsha), transcendental aspect of Consciousness. He is inert, because the Changeless Aspect of the Supreme. In truth She and He are one and the same, being twin aspects of the One who is changelessness in and exists as change."[2] The devout Shākta worshipper who tries to penetrate behind the veil of illusion which envelops this dread aspect of Kālī, the

[1] "The Indian Magna Mater," by Sir John Woodroffe, "Indian Art and Letters," vol. ii, No. 2.
[2] "Garland of Letters," by Sir John Woodroffe, pp. 221-2.

Destroyer of Time, fixes his mind on the light and peace of spiritual liberation to which the Divine Mother leads her children.

The Shākta artist, however, seems to have rarely succeeded in clothing the imagery of these transcendental ideas with dignity and dramatic power. At their best, images of Kālī are a variation of the Natārāja without its superb grace and beauty of design. At their worst, in modern images, a black doll devoid of all artistic feeling serves to symbolise the concept of the great Mother of Nature.

CHAPTER IV

MYTHOLOGY AND METAPHYSICS

MYTHOLOGY, and the doctrine of re-incarnation which is fundamental to all Indian religious teaching, gave a more natural human interest to the metaphysical ideas which the temple sculptor and painter tried to express. The divine Buddha was incarnated as the Sakyan Prince whose life-story and previous births (*jātakas*) were carved or painted on every relic shrine for the edification of pilgrims. By followers of other sects Sakya Muni was regarded as one of the ten incarnations of Vishnu, among which were Rāma, the famous king of Ayodhya, whose adventures were told by every village story-teller, and Krishna, the divine Cowherd and hero of the Great War, who led the Pāndavas to victory. Siva, the Great God himself, lived in his icy cell on Mt. Kailāsa the usual life of an Indian Yogi, served by his other self, his devoted wife, Parvatī, King Himalaya's fair daughter, except when he was helping the other gods in their warfare with the Asuras and showed himself in all the majesty of the Godhead.

There was, therefore, no lack of subjects which the sculptor and painter might use for the decoration of temples, monasteries, kings' palaces, and more humble dwelling-places. But the icon which was the object of worship in the inner shrine of the temple stood in a category by itself, as a special symbol of the divine nature, and demanded the skill of the finest craftsmen. The legends of the Buddha's life on earth coloured the imager's conception of him as the Divine Yogi, and Buddhist art, before Mahāyāna doctrines reshaped it after its own cosmological notions, was so far in sympathy with the Gandhāran school that it never attempted the physiological impossibilities or abnormalities with which Hinduism deliberately invested the Divine Form. The typical Buddha image was in human shape, of a type familiar to every Indian, only made of a purer, finer substance than ordinary flesh and blood.

But orthodox Hindu teaching always held it to be irreverent and illogical to found artistic ideals of the Divine solely upon the contemplation of the human form. "The artist," says Sukrachārya,[1] "should attain to images of the gods by means of spiritual contemplation only. The spiritual vision is the best and truest standard for him. He should depend upon it and not at all upon the visible objects perceived by external senses. It is always commendable for the artist to draw the images of the Gods. To make human figures is bad, and even irreligious. It is far better to present the figure of a god, though it is not beautiful, than to reproduce a remarkably handsome human figure."

"Spiritual contemplation." Here is the keynote of Hindu art, as it was that of the art of Fra Angelico and other great Christian masters.[2] The whole philosophy of Indian

---

[1] Sukrachārya is the reputed author of an ancient Sanskrit work, "Sukra-nitisāra," or "The Elements of Polity by Sukrachārya." The fourth chapter, besides discoursing on politics, law, reformatory institutions, and the punishment of criminals, deals with arts and sciences, the building of castles, temples, bridges, and ships, the making and repairing of images, gardening, and the digging of wells, etc. It was translated into Tibetan in the seventh century A.D.

[2] For an interesting discussion of the processes of artistic creativity in India see Ananda Coomaraswamy, "The Intellectual Operation in Indian Art," *Figures of Speech of Figures of Thought*, London, 1946, pp. 145-157. According to it, there are two stages in the procedure of creating a work of art, the first being directed towards the realisation of a vision by means of contemplation (*yogadhyāna*) and the second the rendering of this vision in concrete form. Coomaraswamy, who has discussed at length the Śukranītisāra passage quoted by Havell in his *Transformation of Nature in Art*, Cambridge, Mass., 1934, also discusses the Kimchit-Vistara-Tara Sadhana published as No. 9 in the *Sadhanamala*, Gaekwad's Oriental Series No. XXVI, further clarifying the process of artistic creativity.—P.C.

Stone image of Prajñāpāramita, from Singhasāri, Indonesia. (*Ethnographic Museum, Leyden*).

PLATE 9

B. Siva-Ardhanáriswara, from Great Cave, Elephanta.
(*Photo Copyright by Department of Archaeology, Government of India*).

A. Hammered copper image of Tārā, from Tibet or Nepal. Height, 15½ in.
(*Calcutta Art Gallery*).

PLATE 10

B. Hammered copper image of Manjusri, Height, 11¼ in. (*Calcutta Art Gallery*).

PLATE 11

A. A Nāga and Nāgini. (*Indian Museum, Calcutta*).

Siva as Bhairava, Fragment from the Great Temple, Elephanta.
(*From a photograph in the India Office Library*).

PLATE 12

art is in these two words, and they explain a great deal that often seems incomprehensible and even offensive to Europeans.

While the Greeks made the perfect human body the highest ideal for an artist, there has been always in Indian thought a deep-rooted objection to anthropomorphic representations of the Divine. The Aryans in early Vedic times built no temples, and image-worship was not recognised in their higher ritual. The Hindu Sāstras hold that it is unlucky to have any representation of a human figure within the inner precincts of a temple. The substitution of a plain stone emblem of phallic origin for an anthropomorphic image in Saiva worship may be due to this feeling. The change appears to have taken place about the time of the great Hindu reformer of the eighth century, Sankarāchārya, who regarded the Lingam as a symbol of the Eternal Unity, or of the "formless god."[1]

In the temple of Chidambaram in Southern India the Cause of all things is represented by space—an empty cell—showing a fine perception of the limitations of art; for how can art, which is knowledge and expression, represent the Unknowable and Inexpressible?

The Mosaic law declares, "Thou shalt not make to thyself any graven image or likeness of anything that is in heaven or earth." The Buddha forbade the decoration of monasteries with human figures. The Sunna, the law of Islam, likewise forbids the representation of animate nature in art.

The Buddhist creed originally was simply a rule of life founded on the precepts of right views, right resolves, right speech, right actions and living, right effort, right self-knowledge, and right meditation. Its ritual at first was purely symbolical and non-idolatrous, though the Buddha's followers in after times adopted the image of the Master, or rather that of his spiritualised Self, as an object of worship. For several centuries this spiritualised human type dominated the ideals of Buddhist art, but when orthodox Brahmanical influence began gradually to assert itself more and more strongly in Buddhism we find Indian artists attempting to differentiate the spiritual or divine type from the human by endowing the former with superhuman attributes, quite regardless of physiological possibilities or probabilities. Indian art has never produced a Phidias or Praxiteles, not because an Olympian Zeus or an Aphrodite of Cnidus was beyond its grasp, but because it deliberately chose imaginative rather than naturalistic ideals of the divine form.

The old Hebraic tradition, like the Greek, declared that God made man in His own image; but the Hindu conception of the Cause of all things was of something much more vast and unapproachable—a vision too tremendous for human eyes to realise. In one of the most striking passages of the Bhagavad Gītā, Krishna reveals to Arjuna the nature of his Divinity. It has been finely rendered into English by Sister Nivedita thus :[2]

"I am the Soul, O Arjuna, seated in the heart of every being. I am the beginning, the middle, and the end of all things. Vishnu among the gods am I, among the lights I am the Sun. I am the mind among the Senses, the moon among the Stars. Amongst the waters, I am Ocean himself. Amongst trees, the Aswattha (Bo-tree) Tree am I ; amongst weapons the thunderbolt ; and Time amongst events. Of rivers I am the Ganges. Of created things I am the beginning, the middle, and the end. Time eternal am I, and the Ordainer, with face turned on every side ! Death that seizeth all, and the source of all that is to be. I am the splendour of those that are splendid. I am Victory, I am Exertion, I am the Goodness of the good. I am the Rod of those that chastise, and the

---

[1] The phallic symbol, though found in the Saiva temples of Java, does not appear to have been the principal object of adoration there, as it is now at Benares, the great centre of Saiva worship in India. From the number of statues of Siva found in Java we may conjecture that the worship of his image in human, or super-human form, was also predominant in northern India, the birthplace of Saivism, before the time of Sankarāchārya, as it still is in the south. At the time of Hiuen Tsang's visit the principal object of worship at Benares was a statue of Siva, a hundred feet high, "grave and majestic, filling the spectator with awe, and seeming as it were alive." If the disuse of anthropomorphic images were only a consequence of the Muhammadan conquest it would have applied to the images of all other Hindu sects.

[2] "Cradle Tales of Hinduism," p. 215.

Policy of them who seek victory. I am the Silence amongst things that are secret, and the Knowledge of those possessed of knowledge. That which is the seed of all things, I am That! Supporting this entire universe with a portion only of My strength, I stand!"

Arjuna begged of his divine Charioteer to show him his Eternal Self, his Universal Form ; but Krishna replied : "Thou art not able to look upon Me with this eye of thine. I will give thee an eye divine. See now My sovereign, mystic nature!"

Then, when Arjuna looked, he saw a resplendent vision, filling all the space between earth and heaven, glowing as a mass of light in every region, bright as the sun, and vast beyond all thought. It was Something with innumerable arms and faces turned every-where, uniting in its body all the gods, all men, and all created things. Even with the supernatural power bestowed upon him Arjuna was appalled by this wondrous trans-figuration and begged of Krishna to resume his milder "four-armed form." He received the solemn warning :

By favour, through my mystic form divine,
Arjuna, thou My form supreme hast seen,
Resplendent, Universal, Infinite,
Primeval, seen before by none but thee.
Yet not by Vedas, nor by sacrifice,
By study, alms, good works or rites austere
Can this My form be seen by mortal man,
O Prince of Kurus ! but by thee alone !

Hindu philosophy thus clearly recognises the impossibility of human art realising the form of God. It therefore creates in Indian painting and sculpture a symbolical rep-resentation of those, milder, humanised, but still superhuman, divine appearances which mortal eyes can bear to look upon. A figure with three heads and four, six, or eight arms seems to a European a barbaric conception, though it is not less physiologically impossible than the wings growing from the human scapula in the European representation of angels—an idea probably borrowed from the East. But it is altogether foolish to condemn such artistic allegories *a priori*, because they may not conform to the canons of the classic art of Europe. All art is suggestion and convention, and if Indian artists by their con-ventions can suggest divine attributes to Indian people with Indian culture, they have fulfilled the purpose of their art. It is the unfortunate tendency of modern European education to reduce art to mere rules of logic or technique, anatomy or perspective, style or fashion, so that the creative faculty on which the vitality of art depends is drowned in empty formularies of no intellectual, moral, or æsthetic value.

A bad craftsman certainly may make multiple arms and heads appear clumsy and ridiculous, but in the finest Indian images, such as Plates 10B, 16A, 12 and 19, they are designed with so much decorative feeling and articulated so skilfully with the normal human body that they appear as natural as the body of a Greek centaur or faun. There are often intense imaginative power and artistic skill in these Indian conceptions, as anyone who attempts to study them without prejudice will realise. What tremendous energy and divine fury are concentrated in the bronze statuette of Dharmapāla (Plate 16A), a manifestation of the Supreme Buddha as Defender of the Faith, trampling under-foot the enemies of religion ! And what a suggestion of majesty and restrained power there is in the Manjusri (Plate 11B), the Bodhisattva representing creative science,[1] dispelling ignorance with his uplifted sword of knowledge ! This is from a gilt copper statuette in the Calcutta Art Gallery, which is interesting as a historical landmark, for the inscription

[1] "Manjusri is the Buddhist analogue of the Hindu Brahmā, or Vishvakarma. He is the great architect who constructs the mansions of the world by the supreme Ādi-Buddha's command, as Padmapāni by his command creates all animate beings."—B. Hodgson, "Languages, Literature, and Religions of Nepal," p. 43.

on it in Nepalese shows that it was made to commemorate the death of a learned pandit and dedicated to a Nepalese shrine in the year A.D. 1782.[1] It has all the fine sentiment and decorative skill of the older work, although the technique, especially in the modelling of the lower limbs, is perfunctory and cannot compare with the much finer execution of the earlier Nepalese school from the same collection illustrated in Plate 17A. This is a three-headed and six-armed divinity cast in copper and gilt, probably representing the Buddhist Triad—Manjusri, Avalokiteshvara (Padmapāni), and Vajrapāni, corresponding to the Hindu Trimūrti, Brahma, Vishnu, and Siva. The modelling and movement of this little image are superb.

Hindu sculpture has produced a masterpiece in the great stone alto-rilievo of Durgā slaying the demon Mahisha, found at Singhasāri, in Java, now in the Ethnographic Museum, Leyden (Plate 14A). It belongs to the period of Brahmanical ascendancy in Java, which lasted from about A.D. 950 to 1500. The goddess is striding over the prostrate carcass of the buffalo, in which disguise Mahisha has concealed himself, and seizing the real dwarf-like form of the demon, she is preparing to deal him his deathblow. Judged by any standard it is a wonderful work of art, grandly composed, splendidly thorough in technique, expressing with extraordinary power and concentrated passion the wrath and might of the Supreme Beneficence roused to warfare with the Spirit of Evil.

The student will find in this phase of Indian imaginative art an intensity of feeling—a wonderful suggestion of elemental passion transcending all the feeble emotions of humanity—a revelation of powers of the Unseen which nothing in European art has ever approached, unless it be in the creations of Michelangelo or in the music of Wagner. But such qualities cannot be adequately realised in isolated sculptures collected in museums and art galleries; to be fully appreciated they must be seen in their proper environment and in the atmosphere of the thought which created them.

In the cave-temples of Elephanta, Ellora, and Ajantā Indian sculptors played with chiaroscuro in great masses of living rock with the same feeling as the Gothic cathedral builders, or as Wagner played with tonal effects, hewing out on a colossal scale the grander contrasts of light and shade to give a fitting atmosphere of mystery and awe to the paintings and sculpture which told the endless legends of the Buddha or the fantastic myths of the Hindu Valhalla.

Though they cannot reproduce this atmosphere the three following plates (12, 13, and 18) will give some idea of the imaginative power and artistic skill of Indian sculptors in dealing with compositions of great dimensions. They are examples of the finest period of Hindu sculpture, from about the sixth to the eighth century A.D., when orthodox Hinduism in India had triumphed over Buddhism, and before Hinduism had succumbed to the Muhammadan invader. The art traditions, however, were a direct inheritance from Buddhism.

Plate 12 is a splendid fragment from the great temple of Elephanta of a colossal sculpture of Siva. It was mutilated by the Portuguese in the sixteenth century, but enough remains to show the noble composition and movement, and the broad but subtle modelling of the head, shoulders, and trunk, suggesting the etherealised divine body, with its broad shoulders, slim waist, smooth skin, and refined contours.

Plate 18 is from the wonderful Kailāsa temple at Ellora, a monolithic idealised rendering of Siva's Himalayan hermitage, intended to suggest to the pilgrims that by the grace of Vishvakarma, the temple craftsman's patron deity, a replica of the Divine Yogi's heavenly cell had been put down for them at this sacred spot, so that they might be spared the long and perilous climb to the real Kailāsa.

The sculpture illustrates one of the weird legends of the strife between Rāvana, the

---

[1] The full inscription, translated, is as follows: "Blessing! Hail, Khagamaju! On the occasion of the death of Buddhacharya Ratna Traya this image of Manjusri was made in the Samvat year 902, month of Kartika, 10th day of the waning moon. Bliss!"

ten-headed demon-king of Ceylon, and Rāma, the hero of the Rāmāyana. Rāvana, finding himself worsted in the fight with Rāma and his monkey allies, flies in his magic car to Kailāsa, and placing himself beneath the mountain, strives with all his demon's strength to lift it up, hoping to carry off Siva and the whole Hindu Olympus, and thus masterfully to compel the great god's aid against his mortal foe.

Rāvana is shown in the cavern he has made beneath Kailāsa, exerting terrific force in his effort to lift it up. The mountain quakes, and Parvati, Siva's wife, startled by the shock, clutches her husband's arm and cries out, "Some-one is moving the mountain ; we shall be overthrown !" Her maid is flying in alarm, but Siva, only raising one foot, presses down Kailāsa upon Rāvana's head and holds him fast.

The rest of the legend says that the wicked demon-king remained a prisoner for ten thousand years, until his grandfather, Pulastya, son of Brahmā, teaches him to propitiate Siva, and obtain pardon for his crimes by performing penances and becoming a devotee of the god.

The story is told with intense dramatic force and imagination in this great sculpture. The whole execution shows an extraordinary command of plastic technique, not only in the grouping and composition of line but in the powerful and subtle treatment of the varied gradations of relief. With the feeling of a Rembrandt for effects of chiaroscuro, the sculptor has concentrated masses of deep shadow and strong broken light upon the crouching, struggling figure of Rāvana, which throws into high relief all the horror of his demoniacal power. On the mountain-top where Siva sits enthroned, the serenity of his paradise—hardly disturbed by Parvati's sudden movement and the alarm of her hand-maid—is finely suggested in quieter alternations and gradations of relief, softened by a veil of half-shade which falls over them from above.

The licence which the Indian artist allows himself, more especially in mythological scenes, of varying the proportions in figures of the same group, has been used here with great judgment and discretion. The two principal figures in high relief, the attendant deities on the right and left, and the crowds of lesser divinities and celestial beings, all play admirably their respective parts in the whole scheme. And the astonishing freedom with which this great sculpture is carved from the living rock, without any of the mechanical aids of the modern sculptor, makes it a splendid *tour de force*, quite apart from its higher artistic qualities.

Both at Ellora and Elephanta, as well as at Ajantā and other places, the sculptures, like the Greek statuettes of Tanagra, were carefully finished with a thin coating of the finest limeplaster, often as a preparation for colour and gilding—a process analogous to the *ganōsis*, or waxing, upon which Greek sculptors placed so high a value. At Ellora the whole of the exterior of the temple was given the effect of polished white marble, to suggest the glittering snow of the real Kailāsa. The interior of the *mandapam* was painted in fresco. This plaster finish has often perished by age, by ill-treatment, or exposure, but frequently it has been deliberately removed by amateur archæologists in their zeal for restoration. The process is still used by Indian sculptors and builders, though common whitewash, carelessly applied, is often substituted for it.

Plate 13 is a fine fragment from the Das Avatāra cave at Ellora, the temple of Vishnu whose cult is the principal modern rival to that of Siva.[1] This sculpture represents a myth connected with Vishnu's appearance on earth as the man-lion, one of his ten incarnations. The story is told in the Vishnu-purāna. Hiranya-kāçipu, king of the Asuras and one of the doorkeepers of Vishnu's paradise, had obtained from Brahmā by severe penances the boon that he should not be slain by any created being. Inflated with pride, he then attempted to usurp the sovereignty of Vishnu, and ordered his

[1] It is not quite correct to say that the Dasavatara at Ellora is a temple of Vishnu. Its sculpture is equally Saiva as Vaishnava in theme, the northern wall being carved with Saiva and the southern with Vaishnava sculpture. The sanctum itself contains a Siva linga which would indicate that the temple was dedicated to Siva and not to Vishnu.—P.C.

Narasingha and Hiranya-Kācipu.   A fragment from the Das Avatāra Cave at Ellora.

PLATE 13

B.   Bodhisattva.   Gandhara School.

A.   Alto-rilievo of Durgā slaying Mahisha.   (*Ethnographic Museum, Leyden*).

PLATE 14

B. The Bodhisattva Maitreya. Gandhara School, 3rd century A.D.
(*Prince of Wales Museum, Bombay*).

A. Statue of a lady. Gandhara period, 3rd century A.D.
(*Prince of Wales Museum, Bombay*).

PLATE 15

A.   Bronze image of Dharmapālā.
(*Batavian Museum, Indonesia*).

B.   Siva as Natārāja.   Copper, 16th century, South India.
(*Courtesy, Museum of Fine Arts, Boston*).

PLATE 16

son, Prahlāda, to offer him the worship due to the god. Prahlāda refused and braved all the wrath of his infuriated father. When Hiranya struck him he only thought on Vishnu, and the blows fell harmless. He was cast into the fire and was not burnt. With thoughts still fixed on the Preserver, he remained uninjured when elephants tried to trample him to death, and when thrown fettered into the sea a fish, at Vishnu's command, carried him safely ashore.

At last, as Prahlāda continued praying to Vishnu and proclaiming that He was everywhere and in everything, Hiranya tauntingly asked, "If that is so, why dost thou not show him to me ?"

Upon this Prahlāda arose and struck a column of the hall in which they stood, and behold, Vishnu issued forth in a Form which was half-man and half-lion, and tore the impious Asura king to pieces.

The sculptor has chosen the moment when the terrific apparition of the Man-lion rushes forth to seize Hiranya, who, taken unawares and with the mocking taunt still on his lips, makes a desperate effort to defend himself.

Any artist will appreciate the technical strength and imaginative power with which the subjects are treated in these sculptures. It would, however, be impossible to give an adequate impression of the great sculptured monuments of India within the compass of a single volume, even if sufficient material were available. But artistic research in India, though it has received a great impetus of late years, is still in its infancy. And even if the opportunities for artists were greater than they are there are some qualities in art which are almost impossible to explain.

No books or illustrations can give the haunting mystery of the Gothic cathedrals, or the subtle influence of the interior of St. Mark's at Venice. That only can be realised by seeing them with a mind and disposition for appreciation. Ruskin has truly said, "The arts, as regards teachableness, differ from the sciences in this, that their power is founded not only on facts which can be communicated, but on dispositions which require to be created." I can only hope in the illustrations I have selected to explain the motives and ideals, and to analyse the principles on which the master works of Indian fine art were based, leaving the rest to those who have the disposition and the opportunities for learning.

Apart from the wanton destruction by bigots and Philistines, and the destructive influences of a tropical climate, there is a special reason why masterpieces of fine art seem to be rare in India compared with their number in Europe. This must always seem to be the case in an art which is entirely creative and imaginative, instead of naturalistic. For while imagination is the supremest virtue of the artist, it is also the most rare. Works of the highest imaginative power have not been more rare in Indian art than they are in any country ; but when a European fails in this highest poetic gift he finds a safe refuge in painstaking naturalism, which, to nine-tenths of the public, appeals more than imagination. The Indian artist is usually left without this resource of mediocrity, for the traditions of his art do not admit naturalism to be the highest aim, or even one of the principal aims—at least not in religious art. When he would play to the gallery he must fall back on extravagance and eccentricity, which excite the ridicule of the ignorant European critic. But more often he relies on his wonderful decorative instinct, and Indian art is always superbly decorative, even when it is wanting in the highest poetic qualities. It is only under European influence that it has fallen into the snare of commercialism, the last and worst vice of decadent intellectual powers.

Art will always be *caviare* to the vulgar, but those who would really learn and understand it should begin with Indian art, for true Indian art is pure art stripped of the superfluities and vulgarities which delight the uneducated eye. Yet Indian art, being more subtle and recondite than the classic art of Europe, requires a higher degree of artistic understanding, and it rarely appeals to European dilettanti who, with a smattering of perspective, anatomy, rules of proportion and design, aspire to be art critics, amateur painters, sculptors, or architects, and these, unfortunately, have had the principal voice in deciding administrative questions which vitally affect India's artistic life. So the question whether Indian art is still a vital force, revealing India's spiritual self, seems to be less important than the question of taste—or whether from the European standpoint India's spiritual self should be allowed to reveal itself in art which the European and the Anglicised Indian do not appreciate or understand.

CHAPTER V

THE DANCE OF SIVA

WE have seen how Indian philosophy symbolises the Deity as pure form in the yantra; as sound in the Divine Voice, represented by the mantras and by the rāgas and rāginis of Indian music; again as pure thought, in the image of the Divine Yogi, and as thought-power in the person of the Divine Mother.

The Power of the Godhead is also conceived by the artist-philosopher in terms of motion or vibration. Siva is the Divine Dancer, who in 108 different movements interprets the mathematical law of the universe. The principal movement, known as the Nādānta dance, is represented with wonderful power in the famous bronze image of the Natārāja, the Lord of the Dance, now in the Madras Museum (Plate 19). Another form of the Dance, known as the Tāndavan, which is similar to Kālī's Dance of destruction, is shown among the sculptures of Elephanta and Ellora.[1]

In the Nādānta dance Siva personifies the kinetic aspect of the Deity, or the Spiral Force of Yoga, regarded as the elemental force through which the universe is created, maintained, and eventually destroyed. In the image of the Divine Thinker, Siva (or the Dhyāni-Buddha) is only the static centre round which the moving cosmic forces revolve, as electrons revolve round the static centre of the atom.[2]

The symbolism of the spiral is universal in primitive art. It occurs frequently in Indian art and mythology in the form of the cosmic Serpent, Ananta, the Endless One, who is the couch and canopy of Vishnu, the Lord of Life. Also in the myth of the Churning of the Cosmic Ocean by the Devas and Asuras in order to obtain possession of the nectar of immortality. In this case Ananta, or Sesha, is used as the rope by which the churning stick is turned. The convolutions of the Sālāgrām stone and of the conch-shell, two of Vishnu's emblems, are other instances. In Vedic times Siva, under the name of Rudra, "The Roarer",[3] was the god of the whirlwind. But in this Natārāja image he is conceived mystically and metaphysically as the Divine Spirit, the Supreme Intelligence, dancing in the human soul, removing sin and the effects of Karma. "They never see rebirths who behold this mystic Dance."

George Boole, the famous logician and mathematician, drew attention to a passage in the New Testament in which Christ uses the metaphor of the spiral in a similar mystic sense—a passage containing, he said, a psychological clue especially worth following up. ' The wind bloweth where it listeth and thou hearest the sound thereof, but canst not tell whence it cometh or whither it goeth : so is everyone that is born of the Spirit" (St. John iii. 8). This, Boole pointed out, could not refer to wind travelling in a straight line, for of such a wind one knows whence it cometh and whither it goeth. In referring to the spiral track of the whirlwind Christ was thus using a familiar symbol embedded in the art of East and West from the earliest times.

According to the philosophy of Yoga, the cosmic spiral force known as Mahā-kundali, "the Great Coiled One," has also its seat in the human body; for the latter, as the microcosm of the macrocosm, is said to have a series of psychic centres, corresponding to the spheres of the cosmic yantra, arranged one over the other from the base of the spine to

[1] See "Ideals of Indian Art," Plates 107B and 108A.
[2] See "Serpent Power," by Sir John Woodroffe (Luzac), p. 69.
[3] Nādānta, derived from the Sanskrit root *nad*, to roar, is a metaphysical interpretation of the ancient Vedic concept. See Woodroffe's "Garland of Letters," p. 190.

the top of the brain.   Each of these centres, in an ascending scale, represents different states of moral, intellectual, and psychic development.   The highest, at the top of the brain, is called the Kailāsa of the body.   By the practice and discipline of Yoga the adept is supposed to move the spiral force to gradually uncoil itself, like a serpent, from its central point at the base of the spine, until, when the Yoga is perfect, it reaches the Kailāsa of the body, and the state of ecstasy (*samādhi*) is produced in which the human consciousness is merged in the Universal and Siva reveals Himself.   The power of the Yogi to achieve this result depends upon the purity of his own spiritual condition : he is following, mystically, or psychically, the ardous winding path by which the pilgrim ascends to Mahādeva's Himalayan hermitage.

The spiral is thus a symbol pregnant in meaning for Indian artists, as it represents the progress of the soul towards Nirvana, and the whole scheme of cosmic evolution.   The Madras Museum Natārāja has been more discussed than any other figure in Indian iconography, but the most significant point conveyed by the main movement—that this is the Divine Yogi manifesting in His own body the spiral law of the cosmos, Mahākundali—has been hitherto unnoticed.   Though this is not explicitly stated in the ritualistic texts, it is clearly shown in the varied movements of the limbs, in the rhythmic design of the contours, and even more emphatically in a very characteristic feature which makes this image unique in the Hindu pantheon—the wavy locks which are spread out as an aureole round Siva's head.   The obvious mythological explanation is that the waves are symbolic of the sacred rivers which descend over Siva's head at Kailāsa, a small image of Gangā being enshrined in them.   But this spreading out of the matted locks round the head, which is not seen in any other Siva image, could only occur in a whirling dance, like that of the modern dancing dervishes whose object is the same as that of the Yogi, to excite in the dancer a condition of psychic clairvoyance.   This dance of Siva is still performed by the Devadāsis in the temples of Southern India, but in a much more stately and solemn tempo.   Modern Saiva ritual does not, as a rule, recognise dancing for men ; but in Vedic India both men and Devas danced, and the appropriate dance for Siva in his Vedic aspect as Rudra, the storm-god, would be the dance of the whirlwind, as shown in the Natārāja image.

The mystic significance of the spiral, suggested by the combined movement of the body and limbs, would only be appreciated by the adept in Yoga.   The more obvious symbolism of the minor gestures (*mudrās*) is explained in the Sanskrit ritualistic texts.   The drum, shaped like an hour-glass and held in the upper right hand, beats the cosmic rhythm-sound representing the primary creative force and the intervals of the beat the time-process.   The flame held in the corresponding left hand is the holy fire of sacrifice.   The other left hand stretched across the body points to the uplifted foot of the Deity as the refuge of salvation.   The upraised hand of the lower right arm, round which a cobra is coiled, assures the devotee of divine protection ; the *torana*, or arch of flame surrounding the image, is the Hall of the Universe in which Siva is dancing.

The demon under Siva's right foot is Muyalaka, the dark cloud of materialism in the Eternal Ether (*Akāśa*), which disappears in the sunshine of the Divine Spirit.   The popular mythological explanation of the Dance, intended for those who would not understand the occult meaning, is as follows : Siva, disguised as an ordinary ascetic, came to a forest hermitage where certain heretical Rishis, his enemies, were assembled.   He easily confuted their arguments ; they, in revenge, tried to destroy him by black magic.   First they created a fierce tiger which sprang out of the sacrificial fire.   Siva seized it in its spring, stripped off its skin with the nail of his little finger, and wrapped it as a garment round his loins.   Then they created a venomous serpent.   Siva took it, wreathed it as a garland round his neck, and began to dance.   Whereupon another evil shape, an ugly dwarf demon, rushed out of the fire.   Siva crushed it under his foot, broke its back, and continued his triumphant dance, while all the Devas and all the Rishis assembled as witnesses of the Great Yogi's power.

Auguste Rodin has written[1] an impassioned appreciation of this splendid bronze from a craftsman's piont of view, protesting against the narrow prejudice which has labelled this art as barbaric.   The tribute from the great French master makes further comment almost superfluous.   It is wonderful how the movement of the Natārāja, in all its seeming *naïveté*, embodies the mystic idea of divine ecstasy.   There is nothing in it of the mere animal gaiety of the Dancing Faun, nor any suggestion of the drunken frenzy of the Bacchanal.   In its technical treatment the figure presents the same broad anatomical generalisation and the type of torso peculiar to the Indian divine ideal.   No one who can appreciate the mastery of the structure of the human figure and the immense technical skill which the Hindu sculptor here shows can believe that it was from want of ability or knowledge that he has suppressed the smaller details of the muscular system.   The Indian artist, as a rule, delights in elaborating detail when he thinks it necessary ; but here, as in all his conceptions of Deity incarnate, he has deliberately left out the human details which he thought inappropriate.

The image belongs to the Chola period, about the tenth or eleventh century, when Indian art generally had lost the grand style of Gupta times.   Compared with the best Elephanta sculptures, there is less impulsive energy in the whole conception, a certain suavity in the mode of expression—"puissamment doux," Rodin calls it.   Another magnificent bronze image of the Natārāja,[2] first published by Mr. O. C. Gangoly, which stands in its original place in the great Tanjore temple, approaches nearer to the forceful-ness of Elephanta in its energetic and passionate action.   The power of its conception is enhanced by its size, for it is considerably larger than any other Natārāja known, the figure itself, excluding the pedestal and the *torana*, being nearly four feet in height.   It is to be regretted that sufficient photographic material does not exist for a detailed com-parison with the better-known images of the Madras Museum.

Though the temple imagers conform to fixed laws of proportion and design, laid down in the Silpā-śāstras, the rules are not so rigid as to suppress artistic individuality.   There is a marked difference of movement and expression in different images : it is quite easy to distinguish the creative artist from the common craftsman who works only by rule.   There are many examples of the Natārāja, good, bad, and indifferent, in the temples of Southern India and in public and private collections (Plate 16B).   Some of the temple craftsmen of the present day show no mean artistry when they are called upon to represent the Lord of the Dance, though modern images cannot compare with the great masterpieces of Chola times.

Siva, as mentioned above, is said to dance in 108 different modes, though very few excepting the Nādānta dance are represented in temple images, probably because the spiral dance of Yoga sums up in itself the whole mechanism of the cosmos.   Most of the other complementary modes of dancing are, however, carved as ornamentation on the gateway of the Natārāja temple at Chidambaram, with Sanskrit labels to distinguish them (Plate 20A and B).   Each dance may be said to symbolise some kinetic attribute of the Godhead ; a separate series of time-beats of the cosmic rhythm, like the musical rāgas ; or variations of the cosmic mathematical law.   A series of serpentine dances is shown, representing spiral or gliding motion, one with a similar significance is named after a flash of lightning.   The discus, or chakra, represents circular motion.   Eight of them are based on the swastika, which probably is a symbol of the movement of the sun across the heavens.   A leaping deer suggests the wave-line which in early Buddhist sculpture was used as a symbol of re-incarnation.   A large number are difficult to identify, either from the sculptures or the texts, but the general idea seems obvious, that Siva, the Divine Guru, teaches the geometrical law of the cosmos by dancing.

Ganesha, or Ganapati, the elephant-headed infant deity, which we may assume to be a

[1] "Ars Asiatica," vol. iii.
[2] See "Handbook of Indian Art," by the author, Plate LXV A.

primitive tribal totem adopted by Brahmanism as a son of Siva, is the popular guardian of households, remover of obstacles, patron of merchants, authors, and schoolboys (for he is the scribe of the gods), and god of common sense, who must be invoked before every enterprise and mentioned before any appeal to the Divine Spirit.   This quaint conception, which strikes the keynote of Indian thought—the intimate relationship between man and beast, is treated by Indian sculptors in different moods, but always with great sympathy and a full appreciation of its artistic opportunities.   In Plate 17B, a fine sculpture from northern India, now in the Indian Museum, Calcutta, Ganesha is shown in a spirit of rollicking fun mimicking with entire self-forgetfulness the tremendous cosmic dance of Siva—a delightful blend of the grotesque with the unconscious charm of infancy, and a masterly study of sumptuous plastic harmonies designed with the unfailing instinct of the Indian craftsman for decorative effect.   The splendid example of Indo-Javanese sculpture, Plate 21A, now in the Ethnographic Museum, Leyden, equally rich and accomplished in technique, shows the god in a graver mood with an air of elephantine sagacity, squatting complacently, in an awkward attempt to assume the ritualistic pose of "regal ease", on a row of human skulls which are a reminder of his descent from the Great Destroyer Siva.   It is of the same school as the magnificent sculpture of Durgā slaying the Buffalo-demon, in the same collection (Plate 14A), and possibly by the same artist.

CHAPTER VI

SCHOOLS OF SCULPTURE AND PAINTING

THOUGH it is impossible to classify Buddhist and Hindu art into distinct schools on the basis of dogmatic differences, Buddhism in practice, if not in the essence of its teaching, was more favourable to the development of the fine arts than orthodox Hinduism, partly because for some centuries it had predominant influence in politics, and thus became more prolific in artistic creation, and partly because Buddhism in its origin was a protest against the tendency of Brahmanical teaching to draw all men away from the realities of life into the metaphysical atmosphere of spiritualistic speculation. On the other hand it was Brahmanical thought which eventually transformed Buddhist ideals and gave art in India its peculiar idiomatic expression.

The typical examples already shown are illustrative of the principal ideals of Indian art, but do not give any clear indication of the separate schools of sculpture which undoubtedly always existed in India, though it has been commonly assumed by European critics that the ritualistic and traditional character of Indian art imposed limitations upon it fatal to individual creative effort.

When Indian art was in its full vigour these limitations had no more restrictive effect upon artistic individuality than those which regulated the pre-Renaissance art of Europe. As in every great art epoch, certain traditional types were established, founded partly on sacerdotal prescription and partly on models created by the recognised masters of different schools.

So far as sculpture is concerned, the field is so wide and so much of it from an artistic point of view remains unexplored, that any attempt at a comprehensive classification of it according to schools must be more or less futile.[1] Historical catalogues, arranged on an archæological basis, often without sufficient artistic discrimination, have little value as history and are often misleading as art. The European method of artistic exegesis, applied to India, will only provide more material for museums, the hobbies of the collector and for dealers in antiquities.

For real lovers of art it must always seem more important, before classifying Indian art according to schools and epochs after the method of the European historian, to realise that India has an unbroken artistic tradition going back for thousands of years. The discovery of a living Indian artist or craftsman, learned in the Silpā-śāstras and connected by a long line of ancestors with the most famous artists and craftsmen of antiquity, gives hope of keeping the springs of Indian craftsmanship flowing and an opportunity of historical study which is altogether denied to European art critics, even to those who search in our English villages for the last vestiges of traditional folk-music and art.

The fact, alluded to by Mr. O. C. Gangoly,[2] that in a village of the Tanjore District there exists at the present day a colony of temple imagers descended from the great school of Chola craftsmen who built, carved, and furnished the famous temple of Tanjore, brings the creators of the Natārāja to life and makes Indian art a reality instead of an academic pose. If it were only realised as such, it would be as significant a fact for India as the discovery of skilled English craftsmen descended from the builders of Westminster

---

[1] This is no longer true, and a great amount of material has been since brought to light, studied and classified. The history of Indian Art, in the stricter sense of the term, has made much progress, and the development of the various schools of architecture, sculpture and painting flourishing all over India is becoming clearer.—P.C.

[2] "South Indian Bronzes," pp. 26-7.

Abbey or Wells Cathedral would be for Mr. Stanley Baldwin.[1]

To bring about a real renaissance of art in India, the problem which must be solved is to find work and greater opportunities for the unemployed, or partially employed, artists and craftsmen who form India's own traditional school of art, not to establish more schools of a modern European type to keep them unemployed. But few of India's political mentors seem inclined to make use of the opportunities they now have of preventing any further wastage of India's artistic resources, or to realise that a vital art tradition once lost is lost for centuries, and can hardly ever be revived. It cannot be taught by schools, exhibitions, or museums, or recovered by the fulfilment of political hopes and ambitions.

For some years the Archæological Survey, under the direction of Sir John Marshall became the best craft school in India by giving employment to many skilful sculptors in restoring the famous monuments their ancestors had built. But since that work was completed many of them have been constrained to go on educating their children for clerical or other occupations, as the present public works system gives them no opportunity for practising their own hereditary crafts. One of the most interesting of the old schools of sculpture thus helped by the Archæological Department is that of Orissa, represented by the splendid temple of Kanārak and by some fine modern buildings at Puri and elsewhere.[2] Because, like the Hindu schools of Southern India, it remained outside the influence of Islam, which emasculated most of the sculpture of the North, it still retains much of its pristine virility and imagination, though the school is fast dying out from lack of recognition.

If the springs of Indian craftsmanship, which have flowed spontaneously for ages, must always be harnessed to Western machinery, driven by European art-mechanics, the inevitable consequence is that they will sooner or later be pumped as dry as similar English springs have been made by the same mechanical process. Indians who care anything for art must, above all things, prevent the mechanising of their traditional schools of craftsmanship. It means not only permanent economic loss but that sterilisation of the creative faculties which has been manifested in the building of New Delhi. Nearly a century after the Anglicisation of Indian education began, departmentalism can discover no Indian with creative powers to build or adorn the Indian capital.

Under the guidance of Dr. Abanindra Nath Tagore, C.I.E., the leader of the new Calcutta School of painting, one family of the traditional school of Orissa is now working at Calcutta. The charming little panel, entitled "The Gardener's Daughter," Plate 21B, by Shidhartha Mahāpatra, a happy blend of the new tradition with the old, shows what may be done by sympathetic and wise encouragement of India's own art, which suffers more from the ban put upon it by Europe than from the iconoclasm of Islam.

A complete survey of the traditional schools of art and craft still existing in India, especially of those which have not been debased by Western commerce, would be of great value, though the remarkable evidence of the vitality of Indian craftsmanship collected in the Report on modern Indian Architecture, 1913,[3] has not persuaded the Public Works Department to revise its devastating methods in art.

The traditional canons of Indian art and craft are preserved in the Silpā-śāstras and other works, but Sanskrit literature makes very little reference to the schools of sculpture and painting attached to the ancient universities and other religious foundations in India. The most circumstantial information regarding the Indian schools of fine art, previous to Mogul times, is that given by Tāranath, a Tibetan Lama, who wrote a history of Bud-

[1] The Prime Minister in an appeal for the preservation of old English cottages says that "we have to see if we cannot once again tap the springs of craftsmanship which have not flowed in this country for so long."
[2] See "Indian Architecture," by the author, Plates CXXVII-VIII.
[3] Government Press, Allahabad.

dhism in A.D. 1608. The last chapter, relating to sculpture and painting, has been translated by Mr. W. T. Heeley, I.C.S., in the "Indian Antiquary," vol. iv, p. 101. It gives many important landmarks in Indian art history.

"In former days," he writes, "human masters who were endowed with miraculous powers produced astonishing works of art. It is expressly stated in the Vinaya-āgama and other works that the wall-paintings, etc., of those masters were such as to deceive by the likeness to the actual things depicted. For some centuries after the departure of the Teacher many such masters flourished. After they had ceased to flourish, many masters appeared who were gods in human form; these erected the eight wonderful chaityas of Magadha—the Mahābodhi, Manjusri-dun-dhūbh-ishvara, etc. [the relic shrines marking the chief sacred places of Buddhism], and many other objects."

This refers to a period of which no known artistic traces exist. There are other references to picture-halls and sculptured images in the Mahābhārata, the Rāmāyana, and in the early Buddhist records, but Indian architecture at that time was almost entirely wooden; the pictures, which were mostly fresco paintings on a foundation probably of wood or of unburnt clay, have entirely disappeared together with the buildings. Tāranath only briefly refers to the important monuments of the great Buddhist Emperor Asoka, *circ.* 274-237 B.C., some of which, such as those at Bhārhut and Sānchī, still exist :

"In the time of King Asoka, Yaksha artisans [a race of demigods or supernatural beings] erected the chaityas of the eight great places, the inner enclosure of the Vajrāsana, etc."

The Vajrāsana, "the diamond-throne," or the place under the bodhi-tree at Gāyā where the Buddha won enlightenment, was enclosed by a sculptured stone railing by Asoka. Part of this still exists.

"In the days of Nāgārjuna," continues Tāranath, bringing us down to about A.D. 150, "many works were performed by Nāga artisans. Thus the works of the Yakshas and Nāgas for many years deceived by their reality. When in process of time all this ceased to be, it seemed as if the knowledge of art had vanished from among men." The principal works of this epoch now existing are the early paintings of the Ajantā caves, the sculptured rail of Amarāvatī and some of the Gandhāra sculptures. "Then," says our historian, "for a long course of years appeared many artistic efforts, brought to light by the striving of individual genius, but no fixed school or succession of artists." After this rather vague and legendary account the Lama gives us some more precise details :

"Later, in the days of Buddha-paksha [the identity of this monarch is uncertain] the sculpture and painting of the artist Bimbasāra were especially wonderful, and resembled those early works of the gods. The number of his followers was exceedingly great, and, as he was born in Magadha, the artists of his school were called Madhyadesha artists. In the time of King Shīla there lived an especially skilful delineator of the gods born in Marwār, named Shringadhara : he left behind him paintings and other masterpieces like those produced by the Yakshas. Those who followed his lead were called the old Western School."

The King Shīla referred to is probably the celebrated Harsha Vardhana Sīladitya (606-647), an account of whose empire is given in the narrative of Hiuen Tsang's pilgrimage. The finest of the paintings and sculptures of Ajantā may thus be attributed to this "Old Western" School.

"In the time of Kings Devapāla and Shrimant Sharmapāla there lived in Varendra (northern Bengal) an exceedingly skilful artist named Dhimān, whose son was Bhitpālo ; both of these produced many works in cast-metal, as well as sculptures and paintings, which resembled the works of the Nāgas. The father and son gave rise to distinct schools ; as the son lived in Bengal, the cast images of the gods produced by their followers were usually called gods of the Eastern style, whatever might be the birthplace of the actual designers. In painting the followers of the father were called the Eastern School ; those of the son, as they were most numerous in Magadha, were called followers of the Madhya-desha School of painting. So in Nepāl the earlier schools of art resembled the Old Western School ; but in the course of time a peculiar Nepalese School was formed which in painting and casting resembled rather the Eastern types ; the latest artists have no special character."

The King Devapāla was the third of the Pāla dynasty of Bengal, and reigned about the middle of the ninth century.[1] Further research among the sculptures scattered about Bihar and Orissa might lead to the identification of Dhimān's and Bhitpālo's work. It is interesting to find that there was a school of painting and metal-work in Nepāl founded on the work of these masters, for the fine copper-gilt image of the Trimūrti (Plate 17A), and other examples of old Nepalese art, collected by the author for the Calcutta Art Gallery, may give an indication of their style. Tāranath proceeds to give some information regarding the Kashmir School :

"In Kashmir, too, there were in former times followers of the Old Western School of Madhyadesha ; later on a certain Hasurāya founded a new school of painting and sculpture, which is called the Kashmir School."

This interesting sketch of Indian art-history concludes with some remarks on the comparative influence of Buddhism, Muhammadanism, and orthodox Hinduism on art-development :

"Wherever Buddhism prevailed skilful religious artists were found, while wherever the Mlechchas (Muhammadans) ruled they disappeared. Where, again, the Tirthya doctrines (Orthodox Hinduism) prevailed, unskilful artists came to the front. Although in Pakam (Burma) and the southern countries the making of images is still going on, no specimens of their works appear to have reached Tibet. In the South three artists have had many followers : Jaya, Parojaya, and Vijaya."

Tāranath's allusion to the inferiority of the Hindu artists points perhaps to some of the esoteric influences in later Hinduism which have contributed to the neglect and contempt into which Indian fine art, especially sculpture, has fallen. It is probable that Sankarā-chārya, the great Hindu reformer and apostle of the Vedānta, who lived about the ninth century, was, if not an iconoclast, like the followers of Islam, as much opposed in principle to image-worship as the Early Vedic philosophers, though tolerating it as a spiritual help for the ignorant masses. Sankarāchārya himself used geometric symbolism in his *sādhana* : the *yantra* called the Srīchakra, said to have been used by him, is preserved in the famous Srīngeri Math he founded in Southern India.

Obviously the Vedantic doctrine of Māyā, which treats all Nature as illusion, might, if pushed to extremes, cut away the ground of all artistic creation just as the intense mental concentration which is the foundation of the Yoga School of philosophy might eventually lead to absolute quietism and intellectual sterility. These two tendencies may, therefore, have had some influence on the decadence of fine art in India.

In the days of Hindu political supremacy the manifold activities of a self-supporting and vigorous national life would tend to stimulate the creative powers of thought and counter-act the depressing influence of a doctrine which led to a kind of intellectual nihilism, as far as sense-perception is concerned. But when these activities became subject to the tutelage of a foreign domination this stimulus ceased to be effective. Intellectual Hinduism gave itself up to its mystic reveries and ceased to interest itself in original artistic production.

Deprived on the one hand of the intellectual stimulus which gave it life, and, on the other, of the physical stimulus of state patronage, promoting a natural and healthy activity, it is not surprising that much of the Hindu sculpture of the present day has become a stereotyped repetition of conventional forms in which the highest poetic qualities of a "fine" art are generally lacking.

[1] "Chronology of India," by C. Mabel Duff, p. 298.

B. Ganesha dancing. (*Indian Museum, Calcutta*).

A. Cast copper image of the Buddhist Trimūrti. Height, 8½ in.
(*Calcutta Art Gallery*).

PLATE 17

Rāvana under Kailāsa. From the Kailāsa Temple, Ellora. (*From a photograph in the India Office Library*).

PLATE 18

Siva as Natārāja.   (*Government Museum, Madras*).

PLATE 19

Dance scenes from Chidambaram temple. (*Photos, A. L. Syed*).

PLATE 20

But this very conventionalism and stereotyped tradition have nevertheless been the means of preserving artistic qualities which raise some modern Indian architectural sculpture far above the level of what Europeans and English-educated Indians perversely substitute for it.

Note : Taranath's remarks on the development of Indian art has recently attracted much attention, and the observations of Khandalavala ("Commentary on Taranath's Chapter on Buddhist Art," *Marg*, Vol. IV, No. 1, pp. 61-63) are particularly interesting. According to him the reference to the *Yaksha* artisans of Asoka might indicate the existence of foreign (*yavana*) craftsmen, a fact not improbable looking to the considerable Achaemenid influence found in Mauryan art. The reference to Nagarjuna is interpreted by him to mean the Kushana period in North India and perhaps also the Andhra period in South India. The succeeding period during which Taranatha says that it appeared as if the knowledge of art had vanished from among men is identified by Khandalavala with the time between the fall of the Kushanas and the rise of the Guptas when the country was devoid of any significant artistic activity. The next period, which was marked by strivings of individual genius according to Taranatha, may refer to the early formative stages of Gupta art, though it is surprising that the Gupta school itself seems to have been ignored by him. The reference to Buddhapaksha might really be a reference to Buddhagupta (A.D. 475 to 495), but he was amongst the last of the Gupta line, when Gupta art was already on the decline. Who Bimbisara, the founder of the Madhyadesa school, was is also not very clear, though Taranatha might be referring to the school of sculpture flourishing in Uttar Pradesh and Bihar from about A.D. 475 to A.D. 600. King Shila is identified by Khandalavala with Harshavardhana, though Dr. U. P. Shah in his recent work tends to identify him with Siladitya of Valabhi. The School of the Ancient West founded by Sringadhara during his reign has no connections with Ajanta and the Deccan, as thought by Havell, but refers probably to the art traditions of Gujarat, the flourishing condition of which is borne out by the excellent sculptures found at Samalaji and other sites in former Idar state, and the great hoard of Jaina images discovered at Akota, which forms the subject of a study by U. P. Shah (*Akota Bronzes*, Bombay, 1959). Devapala is undoubtedly the Pala king of the same name who ruled Bengal and Bihar from A.D. 815 to 853 and Dhiman and Bitpalo are probably the great masters that laid the foundations of the Pala schools that produced works of equal merit in stone and bronze sculpture as well as in painting. With the Muslim invasion of India towards the end of the 12th century, many Pala artists fled to Nepal and Tibet, where they developed new schools of painting and sculpture. In this connection it is difficult to understand Taranatha's remarks regarding the similarity between Nepali schools and school of the Ancient West, though it is also true that some Nepali paintings exhibit characteristics such as angularity of drawing that reveal connections with the art of painting in Western India, preserved chiefly as illustrations to Jaina manuscripts. The reference to Hasuraja and the Kashmir school is also very interesting, and requires further investigation. These indicate the persistence of a distinctive Kashmir School of Painting and Sculpture, and it is held by some authorities that this school survived up to the late 16th century at least, when it helped in the formulation of the early idioms of Mughal painting and subsequently also played a part in the development of the Pahari schools of painting. In his recent work on *Pahari Miniature Painting*, Bombay, 1958, p. 52, Khandalavala feels that the Kashmir school was obviously a school of wall painting, though other kinds of work may also have been done. Taranatha gives no inkling as to the date of Hasuraja and all that we can deduce is that the school founded by him was known in Taranatha's lifetime, that is the last quarter of the 16th and the early quarter of the 17th century. He feels that "if there was a pre-Mughal school of miniature painting in Kashmir, then the possibility of such a school also spreading to the nearby hill states would have to be countenanced," but since no such school has ever come to light, "the probabilities weigh heavily against there being any pre-Mughal school of miniature painting in Kashmir, and in the circumstances no Kashmir tradition of miniature painting could have filtered into the Hills. What Taranatha was referring to as the Kashmir school must be regarded as a school of wall painting or banner painting."—P.C.

CHAPTER VII

THE HUMAN IDEAL AND THE SCULPTURES OF BHĀRHUT, SĀNCHĪ, AND AMARĀVATĪ

WE will now proceed to make acquaintance with a phase of Indian religious art which will appeal to most Europeans more than the study of oriental iconography, for it brings us down from the transcendental heights of philosophic Hinduism to the plane of our common humanity.

It is necessary, however, to bear in mind that though it might be supposed that in rendering the ordinary human form and events of human existence Indian art is exactly in the same plane of thought as European, there is nevertheless a wide difference between them. Greek and Italian art would bring the gods to earth and make them the most beautiful of men ; Indian art raises men up to heaven and makes them even as the gods. And until the fine arts were kept quite apart from religion, as in the Mogul period, the types of divine beauty established by artistic and ritualistic tradition profoundly influenced the artist's outlook upon life and the nature he saw around him.

The ideal of manly beauty he set before himself was not represented by a Rajput warrior, but by the divine Buddha, Krishna, or Siva. His idea of female beauty was not seen in the fairest of Indian women, but in Parvati, or in the heavenly Apsaras. Before, then, we begin to assume that Indian sculptors never attained to the same degree of technical achievement as Praxiteles or Michelangelo, we must always clearly understand how far it is possible to draw any comparison between them ; and except in their mutual reverence for the beauties of nature, and in the important part which art took in national life and education, there are not many points of analogy in the spirit of classic art and Indian.

In an age when reading and writing are rare accomplishments, the arts of painting and sculpture play a part in national life and education hardly to be realised nowadays. In the great epoch of Indian art which we are reviewing, art, religion, and education had no existence apart from each other as they have in this age of specialisation and materialism. They were similar and interchangeable forms and expressions of national thought and culture. The Buddhist monks were often themselves practising artists, and like the Christian monks of the Middle Ages they used the arts, not for vulgar amusement and distraction, but as instruments for the spiritual and intellectual improvement of the people.

And, like all true artists, they were keen observers and lovers of Nature. In choosing the places for their retreats, they always had the keenest eye for the beauties of hill and plain, mountain, forest, river, and sea. Dr. Burgess thus describes the prospect from the Elephanta Caves, the sculptures of which we have already discussed.

"The view from the front of the cave is one of exceeding beauty, commanding the fine bay between Elephanta, Bombay, and the mainland. From the grey dawn of morning till the shades of night close upon it, whether crowded with the white sails of hundreds of fishing craft, or only marked here and there with one or two passenger boats, and perhaps a small steamer, it is an ever fresh and varying scene of beauty. And a few steps from the porch will lead the visitor to the site of an old *bangalá* which commands the prospect to the south-west of Bombay and its splendid harbour, with Butcher Island in the foreground. Any true lover of Nature will feel himself amply rewarded by the magnificent views to be here enjoyed."

36

But beauty, for them, was for religion and love, not for idle pleasure ; they had the artistic insight which sees beneath and beyond the external facts and beauties of Nature. They always sought for and found—

> Tongues in trees, books in the running brooks,
> Sermons in stones, and good (God) in every thing.

The alternative reading of Shakespeare's text would make the philosophic Duke express perfectly the Eastern outlook upon nature.   Mr. J. Griffiths, in noticing the wonderful position of the Ajantā Cave-temples, says :
' All the forces of Nature are considered by devout Buddhists as expressions and symbols of the faith.   For the vulgar, the waterfall or the wind turns the mechanical prayer-wheel, but to those devoted to meditation and the cultivation of a higher life, the mere sound of running water, the rustle of the leaves as the wind plays through them, the movement of the clouds in the sky, and the manifold life and activity of the creatures of the jungle, are so many hymns of praise to the great harmonious law enunciated by the life of Buddha.''[1]
The people themselves shared fully in the feeling of their spiritual leaders.   To take the pilgrim's staff in hand and leave the worldly life, to be one with Nature in all her moods, was the supreme desire of every devout Buddhist or Hindu, whatever his sect might be. The pious Buddhist would set out to follow, step by step, the Master's life on earth, from his birthplace in the Lumbini garden to the final accomplishment of Pari-Nirvāna at Kusināra.   And, as the great story was told again and again round the camp-fires at night, the teeming life of the jungle round about seemed to become part of it, and wondrous legends grew of the jātakas, the Master's pre-existences in the form of bird or beast, preparing by many an act of devotion and self-sacrifice to show the way of release for suffering humanity.
And then, as now, Siva's followers climbed the winding pathway up the steep Himalayan slopes, through a paradise of tree and flower, above the dark forests of mighty deodar, to the region of cloud and mist and eternal ice and snow ; gazing there with awe on the shining glories of the silver mountain where the great god sat in sublime meditation.
Others would explore the country made sacred in national song and legend ; they would tread the sacred hill of Chitrakuta, and track the course of Rāma's and Sītā's wanderings by the banks of the Godavari and in the forests of the Deccan ; roam over the battlefields of the heroes of the Mahābhārata, and the scenes of Krishna's adventures and amours in the pastures of Brindaban.
And wherever the pilgrims went, and whatever might be their creed, the gods were with them always.   They felt their presence in the countless denizens, seen and unseen, of forest, field, or flood.   They heard them in the many voices of the jungle ; in the winds which swept through the forest trees, and in the waters which poured down from their heaven-built Himalayan throne.   They knew their power and beauty by the rising and setting of the sun ; by the radiant light and heat of midday ; by the glories of the Eastern moonlit nights ; by the majestic gathering of the monsoon clouds ; by the fury of the cyclone, the lightning flash and thunder, and the cheerful dripping of the life-giving rain.   From this devout communion with Nature in all the marvellous diversity of her tropical moods, came the inspiration of an art possessing a richness of imagery and wealth of elaboration which seem bewildering and annoying to our dull Northern ways of thinking.
Their art was glowing with spontaneous warmth and fantasy, like the Nature which inspired it.   Yet it was not based upon a sensual Nature-worship, like Hellenic art, but upon Nature regarded as the manifestation of one great Universal Law.   It was less coldly reasoned than the art of Greece, but far more spiritual ; for the poets and philo-

[1] "Ajantā Caves," Introd., p. 1.

sophers of a highly intellectual age joined in using this jungle-lore which clung round national history and popular beliefs as a framework for moral and spiritual instruction, inculcating by poetry, fable, and allegory the supreme law of life which the Buddha preached and the eternal truth of the immanence of God.

The schools of art were not only the courts and palaces of kings, or offices of state, but the monasteries and the sacred shrines at which the pilgrims paid their devotions. The early history of this art and architecture belongs to a period when, the greater part of the country being covered by primeval forests, the most convenient material for building and sculpture was wood. But though in this perishable material no monuments of this earliest period actually survive, we can gather a clear idea of the style from the monuments of Asoka's time, in which all the forms of the ancient wooden construction are reproduced, and from the representations of buildings given at Bhārhut, Sānchī, and elsewhere. The modern wooden architecture of the sub-Himalayan countries, like Nepāl, and that of Burma, has many affinities with it.

It is not, however, the purpose of this book to give a history of Indian fine art, but rather to show the highest development of it at a time when the monasteries and sacred shrines had become great national sculpture and picture galleries ; and when, in the course of many centuries, the traditions of Indian art-practice had become perfected into a science which was afterwards reduced to writing and recorded in the literature of Indian ritual and religion. Modern "educated" Indians, to their shame be it said, are mostly ignorant of or indifferent to this great science, the traditions of which are kept alive by the artistic castes of the present day ; though they are fast being crushed under the vandal heel of what we miscall civilisation, just as the traditions of the medieval artists and craftsmen have been extinguished by a barbarous and godless commercialism.

The practice of circumambulating a sacred shrine or place, one of the oldest of religious observances, gave rise to the decoration of the pilgrim's procession paths with painted and sculptured representations of sacred symbols and images, or illustrations of legendary or historical events. The painted decorations were generally the work of monks or of craftsmen supported by the donations of pilgrims ; the sculptures and images in the precious metals were often the gift of kings or other wealthy patrons.

The sculptured stone rails which enclosed the procession paths at Bhārhut, Sānchī, and Amarāvatī have been minutely described and illustrated in archæological works ; and as apart from their decorative beauty they do not represent the highest type of Indian sculpture, it is unnecessary to enter into detailed critical examination of them. Artistically they are extremely interesting because they illustrate the development of Indian sculpture from the time of Asoka (c. 274-237 B.C.), to whose reign the Bhārhut rail is attributed,[1] down to about A.D. 170, the supposed date of the later Amarāvatī sculptures.

Obviously the construction of these rails is borrowed from wooden prototypes ; but it is not only in constructional forms that they give indirect evidence of the ancient crafts of India, which are frequently alluded to in the Rāmāyana and Mahābhārata. The whole technique of the sculpture is a curious rendering in stone of the craftsmanship of wood-carvers, metal-workers, and painters, and as nothing similar to it is to be found in the sculpture of other countries, it will be interesting to inquire how this peculiar style originated.

---

[1] Havell follows the date given to Bharhut by General Cunningham in *Stupa of Bharhut* published in 1879. This dating has long since been discarded and c. 150 B.C. is now more or less accepted as the period of construction. It is also possible that all parts of the *stupa* were not constructed at one and the same time so that it would be more correct to state that the construction of the railing was begun and finished within the limits of the second century B.C. There is an inscription of a king named Dhanabhuti on the eastern gateway, and another of his son Vriddhapala on a rail-bar, the former containing the words *suganam raje*, in the kingdom of the Sungas. This together with other epigraphical evidence from the site puts the date of the balustrade definitely in the Sunga period between the extreme limits of 184 B.C. and 82 B.C. For an excellent discussion of the epigraphical material see Barua, *Bharhut*, Vol. I, Calcutta, 1934, pp. 29-37.—P.C.

Before the time of Asoka the principal artistic crafts of India, exclusive of weaving, were those of painting, wood-carving, and metal-work. The two former were no doubt practised in the Buddhist monasteries of Northern India, as they are now in Nepāl and Tibet. It must not be supposed that the mason's and stone-carver's art was unknown; but only that, as in all countries where wood is cheap and plentiful, the latter material was generally preferred for structural and decorative purposes; and, therefore, the wood-carvers greatly exceeded in number the craftsmen who worked in stone.

When Asoka succeeded to an empire greater than India had ever known before, and settled down as a devout Buddhist to cultivate the arts of peace, he employed the energies of his subjects in constructing a vast number of monuments and offices for the new state religion and many magnificent public works; and, as he desired them to endure for ever, he made as many as possible of brick and stone.

"Asoka", says Dr. Vincent Smith, "was a great builder, and so deep was the impression made on the popular imagination by the extent and magnificence of his architectural works that legend credited him with the creation of 84,000 stūpas, or sacred cupolas, within the space of three years. When Fa-hien, the Chinese pilgrim, visited Pātaliputra, the capital, at the beginning of the fifth century A.D., in the reign of Chandragupta Vikramāditya, the palace of Asoka was still standing, and was deemed to have been wrought by supernatural agency.

" 'The royal palace and walls in the midst of the city which exist now as of old, were all made by the spirits which he employed, and which piled up the stones, reared the walls and gates, and executed the elegant carving and inlaid sculpture work in a way which no human hands of this world could accomplish.' "—*Early History of India*, p. 144.

This extraordinary activity in building must have created a demand for skilled masons and sculptors much greater than India could supply; and just as in later times Shah Jahān brought masons from Samarkand, Shiraz, and Baghdad to assist in building the Tāj, so doubtless Asoka imported numbers of skilled craftsmen from the great cities of western Asia. We can still recognise their handiwork in the magnificent monolithic pillars, some of which are fifty feet in height and about fifty tons in weight, wherewith Asoka marked many of the sacred places of Buddhism. The finest of these, unearthed at Sarnāth on the spot where the Buddha preached his first sermon, is a perfect specimen of the stone-mason's and carver's art (Plate 23B). The design is a Græco-Persian rendering of the Indian world-pillar, shown in all the buildings represented at Bhārhut and Sānchī.

The chief direction of all these works would have remained in Indian hands, and the great majority of the craftsmen must have been Indian also, and therefore more accustomed to work in wood, ivory, and metal than in stone. The wood-carvers found in the red sandstone which abounds in northern India an excellent material, which could be worked with practically the same tools as they had always used: there was no necessity for them to alter their usual technique. Fergusson thought that the surprising degree of technical skill shown in the Bhārhut sculptures (Plate 23A and C) proved that stone must have been a material perfectly familiar to the craftsmen who executed them, and that their skill in lithic work must have been acquired by centuries of practice as stone-carvers; but on technical grounds it is not necessary to assume this. Even now there is very little difference in the tools used in India for decorative purposes by wood, stone, and metal-workers, and technical skill acquired in one material could easily be transferred to another. The technique of the Bhārhut reliefs suggests that they were the work of skilled wood-carvers attempting for the first time to use stone. This would explain why the sculpture of the early stone monuments of India shows a much higher degree of technical perfection than is found in the first attempts at stone-carving of a primitive state of art-culture. The sculptors are not tyros in craftsmanship, but skilled wood or ivory carvers, or sometimes metal-workers.

Asoka was by principle averse from warfare, and India, under the greater part of his rule, enjoyed a profound peace, through the suppression of the rivalry and jealousy of the numerous petty states, then consolidated into one great empire. There was, therefore, less occupation for those who manufactured and ornamented weapons of war, but a great demand for skilled craftsmen in decorating the sacred shrines of Buddhism. The artist-monks also, now that Buddhism was the state religion, under the patronage of a powerful sovereign, were not satisfied with humble stūpas and monasteries of brick and clay decorated with fresco paintings on plaster; they faced them with stone, and made painted *rilievos* instead of frescoes.

These circumstances explain the peculiar characteristics of the Bhārhut, Sānchī, and Amarāvatī sculptures. So vast was the labour bestowed on the decoration of the great Buddhist monuments that each became a permanent art centre and created a school of its own. The technical traditions were handed on from one generation of craftsmen to another, and so we find that even centuries afterwards when they were dealing with the hard limestone of Amarāvatī, they still reproduced in stone the artistic processes of the days of Asoka. Only in Western India, and some other localities, where Asoka's zeal for the Buddhist faith led to the carving of temples and monasteries out of the living rock, the craftsmen were forced to modify their methods, and other schools were created, with a perfectly lithic style of technique which culminated in the magnificent sculptures of Elephanta and Ellora already illustrated.

The Bhārhut rail (Plate 83A) is, according to Fergusson, the most interesting monument in India from an historical point of view. It is especially important for the study of Indian sculpture, because it shows the degree of technical development the fine arts in India had reached before India came in contact with the Graeco-Roman art of Gandhāra, before the Indian artistic ideal was perfected, and before Indian artistic philosophy had been differentiated from that of classical Europe. Fergusson says:

"It cannot be too strongly insisted that the art here displayed is purely indigenous. There is absolutely no trace of Egyptian influence; it is, indeed, in every detail antagonistic to that art; nor can it be affirmed that anything here could have been borrowed directly from Babylonia or Assyria. The capitals of the pillars do resemble somewhat those of Persepolis, and the honey-suckle ornaments point in the same direction; but barring that, the art, especially the figure sculpture belonging to the rail, seems an art elaborated on the spot by Indians and by Indians only."[1]

Fergusson's judgment in this matter, though disputed by some archaeologists, seems to me to be perfectly sound. We must establish our theories on the style as a whole, taking into consideration the esoteric elements, not the external accretions, as those which determine the character and origin of it. The ordinary archaeological method is rather like trying to ascertain the nature and growth of an oyster by analysing the crust outside its shell, ignoring the living organism, and perhaps a pearl, within.

The Bhārhut sculptures also show the interesting fact that in Asoka's time the worship of the person of the Buddha was not a part of Buddhist ritual. "Everything is Buddhist, but it is Buddhism without Buddha. He nowhere appears either as a heavenly person to be worshipped, or even as an ascetic." The objects which attract the reverent homage of both men and beasts are the symbols of the faith; the sacred footprints, the bodhi-tree in which the Presence dwelt, but not the Presence itself. Much of the figure-sculpture at Bhārhut is very primitive, but there are some which prove that, several centuries before the Gandhāran School had developed its ideal, Indian sculptors without foreign tuition had achieved no mean skill in rendering the human form.

The figure called Sudarsanā-Yakshini (Plate 23A) is one of the best of a series of semi-divine beings which appear as guardians at the four entrances, on the upright supports of the rail. The two most obvious points to be noticed in it are, first, that the technique is entirely that of a wood-carver; and, second, that the treatment is frankly naturalistic.

[1] "History of Indian Architecture," p. 89.

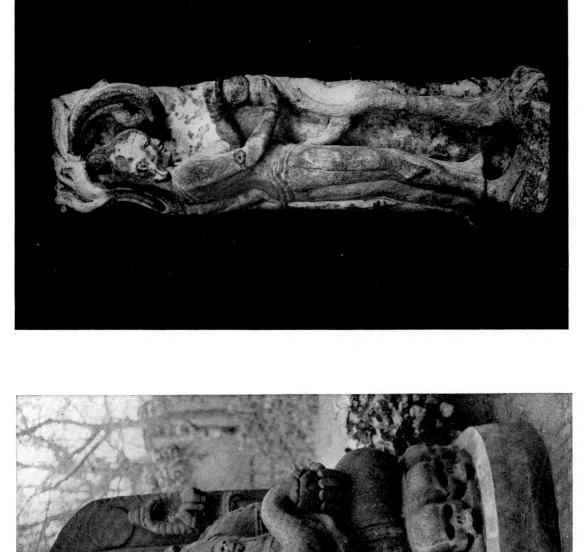

B. The Gardener's Daughter. By Shidhartha Mahâpatra.
Modern Orissa School.
(From photograph supplied by Dr. Abanindra Nath Tagore).

A. Image of Ganesha, Indonesia. (From Ethnographic Museum, Leyden).

PLATE 21

A. The Buddha in preaching attitude. Bronze, Devapala period.
(*Patna Museum*).

B. Nāga couple. Pala School, 11th century A.D.
(*Indian Museum, Calcutta*).

C. "White Tārā." Brass figure from Swayambunath, Nepal.
(*Photo, Tibor Sekely*).

D. Vejra-Tārā. Copper-gilt, 15th century, Nepal.
(*Courtesy, Museum of Fine Arts, Boston*).

PLATE 22

C. Sculpture from Bharhut :
A warrior in foreign dress.
(*Indian Museum, Calcutta*).

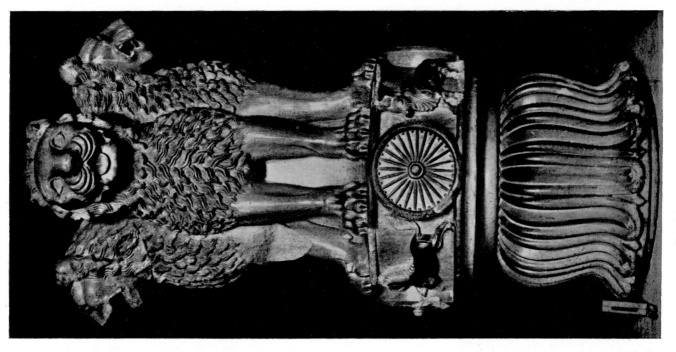

B. Lion Capital, Sārnāth.
(*Photo copyright by Dept. of Archaeology, Government of India*).

PLATE 23

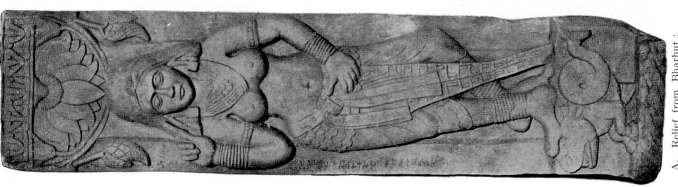

A. Relief from Bharhut :
The Sudarsanā-Yakshinī.
(*From a photograph in the
India Office Library*).

The Eastern Gateway of the Sānchi Stūpa. Inside view.

PLATE 24

There is no attempt to idealise; no indication of the abnormally narrow waist or of the complete suppression of the muscular details which are characteristic of all later Indian sculpture. Here we have "the shoulders loaded with broad chains, the arms and legs covered with metal rings, and the body encircled with richly linked girdles," which, according to Professor Grünwedel, prevented Indian sculptors from producing an anatomically correct form. Yet the main anatomical facts are remarkably well given, especially the difficult movement of the hips. In fact, it is very surprising that in this, one of the earliest known monuments of Indian art, we find such a high degree of technical achievement and such careful study of anatomy.

If we accept the conclusion that the Indian artistic ideal is a feeble attempt to imitate Gandhāran models, or those of Græco-Roman art, we must assume that many centuries later than these Bhārhut sculptures, when every branch of art had progressed and India was the acknowledged head of the scientific world, Indian sculptors and painters had actually retrograded in their art and were less proficient in anatomical knowledge than the artists of Asoka's time. The only alternative to this conclusion is that which I propose, that at some period after the Bhārhut and Sānchī sculptures Indian artists abandoned purely naturalistic aims and perfected an ideal of their own, which was, no doubt, latent in Indian thought even earlier.

The Sānchī sculptures are supposed to cover a period beginning from Asoka's reign, down to about 140 B.C. It would require a whole volume to do them justice,[1] but, except as an important link in the evolution of the Indian ideal, they do not belong to the scope of this work. They are, however, magnificently decorative, and provide a most wonderful picture of Indian life and thought, as described at the beginning of this chapter. The visits of the pilgrims to the sacred shrines, the stories told by the camp-fires, the fabled pre-existence of the Buddha in the form of bird and beast, and all the mysteries of the untrodden primeval forests, are revealed in a series of sculptures which, besides being most valuable for historical purposes, makes a most delightful, original Indian jungle-book. We can see, also, how strongly the idea of the essential unity of creation has taken hold of the Indian mind. For all nature is shown animated by a single purpose; man and beast, gods and demi-gods, and the weird monsters of Indian mythology throng together to join in worship of the emblems of the Buddhist faith.

The Sānchī sculptures are, like those of Bhārhut, entirely naturalistic in the treatment of the human form. As Fergusson says:

"All the men and women represented are human beings, acting as men and women have acted in all times, and the success or failure of the representations may consequently be judged by the same rules as are applicable to the sculpture of any other place or country. Notwithstanding this, the mode of treatment is so original and local that it is difficult to assign it to any exact position in comparison with the arts of the Western world."

It would be better, perhaps, to cease judging Indian art by Western rules, and allow, India the right of keeping her own artistic soul.

The person of the Buddha as a divine being receiving adoration is still unrepresented, though he appears as Prince Siddhartha and as an ascetic. There are some figures of primitive Indian deities, such as Śrī, the goddess of fortune, but they do not seem to suggest any connection with the dhyāna or yoga doctrine, or to represent an idealised type of body. The Indian artistic ideal, if it had been evolved at all, had not yet been adopted by Buddhism.

For European artists the greatest interest of the Sānchī sculptures, apart from their

---

[1] The publication by Marshall and Foucher of three magnificent volumes entitled *The Monuments of Sanchi*, London, n.d., 3 vols., fulfilled adequately the need felt by Havell. The antiquarian remains on the hill date from the time of the Maurya emperor Asoka to the eleventh century A.D. The Great Stupa, the principal monument on the hill, is also a structure built and reconstructed over a long period of time. The railing and the four gateways, however, can be dated to about the middle of the first century B.C.—P.C.

great decorative beauty, will probably be in their wonderfully truthful and skilful rendering of animal life.   This is especially remarkable in the Eastern Gateway, one of the latest of the Sānchī sculptures, illustrated in Plates 24, 25, 26A and B.

Yet some of the single detached figures are extremely good, and show a great advance on the art of Bhārhut, though the style is similar.   Plate 25 is an illustration of a female figure, a dryad, perhaps the sylvan goddess invoked in the Vedas as Aranyāni, singularly fine in movement and skilfully modelled, which forms a bracket on the right-hand side of the same gateway.   The style of it shows no trace of the Hellenic tradition, nor of the idealism of later Indian sculpture.   It is a piece of simple forceful realism by Indian sculptors, before any attempt was made to idealise the human form.   Nevertheless it would be difficult to find among the Gandhāran sculptures anything to surpass it, either in technique or in artistic feeling.

Though the wooden forms of construction are retained, the later sculptures of Sānchī, of which these are examples, show a perfect familiarity with the technique of stone-carving and great freedom of execution.   The best figure sculpture found here, taken in conjunction with that of Bhārhut, make it abundantly clear that before the Sānchī gateways were finished, or before any of the Gandhāran sculptures were executed, India had developed an original school of sculpture, and was no longer dependent upon foreign aid, as it was, to some extent, in the time of Asoka.   Indian art continued to assimilate foreign elements, as every living art will.   The Gandhāran sculptors, no doubt, sometimes found employment in India proper, but they did not come there as teachers, for India had nothing to learn from them in technique, and she deliberately chose ideals different from those of Greece.

The next important series of sculptures representing early Indian life and history are those of Amarāvatī (Plates 27 and 28),[1] a Buddhist settlement on the banks of the Krishna River, in Madras, and probably one of the starting-points of the adventurous emigrants who colonised Sumatra, Java, and Cambodia.   These sculptures are attributed to the last half of the second century A.D., so there is an interval of something like three centuries between them and the later Sānchī sculptures.   It is obvious that a great deal of Indian sculpture must have been produced in the interval, but very little of it remains, no doubt for the same reason that hardly anything has been found before the time of Asoka, namely, because most of it was executed in the wood of the trees consecrated to Vedic ritual.

Asoka's immediate successors did not continue his zealous propaganda of Buddhism, so Indian builders and sculptors naturally reverted to the material most convenient for them.   In the meantime, however, on the north-west frontier of India, the Indo-Baktrian school of Gandhāra arose.   Gandhāra was a country in which suitable stone for building and sculpture was more plentiful than wood ; so while all the wooden, or semi-wooden, buildings constructed in India in this period have totally disappeared, the stone and brick monasteries and the stūpas of Gandhāra have left a great deal of their rich sculptures to posterity.   This, and the fact that Gandhāra was closer to the outskirts of the Roman Empire, and therefore more susceptible to Græco-Roman influences than India, have given the Gandhāran school a rather fictitious importance in the history of Indian art. To understand this early period of Indian art rightly we must always bear in mind that for every monument in stone which now exists, there were perhaps a thousand in less permanent materials, which have completely disappeared.

The Amarāvatī sculptures show the Buddha for the first time in Indian art[2] as a divine

---

[1] Some of them are now in the British Museum, a few in the Indian Museum, Calcutta, but most of the finest and best preserved are in the Central Museum, Madras.

[2] The Buddha and Bodhisattva type of image is found for the first time not at Amarāvatī but at Mathura and images of the Mathura School found at other sites in India.   Of these the earliest include the image of a standing Bodhisattva found at Sarnath and dedicated by Friar Bala in the third year of the reign of Kanishka and the splendid Katra Buddha in the Mathura Museum dated by Vogel to the early Kushana period.   See J. Ph. Vogel, *La Sculpture de Mathura*, Paris et Bruxelles, 1930, pp. 35-36.   The appearance of the Buddha image at Amarāvatī has been dated by Douglas Barrett (*Amaravati Sculptures in the British Museum*, London, 1954, p. 58 ff) to the last two decades of the second

being receiving worship, and as the type of Buddha image closely resembles that of Gandhāra, Professor Grünwedel and other archæologists infer that the Græco-Roman artists of the Kushān Empire supplied Indian Buddhists with the ideal of their divinity. But the Amarāvatī Buddha is not the Indian ideal of divinity : it is a transitional type. In all the art of Amarāvatī we see Indian sculpture passing from the naturalistic school of the Asokan epoch into the idealistic school in which Indian art reached its highest expression. The simple, unsophisticated naturalism of the Bhārhut and Sānchī sculptures is here beginning to change into a very pronounced style of an academic character, but wholly different from the style of Gandhāra, though in the detail Gandhāran or Græco-Roman types frequently occur.

One of the finest and best preserved of the Amarāvatī reliefs is a sculptured slab from the base of the stūpa (Plate 27A) now in the Madras Museum. It represents the stūpa itself, surrounded with its rail, and with a crowd of adoring spirits, the *vidhyādharas*, hovering round its summit. These figures are perhaps the most beautifully designed of all, and they show clearly the idealistic treatment which had developed in Indian sculpture since the Asokan period. The flying movement of these heavenly spirits is conceived with rare artistic feeling and a thorough grasp of the mechanism of the human body, although the details of the muscular system are purposely suppressed.

In the Tusita heavens above the stūpa, supported by the two mystic world-pillars on either side, the Buddha sits enthroned receiving worship.[1] Here and elsewhere in the reliefs he is clad in the same loose robe as the Gandhāran Buddhas. This partially conceals the form and makes the idealistic treatment less conspicuous than it is in the almost nude figures of the *vidhyādharas*, or in the Buddha of later Indian sculpture illustrated previously. In the small upright panels on the right and left of the throne are two very expressive figures of a Nāga Rājā and his wife worshipping. They are well drawn and modelled with more anatomical precision than the *vidhyādharas*, as if to suggest a contrast between ordinary mortal form and the divine one.

This distinction, whether it is intentional or not in this particular case, is not observed throughout the reliefs ; nor is it characteristic of Indian art as a whole. But it is easy to understand that the recognition of a special type of beauty for divine beings would very speedily resolve itself into a general idealisation of the human form in the same direction ; the first step being its application as a mark of distinction for persons of high rank, and the next its adoption as a general academic formula.

The Amarāvatī reliefs, so far from being inspired by Western ideals, indicate the definite evolution of distinctly Indian ones : except for a few obviously borrowed details and motifs there is very little that is foreign about them. The style and whole mode of artistic expression are developments of the Bhārhut and Sānchī school, as can be seen in the beautiful group from the British Museum, Plate 28A. The slim-waisted figure standing by the horse, probably intended for Prince Siddhartha, shows the tendency towards Indian idealism. The two female figures, charmingly natural in pose, are ordinary human beings like those of Bhārhut and Sānchī, but the execution shows no trace of the Western academic style. The exaggerated thinness of the legs of all the figures was,

---

century A.D. The sculpture of Amarāvatī has been divided by Barrett, *ibid.*, p. 99, into three phases, namely, the Early, the Middle and the Late phase, stretching from roughly the second to the middle of the third century A.D. For a different chronology see C. Sivaramamurti, *Amaravati Sculptures in the Madras Government Museum*, Madras, 1942.—P.C.

[1] These mystic world-pillars are interpreted by Coomaraswamy as representations of the Buddha as Supernal Sun. See his *Elements of Buddhist Iconography*, Cambridge, Mass., 1935, Plate I, Figure 2, where an almost identical pillar is reproduced and discussed. The *dharma chakra* on top is supported by four lions of which only two are visible. It has a nave in the shape of a lotus, "the eight petals representing directions ; there are sixty-four spokes ; the triple felly is fringed with twelve *trisula* symbols, representing solar months . . . . The wheel is supported by a column, the Axis of the Universe, corresponding to the trunk of the Tree of Life, and the 'one leg' of the Sun when alluded to as *eka pada*. At the base level there are a throne and a footstool, with wheel marked feet . . . . . These His traces on earth are adored by human worshippers."—P.C.

perhaps, less marked when the sculptures had their finishing coat of fine plaster, though thin legs, like an antelope's, were marks of beauty both for men and women in Indian art.

The foreign elements in all of the Amarāvatī sculptures are not more conspicuous than those usually found in the art of any country which from its imperial position has become a centre of attraction for people of many and diverse nationalities. Nowhere do they justify the assumption that Indian art at this period was in Græco-Roman leading-strings. There is this in common with the Gandhāran sculptures and those of Amarāvatī—that both were inspired by the monastic schools of northern India ; the former employing foreign agents, the latter mostly Indian. The foreign artists of Gandhāra were naturally slower in absorbing Indian impressions, derived from the philosophical schools, than the native artists. The great culture-centres of Asia were at this time the Indian universities of Takshasila, Benares, Sridhanya Kataka, on the banks of the Krishna, and Nālanda : their influence was supreme, and compared with it the whole influence of Hellenism in Indian art may be taken as a negligible factor. It is to the direct teaching and influence of these great educational centres, rather than to the occasional intrusion of foreign suggestions and foreign technique, that we must look for an explanation of the development of Indian artistic ideals. For certainly the teaching of the Mahāyāna doctrine by Nāgārjuna, and the infusion of Brahmanical ideas into Buddhism, were the influences which shaped the ideals of Indian art, not the migration of Western artistic ideas eastwards. India was not then in a state of pupilage, but the teacher of all Asia, and she only borrowed Western ideas to mould them to her own way of thinking. "What Cluny and Clairvaux were to France in the Middle Ages," says Fergusson, "Nālanda was to Central India—the depository of all true learning and the foundation from which it spread to all other lands of the faithful." The whole range of education in these great universities was schemed and co-ordinated with a breadth and largeness undreamt of in modern India. There were schools of painting, sculpture, and handicrafts as well as of mathematics, astronomy, medicine, and other sciences ; at Nālanda religion and philosophy were taught from a hundred chairs. Not less greatly planned were the equipment and environment of the colleges. Hiuen Tsang, who resided at Nālanda for several years, describes it as "an enchanting abode." It had been in existence for seven centuries when he visited it. Six successive Indian kings had devoted their pious efforts to building and adorning it. The last one reorganised the work of his predecessors, opened a number of halls for conferences, and surrounded the whole convent with a single wall. One gate opened into the great college which the Chinese pilgrim thus describes :

"The richly adorned towers were arranged in regular order ; the pavilions, decorated with coral, appeared like painted hill-tops ; the soaring domes reached up to the clouds, and the pinnacles of the temples seemed to be lost in the mist of the morning. From their windows one could watch the movements of the winds and clouds, and above their lofty roofs the sun and moon could be seen in conjunction.

"All around pools of translucent water shone with the open petals of the blue lotus-flower ; here and there the lovely kanaka-trees hung down their deep red blossoms ; and groves of dark mango-trees spread their shade between them. In the different courts the houses of the monks were each four stories in height. The pavilions had pillars ornamented with dragons, and beams resplendent with all the colours of the rainbow— rafters richly carved—columns ornamented with jade, painted red and richly chiselled, and balustrades of carved open work. The lintels of the doors were decorated with elegance and the roof covered with glazed tiles of brilliant colours, which multiplied themselves by reflection, and varied the effect at every moment in a thousand ways."[1]

The groves of mango-trees and the immense tanks still remain as memorials of this splendid convent. There were thousands of these convents in India, though this was the finest of them all. To them students flocked from all parts of Asia, and from them went

[1] "La Vie de Hiouen Thsang," by Stanislas Julien, pp. 150, 151.

out the missionaries who brought Indian philosophy, science, and art to the most distant parts of the continent, China, Korea, and Japan.

Among such surroundings and by such influences were nurtured and developed the culture and ideals which created the great monuments of Indian art, and such was the respect for the dignity of learning inspired by them that, according to the Chinese pilgrim, no single instance of deliberate rebellion against the rules had been known at Nālanda during the seven hundred years since the foundation of the college. Apparently they possessed a secret of which modern India is ignorant. But could love of the *alma mater* ever grow up among the squalid, hideous surroundings, unkept and uncared for, of most Indian colleges ?

The Amarāvatī reliefs are considered by Fergusson and Professor Grünwedel to represent the culminating point in Indian sculpture. But this view can only be held by those who regard as decadence, instead of a new development on a higher plane of thought, the departure from European canons which here took place. Indian sculptors reached much higher imaginative flights and achieved greater technical triumphs, but, after Amarāvatī, they adopted an ideal of beauty totally different from that of Greece. They never attempted such a minute scientific investigation of the human structure as the sculptors of the Italian Renaissance made, because it would have been useless to them in perfecting an idealistic creation based upon imaginative and artistic feeling, rather than upon scientific facts.

Though they are far from showing the highest flights of Indian sculptors, there is much beautiful work in them. The traditions of Sānchī were upheld in the most delightful studies of animal life, combined with extremely refined conventional ornament. The most varied movements of the human figure are drawn and modelled with great freedom and skill. The action and grouping of the figures are singularly animated and expressive. In skilful composition, especially in the design of crowds, a point in which Indian artists always excelled, they far surpass the contemporary school of Gandhāra, and although the sentiment seems sometimes rather forced and artificial, it is much more genuine than the conventional, smug pietism of the Græco-Roman, or Indo-Roman, sculptures.

In Indian art they take much the same place as Cellini's work holds in the sculpture of the Italian Renaissance. But technically the two rails must be considered as painted *rilievos*, rather than true sculpture. The artists relied upon colour, instead of alternation of light and shade, to give emphasis and variety to the composition. Now that the colour has entirely disappeared, the effect of the sculpture viewed at a distance is comparatively cold and lifeless, in spite of the prodigious amount of labour bestowed upon it.

The Indian ideal which we see in process of evolution at Amarāvatī was finally perfected several centuries later. The various types of it have been discussed in the previous chapters. The next great series of sculptured reliefs in which Indian real life is vividly portrayed are those which adorned the great Buddhist shrine of Borobudur, Java's Kailāsa temple. These must be dealt with in greater detail in the next chapter.

Chapter VIII

BOROBUDUR—THE KAILĀSA OF JAVA

The native chronicles of Java, says Sir Stamford Raffles in his History, date the earliest arrival of colonists from India about A.D. 75, when a prince of Gujarāt led an expedition to the island, which did not, however, succeed in making a permanent settlement. In 603, they narrate, a great fleet convoying some 5,000 men, including agriculturists and artificers, established a Gujarātī dynasty in the centre of the island, under whose rule most of the great monuments, including the city of Prambānam and the famous stūpa of Borobudur, were built. But modern archæological research has revealed the fact that about 750, the approximate date of the building of Borobudur, the then ruling power in Central Java had been expelled by a rival Indian dynasty, the Cailendras, established in Sumatra ; the Cailendras, therefore, must be regarded as the builders of Borobudur.

The famous stūpa, the greatest Buddhist monument of the world, has a character of its own quite distinct from any known Indian prototypes. It may rightly be called Indo-Javanese in style, for it was characteristic of the ancient Vedic culture, which spread over so large a part of Asia, that it always adapted itself to its local environment. Yet both in its structural design and in its splendid sculptured decoration, this great monument of Mahāyāna Buddhism in Java is inspired by Indian thought and Indian craftsmanship.

The original Indian stūpa of Vedic times was the funeral mound raised over the ashes of an Aryan chieftain.[1] The early Buddhist stūpas have only the significance of a reliquary or memorial, enclosed by a railing to prevent the intrusion of evil spirits, the umbrella which crowned the summit being only the emblem of the Buddha's rank as a Sākyan prince. But gradually the stūpa was transformed into a religious or metaphysical symbol. The hemispherical dome became the symbol of the inverted sky-lotus. Its pinnacle, a series of umbrellas, piled one over the other and carved underneath with lotuses, stood for the higher spheres, culminating in the planes unconditioned by form and free from sensual desire. When the Buddha himself was deified and translated to Mt. Kailāsa, the central point of the world Yantra, the stūpa was converted into a shrine for his image, and Siva's Himalayan hermitage became the final goal for the Buddhist as well as for the Hindu pilgrim. The Brahmanical doctrine of Yoga, at first regarded by Buddhist teachers as rank heresy, was adopted by Mahāyāna philosophy and inspired the idealism of the Buddhist artist and craftsman. Just as the artist sought by the practice of Yoga to visualise the image of the deity, so the builder, in designing the shrine where the image was to be placed, kept ever in his mind's eye the holy shrine where the Divine Yogi himself dwelt. The traditional rite of circumambulation of the temple, as well as the pilgrim's journey to Kailāsa, became a symbolic act of Yoga, the following of the spiral ascent which brought the Yogi to Nirvāna.

---

[1] For an elucidation of the complex symbolism of the dome see Ananda Coomaraswamy, "Two Reliefs from Bhārhut in the Freer Gallery", *Journal of the Indian Society of Oriental Art*, 1938, pp. 149-162. " . . . . the *thupa*, in representing the complete extinction of the wake, is a representation of the 'whole' Buddha, cosmic and supracosmic, immanent and transcendant, just as the Vedic Fire-altar had been a representation and construction of the whole (*kritsna*) Agni-Prajapati, 'limited and unlimited' (*parimita-parimita*), expressed and unexpressed (*nirukta-nirukta*) together with all the other contraries (not 'opposites', because there is no 'opposition' of finite and infinite of which the former is included in and does not limit the latter as appears in connection with the axis of the whole structure of which axis the undetermined and immeasurable length is not in any way affected by the delimitation of a 'part' of this length by the ground and roof of the *thupa* itself, which represents the Universe, the realm of dimension and number—*mana, sankha*)." Also see the brilliant exposition of the *stupa* as a symbolic architectural form in P. Mus., *Borobudur*, Hanoi, 1935.—P.C.

When the pilgrim had climbed the hill on which Borobudur is built, and the long flights of steps leading to the mysterious hidden shrine which crowns the summit, the prospect would bring many reminiscences of the great northern pilgrimage of India. A wide, fertile plain stretches beneath, like the Ganges Valley at the foot of the Himalayas. In the distance majestic mountain tops tower into the sky : not, indeed, the shining snow-peaks, sources of holy rivers, outwardly so infinitely calm, but covering the intense creative energy latent even in Nature's most peaceful moods. Here are seen grim, grey volcanoes, both extinct and active, which ever seem to threaten with destruction the fair edifice of the Creator. But to the Indian thinker the contrast would seem only to illustrate Nature's law, symbolised in the cosmic Yantra with its two similar equilateral triangles, which interlaced keep the universe in equipoise.[1] Siva was here also, as He was at Kailasa, only in His destructive mood.

Convincing proof that such recollections occurred to the Indian colonists of Java is given by the fact that the highest mountain-top is named Smeru, after Sumeru, the mythical mountain of the Himalayas, while other volcanoes, like Himalayan peaks, bear the names of the Pandava pilgrims. The principal river of Central Java is named after the Himalayan river Sarayu, upon the banks of which Rama's famous city stood.[2]

The builders of Borobudur, therefore, when they created a splendid shrine for all the Buddhas of the Mahayana pantheon, followed the Indian tradition and designed it after the cosmic Yantra, used in the ritual of Yoga, but in three dimensions instead of two. The plane Yantra, Fig. 2, when constructed in three dimensions, becomes a hemispheroid, like an early Indian stupa, with the generating point, the Bindu, or Kailasa, at the top (Fig. 3). It is used in this form in modern Hindu ritual, and is the symbol of the Brahmanda, the cosmic egg or spheroid, with its seven upper and seven lower planes ; but only the upper half is worshipped, as representing the earthly and heavenly spheres.

In the stupa of Borobudur this cosmic symbol is constructed on a colossal scale. It was designed with a square base, like the miniature Yantra used in ancient and modern ritual, and arranged in seven planes after the metaphysical concept. Constructional necessities compelled the builders to flatten the curve of the spheroid considerably, so that pilgrims in their circumambulation might be able to reach the summit. Those who followed the whole procession path up to the stupa's crowning pinnacle were performing symbolically the same rite as the Buddhist pilgrim of to-day, when he first visits the sacred places associated with the various lives of the Blessed One on earth, and then climbs the heights of Kailasa to bow down in worship, as if in the presence of the Lord Buddha.

In exactly the same way the pilgrims at Borobudur, when they entered the lowest procession path, began to pass in review the previous lives of the Buddha, as told in the jatakas, and the story of his last rebirth. Then, as they mounted to the higher circular terraces, they entered the regions of formlessness, the transcendental Himalayas, where the images of the Dhyani-Buddhas (Plate 2A) were only dimly visible through the lattice-work of their bell-shaped Yantras (Fig. 1). Finally, at the summit, they reached Kailasa, the centre of the cosmic Yantra, where Gautama Buddha sat calling earth to witness his Enlightenment, as he had done under the bodhi-tree at Gaya, but invisible, like Siva in his Himalayan cell, except to the adept in Yoga ; for the image was entirely embedded in the masonry of the cupola which crowns the stupa, so that no human eyes could see it, nor human hands touch it. It was thus that the creators of Borobudur symbolised the highest insight, the supreme goal of the devout Buddhist.

The skyline of Borobudur (Fig. 4), with its myriad pinnacles, like mountain peaks, suggested the worlds innumerable from which all the Buddhas had flocked on that great day when Gautama proclaimed his Buddhahood. But architecturally Borobudur, in its incomplete and ruined state, is far less impressive than Ankhor Vat in Cambodia ; chiefly

[1] The equilateral triangle, standing on its apex, is a symbol of water ; reversed it becomes a symbol of fire.
[2] Dr. J. P. Vogel, "Influences of Indian Art" (Indian Society Publication), p. 37.

Fig. 4.—Skyline of Borobudur.

on account of its stunted proportions, which are partly due to the exigencies of the procession paths, and partly to a miscalculation in engineering which obliged the builders to prevent the collapse of the whole edifice by strengthening it with a solid band of masonry at the base.   The height of the walls of the lowest terrace in the original project was thus considerably reduced.   Nevertheless, as the master builder imagined it, with its vast glittering white walls, painted reliefs, and gilded pinnacles and cupolas, it was a noble conception worthy of one of the world's great spiritual Teachers ; a poet's dream of India's heavenly city, Himalaya, the Abode of Snow.

A detailed description of this great architectural *tour de force* does not come within the scope of this book.   The chief glory of Borobudur now is its wonderful series of sculptures, extending in the aggregate for a length of nearly three miles, and expounding in ordered sequence the mythology and philosophy of Mahāyāna Buddhism.   For the devout Buddhist who paced these sculptured galleries they were illustrated scriptures, which even the most ignorant could read, telling in living words the life-story and message of the Master.   We have discussed already the Indian idealised type of Divinity which is represented on the monument in countless images of Buddhas and Bodhisattvas in high and low relief, sculptured in panels and placed in niches above the different galleries. We are now only concerned with the reliefs along the procession paths which exhibit the Indian sculptor's highest achievements in the treatment of scenes of real, or quasi-real, life.   Fortunately, though some have suffered from exposure to the weather, they have escaped the ruthless vandalism to which nearly all works of art in India have been subject.

These reliefs give, in the upper half, one hundred and twenty scenes from the life of the Buddha, following the text of the Lalitavistara, and, in the lower half, a similar number from the jātakas—the legends of his previous existences.   Tradition gives only the name of the chief master-builder, one Gunadharma.[1]   The Indian master-builder is always a skilled carver.   Doubtless some of the principal sculptures were from his own chisel, but in such a vast undertaking a great number of apprentices and inferior craftsmen must have been employed, over whose work the chief designers could only exercise general supervision.   In fact the sculptures show a much more uneven quality of technique than is found in small-scale monuments like Amarāvatī, but the extraordinary beauty of the best of them can be seen in the reproductions given in Plates 29 to 34.   They are from a splendid set of photographs made in 1872 for the Batavian Society of Arts and Sciences by Mr. J. van Kinsbergen.

Evidently there is a close kinship between them and the sculptures of Amarāvatī, but the Borobudur craftsmen have been inspired by the colossal scale of the building to adopt a much more spacious and dignified style of design.   To compare them with the Panathenaic frieze of the Parthenon would serve no useful purpose, though as artistic achievements of the highest class the best Borobudur sculptures would not suffer by the

[1] Dr. N. J. Krom, "The Life of the Buddha on the Stūpa of Borobudur."

comparison. There is as little kinship between the academic refinements of the Parthenon sculptures and this supremely devout and spontaneous art as there is between Indian and Hellenic religious thought. They are much more closely allied in feeling and expression to the sculptures of Donatello and those of the best Italian masters of the fourteenth and fifteenth centuries.

A very near parallel may be found in the celebrated bronze doors of the Baptistery of Florence, by Lorenzo Ghiberti, one of the great masterpieces of Italian art, of which Michelangelo is reported to have said that they were "fit to be the gates of Paradise." In these gates a number of Biblical scenes are treated in a series of relief panels with accessories similar to those used by the Borobudur sculptors, i.e., the figures are accompanied by representations of temples, houses, trees, clouds, water, and landscape.

The Italian master achieved a technical triumph which won for him the rapturous applause of the *virtuosi* of his day, yet by the use of perspective and of an excessive number of planes of relief, in the attempt to produce the illusion of pictorial effects, he sacrificed breadth and dignity and overstepped the limitations of plastic art. In spite of its extraordinary technical qualities the main impression given by Ghiberti's masterpiece is that the artist was more concerned in exhibiting his skill to his fellow-citizens than in producing the most perfect and reverent rendering of the sacred subjects.

The Borobudur sculptors, with much deeper reverence and less self-consciousness, show conclusively that art is greater than artifice. The very simplicity and unaffected naiveté of their style are much more impressive and convincing than the elaborate efforts of the Italian master, who, with all his wonderful technique, is far behind in imagination and poetic feeling. Especially in the magnificent conventionalism of the accessories—the trees, buildings, ships, etc.—does the art of Borobudur rise above the art of Ghiberti. Western artists, also, before their intuitive faculties were atrophied by the pedantic teaching of the schools, saw that their conventional perspective, not strictly bound by optical laws, gave a much greater richness and variety in design. That is why the pre-Renaissance art of Europe has generally a much finer decorative quality than the art of the Renaissance, or the academic art of modern Europe.

The great charm of the Borobudur sculptures lies in their absolute truth of expression, a truthfulness which is the more conspicuous because the artists have not tied themselves to the petty rules and regulations upon which the modern dilettante critic so often bases his judgement of works of art. What modern academician would dare to disregard the relative proportion between human figures and the accessory trees, houses, temples, elephants, oxen, and carts as these men have done—not because they did not *know*, but because they felt the story must be told in that way? And yet the disproportion does not jar, it only contributes marvellously to the strength of the story-telling and to the richness of the decorative effect.

The artists who conceived these sculptures were not aiming at the applause of their fellow-men, but trying to tell the story of the Master in the way they conceived He had told it, offering their labour and skill as a devout gift to His shrine. Art seems to reach its highest and go deepest when all that is small and common is excluded, when the effort of the artist is invisible, and when nature, purified by the God-given powers of man, is, as it were, re-born. The simple life these men led left them in peace to concentrate their whole soul on their work, and kept their minds free and able to listen to the voices of nature and of their own inspiration—the soul of nature speaking to the soul of men.

They loved and reverenced the Buddha with all their heart, and through the directness and strength of this feeling, and because there was nothing to jar on it in their life and surroundings, they, with the great gifts they had, could show what they felt without feebleness and without faltering. The spiritual power of their art has broken the chains of technical rules, risen above all thought of what critics call right or wrong, and speaks with divinely inspired words straight to the heart of the listener. In this heaven-born quality of inspiration European art has rarely equalled, and never excelled, the art of Borobudur.

Just as we have seen in the Indian ideal type, the smaller anatomical details of the figures are suppressed, but the real spark of life, the essence of feeling, is wonderfully manifested. Every group and every figure are absolutely true and sincere in expression of face, gesture, and pose of body ; and the actions which link the various groups and single figures together are strongly and simply told, without any effort or striving for effect—it was so, because so it could only be.

The lower panel in Plate 29 is one of the most beautiful and perfectly preserved of the whole series.[1] We think at once of Tanagra. Yes, but the pretty domestic art of Tanagra produced nothing so great as this. It is Tanagra art, without its coquetry, chastened and strengthened by a profound religious sentiment. The scene is one which may be witnessed every day in any Indian village, but the inspiration of the art which created such a masterpiece lives no longer.

It is only a group of Indian women drawing water from the village tank, under the shade of the sacred tree next to the village temple. One of them bending over the lotus-covered water is just filling her vessel, watching it intently as she draws it up with her left hand, while her right is raised to grasp it when it comes within reach. Some with their vessels filled and balanced truly on their heads are already moving off with queenly steps, and wend their way towards the village shrine. Others are approaching the water with their empty vessels. And one apart from the rest is kneeling at the foot of the Bodhisattva and receiving instructions from him.

The story comes from the jātakas. It tells how the Buddha was once born as the Prince Sudhana, son of a king of northern India. Sudhana falls in love with a fairy princess, who, having incautiously flown down to earth from the Himalayas, had been captured by a hunter with his magic lasso. The prince took her to his father's court, but a crafty Brahman minister having plotted to take her life, the queen helps her to escape. She flies away home, but leaves with a hermit in the forest a ring and instructions by which the prince might find his way into the Himalayan fairyland. After a long and difficult journey the prince reaches it and meets the princess's handmaidens going to fetch water for her bath.

In the series of thirty panels which tell the story is this most delightful one, where the prince sitting under a tree talks to one of the girls and drops the ring into her pitcher, so that the princess might know of his arrival. The artist with a rare touch of genius has conveyed, in the gracious figure of Sudhana and the reverent attitude of the handmaiden, a subtle suggestion of the higher life towards which the Prince was aiming. We know now that in another life he will become the Enlightened One and the Teacher of the Law.

How marvellously the whole scene lives and moves, and what an atmosphere of purity, freshness, and womanly grace breathes through it all. We seem to feel the brightness of the Indian morning and hear the twittering of the birds as they fly from tree to tree and hover round the temple roof. Every figure is full of unconscious grace and dignity ; every movement helps, but there is no posing for effect, no effort of the artist to show his cleverness. The simplicity of the treatment is as wonderful as its strength. Where Ghiberti or any modern European sculptor would use half-a-dozen planes of relief, the Indian artist is content with one or two, and tells his story with much greater vividness and truthful feeling.

And over all there is an undefinable sense of reverent adoration, for the beauty of

[1] With reference to this relief Krom remarks, *ibid.*, p. 259, "The relief is a fine work of art. The sculptor must have worked at it with great pleasure. We can see with what care the pond has been carved, the lotus flowers and leaves, the birds disporting themselves in the water and especially the little delicate plants on the edge of it in front. Above all we admire the graceful figures of the maidens to which he has given such charm. As regards composition and the execution of details, this beautiful relief is one of the best on the Barabudur, undoubtedly the work of a great artist."—P.C.

nature and for the divine wisdom which created it. This is the leading motif in the music of all these panels. It is repeated again and again in different keys and different chords, every note and every phrase helping to make one harmonious sequence of praise and thankfulness.

The upper panel in the same plate is one of the series which tells the marvellous story of the Buddha's last appearance on earth.[1] Queen Māyā, seated in her palace, on the right, has sent a messenger to ask the king to come to her at once, to explain the wonderful dream she has dreamt. King Shuddhodana, to whom a heavenly voice has already whispered the news, receives the messenger as he stands under the state umbrella, with his ministers in attendance, pondering over the strange event. The royal elephant, a noble beast, salutes his master, and seems to say, "Come, let us go to the palace!"

In the upper panel of Plate 30 the King is distributing rewards to ten Brahmans who interpreted the dream. There is wonderful descriptive power and truth of expression in the lower panel of the same plate, a continuation of the story of Prince Sudhana, showing the nautch party performing at his wedding festivities.[2] The dominant note in the composition is given by the Devadāsi, dancing Siva's dance in front of the canopy under which the bridegroom and his bride are seated. The close grouping of the musicians on the left, all absorbed in the accompaniment of the dance, balanced by the group of animals and attendants, all intently listening on the right, helps to fix attention on the superb figure of the dancer whose rhythmic movements and gestures interpret the cosmic law. The Prince himself also listens to the music, but in a pensive mood, for his thoughts are far, far away. This again is a perfectly true note. The instinct which led the artist to express this touches the centre of true feeling.

The two panels in the next illustration, Plate 31, show the same superlative sense of beauty and power of grouping figures together to express varying feelings and emotions. The upper one represents Queen Māyā, seated in her state car and hastening with her retinue to the Lumbini Gardens, where, as she had been told in a dream, her son, who was to be the salvation of the world, should be born. The male attendants surround the car in zealous care of their royal mistress, clearing the path in front of any untoward or unseemly thing, and holding the insignia of royalty proudly over her, while the ladies in her train follow behind in lively converse on the coming event. The expression of queenly dignity in Māyā and the eager expectancy in the throng of her attendants, as well as the movement of the whole procession, are perfectly given. The lower panel, belonging to the jātaka series, shows a princess inside a temple, making offerings at the shrine. Her attendant ladies, waiting outside, make an exquisite group, designed with consummate art.[3] It is one of the gems of Borobudur, evidently the work of a master-craftsman.

We now pass by over twenty panels, all well designed as decoration, but lacking the distinctive touch of the master. We must remember that a great monument like this was a school of traditional craftsmanship, in which the sons and pupils of the masters of the age were allotted their share of the work under their guru's eye, and thus learnt their craft.

In none of these scenes is there any set form or mannerism in the grouping, such as we often observe in Ghiberti's art and in the composition of many of the best Italian masters.

[1] Havell's description of this panel is not quite correct. According to the *Lalitavistara*, Maya descended from her palace into the *asoka* wood after the wondrous dream in which she was visited by the white elephant, and sent a messenger to Suddhodhana requesting his presence. The king proceeded to the *asoka* wood, but on reaching it he hesitated to enter, and he felt his body became heavy. What we actually see in the relief is Suddhodhana standing outside the *asoka* wood reflecting on his strange mental and physical condition. Maya is seen seated in a pavilion to the left though the absence of *asoka* trees is a little perplexing. See N. J. Krom, *Barabudur*, The Hague, 1927, pp. 118-119.—P.C.

[2] According to Krom, *ibid.*, p. 260, the relief represents Sudhana and Manohara enjoying themselves at the court of Druma. The dancer is accompanied by a group of seated musicians playing the flute, pot-shaped drum and a large cymbal. Behind them stand a row of women playing on small cymbals.—P.C.

[3] The lower panel has not yet been identified with certainty. See Krom, *ibid.*, p. 261.—P.C.

The spacing of the figures and their accessories in the panel is by no means haphazard : it is all admirably designed.   But these Borobudur sculptors have known how to convey the essence of truth, as it is found in nature, without obtruding their own personality or the technique of their craft.   Their art, used only in the service of truth and religion, has made their hands the obedient tools of a heaven-sent inspiration ; and their unique power of realising thus, with a depth and sincerity unsurpassed in the art of any land, gives them a right to rank among the greatest of the symbolists in the whole history of art.

Again we must pass by a number of sculptured panels of no special artistic interest : the master-craftsman's touch is wanting, though the uncritical eyes of the pilgrims would not notice the difference, for the story is intelligible and never lacks interest for them. This is not a record of the dead past, but the realisation of the great Teacher's living presence.   Then we come to another fine group, the upper panel in Plate 32, showing Prince Siddhartha in the archery tournament, competing with other Sākya lords, his cousins, for the hand of the fair Yasodharā.   The scene is described by Sir Edwin Arnold in "The Light of Asia:" [1]

> Then Nanda challenged for the arrow-test
> And set a brazen drum six gows away,
> Ardjuna six and Devadatta eight ;
> But Prince Siddhartha bade them set his drum
> Ten gows from off the line, until it seemed
> A cowry-shell for target.   Then they loosed
> And Nanda pierced his drum, Ardjuna his,
> And Devadatta drove a well-aimed shaft
> Through both sides of his mark, so that the crowd
> Marvelled and cried ; sweet Yasodharā
> Dropped the gold sari o'er her fearful eyes,
> Lest she should see the Prince's arrow fail.

The bow first offered him Siddhartha broke in testing, and then called for one "more fit for Sākya lords to use"—the famous bow of Siva, kept in the temple, which no man had yet been able to draw :

> Twice Siddhartha tried
> Its strength across his knee, then spake—"Shoot now
> With this, my cousins !" but they could not bring
> The stubborn arms a hair's breadth nearer use ;
> Then the Prince, lightly leaning, bent the bow.
>   .   .   .   .   .
> Then lifting fair a shaft, he drew and loosed,
> And the keen arrow clave the sky and drave
> Right through that farthest drum, nor stayed its flight
> But skimmed the plain beyond, past reach of eye.

[1] Sir Edwin Arnold's poetic version of the incident leaves several elements in the bas-relief composition unexplained. According to the *Lalitavistara*, which is the Buddhist text chosen by the Javanese sculptor for illustration, the competitors included Ananda who put up an iron drum at two *krosas* as target and also Devadatta, Sundarananda and Dandapani who put up their iron drums at a distance of *four krosas*, six *krosas* and two *vojanas* respectively.   The future Buddha, Prince Siddhartha, set up "an iron drum at ten *krosas*, behind that seven *tala* palm trees and an iron boar on a pedestal."   Each one of the competitors shot their own targets but could not shoot further, but when it came to the turn of Siddhartha, he shot the arrow not only through his own target but also the iron drums of the previous competitors, the seven palm trees, the iron boar, and after that piercing the ground the arrow vanished from sight.   In the Borobudur relief only the seven palm trees through which the Buddha shot his arrow are shown and none of the other objects. For further details see N. J. Krom, *ibid.*, pp. 151-153.—P.C.

The artist has not made an exhibition of his own skill : he knew how to conceal his art. Nor has he tried to indicate any supernatural quality in the Prince's strength. He just shows us the incident as it might have occurred in the court life of his time. The simplicity and unconventionality with which the tale is told gives it its charm, and the student of the present day who reads these panels can enjoy the artist's power, just as the myriads of devout pilgrims who reverently paced the procession paths of Borobudur did in bygone days.[1]

Again we must pass by a long stretch of richly sculptured wall, with only a panel here and there which calls for special remark. Then we find another gem, Plate 33, in the upper part of which the Prince having at last attained Nirvāna, bathes in the River Nairañjanā. Here we have no longer the man with human desires and aims, but the Buddha in the full glory of his divinity. All his struggles and trials are finished now : he has passed through all the gates of difficulty and doubting. Now he is the noble, purified soul, in a noble body filled with heavenly bliss.

Every creature that comes near him is conscious of it. The spirits of the upper air, the Vidhyādharas and Siddhas, whose voices the pilgrims heard so often in their wanderings, flock round him showering scented flowers on the river, feeling and rejoicing in the power of purity which goes out of him. The Nāgas, the water-sprites, raise their heads to do him homage. On the other side of the river, three of the Devas, in the attire of Javanese princes, prostrate themselves before him, and reverently scoop up water, like pilgrims, to carry away with them to their divine mansions.

The doe from the forest knows at once that her Lord and Protector has come, He who in His boundless love once offered His life for hers. She whispers the joyful tidings to her little one, which turns its head in curiosity to look upon Him whom all nature worships. The lower half of the panel, with its magnificently designed ship in a storm, tells another jātaka story, typical of the adventurous life of the Indian colonists.[2] The sailors are trying desperately to furl sails and bring the ship to anchor. On land a benevolent householder and his wife, under the grateful shade of the palm-grove surrounding the house, appear to be distributing food to the survivors of the wreck. The contrast between the fury of the ocean and the peaceful serenity of the land is drawn with the faithfulness and sincerity of feeling characteristic of all these reliefs. The two different incidents and different moods are ingeniously knit together in one rich and harmonious decorative scheme.

The last of the illustrations selected to show the work of the master-sculptor at Borobudur, Plate 34, is one of a series representing scenes in the Tusita heavens, where, according to Mahāyāna teaching, all Bodhisattvas are born before they appear in the world, and where Maitreya, the coming Buddha, now lives.

Here, also, the Buddha, Gautama, having finished his incarnations on earth and accomplished his Pari-nirvāna, is said to have gone to teach and convert his mother Māyā, who died a week after his birth. This is probably the scene represented in the panel.

[1] The lower panel of this plate, not described by Havell, is probably related to legendary story of King Mandhatar. Having conquered the earth, Mandhatar became so powerful that he shared half the throne of Indra, the king of Gods, and helped him in inflicting a defeat on the Asuras. Filled with pride, he wanted to dispossess even Indra of his sovereignty, at which thought he fell from heaven, and knew that death was at hand. According to Krom, *ibid.*, p. 274, the relief represents this scene where Indra, who is shown to the extreme left, is walking away from Mandhatar and on the point of hurling him to the earth.—P.C.

[2] The relief forms part of a long series illustrating the career of the *bhikshu* Mahakatyayana as related in the story of Rudrayana in the *Divyavadana*. The wise ministers Hiru and Bhiru fled from the city of Roruka due to the misbehaviour of the king, and founded the cities of Hiruka and Bhirukachha. The scene represents the landing of Hiru at Hiruka. On the right we see the party of immigrants in a ship and on the left we see them on land being received by a family consisting of man, woman and child. The representation of the ship is very interesting and gives us an idea of the vessels used at that time. The house to the left, standing on piles with room under the floor for servants, is also very interesting. The relief also gives us an idea of the manner in which the Indian emigrants arrived at Java and the hospitable reception accorded to them.—P.C.

The Buddha, enthroned in all the glory of his divinity under a splendid canopy, is preaching the Law to Māyā, who sits in happy ecstasy listening to the inspired words of her son.

The two symbolic trees, magnificently conventionalised, the doves and sacred birds which hover overhead, contribute greatly to the richness of the decorative scheme; but the rare genius of the artist is most conspicuous in the charming group of the Queen's five attendants, leaning forward as far as respect for their royal mistress will permit, and straining their ears so that no word of the Divine Truth may escape them.

Were it not that the reputation of works of art in Europe depends far more upon the label attached to them by the pedantic tradition of our so-called classical education than upon their intrinsic merits, these wonderful sculptures would not have remained in obscurity so long. Mr. van Kinsbergen's photographs, taken in 1872, were buried in the libraries of six learned societies for thirty-six years, before artists in Europe took notice of them. But it can hardly be doubted that had these sculptures been labelled "Greek," "Roman," or "Italian," the volumes of criticism and commentaries on them would have filled many libraries; casts of them would be found in every European art-school and museum; tourists would have flocked to inscribe their names on them or chip off fragments as souvenirs; art-dealers and American millionaires would have jostled one another in eagerness to possess them. But being only Indo-Javanese and memorials of a great Asiatic culture, they were for long years totally unappreciated, though well-known to oriental savants.

And while the living traditions of this great art still survive in India, we establish schools to teach Indians sculpture and painting as they are taught in Europe, and send out sculptors and painters to decorate Indian buildings, under the pretext that we are helping to elevate the taste of the Indian public.

Europe of the present day has far more to learn from India in art than to teach. Religious art in Europe is altogether lost: it perished in our so-called Renaissance. In India the true spirit of it still lives.

Quite apart from its purely æsthetic quality there is in an art like this an ethical value which modern India for the most part seems unable to understand and utilise. It is just in this ethical principle that modern education on classical lines misconstrues the spirit of classical culture and art. Every national art is an expression of national character, and when we compare the devout and reverent outlook upon Nature shown in these Borobudur sculptures with the utter vulgarity of modern India, as we have made it, it is only too evident that in one respect our education falls immeasurably behind that of Greece and of ancient India, through the neglect of Plato's injunction "to use the beauties of earth as steps along which we mount upwards."

India, vulgarised by modern education and by the sordid ideals of modern commercialism, will never compensate humanity for the passing of India with its love of beauty—the perfect law of Nature, in which science and art are one.

CHAPTER IX

HINDU ART IN JAVA AND CAMBODIA
PORTRAITURE

THE Borobudur sculptures are in some respects unique, both in the perfection of their art and in the good fortune which has preserved them from wanton destruction. The obscurity into which the great monument fell was its best protection, saving it from the fate of so many other masterpieces of Indian art. No fanatics, either European or native, have laid sacrilegious hands upon it ; no enterprising builders have made use of it as a stone quarry, or as materials for lime ; no railway contractors or energetic public works officers have broken up its splendid sculptures for ballast or road-mending. What it has suffered has been from natural causes, the destructive influences of a tropical climate, from earthquake, or from mere neglect. In recent years, under the zealous care of the Netherlands India Archæological Department, it has been judiciously restored and is now safe from any vandalism.

Just as in India proper, Buddhist and Brahmanical art in Java had a common philosophy and a common technical tradition. The cult of Siva, says Dr. Vogel,[1] flourished in Java side by side with Buddhism, and, as we have seen in the design of Borobudur, the ideas of both religious schools intermingled.

Some of the finest Brahmanical images of Java have been illustrated in Plates 9, 14A, and 21A. They often bear a distinct impress of Indian origin, and may have been sometimes direct importations from the most famous Indian centres of temple craft, or sometimes the work of royal craftsmen brought from India to give distinction to the great building enterprises of the Indo-Javanese dynasties. Royal courts always vied with each other in the skill of their artists and craftsmen : the latter were always regarded as valuable loot in war, and the loan or gift of a master-craftsman would be a most acceptable proof of friendliness in diplomatic intercourse between the rival dynasties which from time to time held command of the chief Asian sea-routes. In this way there would have been a constant flow of artistic culture from India to her great Eastern colonies, diminishing in force as the colonial rulers obtained a sufficient supply of local craftsmen to meet their artistic requirements. But both in Java and Cambodia art gradually sank down again to its original primitive level when Indian thought ceased to control and inspire it.

Prambānam, the ancient capital of Central Java, has a triple-shrined Saiva temple, dedicated to the Trimūrti, differing in structure from the Borobudur stūpa, but surrounded, like the latter, by an enclosed procession path, on the walls of which is exhibited a long series of sculptured reliefs for the edification of worshippers. The subject, in this case, is taken from the Hindu epic, the Rāmāyana, which was current folk-lore in Java as it was throughout India.

These sculptures are probably two or three centuries later in date than the great Buddhist monument. They mark the climax and the beginning of the decline of Indo-Javanese art. Though there are passages of magnificent design, carried out with a wonderful richness of plastic effect, generally speaking they lack the fine simplicity and restraint of the best Borobudur sculptures. The master-craftsman's personal touch is most conspicuous in the beginning of the series, illustrated in Plates 35 and 36, a splendid rendering of the opening scene of the Rāma legend, of which various versions are known in India and Java. In this case we may accept Dr. Vogel's opinion that it represents the

[1] "Influences of Indian Art," p. 68.

55

version adopted in Kālidāsa's "Raghuvaṃśa," in which the gods, headed by Brahmā, appeal to Vishnu to incarnate himself as Rāma, in order that the world may be saved from the wicked demon-king, Rāvana.

Vishnu is discovered in the depths of the cosmic ocean, which teems with varied forms of marine life, reclining in the formal pose of "regal ease" on the serpent Ananta, the symbol of eternity. The deity's *vahan* or vehicle, the sun-bird, Garuda, sits in his mountain-grot on the left, holding Vishnu's flower, the blue lotus. On the right of the panel the gods approach the Lord of Life with their request.

The next scene, Plate 36, brilliantly composed and evidently by the same mastermason, brings us to the court of Ayodhyā, where Rāma and his three brothers were born to King Dasaratha and his three wives. Here Dasaratha is receiving a chela of the great sage Vishvamitra, who by his Yogic power has learnt the intentions of the gods and sends him with the message that he has wonderful news for the king. The whole series of sculptures is admirably illustrated and described by Dr. Wilhelm Stutterheim in his "Rāma-Legenden und Rāma-reliefs in Indonesien."[1]

The inequality of the sculptures, which is so noticeable at Borobudur, is even more marked in the Prambānam reliefs. Here and there are passages of great beauty of design and fine craftsmanship. But the imagination of the sculptors often runs wild, in trying to depict the exploits of Rāma's monkey allies, and shows a tendency to incoherency in composition and looseness in technique.

Only a passing allusion can be made to the remarkable series of sculptures which adorn the great temple of Nakhon Vat, near Angkor, in Cambodia, a vast structure exceeding Borobudur in dimensions, the outer walled enclosure of it measuring two-thirds of a mile on each of its four sides. We are not, however, concerned with the magnificence of the architecture, details of which are given by Fergusson, but with the sculptures illustrating the Rāmāyana and Mahābhārata which decorate the walls of the temple. They are in very low relief, as they were not, like the Borobudur sculptures, intended for open-air effect, but for the reflected light of the magnificent colonnades under shelter of which they were placed. The whole of them, about six and a half feet in height and of an aggregate length of about two thousand feet, were originally gilt.

Casts of these fine sculptures are in the Ethnographic Museum, Berlin, and in the Trocadéro, Paris, but they are not displayed to great advantage there for lack of space. The most striking subject is the legend told in the Rāmāyana of the Churning of the Ocean by the gods and *asuras*, in order to procure *amrita*, the nectar of immortality. This is treated with immense imaginative power and intensity of movement, but the sculptures as a rule do not possess the peculiar charm of Borobudur and Prambānam.

Most of the other subjects are battle scenes from the Mahābhārata, which are described with extreme elaboration and wonderful vigour. In the treatment of the human figure these Cambodia reliefs are strongly suggestive of the Amarāvatī sculptures.

In Cambodia, as in Java, many fine images of Indian origin have been found, for illustrations of which the reader must be referred to the publications of the École Française d'Extrême-Orient and other works dealing with that special subject.

We have now only to discuss the question of portraiture in Indian sculpture. From numerous references in Sanskrit literature it appears that painted portraiture was quite common in India in pre-Mogul times, but allusions to sculptured portraits, as distinguished from images of the gods, are rare. There are several in the Rāmāyana ; one in which Rāma had an image made of Sītā. This was, however, only to meet the dilemma in which he was placed when, after Sītā's exile, he was advised to perform the great horse sacrifice, a ceremony which demanded the presence of his wife, as co-partner in religious rites. Rāma had a golden image of the Queen made for this occasion, and it was carried in front of the procession by his brother Bharat (*Uttara Kanda*, 25).

[1] Georg Muller, Munich.

A. A dryad from the Eastern Gateway, Sānchī Stūpa.
(*From a cast in the Victoria and Albert Museum, London*).

B. Detail from pillar of Eastern Gateway, Sānchī Stūpa.
(*Photo, A. L. Syed*).

PLATE 25

B. Sakya's Nirvana. Sculpture from the Eastern Gateway, Sānchī Stūpa. (*Photo, A. L. Syed*).

A. Adoration of the symbol of the Dharma. Sculpture from the Eastern Gateway, front view, Sānchī Stūpa. (*Photo, A. L. Syed*).

PLATE 26

A. Sculptured slab from the base of the Great Stūpa, Amarāvatī.
(*From a photograph in the India Office Library*).

B. Pillar from Amarāvatī.
Late 2nd century A.D.
(*Indian Museum, Calcutta*).

PLATE 27

A. Sculptured slab from Amarāvatī. (*From the original in the British Museum*).

B. Carving on coping of rail, Amarāvatī. (*Government Museum, Madras*).

PLATE 28

In two other instances Rāma's demon adversaries had life-like portraits made, but the context clearly shows that this branch of sculpture was considered to belong to the black rather than to the fine arts.   The first was when Rāvana wanted to beguile his unhappy captive Sītā into believing that Rāma was dead.   He ordered a skilful craftsman to make a life-like model of Rāma's head which was brought to Sītā, who,

"Seeing the severed head, and finding in the complexion of the face, in the eyes, in the hair, and in the jewelled knot, a likeness to her husband, and recognising it by all these signs and marks, became exceeding sad, and crying like a *kurari*, denounced Kaikeyi bitterly."—*Lanka Kanda*, 32.

In the same book, Indrajit, the son of Rāvana, had an image made of Sītā, and bringing it on his chariot in front of the contending armies, cut it down with his sword.   The trick was so successful that even the astute Hanuman, Rāma's monkey ally, was deceived, and brought to Rāma the news of Sītā's death.

The word used in the text for a likeness—*māya*, illusion or deception—is significant of the orthodox Hindu attitude towards portraiture.   It was the whole object of Hindu endeavour to get rid of *māya*, the illusive appearance of things, and to penetrate to the eternal Reality which stood behind it.   For the artist to occupy himself with a simple imitation of nature was idle and impious.   His aim must be to show the Divinity, which is the only reality.   By the Hindu Shāstras, as well as by the law of Islam, statues of human beings, as such, are distinctly forbidden.   In the Sukranitisāra, already alluded to,[1] it is said : "Only the images of the gods should be made, for they confer heaven and happiness ; but the images of men and others shut the door of heaven and bring ill-fortune."   Again : "A misshapen image of God is always better than an image of man, however well made the latter may be."[2]   This sufficiently explains why on old Indian coins we rarely find effigies of Hindu rulers.   It also explains why, in Hindu sculpture, the tendency has always been to make representations of human beings, even when intended as portraiture, to conform to the ideal type of Divinity.   It was impious to glorify man in his common personality, but not to explain him as one of the manifestations of the universal, divine nature.   Europe says : "The noblest study of mankind is man" : India declares it to be not man, but God, and Hindu art is only concerned in showing the relationship between the human and divine nature.

In the Buddhist period, however, this prejudice against ordinary portraiture was not so strong, and at Bhārhut and Sānchī there are sculptures of semi-divine beings showing a clearly marked individuality.   One from Bhārhut is illustrated in Plate 23A.   Among the later Gandhāran sculptures there are many strikingly characteristic heads which are so distinctly individual that they are taken by some archæologists to be portraits of Gandhāran kings ; but others consider them to be intended for Bodhisattvas, or for guardian demigods.   Very likely they are idealised portraits of kings, deified after death as Bodhisattvas, according to the custom prevalent in Java and Cambodia.

Early Indian coinage also shows the most obvious portraiture (Plate 37C and D) ;[3] but this is pure Græco-Roman art, untouched by Indian influence.   Evidently Græco-Roman artisans at one time had almost a monopoly of some of the mints of northern

---

[1] *Supra*, pp. 40-1.

[2] The same work, after the most minute instructions as to the correct proportions of images, from the total height down to the circumference of the thumb and great toe, adds the following explanations :

"In order that the form of an image may be brought out fully and clearly upon the mind, the image-maker must meditate, and his success will be in proportion to his meditation.   No other way, not even seeing the object itself, will answer this purpose.

"To every part of the image should be given that grace and ease which is most suitable for it . . . . An image with a wrathful look should not have complacent eyes.   Those images are handsome the measurements of which are in accordance with the rules of the Shāstras.   Some, however, are of opinion that what pleases the heart is beautiful.   But the measurements which do not agree with those given in the Shāstras cannot be pleasing to the cultured."

[3] See frontispiece to Vincent Smith's "Early History of India."

India ; and this was, perhaps, the only craft in which Indians of that time were inferior to foreigners.

When the canons of Indian art were finally fixed as part of religious ritual, portraiture as a distinct branch of sculpture seems to have become almost extinct.   In images of the gods the whole aim was to suggest a type of face as far as possible impersonal—that is, to suppress all the details indicative of human individuality, instead of creating a type of ideal human beauty, as in Greek art.   Similarly at Borobudur we find human beings distinguished from one another, not as individuals, but as typical representatives of the class or caste to which they belong, chiefly by difference of dress, action, and gesture. But there is a great deal of Indian sculpture, especially in Java and Cambodia, in which a distinct ethnical type is taken for the head of a Buddha, Bodhisattva, or Hindu demigod, just as in the medieval art of Europe royal personages and dignitaries of the Church suggested the types of Christian saints.

In this, what we may call uncanonical Indian sculpture, we can find types of physiognomy and character given with the highest art, and with as much variety and power of expression as Greek sculpture can show, though it is not, strictly speaking, portraiture. Here Indian art comes into the same plane of thought as European, and we can fairly draw a comparison between them.   That Indian sculptors did not attempt to portray violent emotions and facial expression in the same way as Europeans must again be attributed to a difference of temperament and difference of thought, not to want of capacity.   Their religion taught them that the way to spiritual advancement was by controlling human passions, and this teaching strongly influenced their art.   But the common idea that Indian sculpture is lacking in power of expression is just as wrong as other uninformed opinions on Indian art.   The best Indian sculpture touched a deeper note of feeling and finer sentiments than the best Greek.

Three ethnical types of extraordinary beauty and character are given in Plates 37A and B and 38A.   According to popular tradition, which may or may not be correct, the two on Plate 37 represent Bhima, one of the heroes of the Mahābhārata, famous for his strength and courage.   They are from an ancient Hindu temple, now named after him locally, built in the plateau of Dieng, Central Java.   The third head, Plate 38A, represents the Buddha himself.   It also comes from Java, but is now in the Leyden Museum.[1]

At first sight the suggestion they give of ancient Egyptian or Greek art is almost startling. There is the same greatness of line, broad generalisation, and profound abstraction of the best Egyptian sculpture, and all the refinement of Greek art.   But the similarity comes only from the kinship which exists between all truly great works of art, for these types are wholly Indian.

The contrast of the two characters is given with a depth of penetration which belongs

[1] For an interesting study of portraiture in South Indian sculpture see T. G. Aravamuthan, *Portrait Sculpture in South India*, London, 1931, together with a foreword by Dr. Ananda Coomaraswamy.   Among the earliest portrait sculpture must be mentioned the bust of a priest wearing a robe with trefoil pattern from Mohenjo-Daro (Plate 82D). The Mauryan heads found from Sarnath are also excellent examples of portraiture, and we also get numerous portrait heads and images of the Kushana period from Mathura, including the marvellous group of Kushana emperors from the so-called Devakula near Mathura.   The portrait sculptures decorating the walls of the Nagesvarasvami temple at Kumbhakonam of the early Chola period are among the finest.   The interested reader is also referred to Ananda Coomaraswamy, "Traditional Conception of Ideal Portraiture," *Why Exhibit Works of Art*, London, 1943.   Coomaraswamy distinguishes between two different traditions of portrait sculpture in India, one being "posthumous, hieratic and ideal on the one hand, and taken from life, profane, and sentimental on the other," the former being represented by several images that have survived to the present day.   These are marked by an ideal expression without reference to individual peculiarities.   Numerous references are also found in ancient literature to portraits where a real likeness to the subject portrayed was insisted upon, though of the examples that survive there are few; if any, earlier than the Mughal period. This difference can only be understood by references to the Indian doctrine "in which a distinction is drawn between the appearance of the man on one hand, and on the other the interior image of the very man invisible to the physical, but accessible to the eye of contemplation."—P.C.

only to the finest portraiture. In the two Bhima heads the artist, with a few bold clearly-drawn forms, shows us the born fighter and leader of men. In the large square forehead, the full firm jaws, the eyes set wide apart, and the determined mouth—half-savage, even cruel when his blood is roused—we recognise a young Alexander, a fighter who knows his strength and revels in it. All his desires are human, yet there is nothing low or brutal in his nature. He is a great national hero, a war-lord fit to lead and command a noble, free-born race.

Compare this with the head of the Buddha, Sākya-Muni. There is an infinity of difference in the type, yet the art is the same in its greatness and its inwardness. It is a true portrait-type of a high-bred intellectual Indian, but all that is pure, spiritual, and holy in Indian thought and religion is summed up in this supremely lovely face. The perfect oval shape, the small refined chin, and the finely chiselled features, speak of the god-like man who chose to leave all that was his—a royal throne, wealth, and earthly happiness —only to find the Way to help his suffering fellow-men.

The nobly vaulted brow and exquisitely formed eyes, with half-fallen meditative lids, tell us of infinite spiritual strength. A touch of sadness seems to rest on the full and tender lips, yet we can almost see them wreathed with a consoling, loving smile, and hear them utter words of blessing and perfect peace.

Compare it, if you will, with its assumed Gandhāran prototype, or with the Grecian models which Gandhāra had in its mind ; but there is in this art a depth and spirituality which never entered into the soul of Greece.

The method of treating the hair in formal curls, which is characteristic of the Indian ideal of the Buddha, has given rise to much archæological speculation and condemnation. The general conclusion, founded on the assumption of Indian artistic incapacity and bad taste, has been that Indian sculptors found the Grecian treatment, generally adopted in the Gandhāran sculptures, too difficult to imitate, and that in consequence they fell back upon this which Vincent Smith called "the feeble conventionalism of ordinary Indian art."[1]

If we adopt the alternative hypothesis that Indian artists possessed quite as much artistic sense as others, the explanation is not very far to seek. In endeavouring to differentiate divine beauty from that of mortals they look for those characteristics which are uncommon in human beings. To this day anything rare or abnormal is popularly regarded in India as a special manifestation of the divine nature. Among Indians of the highest castes, descended from the pure Aryan stock, short curly hair is unusual, and held as a sign of special distinction or good fortune. Naturally enough, it was adopted by Indian artists as one of the marks of divine beauty.

The formalism is only another Indian method of showing that the divine nature transcends that of common humanity. And when this conventionalism is thoroughly well carried out and is a true expression of Indian thought there is no justification for calling it "inartistic" or "depraved," except in the minds of those who are convinced beyond argument that there is nothing admirable in any art the ideals of which differ from those of Greece and Italy.

Java and Cambodia are so rich in beautiful types of sculpture of this class that volumes might be filled with them. But we must now return to India, the fountain-head, where the old art traditions are still alive, whereas the art of Borobudur and Prambānam was practically extirpated in Java by the conversion of the islanders to Islam about the fifteenth century. The next illustration, Plate 39, one of the grandest examples of Indian sculpture extant, not only shows the versatility of Indian sculptors in the past, but points to one of the many potential opportunities which might be opened to their descendants in the present day[2] if Anglo-Indians, instead of regarding them as ignorant

[1] "Journal of the Asiatic Society of Bengal," vol. lviii, 1889, p. 128.
[2] The work of a traditional sculptor of the Orissa School now living is shown in Plate 21B.

children, would learn to make use of the extraordinary artistic resources of the land in which they live and rule. For certainly among all the commonplace statues of British Viceroys and Generals set up on the *maidans* of Calcutta and Bombay, there is not one to be placed in the same category as this. But as our own national craftsmanship has been practically exterminated we have only brought into India the bookman, the paper architect, and the eclectic or amateur artist, who find little beauty in Indian art and can do nothing with it but debase it.

Again, the thought occurs that had it by chance been labelled Roman or Greek, this magnificent work of art would now be the pride of some metropolitan museum in Europe or America. It is one of the two colossal war-horses adjoining the southern façade of the Kanārak temple in Orissa, said to have been built by Marasimha I, about the middle of the thirteenth century. The companion horse is completely mutilated, but this one, apart from the broken ears and the missing head of the charioteer leading it, is almost intact, or was so not many years ago. Its surface, however, has suffered considerably from the weather, and from its exposed position it is likely to suffer more.

Visions of the Mahābhārata, of the clash of battle in heroic ages, and the memories of the past triumphs of Indian chivalry must have inspired the sculptor of this noble figure and his prancing, war-harnessed steed, pacing grandly forward over his prostrate foes. Here Indian sculptors have shown that they can express the pride of victory and the glory of triumphant warfare with as much fire and passion as the greatest European artists : for not even the Homeric grandeur of the Elgin Marbles surpasses the magnificent movement and modelling of this Indian Achilles, and the superbly monumental war-horse in its massive strength and vigour is not unworthy of comparison with Verocchio's famous masterpiece at Venice.

The art we see here is not the less great because there is a great deal in equine anatomy which this unknown sculptor has not cared to emphasise. As he had no modern dilettante critic to satisfy, he was free to make his statement of facts as simple and general as his artistic consciousness dictated, and to strike a note of epic grandeur hardly ever heard in any modern art.

The next illustration, Plate 40A, is of a very different type, and belongs to another school. It is a copper-gilt statuette from Nepāl, now in the Calcutta Art Gallery, representing a demigod, probably Kuvera, the god of worldly prosperity. Divested of his divine attributes, the crown and two supplementary arms, it is a vivid and speaking portrait of a well-fed, self-indulgent Lama or Brahman priest, fond of good living and of all things which make life easy and comfortable.

The contrast between this very mundane deity and the idealised spiritual type we have seen before is very striking. Here the artist has only wanted to show the human body without the divine soul, and in this animated and strongly modelled figure it is evident that he is as capable of doing this as any European sculptor.

It is thoroughly modern and European in all its sentiment. There are no dreams, no religious ecstasy, no high spiritual ideals. It is a personification of materialism and the worldly life. The movement of the fingers speaks of prayer, but the prayers are for worldly, not spiritual benefits. The coarse, strong features and very lively expression of the face indicate sensuality and intellectual power of a low, self-seeking kind, combined with an infinite capacity for the enjoyment of the pleasures of life. The body, well-fed and rounded in every limb, makes it clear that hard work and abstinence is not part of the gospel he preaches. European artists who have neither the time nor the opportunity to study Eastern art commonly assert that the oriental can neither draw nor model the human figure correctly, although oriental life gives far better opportunities for the study of the nude than the artist has in Europe. The criticism is as superficial as it is unjust. The Eastern artist, like the Western, draws what he wants to draw and models what he wants to model. The failure of the European to understand oriental draughtsmanship

Relief from the procession path, Borobudur, Indonesia. (*From a photograph by Van Kinsbergen*).

PLATE 29

Relief from the procession path, Borobudur, Indonesia. (*From a photograph by Van Kinsbergen*).

PLATE 30

Relief from the procession path, Borobudur, Indonesia. (*From a photograph by Van Kinsbergen*).

PLATE 31

Relief from the procession path, Borobudur, Indonesia. (*From a photograph by Van Kinsbergen*).

PLATE 32

Relief from the procession path, Borobudur, Indonesia. *(From a photograph by Van Kinsbergen).*

PLATE 33

Relief from the procession path, Borobudur, Indonesia. (*From a photograph by Van Kinsbergen*).

PLATE 34

comes either from his inability, or from his unwillingness, to understand the intention of it.

I will conclude this brief study of Indian portrait sculpture with another example of the Nepalese School, a copper-gilt statuette of a Tibetan nun, or abbess, holding the usual sacerdotal drum, made of human skulls, in the right hand, and a beggar's bowl in the left (Plate 40B). The original, like the last example, belongs to the collection which the author made for the Calcutta Art Gallery.

This is another delightfully conceived and admirably executed portrait study of an ordinary human being. The real type the artist knew was, perhaps, a frowsy, unkempt, ugly, and awkward Tibetan woman, mumbling an empty formula, with a dull monotonous drum-beat as an accompaniment. But guided unconsciously by his inherited art-traditions, and without any desire to flatter or idealise, he has succeeded in expressing, in the whole attitude and in the treatment of the dress and all the accessories, that style and dignity which national feeling and respect for the spiritual calling of his subject demanded, even though individuals should be found unworthy of it. In all these portrait types, reflecting so sincerely and truthfully the soul of the people, we can feel the different outlook of a great hereditary artistic tradition, compared with that of the petty individualistic art of modern Europe, with all its narrowness, self-consciousness, and provincialism. "Whole æras," said Ruskin, "of mighty history are summed and the passions of dead myriads are concentrated in the existence of a noble (national) art ; and if that art were among us we should feel it and rejoice."

We Europeans who live in India to-day have such an art still living amongst us ; but the history is not our history. The passions of those dead myriads do not move us. So we neither feel it nor rejoice, but rather trample it heedlessly under our feet.

PAINTING

Rāmāyana relief, Prambānam, Indonesia. *(From a photograph by the Archaeological Survey of Netherlands India).*

PLATE 35

Rāmāyana relief, Prambānam, Indonesia. (*From a photograph by the Archaeological Survey of Netherlands India*).

PLATE 36

A, B. Two heads of Bhima, from the Bhima Temple, on the Dung Plateau, Indonesia.

C. Portrait of Chandragupta II Vikramaditya on a coin.
(*Prince of Wales Museum, Bombay*).

D. Portrait of Vasisthiputra Satakarni on a coin.
(*Prince of Wales Museum, Bombay*).

PLATE 37

A. Head of the Buddha. (*From the original in the Ethnographic Museum, Indonesia*).

B. Head of the Buddha, Bronze. (*Patna Museum*).

PLATE 38

Horse and Charioteer, Kanârak, Orissa.   (*From a photograph in the India Office Library*).

PLATE 39

A. Gilt-copper image of Kuvera.
(*From the original in the Calcutta
Art Gallery*).

B. Gilt-copper image of a Tibetan
nun.   Height, 10 in.
(*From the original in the Calcutta
Art Gallery*).

PLATE 40

CHAPTER **X**

INDIAN MURAL PAINTING

THE building of New Delhi has not, apparently, provided any opportunities for Indian painters, but it has drawn attention to the subject of mural painting, now reckoned, like architecture, among the lost, or forgotten arts of India.

As in other countries the art of painting in India became a potent force in national culture in the great schools of mural decoration, and gradually lost touch with real life when pictures came to be regarded more as articles of luxury for the connoisseur than as a means of instruction and spiritual uplift for the whole community.

It is evident from early Buddhist records how closely painting was associated with popular festivals and with civic life in ancient India. No town or village festival was complete unless the streets were made gay with pictures painted on the house-fronts or on scrolls and banners hung on temporary screens of bambu. The traditions of this folk-art are still alive.

While painted stone or wood-carving gradually superseded mural painting in the great temples and stūpas, built to last for ages, painting of the highest class held its own in the *chitra-sālas* of kings' palaces, which were more or less of a temporary character. A *chitra-sāla*, or gallery of mural paintings, was an indispensable annexe to a Hindu palace until quite modern times, or until Indian art fell into disrepute and it became fashionable for Indian princes to import inferior European oil-paintings and European furniture.

The process employed was usually that which is known in Italy as *fresco buono,* in which colours mixed with lime-water are applied to a prepared surface of the finest plaster, while it is still wet, so that they are chemically united with the ground. Indian *fresco buono,* when the wall is a suitable one, is an exceedingly permanent process for interior decoration, and much more durable in a tropical climate than oil-painting. But as it was largely used in exposed situations or in buildings which were not in themselves of a permanent kind, very few of the early Indian fresco-paintings have survived.

These palatial *chitra-sālas* were quadrangular cloisters surrounding one of the palace gardens or pavilions, sometimes reserved for the ladies of the zanana and sometimes apparently a public resort. There are many allusions to them in Sanskrit literature. The Rāmāyana describes Rāvana's palace in Ceylon, where

> Gay, blooming creepers clothed the walls,
> Green bowers were there and picture-halls,
> And chambers made for soft delight.[1]

But the most detailed and interesting description of them is given by Bhavabhuti, the great dramatist of the sixth century, in his "Uttara Rāma Charita," translated by Wilson. Here a whole scene in the first act is devoted to an animated description of a series of pictures illustrating the Rāmāyana, like the reliefs sculptured in the courtyard of the Siva temple at Prambānam described above. The *dramatis personæ* are Rāma, king of Ayodhyā, Sītā, his queen, and Lakshman his brother and faithful companion in exile.

Lakshman invites Rāma to come and look at the pictures:

[1] "Sunda Kanda," Griffiths' trans., Book V, Cant. VI, p. 297.

Come, my most noble brother, on these walls
Behold a skilful artist has portrayed
Your story as he learnt it late from me.

The next scene, called "the contemplation of the picture," is laid in a pavilion in the
garden of the palace. The walls on which the pictures were painted were those which
enclosed the garden and pavilion.

Enter LAKSHMANA, SĪTA, *and* RĀMA

LAKSH. Behold the picture.
SĪTĀ. What are these that crowd
    Around my lord, and seem to hymn his praises ?
LAKSH. These are the heavenly arms,[1] that Vishvamitra,
    The holy sage from Kusa sprung, the friend
    Of all mankind, obtained from great Krisawa,
    And gave them to the prince to wage the fight
    With that malignant demon Taraka.

The next panel of the painting showed Rāma when as a youth he competed for the
hand of Sītā at the court of her father, Janaka, king of Videha, breaking the famous bow
of Siva which no other suitor had been able to bend.
Sītā herself describes the picture :

    Yes, I see my lord.
Dark as the deep blue lotus is his hue,
And strength and grace in every limb appear,
Paternal looks dwell wondering on his face,
Lovely with graceful curls, whilst high disdain
Swells every feature, as with force divine
He snaps asunder the celestial bow.

The relief at Borobudur, illustrating the similar episode in the legendary life of the
Buddha (Plate 32), will give us a suggestion of this painting.
The next panel depicted the marriage of Rāma and Sītā and those of his three brothers :

SĪTĀ. A solemn scene, where gifts of kine secure
    Auspicious destiny, and four bright youths
    Are knit in marriage bonds with four fair maids ;
    I recognise you all—and there, and there am I.

Farther along the wall Rāma recognises the picture of his bride when he brought her
back to his father's palace at Ayodhyā, before the cruel decree of banishment drove them
both to the seclusion of the forest :

    RĀMA. Ah, too well,
Too well does memory bring back the time
When yet an honoured sire was alive,
Whilst yet a mother's love watched o'er our being ;
When all was joy. Ah me, those days are gone !
But here behold—see how the youthful bride,

---

[1] The arms with which Rāma fought against his demon adversaries, personified.

Sketch showing the full design and
proportions of the painting illustrated
on the right.

B. The Buddha's return to his home.   Painting in antechamber, Cave XVII, Ajantā.
(From a photograph by the Archaeological Department, Hyderabad).

PLATE 41

Yasodharā and Rāhula. Detail from the painting of the Buddha's Return.
(*From a photograph by the Archaeological Department, Hyderabad*).

PLATE 42

A. Head of Bodhisattva. Painting in Cave I, Ajantā. (*From a photograph taken for M. Victor Goloubeff*).

PLATE 43

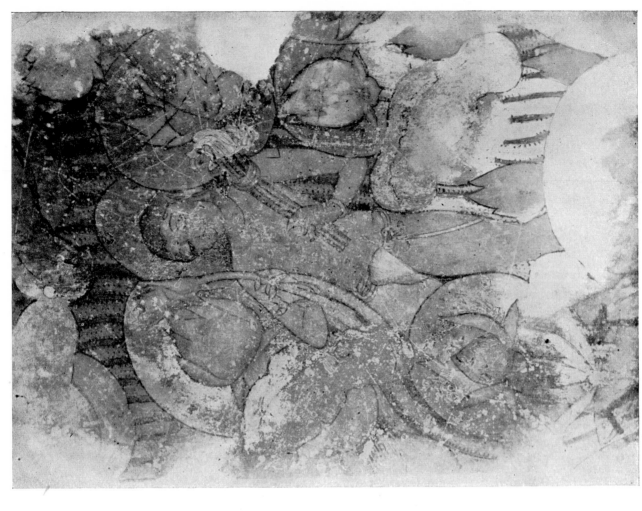

B. Fresco at Sittannavasal. (*From a photograph by S. Raja*).

A. Modern mural decoration in Indian *fresco buono*. In entrance hall of Calcutta School of Art.

PLATE 44

Fair Sītā, wins maternal admiration ;
Her smiling countenance resplendent shines
With youth and loveliness ; her lips disclose
Teeth white as jasmine buds ; her silky curls
Luxuriant shade her cheeks, and every limb
Of brightest texture moves with natural grace,
Like moonbeams gliding through the yielding air.

The dramatist skilfully indicates the varied emotions of the royal spectators, as they review all the incidents of their past life depicted on the walls—their happiness in the jungle hut on the banks of the Godavery :

RĀMA.   Recall'st thou, love, our humble happy dwelling,
   Upon the borders of the shining stream,
   Where every hour in fond endearment wrapped,
   Or in the sweet interchange of thought engaged,
   We lived in transport, not a wish beyond
   Each other, reckless of the flight of time ?

Their encounter with the demons, the abduction of Sītā and the distracted grief of Rāma, the devotion of the eagle-king, Jatayu, killed by Rāvana while desperately struggling to rescue Sītā ; the valour of Rāma's monkey allies, and the heroic deeds by which the demon's stronghold in Ceylon was at last captured and Sītā's release effected, were all depicted on the walls of Rāma's *chitra-sāla*.

In classical Sanskrit literature painting is considered an occupation not unworthy of princes.   In the Nāgānanda, a drama attributed to King Harsha of Kanauj (606-47), a prince of the Vidhyādharas whiles away his time by drawing the portrait of his beloved, Malayāvatī.   He asks for a piece of red arsenic to draw with and his attendant picks up from the ground pieces of clay or stone of five different colours—blue, yellow, red, brown, and grey.   Malayāvatī unobserved watches her lover at work, but the portrait is so indifferent that she believes it is intended for some other fair maid and faints away from jealousy.

There are so many references to painted portraits in Sanskrit literature that evidently the prohibition in the Silpā-sāstras applied only to temples and other sacred buildings and not to the practice of painting as a secular accomplishment.

In a play attributed to Kālidāsa the heroine is the Queen Dhārinī's beautiful attendant, Mālavikā, who is a skilful musician and dancer.   The Queen carefully keeps her attractive handmaid from the presence of the King, Agnimitra, but foolishly caused Mālavikā's portrait to be painted on the walls of the *chitra-sāla*.   The plot of the play discloses the disastrous consequences of the King's next visit to the picture gallery.

In Kālidāsa's famous play, Sakuntala, a considerable part of Act VI is taken up with a painted portrait of the Queen, with which the King Dushyanta, half-demented with grief and remorse for his desertion of Sakuntala, attempts to console himself.   In the text translated by Sir William Jones, this portriat is said to be painted by a lady of the Court, but the more recent version of Monier-Williams makes the king himself the artist.

The picture represented Sakuntala and her two attendants in the garden of the hermitage where Dushyanta first saw them.   Sakuntala herself is leaning "apparently a little tired against the stem of a mango-tree, the tender leaves of which glitter with the water she has poured upon them.   Her arms are gracefully extended ; her face is somewhat flushed with the heat, and a few flowers have escaped from her hair, which has become unfastened and hangs in loose tresses about her neck."

The king, looking at the picture, declares that the background is unfinished and sends an

attendant to fetch the painting implements.   He will have the River Mālinī portrayed
in it :

> Its tranquil course by banks of sand impeded,
> Upon the brink a pair of swans ; beyond,
> The hills adjacent to Himalaya,
> Studded with deer ; and near the spreading shade
> Of some large tree, where 'mid the branches hang
> The hermits' vests of bark, a tender doe,
> Rubbing its downy forehead on the horn
> Of a black antelope, should be depicted.

Then he would add some ornaments to the figure of Sakuntala :

> A sweet Sirisha blossom should be twined
> Behind the ear ; its perfumed crest depending
> Towards her cheek ; and resting on her bosom,
> A lotus-fibre necklace, soft and bright
> As an autumnal moonbeam.

His companion, Māthavya, notices that Sakuntala is covering her lips with one hand as if
to prevent a bee, which "intent on thieving honey from the flowers seems to have mistaken
her mouth for a rosebud," from settling on her lips.   This was an incident which had
actually occurred at the King's first meeting with Sakuntala, as described in the first act,
and Dushyanta, led on by the vividness of the painting to imagine that it was reality,
calls out :
"A bee ! drive off the impudent insect, will you ?"
The story will recall similar ones recorded of ancient Greek artists and their skill in
imitative painting.   A very similar one is told of the first Chinese painter known in
history, Tsao Fuh-king, the court painter to the Emperor Sun K'uan, in the third century
A.D.   In this case a fly was so skilfully imitated that the Emperor raised his hand to
brush it off.[1,2]
Both of Kālidāsa's translators use the word "canvas" in describing the picture.   Some
of the old Central Asian paintings discovered by Dr. von Lecoq are painted on cloth
prepared with a ground of lime like some modern Tibetan paintings, so it is not unlikely
that a canvas of this kind was used by Indian painters in the time of Kālidāsa.   But
from the Sanskrit text it would appear more probable that a wooden panel is intended.
Of this secular art of painting of pre-Muhammadan times there are no Indian examples
extant, but from what we know of the religious sculpture and of the technical excellence
of the best paintings of the Ajantā School we can fairly assume that the merit ascribed to
it by Sanskrit writers was not overrated.
The period covered by the Ajantā paintings is supposed to extend over some six centuries, or from about the second to the seventh century A.D.[3]   Though these wonderful
viharas when they were inhabited must have been extraordinarily beautiful, it must not

---

[1] Anderson, "Pictorial Arts of Japan."

[2] For literary references to painting in ancient India see C. Sivaramamurti, "A Passage on Painting in Potana's
Bhagavata," *Journal of Oriental Research*, VI (1932), pp. 184-187 ; "Painting and Allied Arts as Revealed in Bana's
Works," *ibid* VII (1933), pp. 59-82 ; "Kalidasa and Painting, *ibid.*, pp. 160-185 ; "Sri Harsha's Observations on Paint-
ing with Special Reference to the Naishadhiya Charita," *ibid.*, pp. 331-350 ; and "The Artist in Ancient India," *ibid.*,
VIII (1934), pp. 31-45.   Also see V. Raghavan, "Some Sanskrit Texts on Painting," *Indian Historical Quarterly*, IX
(1933), pp. 898-911.—P.C.

[3] The painting at Ajanta according to the latest researches extends from about the second century B.C. to the sixth
century A.D.—P.C.

An Apsara or heavenly dancer. A fresco from Sittanavasal. Pallava period, 7th century.
The supple movements of the figure have been rendered with the ease and sureness of touch
borne of close observation and aesthetic insight.

(From *Studies in Indian Painting* by N. C. Mehta)

be supposed that the object of the paintings was to provide entertainment for, or to gratify the æsthetic tastes of, the Buddhist monks—the walls were the picture-books used for instructing the pilgrims and novices of the Order in the events of the Buddha's many existences.   If sometimes the subjects seem to be out of keeping with the ascetic life of a monastery, it is only because the Master had experienced life in every phase before he reached Nirvāna, the perfect experience.   And though incidentally the pictures give an intimate revelation of Indian life of the period, it would be a mistake to suppose that the painters intentionally recorded current events as history.

As works of art the Ajantā paintings, like the Borobudur reliefs, are of unequal merit, though some are worthy to rank among the great pictures of the world.

It is often said that Indian painting is to be distinguished from that of the West as being an art of line only, that is Indian paintings are not true pictures in the European sense, they are only coloured drawings.   This is true of the earlier and of most of the later schools of Indian painting.   But it is not true of the grand school of Indian mural painting, in the highest development it reached at Ajantā, Bagh, Sigiri, and in the recently discovered Pallava paintings at Sittannavāsal (Plates 41, 42, 43, 44B, 45, 46A, and 47).

In the great flowering time of Buddhist-Hindu art, from Gupta times down to the Muhammadan invasions, there was a marked tendency to prefer painted reliefs to simple fresco and tempera paintings for the decoration of temple walls ;[1] though the painters'

[1] We have examples of wall painting of the post-Gupta period both in North and South India, notably in the Kailasa temple at Ellora (8th century A.D.) the temple at Madanpur (A.D. 1130 to 1165), the Brihadisvara temple at Tanjore (late 10th century), and the temple at Tirumalai (11th or 12th century).   From their study it is now becoming increasingly evident that the art of painting underwent a degeneration, less rapid in the South, and instead of the free and plastic forms of Ajanta a definite conventionalisation and stiffness set in.   The lines become angular and sharp, and the drawing has none of the suavity and fineness of the Gupta schools.   Aside from the unbroken space provided by the few cave temples of this period there was just no longer sufficient space for the wall painter to practise his craft, the interior of mediæval temples being quite insufficient.   The evolution of painting, therefore, did not parallel the styles of sculpture of this period.   It is true that the sculpture itself was plastered and painted over, but the style of this over painting could not have been different from the other examples of painting that survive from that time.   Judging from these, it does not appear to be correct to state that the painters tried to imitate plastic effects.   Instead we have an art that is shorn of plasticity, with flat compositions and a highly conventionalised and stiff draughtsmanship, as is apparent from the 9th century paintings at Ellora.

The decline in the art of wall painting was followed by the growth of styles of painting more often confined to book illustration, namely, the Pala school of Bengal and Bihar (Plate 51A), and the Western Indian school.   The Pala school, which came to an end about the late 12th century, preserved the traditions of Ajanta to a greater extent, though these were cramped and confined within the small painting space available, and lack the sweeping freedom afforded by the large wall spaces of Ajanta.   The paintings consist mainly of illustrations to Mahayana Buddhist texts and are iconographic in character.   The colours employed are few, and we get a somewhat slavish imitation of the mannerisms of Ajanta art.   The school came to an end with the Muslim invasion at the end of the 12th century A.D.

The earliest examples of the Western Indian style, as preserved in illustrations to Jaina palm leaf manuscripts, continue the style as found at Ellora, the angularity of drawing being more accentuated and the draughtsmanship careless and crude.   In the depiction of the human figures, ancient ideals are still followed, but the result of the artists' work is astonishingly different.   The faces are almost always shown in profile, the noses are sharp and pointed, and the chins small and protruding.   The eyes are set close to each other, one of them projecting in a rather clumsy way outside the face, the poses of the figures are still, and the little movement that is shown is puppet-like.   The treatment of nature is conventionalised and decorative, and the birds and animals turn out looking like pretty wooden toys.   The Western Indian style was also extraordinarily conservative, sticking with great tenacity to these characteristics for a period of over 500 years, almost to the end of the 16th century, though certain stylistic variations and elaborations are to be noticed in the various phases.   The early paintings on palm leaf have a simple primitive vigour that is associated with the terse and direct expression inaugurating a new style.   As time progresses the art tends to become more elaborate and refined, and the paintings of the first paper manuscripts, which begin to appear about the middle of the 13th century, are among the finest examples of this school, combining successfully the early strength with a subtler draughtsmanship and exquisite love for detail.   The colours too are more refined, and used with greater effect, but gold and blue, so lavishly used by the painters of the next period, are as yet unknown.

By the middle of the 15th century palm leaf manuscripts disappear entirely, and the paintings on paper manuscripts become extremely opulent, employing a great deal of blue and gold, probably the result of increasing Persian contact.   Among the finest examples of this phase are the manuscripts of the *Kalpasutra* painted at Mandu in 1439, another painted at Jaunpur in A.D. 1465 (Plate 75C and D), and the magnificent *Kalpasutra* of about the same date in the col-

share in the work was an important one, for without the eye-painting ceremony with its appropriate mantras a stone image was not "alive," or filled with the Divine Presence, and could not, therefore, be worshipped.   The combination of sculpture and painting, often practised as a single craft, was the highest form of religious art, being more difficult and costly than simple painting, and therefore conferring more merit both on the artist-devotees and their patrons.

The religious sentiment had its natural re-action on the practice of fresco and tempera painters.   They tried to imitate plastic effects ; not to produce the atmosphere of Western painting, but to give their work the solidity and reality of sculpture.   The classic examples of Indian pictorial art, therefore, show something more than an art of line.   These Indian painters did indeed rival the best Chinese masters in their wonderful power of delineation, but they also excelled in the subtle modelling of surfaces.   Whether they were modelled by the painter or the sculptor, the finishing brush-outline gave life to the forms.

Writing on the technique of the Ajantā paintings Mr. J. Griffiths says :

"The artists who painted them were giants in execution.   Even on the vertical sides of the walls some of the lines which were drawn by one sweep of the brush struck me as being very wonderful ; but when I saw long delicate curves drawn without faltering, with equal precision, upon the horizontal surface of a ceiling, where the difficulty of execution is increased a thousandfold, it appeared to me nothing less than miraculous.   One of the students, when hoisted up on the scaffolding, tracing his first panel on the ceiling, naturally remarked that some of the work looked like child's work, little thinking that what seemed to him, up there, rough and meaningless, had been laid on with a cunning hand, so that when seen at its right distance every touch fell into its proper place."[1]

A great deal of misconception of the true character of these paintings is due to the fact that nearly all the published material for the study of them has been derived from copies, carefully traced by hand, which give a very faint impression of the marvellous beauty and freedom of the brush-outlines, the masterly plastic treatment of the surfaces, and the exquisite delicacy and refinement of ornamental details.   These copies, made under great difficulties, are by no means to be depreciated.   They are most useful records of the general design, and in some cases supply details which cannot be distinguished by the camera.   But it cannot be too strongly insisted that hand-copies must be supplemented by the best reproductions which scientific photography can make.   For artists and art-students a first-rate photograph is infinitely more valuable than the best hand-copy.[2]

For the first edition of this book the only materials available were the copies made by the students of the Bombay School of Art, published by Mr. Griffiths in his work on Ajantā, and these furnished the only illustration given of the Ajantā School, a very in-adequate and incomplete copy of the wonderful painting in the antechamber of Cave

---

lection of the Devasanapada Jnana Bhandar in Ahmedabad (Plate 75B).   In spite of all the lavishness, however, one cannot escape the feeling that the art is really getting poorer, and in spite of all the elaborate attention to iconography, lacks inner spiritual vitality.   Western Indian painting is thus a superstitious art in the sense that it is something that stands over from the past, the forms themselves being devoid of inner meaning.   Convention and formula are repeated in a mechanical manner and the decorative and ornamental qualities, instead of being an incitement to the release of more abundant energy, become gross and superfluous embellishment.

The subject matter of most of these paintings is Jaina, illustrating the cyle of legends related in the *Kalpasutra* and *Kalakacharyakatha*.   The latter is the story of Kalaka, the Jaina monk who is reputed to have invited the Sahi kings to destroy Ujjain in retaliation for the abduction of a nun by the king, while the former tells in brief the life of the various Jaina Tirthankaras.   In addition to Jaina works, Hindu themes also form the subject matter of paintings in the Western Indian style, and those illustrating Vaishnava works like the *Bagalopalastuti* are full of a delightful poetic atmosphere. For an exhaustive discussion of this school of painting, see Moti Chandra, *Jaina Miniature Painting from Western India*, Ahmedabad, 1949.—P.C.

[1] "Indian Antiquary," vol. iii, 1874, p. 26.

[2] These have since been published by the Government of Hyderabad in four magnificent volumes : G. Yazdani, *Ajanta* : The colour and monochrome reproductions based on photography, Vol. I, 1930 ; Vol. II, 1933 ; Vol. III, 1946 and Vol. IV, 1955.—P.C.

Bharata Requesting Rama to Return to Ayodhya. Popular Mughal School,
c. 1610 A.D. From a *Ramayana* series, here Rama is being requested by Bharata and
Satrughna to return to Ayodhya from his self-imposed exile. The picture effectively
combines the technique of the Akbar School with the brilliant colour scheme of
Rajasthani art.

(Courtesy, Prince of Wales Museum of Western India, Bombay)

XVII, undoubtedly the greatest achievement of the school.   The same group, inexplicably divorced from its context, was illustrated in Lady Herringham's work.   A complete, but not quite accurate copy, showing the colour-scheme and the whole design, was subsequently made by Mr. Mukul Chandra Dey and published by him in his "Pilgrimages to Ajantā and Bagh."[1]

The long wanted photographic survey of the paintings, commenced by M. Victor Goloubeff in 1911, is now being completed by the Archæological Survey of Hyderabad, and through the kindness of the Director, Mr. G. Yazdani, I am enabled to give more satisfactory reproductions of the painting (Plates 41, 42, and 43) of which a very discerning critic, Mr. Binyon, has said that no picture anywhere is more impressive in grandeur and tenderness.

Though the unknown Ajantā artist has not followed strictly the authorised version of the legend, there can be no doubt as to the subject of the painting.[2]   It is the legend of the return of the Buddha to his home, after the Enlightenment.   One spring morning, eight months after he had attained Buddhahood, the Blessed One resolved to revisit his native city, Kapilavastu.   Travelling on foot and begging his food from door to door, as was the custom of all the Buddhas, he reached the city after a two-months' journey. The Sākya princes, his former companions, went out with flowers in their hands to greet him and led him to a pleasant grove in the outskirts of the city.   But, regarding him as a younger brother, they would not do obeisance to him until he assumed his Divine Form and rising into the air filled the whole universe with his Presence, performing many miracles which made the King, his father, and all his courtiers fall down in worship.

The next day the Buddha went into the city to beg for alms.   Lotus-flowers sprang up beneath his feet, a glory shone round his head, and he comes at last to the door of his own palace presenting his begging bowl.   Yasodharā, his wife, leading Rāhula, now seven years old, comes out and worships him, saying, "O Siddhartha, that night Rāhula was born you rejected your kingdom and went silently away.   Now you have a more glorious kingdom instead !"

The wall-space chosen by the artist lends itself admirably to the noble design of the picture.   It is a narrow upright panel at one end of the antechamber, framed on the right-hand side by the richly carved architrave of the doorway leading into the shrine. The palace walls are cunningly made to abut on to the architrave of the doorway, leaving a narrow upright space filled by the majestic figure of the glorified Buddha towering over the palace roof.   A Vidhyādhara, flying over the Buddha's head and holding over it a flower-decked umbrella, fills the upper part of the panel which is narrowed again by the projecting lintel of the doorway.

Yasodharā, wearing on this day of gladness the jewellery she has discarded for seven long desolate years, stands at her door, gazing up in adoration at the glorious apparition in front of her and holding out caressingly the precious gift she offers to the Divine Beggar, her darling child.   The Buddha, graciously bending his head, accepts Rāhula as his disciple.

The artist has indeed been wonderfully inspired, in the grand spacing out of the whole design, in his conception of the Divine Form, majestic in its simple and austere lines, and in the tenderness and pathos he has given to the figures of the mother and child, drawn in rhythmic brush-lines with exquisite delicacy and charm (Plate 42).

Like all the Ajantā paintings, this masterpiece has suffered irremediable damage, the lower portion having been almost completely destroyed.   But the entire spacing out of the panel and the true proportions of it can be seen in Pl. 41B.   The photographic reproduction, Plate 41A, unfortunately has stunted the proportions of the Buddha by omitting both the lower part of the panel, where a portion of the lotus-flower springing

---

[1] The copy is now in the Oriental Department of the British Museum.

[2] A very inferior painting of the same subject in Cave XIX is illustrated in Griffiths' "Ajantā" (Plate 89, Fig. 5) and in Vincent Smith's "History of Fine Art in India and Ceylon," 3rd Edition, Plate 88.

under his feet is to be seen, and also the blackened upper part filled by the umbrella.

It is very much to be desired that all the resources of scientific photography may be applied to the task of making the best possible record of this great painting and others which have not yet been worthily reproduced. Such reproductions, enlarged to full size, might provide material for an "Ajantā Museum," worthy of India, designed to give a complete replica of two or three of these magnificent monastic halls, and to demonstrate the perfect co-ordination of building design, sculpture, and painting into a higher organic unity, which, as Professor Lethaby has said, is the true test of noble architecture. Thus India might hand down to posterity a complete record of the golden age of her art, and help to revive the grand traditions of her own school of mural painting, not yet extinct.

The lovely head of the Bodhisattva in Cave I, Plate 43, from a photograph kindly provided by M. Goloubeff, will give, in spite of its damaged condition, a good impression of the broad plastic treatment of the later Ajantā paintings. The brush-outlines here visible are not the foundation of the painting, but the finishing touches which give emphasis and reality to the surface modelling.

There has been much discussion regarding the exact process used by the painters of Ajantā and Bagh, and much difference of opinion among experts. Sir John Marshall says that it is tempera painting, not *fresco buono*. There cannot be any doubt, however, that the true fresco process has been practised in India for many centuries. It was used by Akbar's painters in the decoration of Fatehpur-Sikri, and is still used by the temple craftsmen of Rajputana, or was so about twenty years ago, when I engaged a Jaipur painter to decorate the entrance hall of the Calcutta School of Art and to give instruction to the students. The process is described in the Appendix. Plate 44A shows part of the wall decoration of the school executed throughout in *fresco buono*, and Plate 68 a fresco panel painted at the same time by Dr. Abanindra Nath Tagore, C.I.E. No attempt was made to imitate the technique or style of the Ajantā school, but simply to open a door for the revival of art in India which departmentalism has long kept shut.

It cannot be supposed that the process was introduced into India by the Moguls, and one would certainly expect to find it used by the earlier schools of Indian mural painting. As a matter of fact the *intonaco*, the thin plaster ground at Ajantā, Bagh, and elsewhere, is exactly the same as that used by the Rajput temple craftsmen at the present day. M. Goloubeff, in his admirable monograph on Ajantā,[1] says that the paintings are true frescoes, though some of them have been finished or retouched by a process analogous to tempera. In other words the Ajantā paintings seem to be a combination of *fresco buono* and *fresco secco*. This view is supported by very good historical evidence, the hereditary craft-tradition of Indian mural painting.

It is hardly necessary now, as it was twenty years ago, to insist that the Ajantā School is purely Indian and not, as Dr. Vincent Smith maintained, "a local development of the cosmopolitan art of the contemporary Roman Empire." The painting in Cave I, described by him as a "vivid representation of the ceremonial attending the presentation of their credentials by the Persian Envoys" (from Khushru II of Persia to Pulikesin of Mahārāshtra, in the thirty-sixth year of his reign, A.D. 625-6), and cited as a signal proof of the derivative character of the Ajantā School, has been shown by M. Foucher to be no historical painting, "a landmark in the history of art," but an illustration of a jātaka story, like most of the other paintings in the Caves.

The discovery in 1920 of fresco paintings (Plates 44B and 46A) in a rock-cut temple at Sittannavāsal in the ancient Pallava country, not far from Pudukkottai, through the brilliant archæological researches conducted by Professor Jouveau-Dubreuil, has added an important chapter to the history of the great school of Indian mural painting. Mr. N. C. Mehta, I.C.S., in his "Notes on Indian Paintings,"[2] has published coloured sketches of

---

[1] "Ars Asiatica," vol. x.

[2] Taraporevala Sons & Co. Private Ltd., Bombay.

A.   Two paintings from Sigiri, Ceylon.   (*From photographs by the Archaeology Survey of Ceylon*).

B.   Fresco from Sigiri, Ceylon.   (*Photo Copyright by Archaeological Department, Ceylon*).

PLATE 45

A. Wall painting from Jain Caves, Sittannavasal. 7th Century A.D., Post-Gupta period.
(*Photo Copyright by Prince of Wales Museum, Bombay*).

B. Wall painting from Badami. (*Photo Copyright by Prince of Wales Museum, Bombay*).

PLATE 46

A group from the great fresco of the Rang Mahall, Bagh.   (*From a copy by Mr. Asit Kumar Haldar*).

PLATE 47

The birth ceremony of the infant Krishna. Kangra School brush drawing, 18th or 19th century. Author's Collection.

PLATE 48

some of them, but the scientific photographic survey necessary for the full appreciation of their artistic value has yet to be made.[1]

They are attributed by Professor Jouveau-Dubreuil to the reign of Mahendravarman I, *circ.* A.D. 600-25, one of the great Pallava dynasty which dominated the south for two centuries and gave to Indian art the wonderful sculptures of Māmallapuram (Plates 103B, 104A and B). They therefore seem to be contemporary with the finest paintings of Ajantā. The principal subject, says Professor Jouveau-Dubreuil, is a grand fresco which adorns the whole of the ceiling of the verandah, representing a lotus tank enlivened with fish, geese, buffaloes, elephants, and three human or divine figures, devotees or Gandharvas, holding in their hands the lotus flowers and leaves they are gathering. On two of the pillars of the façade are two paintings of Devadāsis dancing the dance of Siva. Unfortunately the photographs of these most impressive fragments which I have been able to secure, though they prove them to be the work of a great artist, are not suitable for reproduction. But Plate 44B, for which I am indebted to the kind help of Mr. S. V. Ramasami Mudeliar of Madras, will indicate that the painters of Sittannavāsal were in no way inferior to the best of the Pallava sculptors. The youth whose graceful figure makes rhythmic play with the lotus leaves and flowers is drawn with all the power and freedom of the classical Indian school at its best. It is interesting to note that the design has been put on the wall or ceiling in the first instance by stencilling, the dots of the pouncing being clearly visible under the vigorous strokes of the finishing brushwork. In the Sittannavāsal frescoes also the different quality of the master-painter's work and that of his assistants or apprentices, can be clearly distinguished in different parts of the decorative scheme. Plate 44B undoubtedly shows the hand of the master himself.

Ceylon, which is very rich in sculptured monuments of Indian origin, also furnishes some remarkable remains of mural paintings (Plate 45), well worth a separate monograph, apparently derived from the great school of Ajantā. They are situated in two caves excavated on the western face of the wonderful Sigiri rock in the central province of the island, and it has been assumed that they are the work of the court painters of the parricide King Kāsyapa I (A.D. 479-497), who made this impregnable rock his stronghold, and that they represent his queens with their attendants going to worship at the neighbouring Buddhist monastery. No satisfactory explanation has been given of the reason why the queens and their hand-maidens appear as if half immersed in clouds, the usual convention of the heavenly spheres. The suggestion that this was merely a device to make up for the cramped space which the painters had to fill is very unconvincing. But if we imagine that one of the royal ladies dreamed of a visit to the Tusita heavens, and that the court painters, or those attached to the monastery, took this for their subject as an everyday event in Buddhist religious life, the difficulty would be removed.[2]

[1] The Sittannavasal temple is dedicated to the service of the Jaina religion, and was constructed by Mahendravarman I, the remarkable Pallava artist king probably before he was converted to the Saiva faith by that saint Appar. The paintings that have survived consist of heavenly nymphs dancing in the clouds, a royal couple identified with the king and his consort, and two ceiling panels, the first depicting a lotus pond filled with aquatic flowers, geese and a human figure (Pl 44B) and the second also representing a similar lotus lake. The paintings have been discussed at length by Stella Kramrisch, "Dakshinachitra," *Journal of the Indian Society of Oriental Art*, Vol. V. The lotus ponds have been interpreted as a part of a *samvasarana*, or a resting place made by gods for a Tirthankara after he has attained *kaivalya*.—P.C.

[2] For some decent colour reproductions of the paintings at Sigiri, see W. G. Archer and S. Paranavitana, *Ceylon: Paintings from Temple, Shrine and Rock*, UNESCO World Art Series, 1957, Pls. I-X. Paranavitana has also given a correct explanation of the meaning of these paintings in "Sigiri, the Abode of a God-king," *Journal of the Ceylon Branch of the Royal Asiatic Society*, New Series, I (1950), pp. 129-162. According to him " . . . . . . the plan of Sigiri as a whole has been devised as an earthly representation of the Paradise of Kuvera on Mount Kailasa. In fact the old chronicler explicitly states that Kassapa's city of Sigiri resembled Alakamanda and that the king dwelt there in the manner of Kuvera (the God of Riches). The purpose of the paintings, therefore, must have been to carry out the scheme in all its details, and they must represent Clouds and Lightning moving about the peak of Kailasa. There is in fact a reference in the historical writings of Ceylon to "Cloud-damsels" and "Lightning-princesses" as subjects represented in Sinhalese art."—P.C.

Fortunately a complete photographic record of the paintings, which owing to their inaccessible position have been much better preserved than those of Ajantā and Bagh, has been made by the Archæological Survey of Ceylon. There are twenty-one figures in all, five of which are shown in Plate 45. As usual, some of them are by the hand of a master-painter and others by the pupils working with him ; this was the way the master passed on the torch his ancestors had lighted for him to the next generation. The monuments we guard to-day as archæological treasures served the purpose of modern art galleries and schools of art.

There is a peculiar charm about these Sigiri paintings in the expression of the wonder and delight felt by the visitors to the celestial spheres, in the grace and spontaneity of movement, quite free from any academic pose, and in the strength and vitality of the drawing and modelling.

The Bagh rock-cut viharas, in the Gwalior State, contain some of the most important remains of the grand school of Indian painting, in its best period, about the seventh century A.D. A good set of copies of the principal frescoes, made for the Gwalior Durbar, a duplicate of which is in the British Museum, gave the material for a recent publication by the India Society, but the indispensable photographic survey has not yet been made and it is improbable that any measures taken for the preservation of the paintings *in situ* will stop the progress of the rapid decay which has already destroyed the greater part of them. Indian art will surely suffer further irreparable loss unless these precious fragments are removed from the walls of the viharas and placed under proper care in a suitable museum or art gallery.

The sympathetic copy of the fascinating group of dancers and musicians, Plate 47, made by Mr. Asit Kumar Haldar in a limited time under considerable difficulties, gives a good impression of the life and movement of one of the most attractive passages in the great fresco of the Rang Mahall, Cave IV, though only a photograph can reproduce the consummate technique of the brush-lines and the surface modelling. The subject, a group of girl musicians gathered in a ring round two male dancers, suggests a variation of the Indian artist's central theme—the universal Dance of Siva. The rhythmic curves of their vividly striped dresses give the impression of a band of nereids sporting in a sea of music, keeping time with the ripple of the waves.

This, however, is only an incident in the main subject of the fresco, a great procession of horsemen and elephant riders sweeping across the wall in a stately city pageant, representing undoubtedly, not a contemporary event, but some familiar tale told by the monks for the edification of the pilgrim visitors.

The technical tradition of the great school of Indian mural painting survives, as we have seen, in the temple craftsmanship of the present day in Rajputana. The Ajantā tradition was also brought down to modern times in the numerous paintings and drawings, mostly by Rajput and Kangra artists, illustrating in miniature Vaishnava and Saiva myths and legends as they were depicted formerly on the walls of Hindu *chitra-sālas*.[1] Plate 48, "The Birth Ceremony of the Infant Krishna," a brush drawing of the Kangra

---

[1] For a differing point of view see Karl Khandalavala, *Pahari Miniature Painting*, Bombay, 1958, p. 19. In spite of a common poetic beauty and earnest religious feeling, there is little in common between the tradition of Ajantā and the miniature paintings of the Kangra artists. They are separated by a gap of over a thousand years not satisfactorily explained, and to quote Khandalavala, "One cannot but feel that Rajasthani and Pahari miniature painting never stepped from the walls of shrines and palaces but was a Hindu corollary, albeit different in spirit, to the Mughal miniatures, ... Every discovery of Rajasthani and Pahari masterpieces goes to confirm the view that not only were these miniatures suited to portfolios but were in fact always regarded as portfolio pictures . . . . . The true miniature implies fineness in general execution and detail, compact and tidy composition, smooth brushwork, and a proper appreciation of how to organise forms and colour in a format of small dimensions. Judged by these standards, Rajasthani and Pahari painting do on the whole recognise the requirements of a miniature art. If however they were transplanted on to walls in an enlarged size, they would, I fear, ill-fulfil the requirements of great fresco painting, such as breadth of treatment, forceful sweeping brushwork and an avoidance of the meticulous."—P.C.

Pl. C

Camel-fight. Mughal School (Delhi), 1st quarter of the 17th century. This is an interesting representation of a camel-fight, a favourite sport of Mughal times. The ferocity of the fight is emphasised by the vicious grasp of the animals. Though the hair of the camels is represented with very fine brush strokes. The colouring is subdued, a rich effect has been achieved.

(Courtesy, Prince of Wales Museum of Western India, Bombay)

School, carefully shaded to give an impression of relief, puts the Krishna legend in a modern Rajput setting, but preserves the spirit which informed the great art of Ajantā and very much of its technique.

The painted icons used in Vaishnava household worship formed another link, now almost broken, which connected classical Indian art with modern times. A very interesting example, probably of the eighteenth century, Plate 49A, represents in iconographical form the Coronation of Rāma and Sītā at Ayodhyā after the overthrow of Rāvana and the termination of their exile. Rāma's sword and the famous bow of Siva are on the ground in front of him; Hanuman the monkey-king, his faithful ally, kneels and clasps the King's leg. His three brothers are in attendance on Rāma's right hand; on the opposite side a bevy of court ladies and musicians wait on the Queen.

The details of the throne, the royal crowns, and the umbrella are rendered in relief with gilt gesso and glass. Real pearls are used in the ornaments. In the background is given a realistic picture of the palace and citadel of Ayodhyā, with its inhabitants; courtiers, men-at-arms, richly caparisoned elephants and war-horses; the temples and sacred cows, the public bathing tank, the city walls, the river, and the country beyond—a perfect microcosm of the life and ceremonial of a royal Indian city.

The still living Tibetan school of painting and sculpture is an offshoot of Nepalese Buddhist art dating from the time of King Srong-tsan-gampo in the seventh century A.D. The craftsmen of the Tibetan monasteries, painters and sculptors, cling tenaciously to the old traditions, and much might be learnt from them, though it is in technique rather than in spiritual outlook that they stand in close relation with the art of India. Tibet is part of the hinterland of Indian art, half-way between India and China, which can only be dealt with satisfactorily in a comprehensive monograph, but a few suggestions on colour symbolism which Tibetan artists borrowed from Buddhist India may be noted:

The Manikabum, a Tibetan work of the seventh century, gives the symbolic colours appropriate for each of the six syllables of the famous Sanskrit Mantra AUM MANI PADME HUM, which is said to save from rebirth in either of the six conditions, i.e. as a *deva*, *asura*, man, animal, goblin or hopeless being, or as a devil.

The colour of AUM, the heavenly state, is white. White, both in Buddhist and orthodox Hindu symbolism, signifies heavenly purity and bliss. It is a symbol of Siva and of his snow-clad paradise, and also of Parvati, his consort. It may also represent water.

The colour of MA, the *asura* state, is blue. In Hindu orthodoxy blue is the colour of Vishnu, the Preserver, and of his incarnations, Krishna and Rāma.

The colour of NI, the human state, is yellow, like the ascetic's robe.

Images of Buddha, as well as those of Maitreya and Manjusri, are painted a golden yellow. It is also the symbol of earth.

The colour of PAD, the animal state, is green, while that of ME, the state of a hopeless being or goblin, is red. This is in direct opposition to Brahmanical symbolism, in which red is the colour of the sun-god, Sūrya, of the solar sphere, the abode of spirits whose earthly migrations are finished, and also of Brahmā, the Creator. King Harsha's father is said to have offered daily to Sūrya a bunch of red lotus-flowers, in a vessel of ruby red.

The colour of HUM, the state of a devil, is black.

But in the Hindu Sāstras black symbolises the formless unconditioned state which existed before Creation, personified by Kālī, the Mother of the Universe and the Great Destroyer. The Nirvāna Tantra says, "As the lightning is born from the cloud and disappears within the cloud, so Brahmā and all the gods take birth from Kālī and disappear in Kālī."

The three *gunas*, or qualities of Matter, have their colour symbols—*sattvam*, white; *rajas*, yellow or red; *tamas*, blue or black.

According to the Vishnudharmottaram,[1] a Sanskrit treatise on painting, the colouring

[1] See Dr. Stella Kramrisch's translation, pp. 16-17.

of things seen should be true to nature, but the colouring of images and also that of a certain category of pictures descriptive of the *rasas*, or emotions, must be according to the rules of symbolism. Every *rasa* had its appropriate colour : the emotion of love, dark blue ; of laughter, white ; of compassion, grey ; of rage, red ; of valour or heroism, yellowish white ; of terror, black ; of astonishment or feeling of the supernatural, yellow ; and of loathing, indigo blue.

The specialised schools of painting mentioned above, which were developed as part of the culture of the Buddhist or Hindu monastery, temple, or court, grew up from a broad substratum of popular pictorial art, some of it very primitive, some of it, like the "Pat" drawings of Bengal described by Mr. Asit Ghose,[1] showing a technical skill of a high order. From very early times this substratum served as a means of religious propaganda among the illiterate masses. In the Sārattha-Pakasini, says Dr. Kramrisch, allusion is made to a class of Brahmans known by the name of Nakha, who wandered about with pictures mounted on a portable framework, showing "scenes of good and evil destinies, of fortunes and misfortunes," and pointing out that "by doing this deed one attains this, and by doing that one attains that." The moral and religious teaching of the great Hindu epics was, and still is to a certain extent, popularised in a similar way by minstrel-painters wandering from village to village, but the scheme of modern progress elaborated by the educated townsman has no use for this traditional method of popular culture, so the Indian villager desirous of recreation or edification must wait patiently until the cinema points the modern way to spiritual enlightenment, or prostitution.

[1] "Indian Art and Letters," vol. ii, No. 2, 1926.

A.   The Coronation of Rāma and Sītā.   (*From a painting in the Calcutta Art Gallery*).

B.   Camels Fighting.   Mughal School, C. 1615 A.D.   (*Prince of Wales Museum, Bombay*).

PLATE 49

A nautch party at the court of Muhammad Tuglak, by Shapur of Khurasan. (*From a painting in the Calcutta Art Gallery*).

PLATE 50

A. Detail from a palm-leaf folio of a Ms. of *Prajnaparamita*. Pala School, late 12th century A.D.
(*Prince of Waels Museum, Bombay*).

B. Portrait of Abdur-Rahim Khankhanan.   Mughal, School, early
17th century A.D.   (*Prince of Wales Museum, Bombay*).

C. Portrait of a divine, by Farrukh Beg, the Kalmuck.
Mughal School, C. 1610 A.D.   (*Khudabux Library, Patna*).

PLATE 51

B. A lily, by Muhammad Nazar Samarkandi. Mughal,School,C. 1610 A.D.
(Collection of Sir Cowasji Jehangir, Prince of Wales Museum, Bombay).

A. A duck. Mughal School, C. 1615 A.D.
(Collection of Sir Cowasji Jehangir, Prince of Wales Museum, Bombay).

PLATE 52

CHAPTER XI

PAINTING IN MOGUL TIMES

WE have seen in the last chapter that in the pre-Muhammadan period the art of painting was cultivated as a dilettante amusement or accomplishment in the courts of Buddhist and Hindu sovereigns, but it was not until Mogul times that a distinctly secular school of painting, derived originally from Persia, arose in India. This secularisation of art in the Mogul period in India may be compared with the Renaissance in Europe.

The direct origin of this secularisation was the formal prohibition by the Muhammadan law of the representation of animate nature in art. The effect of this law was virtually to suppress the practice of painting and sculpture as fine arts in all countries under Muhammadan rule, from the founding of the Caliphate of Baghdad down to the beginning of the thirteenth century.

With the decline of the spiritual power of the Caliphs the prohibition ceased to have full effect, but the revival of pictorial art in Persia did not really begin until the overthrow of Arab rule by the Mongols, about the middle of the thirteenth century.

It is interesting to notice how, both in Europe and in Asia, such rude barbarians as the Mongols, who revelled in rapine and bloodshed and marked their progress with monuments of human skulls, were, like other scavengers of civilisation—the Goths, Vandals, and Huns—the means of moving the intellectual waters and of bringing new inspiration into art.

The effect of the Mongol invasion on the civilisation of Western Asia is well summarised by Professor E. G. Browne in his "Literary History of Persia" :

"Infinitely destructive and disastrous as it was to life, learning and civilisation, and especially to the Arab culture, which, as we have already seen, maintained itself with such extraordinary vitality in Persia for six centuries, long after the war of Arab conquest had utterly subsided, the Mongol invasion did, perhaps, contain some quickening elements, and the Mongol character, for all its reckless ferocity, some potentialities of good. One of its few good effects was the extraordinary intermixture of remote peoples, resulting in a refreshing of somewhat stagnant mental reservoirs, which it brought about. In Europe it was a cause, if not the chief cause of the Renaissance, for it thrust the Ottoman Turks out of the obscurity of Khurāsān into the prominence of Constantinople and was thus ultimately responsible for the destruction of the Byzantine Empire and the dispersion of the Greeks and their treasures into Europe . . . . And within Asia it brought together, first in conflict and then in consultation, Persians and Arabs with Chinese and Tibetans, and confronted, on terms of equality which had not existed for five or six centuries, the doctors of Islam with Christian monks, Buddhist Lamas, Mongol *bakhshīs* or medicine men, and the representatives of other religions and sects" (pp. 441-2).

It is very important to remember also that from motives of self-interest, and not from any respect for art, these ferocious invaders, who massacred wholesale men, women, and children of the general population, usually spared the artisans and craftsmen, and thus preserved for their own uses the art-traditions of the countries they ravaged and desolated. Skilled craftsmen were always the prizes of war, and when an uncivilised race like the Mongols triumphed over a highly cultivated one the craftsmen of the defeated became the teachers of the victors ; this transplantation into a new soil brought new vigour into art, and was the beginning of great developments. When Timur, the ancestor of the Indian Mogul dynasty, withdrew his hordes from northern India in 1398, after ravaging it with fire and sword, he took back with him as captives all the masons who had built the famous mosque of Ferozabad, in order that they might build one like it at Samarkand. Thus Indian art fulfilled once more its civilising mission, and when two and a half centuries later Timur's descendant Shah Jahān was building the famous Tāj Mahall at Agra (Plate 97), some of the principal masons were brought from Samarkand—probably descendants of Timur's captives.

The important part which craftsmen, more especially oriental craftsmen, have always played in the world's history as missionaries of civilisation, culture, and religion, is not generally recognised by bookmen. Even at the present day the Indian craftsman, deeply versed in his *Silpā-śāstras*, learned in folk-lore and in national epic literature, though excluded from Indian universities—or rather, on that account—is often more highly cultured intellectually and spiritually than the average Indian graduate. In medieval times the craftsman's intellectual influence, being creative and not merely assimilative, was at least as great as that of the priest and bookman. The Founder of Christianity was Himself a craftsman, and in those noblest monuments of the Christian faith—the Gothic cathedrals of medieval Europe—we can see that the splendid craftsmen of the Middle Ages preached and practised a religion like their Master's, pure and undefiled before God, while philosophers and bookmen wrangled over its dogmas.

It is curious that archæologists, who are so concerned in trying to prove that nearly all Indian art was derived from the West, should seem to be only dimly aware of the immeasurably greater debt which European art and science owe to India, for they very rarely dwell upon it. From the time of the break-up of the Roman Empire, and even some centuries before, down to the days of the Renaissance, there was flowing into Europe a continuous undercurrent of Indian science, philosophy, and art, brought by the art-workers of the East. In the nature of things, what could have been the effect of Alexander's raid, or even the more lasting influence of the Græco-Baktrian kingdom, compared with that of the successive streams of Asiatic invaders (barbarians, if you will) which century after century poured into Europe, bringing with their armies skilled craftsmen as engineers and armourers, followed by artisans of every kind, when, as often happened, a permanent occupation of a country took place ?

Even uncultured marauders, like the Huns and Mongols, brought with them non-combatant craftsmen to help them in their attacks on walled towns, and to keep their fighting equipment in order ; so that, while the fighting men of East and West were busy cutting throats, the craftsmen of both sides fraternised in a secret freemasonry, founded on common artistic interests.

Indian idealism during the greater part of this time was the dominant note of the art of Asia which was thus brought into Europe ; and when we find a perfectly Oriental atmosphere and strange echoes of Eastern symbolism in the medieval cathedrals of Europe, and see their structural growth gradually blossoming with all the exuberance of Eastern imagery, it is impossible to avoid the conclusion that Gothic architecture and Gothic handicraft owe very much to the absorption, by the *bauhütten* of Germany and other Western craft-guilds, of Asiatic science and art, brought by the thousands of Asiatic craftsmen who entered Europe in the first millennium of the Christian era ; a period which in the minds of Europeans is generally a blank because the "Great Powers" were then located in Asia instead of in Europe.

Byzantine art and Gothic art derived their inspiration from the same source—the impact of Asiatic thought upon the civilisation of the Roman Empire. The first shows its effect upon the art of the Greek and Latin races, the other its influence upon the Romanesque art of the Teutonic and Celtic races. The spirit of Indian idealism breathes in the mosaics of St. Mark's at Venice, just as it shines in the mystic splendours of the Gothic cathedrals ; through the delicate tracery of their jewelled windows, filled with the stories of saints and martyrs ; in all their richly sculptured arches, fairy vaulting, and

Pl. D

Meeting of Rama and Parasurama. Rajasthani School (Mewar), A.D. 1649. This is a folio of Ms. of the Balakanda of Valmiki's *Ramayana* painted by Manohar, for Acharya Jasavant. To the left are Rama and his brothers on chariots accompanied by Dasaratha on a white horse. In the centre they are shown after dismounting, while opposite them is the gigantic Parasurama holding an axe and with gods behind him. Below we again see Rama and Parasurama facing each other. The artist has combined three scenes in one picture, namely, the marriage procession, the encounter between Rama and Parasurama, and Parasurama's departure.

(Courtesy, Prince of Wales Museum of Western India, Bombay)

soaring pinnacles and spires.   The Italian Renaissance marks the reversion of Christian art to the pagan ideals of Greece, and the capture of art by the bookmen, leading to our present dilettantism and archæological views of art.

When a new inspiration comes into European art it will come again from the East ; but what irony there is in the present spectacle of the Christian nations of Europe, in the twentieth century, using their influence to paganise the art of Asia !

To return to the history of Mogul art—the revival of painting in Persia under Mogul rule was very largely due to the influence of the Chinese schools, which again owed their inspiration originally to the great schools of India.   In the early centuries of the Christian era the traditions of Indian religious art had been brought into Turkestan and China by Indian Buddhist missionaries and craftsmen, and by Chinese students taught in Indian universities.   There they were acclimatised, and by the fusion of Indian idealism with the naturalism of the indigenous schools the modern schools of China and Japan originated, which are more familiar to European artists and art critics than the art of India, to which they owe so much.

Under this Indian inspiration Chinese painting had reached by the seventh century (which may be considered as the zenith of pictorial art in India) an extraordinary degree of eminence, far surpassing the contemporary art of Europe.   Dr. W. Anderson, in his great work on Japanese and Chinese painting, says :

"There is, perhaps, no section of art that has been so completely misapprehended in Europe as the pictorial art of China.   For us the Chinese painter, past or present, is but a copyist who imitates with laborious and indiscriminating exactness whatever is laid before him, rejoices in the display of as many and as brilliant colours as his subject and remuneration will permit, and is only original in the creation of monstrosities.

"Nothing could be more contrary to fact than this impression.   If we omit from consideration the work executed for the foreign market—work which every educated Chinese would disown—the old Masters of the Middle Kingdom, who as a body united grandeur of conception with immense power of execution, cared little for elaboration of detail, and except in Buddhist pictures sought their best effects in the simplicity of black and white, or in the most subdued chromatic harmonies . . . .

"If we endeavour to compare the pictorial art of China with that of Europe, we must carry ourselves back to the days when the former was in its greatness.   It may be safely asserted that nothing produced by the painters of Europe between the seventh and thirteenth centuries approaches within measurable distance of the works of the great Chinese masters who gave lustre to the T'ang, Sung, and Yuën dynasties ; nor—to draw a little nearer to modern times—is there anything in the religious art of Cimabue that would not appear tame and graceless by the side of the Buddhistic compositions of Wu-Tao-Tsz', Li Lung-yen, and Ngan Huru.   Down to the end of the Southern Empire in A.D. 1279, the Chinese were at the head of the world in the art of painting, as in many things besides, and their nearest rivals were their own pupils, the Japanese."[1]

The artists of this new Iranian school of painting, revived by an infusion of Indian art traditions naturalised in China, were the court painters of Bābur, the first Mogul Emperor of India, who thus brought them back to the fountain-head of their art.[2]   But Mogul painting was, unlike Indian, a purely secular school.   The general ban of the fine arts was not removed even by the Mogul Emperors, and it continued to have full effect so far as religious art was concerned.

Painting as a fine art became a diversion for the Mogul Emperors and their nobles ; the artists of the courts of Akbar, Jahāngīr, and Shah Jahān, both Hindu and Muham-madan, were greatly encouraged, in drawing portraits, in illustrating legend and history or contemporary life, both in fresco on the walls of palaces and villas and in exquisite

---

[1] "Pictorial Art in Japan," vol. ii, p. 262.

[2] This seems to be overstating the case by far, and would be difficult to prove on the basis of stylistic evolution.—P.C.

miniature paintings on paper, usually intended for book illustration. But not even Akbar, who took a most liberal and enlightened view of art, permitted the representation of a human being, or of the Deity, in a mosque or building consecrated to religion. Nor did he attempt to revive a school of religious painting. The rule of the Sunna is scrupulously observed in the decoration of the great mosque at Fatehpur-Sikri, where Akbar promulgated his new religion, "The Divine Faith."

The fresco paintings of the Mogul period, like those of Hindu times, have nearly all perished, only a few fragments remaining of the decoration of Akbar's palace at Fatehpur-Sikri.[1]

Our present knowledge of Mogul painting is almost entirely derived from the pictures, nearly always painted on very fine Indian or Chinese paper, which in spite of the delicate material have more often survived, as they were frequently carefully preserved in royal libraries or in private collections.

In early Mogul times oil painting was not practised by Indian artists, and it should be understood that these pictures by the Mogul court painters were not, as a rule, hung on the walls of apartments, or used for decoration, like modern European cabinet pictures. The pictures of the Indian *chitra-sālas* were always painted directly on the walls in fresco or tempera, but the Indo-Muhammadan paintings were kept like valuable manuscripts, and only brought out occasionally to be handed round for discussion and criticism ; just as in Japan to-day the painted silk scrolls, called *kakemonos*, are displayed one at a time at a tea-party and afterwards carefully packed away. The refined artistic sense of the true Oriental dilettante would be outraged by the hideous jumble of heterogeneous pictures which we crowd together in modern exhibitions and use to "decorate" our houses.

The early Mogul paintings, or those dating from the first half of the sixteenth century, in the reigns of Bābur and Humāyūn, are all of the Persian school, which absorbed many Central Asian elements. The effect of the Islamic ban on the fine arts is very strongly marked in all of them. Muhammadan calligraphists were craftsmen of the highest rank, but when they turned to picture-painting and were released from the rule prohibiting the delineation of the human form they took a long time to shake off the tradition of centuries which had confined them to the elaboration of geometric patterns. They showed little of the genius of the old Buddhist mural painters for vivid narration, for depicting life, buoyant, throbbing, exalted, stirred by passionate spiritual impulses. They had an intense delight in the beauty of a tree or flower, and an unerring intuitive feeling for decorative fitness, but no interest in humanity as a revelation of life. They continued to regard a human figure or crowd with the eye of a geometrical designer, only as a pattern giving opportunities for delightful colour harmonies and intricate combinations of lines. Somewhat in the manner of the modern cubist, only without self-consciousness and aggressiveness, Indo-Muhammadan calligraphists reduced pictorial art to a geometric formula.

The contact of Persia with China and to a certain extent with Europe gradually helped the Muhammadan calligraphers to bring more life into their pictorial efforts, and about the end of the fifteenth century a famous painter Bihzād, at the court of Sultan Husain of Khurasan, founded a new school distinguished by minute finish and careful observation of nature, especially of animal life. It was from this school that Bābur and Humāyūn, the two first Mogul emperors of India, drew most of their court painters.

Nevertheless the gulf which separated them from the early Indian schools of mural painting was very wide. A comparison of a painting by Shapur of Khurasan, who was probably attached to Humāyūn's court, with the Ajantā and Bagh paintings, will show what a world of difference there was between the outlook of the Muhammadan

[1] The most interesting of these is a full-length portrait of a lady, painted on a panel inside the building known as 'Mariam's House," probably the residence of Mariam Zāmāni, the mother of Jahāngīr.

A. Unfinished painting showing the initial stages of a painter's work. Pahari School (Kangra), late 18th century A.D. (*National Museum of India, New Delhi*).

B. Meeting between Rāma and Bharata. Page from a Ms. of the *Rāmāyana*. Mughal School, A.D. 1600 (*Prince of Wales Museum, Bombay*).

PLATE 53

Two brush-line portraits, School of Shah Jahān. (*Lady M. D. Scott-Moncrieff's Collection*).

PLATE 54

B. Folio from a Ms. of *Syar-i-Danish*. Mughal School, late 16th century A.D. (*Collection of Sir Cowasji Jehangir, Prince of Wales Museum, Bombay*).

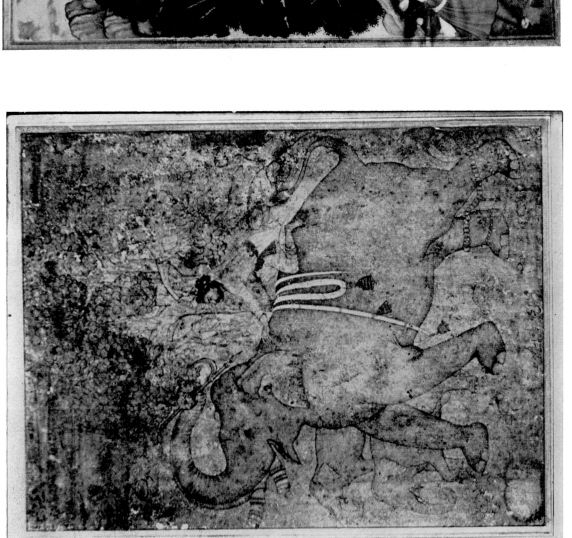

A. Prince Muhammad Murad on the elephant Iqbal. From a drawing by Ghulām, A.D. 1610. (*From a shaded brush drawing in the Calcutta Art Gallery*).

PLATE 55

B.   Muhammad Jam Qudsi, Shah Jahan's Poet Laureate, by Bichitr.
(From a coloured brush drawing in the Calcutta Art Gallery).

PLATE 56

A.   Portrait of Sultan Muhammad Kutb Shah of Golconda, by Mir Hashim.
(From the original in the Victoria and Albert Museum).

artist-scribe and that of the Buddhist mural painter. Shapur's picture (Plate 50), now in the Calcutta Art Gallery, is dated 1534[1] and represents a nautch party at the court of Muhammad Tuglak—a somewhat similar scene to that depicted on the walls of Bagh ten or eleven centuries earlier. Shapur draws his group diagrammatically on a rich gold background with the neatness and precision of an accomplished scribe, making delicious colour harmonies with a pale blue carpet and the orange, green, lilac, and lemon coloured costumes, but the figures, though well-spaced for decorative effect, seem like puppets pulled by strings compared with the intensely alive and human group of Indian minstrels and dancers at Bagh.

It was not until the time of Akbar and of his son Jahāngīr that the Mogul court painters of India began to throw off the stiffness and formality of the old tradition, and to draw fresh inspiration from the study of nature which the Muhammadan law, as interpreted by the Caliphs, had denied them.

The new departure was due partly, perhaps, to the influence of the Hindu painters employed at the Mogul court, but we need not assume from Abul Fazl's admiration for their art that Hindu painting in the sixteenth century retained the freshness and vitality of the Ajantā school or that the renaissance of art under the Mogul Emperors achieved results at all comparable with the sculpture and painting of pre-Muhammadan times. Judging from the works of Akbar's Hindu painters which have come down to us, it would seem that Indian painting, like Indian poetry, had become intensely formal and ritualistic. The Hindus were generally more proficient in drawing the human figure, but both Hindu and Muhammadan artists seemed to be cramped by the Islamic tradition, thinking more of the geometric pattern of the picture, as providing the framework for their brilliant colour-schemes, than of the representation of animate things.

Abul Fazl, Akbar's Prime Minister and devout admirer, records in the courtly language of the Aīn-i-Akbāri the Emperor's practical interest in the fine arts and the prejudices of the orthodox Musalman :

"I have to notice that the observing of the figures of objects and the making of likenesses of them are, for a well-regulated mind, a source of wisdom, and an antidote against the poison of ignorance. Bigoted followers of the letter of the law are hostile to the art of painting, but their eyes now see the truth.

"One day, at a private party of friends, His Majesty, who had conferred on several the pleasure of drawing near him, remarked : 'There are many that hate painting, but such men I dislike. It appears to me as if a painter had quite peculiar means of recognising God, for a painter, in sketching anything that has life, and in devising the limbs one after another, must come to feel that he cannot bestow personality upon his work, and is thus forced to thank God the Giver of Life, and will thus increase his knowledge.'

"Akbar," says Abul Fazl, "had from his earliest youth shown a great interest in painting, and given it every encouragement, regarding it both as a means of study and as an amusement.

"The works of all painters are weekly laid before His Majesty by the Darogahs and the clerks ; he then confers rewards according to excellence of workmanship, or increases the monthly salaries. Much progress was made in commodities required by painters, and the correct prices of such articles carefully ascertained. The mixture of colour has especially been improved. The pictures thus received a hitherto unknown finish.

"Most excellent painters are now to be found and masterpieces worthy of a Bihzād may be placed at the side of the wonderful works of the European painters who have attained worldwide fame. The minuteness in detail, the general finish, the boldness of execution, etc., now observed in pictures are incomparable ; even inanimate objects

---

[1] It is impossible for Pl. 50 to be dated A.D. 1534. It is without a doubt an example of Mughal painting of the late 18th century and not earlier. Inscriptions on Indian paintings should be critically studied before they are accepted as genuine or the critic is likely to fall into serious errors.—P.C.

look as if they had life. More than a hundred painters have become famous masters of the art, while the number of those who approach perfection, or those who are middling, is very large. This is especially true of the Hindus : their pictures surpass our conception of things. Few indeed in the whole world are found equal to them.

"The number of masterpieces of painting increased with the encouragement given to the art. Persian books, both prose and poetry, were ornamented with pictures, and a very large number of paintings were thus collected. The story of Hamzah was represented in twelve volumes, and clever painters made the most astonishing illustrations for no less than one thousand and four hundred passages of the story. The 'Chingiz-namah,' the 'Zafar-nameh,' this book, the 'Razm-nameh,' the 'Ramayan,' the 'Nal Daman,' the 'Kalilah Damnah,' the 'Ayār Dāmsh,' etc., were all illustrated.

"His Majesty himself sat for his likeness,[1] and also ordered to have the likenesses taken of all the grandees of the realm. An immense album was thus formed ; those that have passed away have received a new life, and those that are still alive have immortality promised them."[2]

Abul Fazl gives a list of the celebrated painters of the Court. He singles out four for special mention :

"Mir Sayyid Ali, of Tabriz." [Translator's note : "Better known as a poet, under the name of Juddi. He illuminated the story of Amir Hamzah, mentioned above."]

"Kwājah Abduççamad, styled Shīrīnqalam, or 'Sweet Pen.' He comes from Shiraz.

"Daswanth. He is the son of a palkee-bearer. He devoted his whole life to the art, and used, from love to his profession, to draw and paint figures even on walls. One day the eye of His Majesty fell on him ; his talent was discovered, and he himself handed over to the Kwājah. In a short time he surpassed all painters and became the first master of the age. Unfortunately the light of his talents was dimmed by the shadow of madness. He committed suicide. He has left many masterpieces.

"Basāwan. In backgrounding, drawing of features, distribution of colours, portrait-painting, and several other branches, he is most excellent. So much so that many critics prefer him to Daswanth."

The following thirteen painters are also mentioned as being famous :

Kesu, Zāl, Mukund, Mushkin, Farrukh the Qalmaq, (Plate 51C) Mādhū, Jagan, Mohesh, K'hemkaran, Tārā, Sānwlah, Haribans, Rām.

A considerable number of the works of these painters are still in existence, and in the last twenty years have emerged from obscurity and furnished materials for many learned critical studies which have done much to create an interest in Indian art, at least as a cult for the connoisseur, if not in a deeper sense. It is impossible here to enter into all the technical details which are of such absorbing interest for the collector.[3]

Akbar was certainly something more than a connoisseur. He approached art in a religious spirit and with a profound view of statesmanship, regarding it as a spiritual force which makes for peace, reconciliation, and enlightenment. The early works of his court painters, such as the illustrations of the story of Amir Hamzah and of the Akbar-nāma, exhibit a patchwork of all the contemporary calligraphic styles, Persian, Central Asian, Chinese, and Indian, the predominant tendency being towards fine pattern-making, more suggestive of Chinese cloisonné enamel and faience than of pictorial art, as it is understood in Europe. Akbar's aim apparently was to create a new synthesis of art out of all the heterogeneous racial elements which were gathered in his court in the

---

[1] A portrait of Akbar, bearing Jahāngīr's seal, formerly in the Calcutta Art Gallery, is now in the Victoria Memorial Collection.

[2] Blochmann's translation, vol. i, pp. 107 *et seq.*

[3] For a recent discussion of Mughal painting during the period of Akbar, see Emmy Wellez, *Akbar's Religious Thought as Reflected in Mughal Painting*, London, 1952. The finest discussion of Mughal painting is still to be found in Stchoukine, *La Peinture Indienne*, Paris, 1929.—P.C.

Pl. E

Snake-charmer.   Rajasthani School (Bundi), c. 1760 A.D.   This is a study from the everyday life of the people—the snake-charmer playing his pipe before the snake that has raised its hood.   The attendant mangooses its nearby, ready for the traditional snake-mongoose fight.   On the left are three lovely girls watching the performance while Sri Krishna watches from the balcony above.

(Courtesy, Prince of Wales Museum of Western India, Bombay)

same way as he sought to unite all the religious elements in his imperial Order, the Dīn-i-Ilāhi ; his method being to bring out individual talent by the spur of competition under his own eye. Eventually a definite Mogul style which was really Indian evolved out of this clash of racial æsthetics, but, as Dr. Heinrich Gluck remarks in his sumptuous volume on the Hamzah series in the Vienna Museum of Art and Industry, painting under Akbar and his successors

"became a thing which was specially perfected in certain departments, e.g. portraiture and group-portraiture, but which invariably remained confined to the court and to which somehow the character of the conscious and of something artificially produced ever clings. For it is true that at a later period this art also came, here and there, into touch with popular sources, but very much as an eccentric wealthy man surrounds himself with a collection of popular objects. This art was not produced out of the unconscious popular spirit, out of the crystallisation of this spirit in a dominant will, and therefore could not flow back into it."[1]

Yet it must be remembered that Akbar's personal influence extended over almost the whole range of art and must not be reckoned solely by the works of his court painters. He was a great builder, and the numerous state-workshops which he established and supervised with his indefatigable energy were admirable schools of arts and crafts. But Akbar's reign was a period of transition and reconstruction, and his influence upon the art of his time was most apparent after his death.

Jahāngīr, Akbar's intemperate son (1605-28), inherited few of his father's higher qualities, but was equally devoted to the fine arts. His memoirs contain many evidences of the keen personal, even affectionate, interest which he took in his court painters and their work. He treated them as intimate friends and frequently bestowed upon them the highest distinctions. Jahāngīr himself tells us that he raised Sherif Khan, the son of Abdul Hamad—one of Akbar's portrait-painters—who had grown up with him from infancy and upon whom, while heir-apparent, he had conferred the title of Khan, to the position of premier grandee of the empire.

In the thirteenth year of his reign the memoirs record :

"This day Abul Hasan, a painter who bore the name of Nādiru-Zamān, drew a picture of my court and presented it to me. He had attached it as a frontispiece to the ' Jahāngīr-nāma.' As it was well worthy of praise, I loaded him with great favours. If the celebrated Abul Haī and Bihzād were alive they would do him full justice for his exalted taste in painting.

"His father, Aka-Rāza, was always with me when I was a prince and his son was born in my household. However, the son is far superior to his father. I gave him a good education, till he became one of the most distinguished men of the age. The portraits furnished by him are beautiful.

"Mansūr is also a master of the art of drawing and he has the title of Nādiru-l-Aslī. In the time of my father and my own there have been none to compare with these two artists."

Neither Abul Hasan nor Mansūr is mentioned in Abul Fazl's list. They came into prominence in the later period of Akbar's reign. Mansūr is chiefly known for his wonderful studies of bird life, which are noticed further on, but he was also one of the best of the Mogul portrait-painters.

Jahāngīr prides himself on his ability as a connoisseur and alludes to the practice of dividing the work of painting a picture between several artists :

"I am very fond of pictures, and have such a discrimination in judging them that I can tell the name of the artist, whether living or dead. If there are several portraits (in the same picture) painted by several artists I could point out the painter of each. Even if one portrait were finished by several painters I could mention the names of those

[1] Translated in "Rūpam," No. 29, Jan. 1927.

who had drawn the different portions of that single picture. In fact I could declare without fail by whom the brow and by whom the eyelashes were drawn, or if anyone had touched up the portrait after it was drawn by the first painter."

When his zoological collection was enriched by a number of rare birds and animals from Goa he ordered paintings to be made from them, and observes :

' The Emperor Bābur has in his memoirs given an able description and pictured representation of several animals ; but it is most probable that he never ordered the painters to draw them from the life."

It was, no doubt, the practice of drawing from the living model, enjoined by Akbar and Jahāngīr on their painter-calligraphists, which led to the very remarkable achievements in portraiture and direct representation of animal life of the best artists of Jahāngīr and Shah Jahān. This practice and the division of labour in making up a picture to which Jahāngīr alludes may also account for the disjointed design of many of the Mogul paintings. The miniature painters of the Mogul School painted as exquisitely as the *petits maîtres* of Europe, but they cannot be put in the same class as the great masters of Ajantā and Bagh, who followed their own traditions and were not under dilettante dictation. The painters of the Hindu School, whose superiority as artists impressed Abul Fazl so strongly, did not take "drawing from the life" in the same sense as the modern European academician. It did not mean that the student sat down in front of his model and reproduced as closely as possible the reflection of it on the retina of his own eyes ; but that after the most careful observation he went away to record his mental impression of it, returning occasionally, if necessary, to refresh his memory. In this way the artist's memory and powers of observation were developed to an extraordinary degree, as we can see in the wonderful memory paintings of the Ajantā and Bagh viharas.

An amusing passage in the memoirs of Sir Thomas Roe, who was sent by James I to the Court of the Great Mogul in the interests of the East India Company, is concerned with Jahāngīr's pride in the technical skill of his painters. The directors of the Company knowing what were the most acceptable presents at the Mogul Court had sent some pictures with the ambassador : they had previously sent out portraits of James and his Queen, Anne of Denmark, as well as one of Sir Thomas Smyth, Governor of the Company, which was much prized by Jahāngīr as his painters, so it was said, confessed their inability to imitate it.

Finding that Jahāngīr was more pleased with pictures than with anything else, Roe presented him with one of his own :

"A Pickture of a friend of myne that I esteemed very much, and was for Curiositye rare, which I would give his Maiestie as a present, seeing hee so much affected that art ; assuring myselfe he never saw any equall to it, neyther was anything more esteemed of mee."

This was a painting by Isaac Oliver, the English miniaturist.

Jahāngīr was delighted with the picture, but offered to bet with the ambassador that his own painters would make a copy of it which Roe could not distinguish from the original. After some diplomatic fencing, Roe, who had formed a very poor opinion of Indian artists, agreed to "lay a good horse" with the Minister, Asaph Khan ; but the latter, he noted in his diary, "recanted in Priuat."

Some weeks afterwards the ambassador was summoned to the Durbar and was first asked by Jahāngīr what he would give the painter if his copy fulfilled the terms of the wager.

' A painter's reward—50 rupees," said Sir Thomas, rather contemptuously. Jahāngīr replied that this was insufficient, for his painter was "a Cauallero"—a gentleman. The copies, when produced, were five in number, pasted together with the original "on one table," and so like that Roe was—

"By candlelight troubled to discerne which was which ; I confess beyond all expecta-

The Heroine Garlanding the Hero. A leaf from the *Amarusataka*. School of Malwa, c. 1680 A.D. The love lyrics of the *Amarusataka* are famous in Sanskrit literature for their diction and sensuousness. Under a pavilion the heroine is putting a garland round the neck of the hero, while her attendant is trying to persuade her not to do so. The brilliant colour patches in the background, the colourful architecture and the carefully depicted details of the costumes and the ornaments are typical of the School of Malwa.

(*Courtesy, Prince of Wales Museum of Western India, Bombay*)

tion ; yet I showed myne owne and the differences which were in arte apparent, but not to be judged by a common eye. But for that at first sight I knew it not, hee [Jahāngīr] was very merry and joyfull, and craked like a Northern man."

Jahāngīr again exultingly insisted upon knowing what reward Roe would give to his painter, and refusing a gift of money, finally settled that for one of the copies which Jahāngīr gave, the artist should choose one of the English "toyes" Roe had brought with him.

Though the test imposed by Jahāngīr was one of ordinary technical skill and not very convincing, there is no doubt that there were many distinguished artists among his court painters. The subtle refinement of the Indian miniaturist's art was evidently lost upon Roe, and the more obvious realism of European painting appealed to him, just as it does to "a common eye" in India to-day.

It is interesting to note that about this time one of the greatest of European artists, Rembrandt, was making use of Indian miniature paintings in his work. Among Rembrandt's pen-and-ink studies collected in the British Museum a number have been identified as copies or adaptations of Indian miniatures, and it has been shown that from them chiefly Rembrandt derived the atmosphere for his Biblical subjects.

Professor Sarre, in his monograph on the subject,[1] compares reproductions of the original Mogul miniatures with Rembrandt's pen-and-ink sketches. The British Museum possesses a drawing by Rembrandt copied from a Mogul miniature of "Akbar (?)[2] on his Throne," now in the Ethnographic Museum, Berlin. The latter has also an original Mogul painting of an "Indian Prince on Horseback," of which Rembrandt's copy is in the British Museum. The Louvre has another study by him of "Timur on his Throne," copied, with a few variations, from an Indian miniature now in Berlin.

It appears that in 1631 Rembrandt resided at Amsterdam, then the headquarters of the Dutch East India Company. In 1642 he painted the portrait of Abraham Wilmerdonks, a Director of the Company, who had a considerable oriental collection.

Rembrandt himself collected oriental costumes, wood-carving, and paintings. In the inventory of his effects made after his bankruptcy in 1656, there is an entry of "a book of curious miniature drawings," which may have been the Mogul miniatures from which he made his studies.

Professor Sarre is doubtless right in pointing out that, though Rembrandt made use of these miniatures for the oriental accessories of his pictures, it cannot be said that his art was influenced by them in a deeper sense. European critics do not always show such discernment when they discover Indian artists borrowing Western details for their own use.

Both Akbar and Jahāngīr admired the realism of the European paintings which were brought to them as presents. They had them copied and hung them on the walls of their palaces as modern Indian Princes do. The best Mogul painters used them in their original work in the same way as Rembrandt and many Italian masters used oriental material, not imitatively but artistically. Indian art thus preserved the intrinsic qualities which give it value and interest to Western artists. When it loses its Indianness it loses everything.

The middle of Shah Jahān's reign (1628-58) may be said to mark the zenith of the Mogul Court painters' art, though there is no record of such intimate personal relations between the Emperor and his artists as that which Jahāngīr has given us. The unhappy Dārā Shikoh, Shah Jahān's eldest son, has left a token of his personal interest in painting in the album which is now one of the historic treasures of the India Office Library. It is dedicated to his cousin and favourite wife, "his nearest and dearest friend, the Lady Nādirah Begum," in the year 1051 A.H. (A.D. 1641-2). Her tragic fate, seventeen years

[1] "Jahrbuch den Kön. Preuszischen Kunst Sammlungen," xxv, Berlin, 1904.
[2] Mr. G. P. Rouffaer has pointed out that this is Jahāngīr.

later, is told by Tavernier. She died of heat and thirst in the deserts of Sind, while following her husband in his flight from the victorious forces of Aurangzīb. Dārā Shikoh himself, distraught with grief, was betrayed into his brother's hands shortly afterwards and murdered in prison.

The sorrowful story lends a pathetic interest to the fine portrait of the Prince as a youth gazing at his beloved's picture (Plate 57), now in the Victoria Memorial Collection, Calcutta, which will be noticed later on.

The accession of Aurangzīb in 1658 completely altered the privileged position which artists had enjoyed at the Mogul Court, and from that time interest is mainly concentrated on the independent Hindu schools, the most important of which were located in Rajputana and Gujarat, and later on in some of the sub-Himalayan principalities.

Study of a Woman by Govardhana.   School of Jahangir.   The brush work is very fine, the colour scheme sumptuous and the treatment of the hands sensitive.   The face of the figure is beautiful and full of charm.   This miniature is altogether a dainty specimen of the Mughal art at its zenith.

(From *Studies in Indian Painting* by N. C. Mehta)

Chapter XII

TYPICAL INDIAN MINIATURE PAINTINGS

There were, as Abul Fazl indicates, two formative elements in the school of painting established by Akbar, one which was mainly foreign, derived from the different Islamic schools of book-illustration and calligraphy, the other indigenous and Hindu, which must also be taken as a general term for Indian art, derived from folk-traditions and from the ancient schools of mural painting.[1]   In course of time the two amalgamated and formed a distinct school, called Mogul to distinguish it both from the foreign schools and from the contemporary Hindu and Jain schools which had an independent existence.

The nucleus of the school was formed by the foreigners brought into India by Bābur and Humāyūn, but under Akbar the Hindu element became the strongest both in numbers and as a creative force, for the Indian painters had an age-long tradition of art-practice behind them closely bound up with religious and social life and only fettered by puritanical restrictions when they were obliged to consider the feelings of their Muslim rulers. Yet the indigenous schools must have suffered much from the disrepute in which pictorial art was held by Muhammadan orthodoxy and by the strict enforcement of the law of Islam in the previous centuries.   A Hindu who wished to avoid offence to his Musalman neighbours, or to cultivate their friendship, would not care to decorate the walls of his guest-chamber with paintings banned by the law of Islam.   But he could indulge his personal taste and that of his Hindu friends secretly with the art of the miniature painter.

Abul Fazl only makes a passing allusion to wall-painting.   Like every strict Muhammadan he valued calligraphy as a finer art than that of the picture-painter and not suspect as irreligious.   "The letter, a magical power, is spiritual geometry, emanating from the pen of invention ; a heavenly writ from the hand of fate."   There were eight calligraphical systems recognised in the Muhammadan world.   In China writing and drawing have been recognised as sister arts from the days of the legendary monarch Fa-hi in the third millennium B.C. who is said to have made drawing one of the six branches of calligraphy.

The character of the handwriting to which he was accustomed naturally influenced greatly the style of the artist's drawing.   The great variety of the strokes in Chinese and Japanese ideographs has given an immense fluency and variety to the brush-outlines of the artists of those countries : in Japan ten different styles of line-drawing are recognised, each style representing a special character or mode of expression.   The Indo-Persian scribe, on the other hand, used a reed-pen in writing and as a miniature painter his line acquired thereby more uniformity and regularity, the precision of a medallist rather than the fluency of the habitual brush-writer.   Owing to the generally small scale of the Mogul drawings it was a line of wonderful delicacy, though the rhythmic flow of the Ajantā

---

[1] Various opinions are held on the existence of a Hindu school previous to the Mughal school, and different from the Jaina school.   Some authors hold that this was not the case, at least as far as Rajasthan is concerned, while others hold a contrary view.   Recently discovered documents of painting including the Mandu *Kalpasutra* of A.D. 1439, the Jaunpur *Kalpasutra* of A.D. 1465 (Plate 75C and D), the *Niamat Namah* of the early 16th century, probably done at Mandu in Malwa and published by Robert Skelton in *Marg*, 1959, the *Adipurana* Ms of A.D. 1540 done at Palam near Delhi, the *Lor-Chanda* set of the Prince of Wales Museum of Western India, to be shortly published in a monograph by Moti Chandra and Karl Khandalavala, a set illustrating the *Mrigavati* in the Bharat Kala Bhavan, Banaras, and paintings done in the style of the "Laur Chanda" and "Chaurapanchasika" group (see Karl Khandalavala, "A Gita Govinda Series in the Prince of Wales Museum," Bulletin of the Prince of Wales Museum, No. 4, 1953-54, pp. 1-18) would indicate the existence of a style different from that of the Mughal and Jaina styles in Northern India, in the general area of Malwa and Uttar Pradesh.   See Appendix II.—P.C.

brush-lines, controlled by the arm and wrist rather than by the fingers, is generally wanting. The Ajantā technique is more apparent in the drawings of Hindu artists, who practised both fresco and miniature painting and did not specialise in calligraphy. As they had the predominating influence at the Mogul Court the stiffness and conventionality of the early school of Akbar gradually disappears, though the calligraphic style left its mark on the character of most Mogul painting.

Indian connoisseurs distinguish the various styles of draughtsmanship which developed in different localities or different families of painters by the term *kalam*, pen or brush— the lines being drawn with a fine brush usually made from the hairs of a squirrel's tail.

A preliminary outline sketch was made in Indian red, used without gum so that when dry the colour could be brushed away, leaving a very faint indication of the drawing (Plate 53A). The finished line was then drawn with lamp-black, specially prepared by burning a camphorated cotton wick in a mustard-oil lamp. Sometimes the drawing was delicately shaded, and some of the details heightened with gold or tinted. The artists prided themselves on the fineness of their brushes, and the test of supreme skill was to finish the detail with an *ek bāl kalam*, a one-haired brush, which seems to have been used for microscopic stippling as well as for the finest lines.[1]

The illustrations will give some idea of the great distinction, delicacy, and charm of the best Mogul court painters' brush-drawing. With all the sincerity, truthfulness, and perfect finish of the old Dutch and Flemish masters, these Indian drawings have a subtlety and sensitiveness of their own suggestive of the songs of Hafiz and Omar Khayyam and of the music of the *vina* to which the dilettante of the Mogul Court listened as the portraits passed from hand to hand. Sometimes delicately shaded and embellished with discreet touches of gold, they are completely satisfying as works of art, the strength and sureness of the brush-lines giving them then the precision of fine sculpture.

Plate 54 shows two admirable brush-line studies by an unknown artist of two of Shah Jahān's courtiers, Mirza Sultan Nazir (left) and Afzal Khan, from Lady Scott-Moncrieff's collection. A more highly finished drawing shaded and embellished with gold, reproduced in Plate 55A, bears the inscription in Persian, "Prince Murad, son of Shah Jahān, on the elephant Iqbal, drawn by Ghulām, 1030 A.H. (A.D. 1621)." Interest is concentrated on the great elephant, which has evidently become unruly, as he is flourishing the mahout's goad in his trunk and trumpeting with rage. The Prince has climbed on his back to take the mahout's place while the latter, or one of the attendants, is chaining the elephant's legs. The excited action of the great beast is splendidly given, while the vigour of the composition is not less striking than the finished technique, both in the drawing of the three elephants and in the careful study of the banyan-tree behind.

In the portrait of Shah Jahān's Poet Laureate, Muhammad Jam Qudsi (Plate 56B), the artist Bichitr reveals himself as one of the most accomplished masters of the Mogul Court. This delightful coloured drawing, one of the collection made by the author for the Calcutta Art Gallery, bore on the mount an inscription by the court scribe or a former owner, "A Portrait of Sa'di of Shiraz (may God sanctify his tomb !)," but a more authentic inscription on a similar portrait published by Major D. Macaulay in the "Burlington Magazine"[2] gives both the name of the artist and the subject of the portrait as above.

Though it is unmistakably a study from life, it is not surprising that it should be taken for a portrait of the more famous Persian poet of the fourteenth century. There was a regular demand at the Mogul Court for traditional portraits, such as those of the Padshah's ancestors, or other great historical personages, and such portrait types, more or less authentic, were handed down in the artist's families from one generation to another as part of their stock-in-trade.

[1] See Moti Chandra, *Technique of Mughal Painting*, Lucknow, 1949, for an exhaustive exposition of the technique and materials of the Mughal painter.—P.C.
[2] February, 1925.

Prince Dārā Shikoh. (*From the original in the Victoria Memorial Collection, Calcutta*).

PLATE 57

B. A pair of cranes. Mughal School, C. 1615 A.D.
(Collection of Sir Cowasji Jehangir, Prince of Wales Museum, Bombay).

A. A turkey-cock, by Ustād Mansūr.
(From the original in the Calcutta Art Gallery).

PLATE 58

Two Sāras, by Ustād Mansūr. (*From the original in the Victoria and Albert Museum, London*).

PLATE 59

B. Portrait of Babar. Mughal School, early 17th century A.D.
(*Prince of Wales Museum, Bombay*).

A. A black buck, by Manohar.
(*From the original in the British Museum*).

PLATE 60

The dignified old poet of Shah Jahān's Court, with a face so strong and full of character, might very well have posed for the adventurous Sa'di, whose sonnets often served as decoration on the illuminated mounts which framed the Mogul miniatures so exquisitely. When the great masters of calligraphy thus collaborated with the miniature painters the taste of the Mogul connoisseur who gave the frame a higher value than the picture is sometimes hardly to be criticised. The mounts of Jahāngīr's miniatures are often embellished with admirably designed floral patterns, in which may be seen the original suggestions for the *pietra-dura* decoration of the Tāj, wrongly attributed by Anglo-Indian tradition to the French adventurer at Shah Jahān's Court, Austin de Bordeaux.

Calligraphy, however, must be treated as outside the scope of this book, except as an influence bearing on the art of the Mogul miniature painter. In Bichitr's drawing, moreover, the artist has the field to himself, for the mount is a simple one, discreetly splashed with gold. The strength and thoroughness of his draughtsmanship can only be appreciated by examining the original with a magnifying glass.

Portraiture and brilliant court ceremonials were the subjects of most of the Mogul miniature paintings. The Padshah and his favourite generals and courtiers were drawn and painted, singly and in groups, assembled in Durbar, in shooting or hawking parties, sometimes in battles or sieges. The illustrations to the Akbar-nāma give vivid impressions of the great Emperor's manifold activities, but are more interesting as historical documents than as works of art. A rigid code of etiquette prevents the artist from penetrating deeply the human side of Mogul Court life. Religious subjects are studiously avoided, except for a formal visit to a sacred shrine, or an interview with a Muslim saint.

Restricted to a very limited range of ceremonial poses, nearly always in profile, the court portrait-painters could yet show their high capacity as delineators of character, while they revelled in delicate finish and in gem-like combinations of colour, which gave currency to the legend that they used precious stones as pigments. The best Mogul miniatures, therefore, have a high æsthetic value, apart from their historical importance, in spite of the artificial atmosphere in which the artists lived.

The portrait on Plate 56A of Sultan Muhammad Kutb Shah of Golconda, by Mir Hashim, one of Shah Jahān's court painters, might be taken to represent the acme of elegance and distinction attained in Mogul painted portraiture. In the fine sensitive drawing of the head and hands Mir Hashim shows himself Bichitr's equal. Like the latter he has got entirely free from the somewhat tiresome mannerisms of the calligraphic school, while retaining its cameo-like precision and delicacy of finish. The conventional profile pose is made natural and unaffected, the perpendicular lines of the long sword and the fall of the brocaded edges of the Sultan's muslin shawl giving it a statuesque dignity. The pearly hues of the white drapery, faultlessly rendered, are set off by sparkling contrasts of emerald, ruby, gold, and jade. Other Mogul portraits may show a more sumptuous palette and subtler gradations of colour, but few have the brilliancy and charm of this little gem of Mogul art. It seems to suggest a wall painting in miniature, and as mural decoration, life-size, it would have been a noble ornament for the Sultan's palace.

Jahāngīr was as fond of decorating the walls of his summer-palaces with pictures, especially portraits, as the old Hindu rulers had been. We occasionally get direct evidence of the art of the *chitra-sāla* in Mogul times in large-scale portraits drawn or painted on paper. An exceptionally fine example is the painting reproduced in Plate 57, which gives a very sympathetic presentment of Dārā Shikoh as a youth, by an unknown artist. The Prince is painted quarter-length, standing within one of the white marble balconies of the Delhi Palace, holding in his hand a portrait of "his nearest and dearest friend," the Lady Nādirah Begum. Rich colour contrasts are obtained by an effective use of silken purdahs and awnings, but the *pietra-dura* decoration of the architectural setting is rather weak and over-elaborated. The portrait itself, drawn with great sincerity and feeling, and delicately modelled in the manner of the later Ajantā School, gives us an insight into the temperament of the high-minded but headstrong Prince. The melancholy mood of a lover or a foreboding of the tragic end of the devoted couple is reflected on his refined but rather effeminate features.

A remarkable but less sympathetic portrait of Dārā Shikoh in later life, on a still larger scale, is given by Mr. Percy Brown in his "Indian Painting under the Mughals," Plate XXIX. It is by Hunhar, a very able Hindu artist, c. 1650.

Ustād Mansūr, upon whom Jahāngīr bestowed the title of "Wonder of the Age," was one of the most famous of the Mogul portrait-painters, though comparison of his known works with those of Bichitr and Mir Hashim is hardly to his advantage. The Wantage Collection at the Victoria and Albert Museum has a portrait by him of Khwāja Kalān Beg which gives the impression of being an excellent likeness of an obsequious old courtier, bordering on senile decay, but it lacks the freshness of Bichitr's and Mir Hashim's technique, and the elaborate stippling of the drapery, in imitation perhaps of European miniatures, is rather overdone.[1]

Mansūr's claim to distinction rests rather upon his admirable portraiture of birds and animals. The atmosphere of the court under Jahāngīr and Shah Jahān was too materialistic to produce devout lovers of nature like the Chinese and Japanese, or the Indian Buddhist painters. Mansūr, Manohar, and others were only permitted to study birds and animals as zoological ornaments of the Mogul Court, posing for their portraits as the Padshah's protégés, never whirling in flight across the heavens or enjoying the freedom of the forest.

Not that Jahāngīr himself did not feel delight in the beauties of nature : his memoirs give sufficient proof of his keen artistic temperament. But he lacked the sincere religious feeling of his father, and was too self-centred to inspire great art. Yet within the limitations imposed by the environment in which they were produced the studies of bird and animal life by Mansūr and Manohar are unsurpassed for scientific exactness and superb craftsmanship.

Jahāngīr mentions the occasion which led him to give orders for a series of paintings from his zoological collection to adorn the pages of the Jahāngīrī-nāma. Mukarrah Khan in the seventh year of his reign had been sent on a mission to Goa, and returned with some rare birds and animals which Jahāngīr had never seen before. Among them was a turkey-cock, of which Jahāngīr gives a graphic description :

"One of the birds resembled a peahen, but was a little larger in size, though less than a peacock. When he was desirous of pairing he used to spread his tail and feathers and danced about like a peacock. His beak and feet resembled those of a barn-door fowl. His head, neck, and throat changed their colour every minute, and when anxious to pair he became a perfect red and seemed to be a beautiful piece of coral. After sometime he was as white as cotton, and sometimes he got as blue as a turquoise, and in short turned all colours, like a chameleon. The piece of flesh which is attached to his head looks like the comb of a cock. But the curious part of it was that that piece of flesh, when he was about to pair, hung down a span long, like the trunk of an elephant, and when again restored to its position it was erected over the head to the height of two fingers. The part round his eyes remained constantly of a blue colour, and was never subject to change, which was not the case with his wings, which were always changing their colour, contrary to those of a peacock."[2]

This turkey-cock is the subject of one of Mansūr's best studies (Plate 58A), now in the collection of the Calcutta Art Gallery. It bears the imperial seal and is mounted on a

[1] The Wantage Collection of the Victoria and Albert Museum, London, contains a number of paintings that are not genuine and belong to the late 18th century. The portrait of Khwaja Kalan Beg is not an original work by Mansur, but a later copy, the stippling referred to by Havell being a late characteristic. For a discussion of this problem, see Moti Chandra, *Technique of Mughal Painting*, pp. 80-84.—P.C.

[2] Translated by Elliott, "History of India," vol. vi, pp. 331-2.

Pl. H

An European Embassy. Mughal, 17th century. The Emperor Shah Jahan is seated in the Diwan-i-Khas with two royal princes behind him and two in front. The exact historical incident forming the theme of this magnificent miniature is uncertain.

(From *Studies in Indian Painting* by N. C. Mehta)

magnificent specimen of calligraphy, embellished with flowers of the Kashmir valley, the beauty of which attracted Jahāngīr so much that he employed Mansūr in painting a series of them. The Wantage Collection of the Victoria and Albert Museum has another painting of the turkey and several other fine bird-studies by Mansūr, including the admirable painting of two Indian *sāras* (Plate 59), probably the portraits of the two pet birds to which Jahāngīr gave the name of Majnūn and Lailā. This is the nearest approach to romance in real life which Jahāngīr's portrait-painters give us. The Padshah's own romance, his attachment to Nūr Jahān, was not a subject for the painter's brush. None of the so-called portraits of her can be considered authentic.

Among other pet animals portrayed by Jahāngīr's artists was a black buck, used as a decoy in hunting. Two very fine studies of it by Manohar are known, one of which (Plate 60A) is in the British Museum and the other in the Wantage Collection at South Kensington.

The Mogul painters naturally took infinite pains in depicting the glitter and tinsel of court ceremonial with all its sumptuous paraphernalia—brocaded canopies and silken carpets, costly jewellery and golden thrones—as a great number of gorgeously decorative paintings testify. But the exuberant elaboration of works of this class, more calligraphic than pictorial, loses all its finesse and colour-charm in reproduction. The subtler qualities of Mogul art are more conspicuous in individual portraiture and in genre painting.

Bichitr shows his quality as a genre painter in his picture (Plate 61A) called "The Tambura Player," for want of a more explanatory title, in the Wantage Collection at South Kensington. It is a very piquant little scene, closely studied from life, in which a one-eyed musician is singing with great gusto a song which excites the hilarity of his listener, the bowman holding an arrow in his left hand and apparently beating time with his right foot. The facial expression of both is admirably rendered, and the imperturbable countenance of the servant squatting in the foreground, with his bundle between his legs, is equally true to life.

The realism of this remarkable little picture might suggest that Bichitr was trying to imitate European painters of genre, but more likely it only points to the natural bent of Mogul art when it shook off the traditional conventions of the calligraphic school. The Mogul Court painters were temperamentally realists, and therefore inclined to admire the realism of the European pictures they saw. But, except under Jahāngīr's dictation, they did not copy them as the modern Indian student does, consciously or unconsciously at the suggestion of his European teachers. They saw life as a materialist sees it, not as a poet or mystic, but did not borrow European spectacles to see it with. They had not the spiritual vision of the Ajantā School, but they were quite sincere students of nature and had something interesting to say about it. Within their limited range the Indian painters of the Mogul Court kept alive the great traditions of the Ajantā School.

But to appreciate the qualities in Hindu painting which are intimately related to Indian life and thought one must get away from the rather stuffy atmosphere of the Mogul Court into the fresher air of the provinces of the empire, where art had always grown freely under natural conditions, not merely as an exotic cultivated by pampered æsthetes who rebelled against puritanical laws. Here, both in subject-matter and in æsthetic quality, we come at once into contact with the romance of Indian life which was hardly ever touched by the artists of the Delhi Court : themes of the country-side its myths and legends, passionate stories of court-life told by the village *kathak*, even glimpses of life behind the zanana walls.

India has never had any separate school of landscape painting, like China and Japan, but in landscape settings to figure subjects of this kind Hindu painters of the Mogul period and later, show a full appreciation of the true function of fine art, as Emerson has nobly expressed it in his Essay :

"In landscapes the painter should give the suggestion of a fairer creation than we

know.   The details, the prose of Nature, he should omit, and give us only the spirit and
the splendour.   He should know that the landscape has beauty to the eye because it
expresses the thought which is to him good, and this because the same power which
sees through his eyes is seen in that spectacle ; and he will come to value the expression
of Nature, and not Nature itself, and so exalt in his copy the features which please him.
He will give the gloom of gloom and the sunshine of sunshine.''

Night and effects of artificial light have an especial attraction for the Indian painter of
Mogul times, though in his thoughts of night there is seldom a connotation of fear.   It is
rather as the joyful time when lovers meet, or as the day's nirvāna, when the pure white
lotus of heavenly bliss is open, a time for meditation and spiritual gladness, that he feels it.

Plate 62, probably a late eighteenth-century work, illustrates the romantic story of
Bāz Bahādur, the Mogul governor of Mālwā, and his love for the beautiful Rajput poetess,
Rūp Mati.   They are seen riding by night through the wooded hills of Mandu, an attendant walking on foot between them ; a masalchi in front shows the way with a lighted
torch.   The darkness closes round the group and pursues the torch's glare.   Rūp Mati is
pointing eagerly forward ; the crescent moon peeps behind a hill and there is a glimpse of
a river in the plain below.   The blaze of the torch throws the high-mettled steeds and
their riders into a warm relief of vivid colour betwen the darkness and the light, half-
revealing, half-obscuring the precipitous rocks behind fringed by a strip of forest.
Through the gap between the hills the sky is seen faintly lighted by the moon.

The largeness and simplicity of the treatment are qualities which modern European
painters of the impressionist school have often aimed at, but seldom realised with so much
spontaneity and true poetry as this little Indian picture, for here there is no conscious
effort to produce an effect called artistic, but unaffected interpretation of Nature as it
revealed itself to the artist.[1]   Compared with the more sophisticated works of the Mogul
Court painters the drawing of the figures and horses is naïve and primitive, though the
design shows a fine sense of dignity and rhythmic beauty.   Any lack of academic learning
is more than atoned for by its romantic charm.

The orthodox critic in Europe is inclined to treat impressionism as a somewhat peculiar
development in modern art, towards which he ought to maintain a strictly guarded, if not
hostile attitude.   It is sometimes a speciality, but more often a fad.   To the academic
professor it is a dangerous tendency, almost a vice, which should be sternly repressed in
all students.   The true oriental artist regards it as the breath of life, the end of all art ;
he thinks that of all artistic faculties, the one which must be trained and developed to the
highest degree is the faculty of realising thought-impressions.

But his impressionism is not merely a blurred vision of natural appearances, as it
often is in modern European art.   To see with the mind, not merely with the eye ; to
bring out the essential quality, not the common appearance of things ; to give the movement and character in a figure, not only the bone and muscle ; to reveal some precious
quality or effect in a landscape, not merely physiographical or botanical facts ; and,
above all, to identify himself with the inner consciousness of the Nature he portrays, and to
make manifest the one harmonious law which governs Nature in all her moods,—these
are the thoughts which he always keeps uppermost in his mind as soon as he knows how
to use his tools with tolerable facility.   It is considered of the most vital importance to
train the faculty of mind-seeing from the earliest youth, when impressions are strong and
vivid, instead of leaving this development to the end of his academic career, as we usually
do in Europe.   The oriental artist does not neglect detail—witness the wonderful studies
of Japanese masters, and those by Indian artists here illustrated.   But the first principle

[1] The painting is really quite ordinary, and it is difficult to understand the lavish praise heaped upon it by Mr. Havell.
Night scenes become popular in Mughal art after the period of Aurangzeb. The technique was to mix gray in the
colours so that the total effect was dominated by that tone, giving an impression of darkness. Plate 63 is another
ordinary painting of little merit.—P.C.

B. Worshipping Sivā at night. Mughal School, 17th century A.D.
(*Prince of Wales Museum, Bombay*).

A. The Tambura Player, by Bichitr.
(*From the original in the Victoria and Albert Museum*).

PLATE 61

Bāz Bahādur and Rūp Mati. (*From the original in the Calcutta Art Gallery*).

PLATE 62

Deer-hunting by night. (*From the original in the Calcutta Art Gallery*).

PLATE 63

B. An illustration from a Ms. of *Tawarikh-i-Khandaw-i-Taimuniya*. Mughal School, C. 1600 A.D. (*Khudabux Library, Patna*).

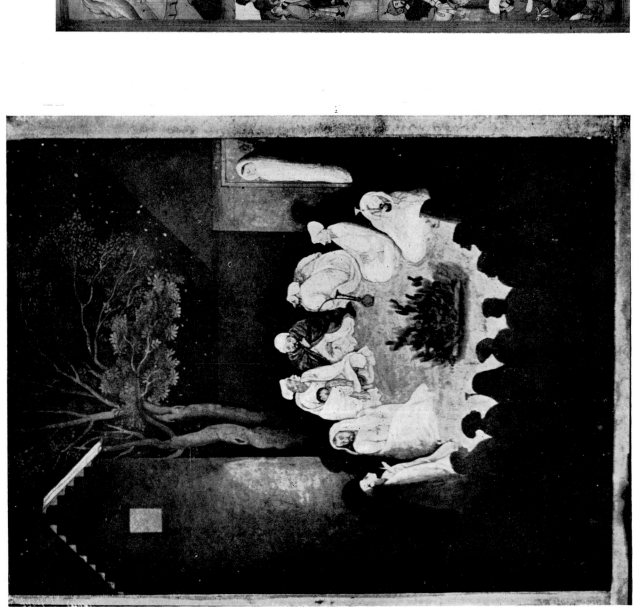

A. Travellers round a camp-fire. (*From the original in the Calcutta Art Gallery*).

PLATE 64

of oriental art-practice is to develop a habit of concentrated thought at the same time as imitative skill is being acquired by practice. In modern European academies the creative power usually lies dormant in the most important years of a student's mental development, while the imitative skill is accumulated by a dreary routine of more or less mechanical exercises. In this respect art teaching only repeats the errors of what we miscall "classical education" in public schools; but the habit thereby engendered of regarding art as a technical process, rather than a creative faculty, explains to a great extent the archæological critic's standpoint in regard to Indian art.

"Deer-hunting by Night," Plate 63, is another characteristic example in which the artist is more engrossed with the beauty of the night than with the action of the figures. It probably illustrates the story of Rāma and Sītā's exile in the forest by the banks of the Godāvari. The hunters are scantily dressed like forest hermits. The woman, concealed behind a bush, holds a lantern and tinkles a small bell to attract the herd of deer. The man armed with bow and arrows has just shot the leader of the herd, the terrified does scattering in all directions. The gleam of the lantern is given by discreet touches of gold.

The interest of the picture does not, however, lie in the figures, but in the charm of the landscape setting and serenity of its translucent chiaroscuro, which makes one feel the stillness of the night, broken only by the tinkling of the hunter's bell and the scampering feet of the frightened deer. The upper part of the picture is simply but beautifully composed with a broad, winding river, a thick clump of trees, and the starlit sky; the dark, heavy foliage massed against the sky, and the silver-grey reflection on the water. Rocks and stunted shrubs and a suggestion of a mountain stream fill up the foreground. The picture is painted in a very low key, but the colour is luminous and full of atmosphere; there is a beautiful sentiment in the whole design, like Mozart's music in its limpid, flowing melody.

The art of the Moguls was not suppressed by the interdicts of Aurangzīb, and did not die with the Mogul dynasty, for though, like our modern art, it was divorced from religion and regarded by the Court only as a distraction and amusement, it was grafted upon the older Buddhist and Hindu schools, upon a truly Indian tradition which was never uprooted, and continued to flourish long after the glory of the Moguls had departed.

Throughout the stormy period of the eighteenth century and even under the depressing influences of the nineteenth Indian artists and craftsmen could create things of beauty recalling the strength and spiritual fervour of former days, and there still survive painters following the old traditions who, but for the generally vitiated taste of the "educated" classes in India, would be honoured as artists of distinction were under Hindu and Mogul rule.

Plate 64A, "Travellers round a Camp-fire," is a late eighteenth-century work of an unknown artist, possibly a descendant of the painter of the Bagh fresco[1] (Plate 47), who in a different milieu recorded his impression of Indian life as faithfully as his ancestor did in the old Buddhist vihara. A party of travellers is seated round a blazing fire—painted in gold—in the compound of a *dharmsāla*, a native rest-house. The artist has been attracted by the effect of the firelight in the darkness, and with the simplicity and directness of true genius he has given a wonderful "impression" of it—what Whistler would have called a symphony in black, gold, and green. We see some figures in the full glare of the firelight placed in bold relief against the darkness of the night; others silhouetted against the blaze; the reflection on the walls, the trunks, and lower branches of the trees; the flash on the window and under the eaves of the house; the ghostly shadows and the depths of the all-environing gloom, relieved by the glimmer of the starlit sky.

Everyone familiar with Indian mofussil life will recognise the truthfulness of the native

[1] Plate 64A is an excellent painting attributed to the pre-Kangra phase of Pahari painting, though it is difficult to see what connection it has with the Bagh fresco.—P.C.

types given with such intense concentration and dramatic skill.   The young man, half in shadow, telling a story ; the old man with a sleeping child on his lap, and the two old men with whom he is conversing—one smoking a hookah, the other resting with his hand under his chin, are all masterpieces of characterisation.

The original of Plate 65, which may be somewhat earlier in date than the last,[1] gives a more familiar aspect of Indian art, for here we have a rendering of daylight with the full strength of the Indian painter's palette, when he revels in the glow and warmth of tropical sunshine.   It suggests a *motif* for the decoration of the *chitra-sāla* of an Indian garden-house, which must have been as delightful as a Pompeian villa when its walls were adorned like this, and not disfigured with vulgar modern gewgaws.

In its unfinished state the picture illustrates the painter's method of work.

The centre of the picture is filled by three young and high-born Muhammadan ladies—whose fair and finely chiselled features are drawn with a Botticellian grace, sitting by the side of a lotus-pool, taking refreshments and conversing gaily.   Unobserved and at their ease in the seclusion of the zanana garden, they have thrown aside their veils and are cooling their feet in the water.   The necessary floral ornaments of the pool, the lotus-flowers, are left unpainted, as well as some of the details of dress.   Under the shade of the trees behind another fair lady with a dusky Hindu companion are standing ; an attendant bringing wine or rose-water finishes up the group.   There is no suggestion of individual portraiture, as in most Mogul composition, but a fine feeling for rhythmic line and harmonious spatial design.

The form and structure of the trees are explained with breadth and simplicity as a foundation for the finishing touches which are wanting.   The vivid contrasts of pure colour, laid on uncompromisingly without softening or half-tones, give the warmth and brightness of an Indian atmosphere and help to sustain the dominant note of youthful vivacity and enjoyment.

"A Music Party," Plate 66, is an example of the popular art of the nineteenth century,[2] founded on the old traditions, which has nearly succumbed to the debasing influences of modern Indian life.   There is an artistic quality in this picture which, in spite of the crudeness of the drawing, gives it a far higher value than any of the Anglicised and commercialised Indian art, sometimes more sophisticated and pretentious, but always insincere, which is supplanting it.

Like the pure melody of an old folk-song, it is a true creation of national sentiment, of the poetic impulse which flows spontaneously from the heart of a people inspired by the joy of life and love of beauty.   In the previous illustrations we have seen how an Indian artist shows the "gloom of gloom" ; here we have the "sunshine of sunshine," given with the same pure delight with which the lark trills his song of joy in the high heavens on a summer morning.   The figures in the picture are by no means attractive types, or very deeply studied as to character ; but their glowing draperies and the gay colours of the musical instruments, together with the pearly whiteness of the marble and the bright hues of the flowers, serve the purpose of the artist—to express the beauty and gladness of the radiant Indian sunlight.

And, just as in Indian music there are no complicated harmonies, but a subtle flow of pure intensive melody, so in painting, too, the Indian artist eschews strong shadows and broken colours, producing an effect of light and atmosphere by the perfect rhythm of his colour-music.

In all Indian paintings, when the art is spontaneous and unaffected, the very Indian qualities of infinite patience and perfect self-control are strongly manifested.   Patience unlimited is bestowed upon detail, apparently the most insignificant, which the artist

[1] Pl. 65 belongs to the Mughal school of about the mid-18th century, probably to the reign of Mohammad Shah, A.D. 1719-1748.—P.C.

[2] This plate belongs to the Sikh school of the early 19th century.—P.C.

Pl. 1

A **Pi**ous Conclave. Mughal, probably from the earlier years of Shah Jahan's reign. The miniature is notable for its fine craftsmanship, finished colouring and extraordinary finesse of the brush work. The characterisation of the figures is marvellous — the gorgeously attired prince, the shrewd courtier in a flowered coat, the aged ascetic and the young anchorite.

(From *Studies in Indian Painting* by N. C. Mehta)

values, but everything is rigorously excluded which he thinks foreign to his purpose. There is no self-advertisement, no cheap effects to attract the applause of the ignorant, no vulgar trickery or playing to the gallery. This restraint and self-control the inartistic mind, accustomed to the loud self-assertion and aggressive realism of common modern painting, often mistakes for defective power of expression.

A Japanese writer of the eighteenth century, quoted by Dr. Anderson, gives a very keen criticism of the realistic tendency of modern European art. "It is the fault of foreign pictures that they dive too deeply into realities, and preserve many details that were better suppressed. . . . Such works are but groups of words. The Japanese picture should be a poem of form and colour."[1]

It is just in this different idea of realism and different outlook upon nature that we find the gulf which separates Eastern art from the academic art of Europe. The difference which the European and Anglicised Indian attributes to defective technical powers or undeveloped intellect, is really due to a different intellectual atmosphere and a different artistic temperament, created by the different answers which East and West give to the question—what is reality?

It is chiefly because the modern European usually refuses to recognise anything which is not evident to his own perceptive faculties that he finds the difference so irreconcilable and the gulf so impassable. The Indian artist lives in a world of his own imagination, where the stolid Anglo-Saxon is unable to follow him ; but until the Western pedagogue brought Indian culture into contempt and stifled the inherited artistic instincts of Indian youth with his own pedantic formulæ, the Indian artist found that his traditional methods were perfectly adequate for obtaining that response from his public which every artist needs.

It is one of the characteristics of a healthy national art that the artist has no need of vulgar extraneous efforts to make himself appreciated by his public. He is the exponent of national art culture, not a specialist shut up in a narrow domain of knowledge from which the world at large is excluded. Therefore he can be sure that a suggestion of his own thought-impressions will evoke a response from his public, just as a note of music finds a response in every wire tuned to the same pitch through which the vibration passes. Relying on his knowledge of sympathetic response from his public, he develops his representation of the natural facts and phenomena which form the framework of his art just to the point at which he knows it will communicate to others the exact impression of his own mind, and does not attempt a laboured and superfluous explanation of irrelevant facts. The imagination of the public he is addressing supplies the complement of the imagination of the artist.

Since the pernicious principles of the Italian Renaissance, the bigotry of Puritanism, and the pedantry of pseudo-classical education combined to destroy the national art of Europe, the public has demanded from the artist not imagination and ideas, but facts— archæological, historical, biographical or otherwise, relevant or irrelevant—only facts which it can understand. When an imaginative artist appears he must now address an unimaginative public through a middleman, an art critic, who explains as best he can in words what the artist intends to convey with his pencil, brush, or chisel, so that society, which does not like to confess itself Philistine, may talk glibly of what it does not know or feel.

Art limps badly upon these literary crutches, and in the artificial conditions of modern life there is no longer that mutual understanding between the artist and his public which existed when art was a popular language of much greater intellectual and moral influence than mere book-learning. The curse of our false classicism, so utterly inconsistent with the true spirit of ancient culture, now hangs heavy upon the national art of India, and the educated Indian, trained in the sordid and squalid atmosphere of Indian universities,

[1] "Pictorial Arts of Japan," vol. ii, p. 242.

becomes completely out of touch with his own national artistic thought, and attributes to Indian art the defects which should properly be ascribed to his own lack of artistic development.

The next two illustrations, Plates 67 and 70A, show how Indian artists in the early days of British rule, before schools of art imposed their pedantic recipes upon them, were employed by their European masters, as their ancestors had been employed at the Court of the Great Mogul. This occupation has been lost to them by the development of photography and by the changed conditions of Anglo-Indian life, which give greater opportunities for the employment of European portrait-painters, but have certainly not raised the standard of public taste. At the same time the spread of the belief in the inferiority of Indian art, which English education does so much to foster, has taken away from Indian portrait-painters the patronage of their wealthier countrymen.

These interesting drawings of Anglo-Indian *burra-sahibs* and *mem-sahibs* as they lived in Bengal in Georgian times were presented to the Calcutta Art Gallery by Dr. Abanindra-nath Tagore, C.I.E. They were found in the possession of a native artist of Calcutta, one of whose ancestors, Gulab Lal, was employed at the Mogul Court about the year 1719, in the reign of Muhammad Shah. Though lacking the wonderful finesse of the best Mogul miniaturists they are of considerable artistic merit and give very amusing glimpses into the Anglo-Indian life of the period.

They were probably executed by one of the same family who was working at Murshi-dabad in the employ of the Nawab Nazim of Bengal, about 1782.[1] The living repre-sentative of this artist family, when I discovered him, had been obliged, from want of encouragement for his art, to give up the profession of a miniature painter, and to look for more remunerative employment in drawing patterns for a European firm which imported Manchester piece-goods. He has now an appointment as teacher in the Calcutta School of Art.

The condition of most other descendants of the great artists of the Mogul Courts is an equally painful commentary on the decadence of fine art in India. There are still a few at Delhi and Agra who find employment at photographic establishments, or in painting the well-known miniatures on ivory which are bought by tourists as Indian "curiosities." A few of the Indian Princes continue to employ court painters of the old school, though it is considered unprogressive to do so. If they take any practical interest in art it nearly always means that the painters are sent to Europe or to an Indian school of art, so that all the Indian traditions they have inherited may be uprooted.

There is, however, in India a not inconsiderable survival of genuine folk-art and of the fine traditions of the temple artist-craftsman, which, if Indians were to take an intelligent and serious interest in them, would be the surest foundation on which to build up the revival of Indian painting. But neither the teaching of schools of art nor that of the universities seems likely to stimulate greatly public interest in art, except as a hobby for the collector or as a plaything for the politician.

---

[1] For a recent discussion of the Murshidabad school see Robert Skelton, "Murshidabad Painting," *Marg*, 10, (December 1956), pp. 10-22.—P.C.

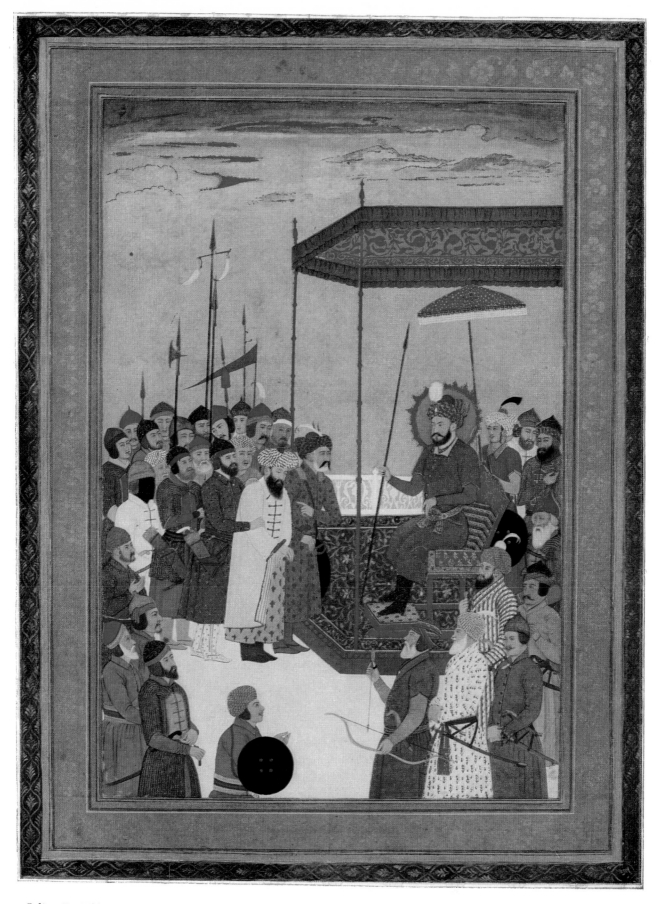

Sultan Bayezid as a Prisoner before Taimur Shah. Mughal. The Turkish Emperor Bayezid I, was captured in A.D. 1402 at the battle of Angora. The painting shows Taimur Shah on a golden chair, looking at the prisoner with an expression of mingled sarcasm and contempt.

(From *Studies in Indian Painting* by N. C. Mehta)

CHAPTER XIII

THE FUTURE OF INDIAN ART

IN the foregoing summary review of Indian sculpture and painting, I have endeavoured to indicate, by the aid of some of those masterpieces, unfortunately few, which have been salved from the wreckage of a great civilisation and culture, the principal psychological impulses through which the ideals of Indian fine art were created. We have seen first an epoch inspired by intense religious fervour, analogous to the Romanesque and Gothic epochs of European art, in which the Indian people, dissatisfied with philosophical abstractions and yearning for tangible symbols of their spiritual desires and beliefs, used the means provided for them by an alien faith and art—just as the early Christians adopted the art of pagan Greece and Rome. Gradually the Indian consciousness, asserting itself more strongly, evolved its own artistic ideals—ideals as different from the original foreign types as Gothic art differs from Roman—and thus created that Indian art which gave its inspiration to the æsthetic thought of all Asia.

The illustrations of some of the masterpieces of that great epoch of religious art, and the explanation given, have been, I hope, sufficient to show that the ideals thus realised were not, as some archæologists aver, the result of the feeble efforts of undeveloped artistic powers to imitate decadent types of the Hellenic school, but original, imaginative conceptions which, rightly understood, are worthy to rank with the noblest conceptions of the West.

After many centuries, when the spiritual fervour which had created the classic art of Ajantā, Ellora, and Borobudur ran riot in a maze of elaborate ritual in which religious symbolism usurped the function of the artist's creative mind, Indian imagination began to spend its vital force in a repetition of æsthetic formularies to which all the virtue of the Brahman's mantras was attached. Yet even in this jungle of exuberant ritualism a great tradition maintained itself, and much noble art towered over the tangled undergrowth, which reformers like Sankarāchārya tried to cut away—the temples of the Cholas with their Natārājas, and the great cities of the north, Mathurā, Kanauj, and Somnath, whose unrivalled beauty and magnificence excited the cupidity and admiration of Mahmūd of Ghazni.

The Muhammadan conquest brought into India another clash of ideals, a puritanical movement, in which the fine arts were banished from places of worship, and an orgy of reckless destruction began, through which the followers of Islam, like the Puritans of Europe, hoped vainly that human nature could be purged of hypocrisy, worldliness, and superstition. Indian sculpture and painting under the influence of Islam was limited to a very narrow range ; the effect of the restriction in emasculating architectural sculpture can be seen in northern India to-day. But though the vision of the artist was thus limited, the instinct for artistic creation did not wither, the old craft traditions renewed their life in working out new problems of construction and design. Thus the Hindu genius in the service of Islam created a noble idealistic architecture, and, under the enlightened patronage of Akbar, a secular school of Indian painting arose, which, though it lacked the high spiritual purpose which inspired the old religious schools, nevertheless deserves the appreciation and careful study of all artists for its perfect sincerity and high technical distinction—qualities which are conspicuously wanting in the degenerate Anglicised art of the present day.

I think my illustrations will show that when the Indian artist finds himself on the same plane of thought as the European he does not lack the capacity for drawing correctly, according to academic rules, or for making truthful transcripts from Nature.

Hindu painters, even when working in the narrow groove of the Mogul Court, did not quite forget that art has a higher aim, to penetrate the soul of things and to bring us into closer relation with Nature's eternal verities. But when art gave up its birthright as the ethical teacher and spiritual helper of mankind, only to minister to the vanity and self-indulgence of the wealthy and indolent ; when man ceased to use his highest creative faculties in the daily worship of his Creator, the Decadence, miscalled in Europe the Renaissance, had already begun. India's loss of spiritual power is the measure of the degradation of her art.

When at last India began to emerge from the political chaos of the eighteenth century and all its attendant miseries, the fine arts not only ceased to have the encouragement of state patronage which had been so lavishly bestowed upon them by the Great Moguls, but the idea that the Indian intellect had always been artistically inferior to the European penetrated the whole fabric of art creation like dry rot. The unimaginative Anglo-Saxon succeeded the imaginative Mogul in the sovereignty of India, and the people, distracted by long years of anarchy, accepted the change gladly. We have fulfilled our duties as policemen, and take a just pride in the organisation, peace, and security which we have substituted for chaos, bloodshed, and general brigandage. It is not a small thing, as Sir Mountstuart Grant-Duff said in one of his Elgin addresses, "to keep the peace between 250,000,000 of men." But it was inevitable that our success in this direction should lead to even greater responsibilities being thrust upon us. The East came to learn the wisdom of the West, and *nolens volens* we have been compelled to undertake the much more difficult duties of teacher and spiritual adviser, as well as those of policemen.

The critic who endeavoured to form a just estimate of the results we have achieved in the two former capacities would naturally take into consideration the present condition of art in India, for as a symptom of intellectual, moral, and spiritual progress the condition of a national art is a more certain guide than any blue books or statistics. Such a critic would perhaps be inclined to regard the degeneration and decay of Indian art, which have certainly been much more rapid under the peace and security of British rule than under the most chaotic period of native government, as a very unfavourable indication—and, so far as it goes, it may be regarded as such. But it may be that this seemingly inexplicable decay in spite of the blessings of order and settled government which we have conferred upon the country is due to causes which, in process of time, may be removed. One of the most conspicuous of these causes is the pernicious example we have held up in Anglo-Indian art, more especially in the architecture of public buildings—always the outward and visible sign of the inner civic consciousness.

If art is the mirror of the age, it must always be humiliating to any artistic Englishman to contemplate our make-believe Gothic and Classic cathedrals, churches, colleges, schools, offices of state, and historical monuments, and compare their banality, ugliness, and squalor with the dignity, strength, and fine craftsmanship of the splendid monuments of the Mogul Empire. It must be equally humiliating to any artistic Indian to find his educated fellow-countrymen imposed upon by these deplorable makeshifts, and using them as models instead of the great masterpieces of their own national architecture.

But when all these things are seen in their true perspective the future historian of British India will be able to find, even in our blunders, sufficient evidence of high endeavour and moral earnestness. We live in an age of transition, and in India the ideals of two great civilisations are now in the melting-pot—the dross will accumulate on the surface, but when that is cleared away the pure gold that is in both will be found beneath. The art of present and past generations of Anglo-Indians reveals the dross ; we may hope that the art of the New India which is forming will show the precious metal.

The Village Beauty by Manaku.   Court-art of Tehri-Garhwal, 19th century.   The artist has succeeded
in producing a delightful and original study of pastoral costume, at once beautiful by its charming
simplicity and practical utility.

(From *Studies in Indian Painting* by N. C. Mehta)

At a time when our own national education was miserably defective, and when our own national art had lost all its vitality and sincerity, we undertook to hold up the torch of European civilisation and progress in the East. And of the two statesmen, Bentinck and Macaulay, who laid the foundations of Western Education in India, the first considered Indian art so lightly that he was only diverted from selling the Tāj Mahall for the value of its marble because the proceeds of a test auction of materials from the Agra Palace proved unsatisfactory, and the second did not hesitate to declare his conviction, after an absurdly inadequate acquaintance with India, that the whole of Indian and Arabic literature was not worth a single bookshelf of a good European library. *Tempora mutantur*, and it is now largely due to the work and appreciation of European scholars and men of letters that New India has been aroused to undertake for herself researches into the priceless stores of oriental literature which had been so long neglected. What we have not yet accomplished is the proper application of our improved knowledge of Indian culture and civilisation to the administrative work of the Empire, especially in matters of education.

The great problems of education in India, which should command Great Britain's highest statesmanship and best intellect, have generally since Macaulay's time been relegated to the pedagogic specialist, often narrow and provincial in his views, and as a rule entirely out of touch with real Indian life and thought.

The statesman has not yet appeared to organise an Indian university affording to Indian youth the best fruits of both Eastern and Western culture, and fit to be a successor of the great universities of Buddhist and Hindu rule in stimulating the national artistic genius—that creative power of the people in the exercise of which will always be found one of the surest guarantees for national prosperity and contentment.

The late Dr. A. C. Benson, Master of Magdalene College, Cambridge, in a trenchant criticism of public school education in England, condemned "the intellectual tyranny that sits enthroned in the centre, a monopoly sustained by specialists, a despotic, inelastic, devastating theory. It is the foe of liberality of thought, mental expansion, intellectual progress, because it substitutes for the intellectual spirit a small and minute image of its own devising . . . . For the majority of boys the classical system, simply because it is the rigid application of a very special subject to the mental needs of an infinite variety of minds, is not only no education at all, but a deliberate sterilisation of the intellectual seed-plot, a perverse maltreatment of the ingenuous mind."

These words, *mutatis mutandis*, may be taken as very applicable to our system of higher education in India ; only the evil of it is there intensely aggravated because Indian students are practically denied any other means of education than the university courses. Our universities have always stood in the eyes of India as representative of the best light and leading of the West ; yet the disabilities and injuries which they, as exponents of all learning recognised by the State, inflict upon Indian art and industry are incalculable, for not only do they refuse to allow art its legitimate place in the mental and moral equipment of Indian youth—the average Indian graduate, with all his remarkable assimilative powers, is often less developed artistically than a Pacific islander—but by practically excluding all Indian artists of the old hereditary professions from the honours and emoluments of state employment, they lower the status of Indian art and give a wholly unjustifiable preference to the art imported from Europe, which comes with the prestige of a presumed higher order of civilisation. The building of New Delhi has demonstrated on a grand scale how "the sterilisation of the intellectual seed-plot" by the universities is withering the roots of Indian art and craft.

It is only necessary to compare the present position of Indian artists with that of their forefathers to see the evil our whole administrative system works upon art in India. In the time of Akbar, Jahāngīr, and Shah Jahān the best artists became grandees of the Court and sometimes intimate friends of the Emperor himself. In Rajputana also, under

Hindu rule, painters and architects held dignified positions at Court, and besides liberal pecuniary rewards they were often given special honours and grants of land. In the Imperial Library at Calcutta there is preserved a Persian manuscript giving the names of the designers and chief constructors of the Tāj Mahall and the salaries they received. The three principal designers were each paid a thousand rupees a month; another received eight hundred; six others four hundred; and nine others from two hundred to four hundred a month. These salaries would represent a considerably larger sum in present Indian currency. But the descendants of these men in India, who practise their professions now with little less ability, though their opportunities for exercising it under our Public Works system are miserably few, are considered well paid at thirty, forty, or sixty rupees a month.

The question of remuneration or reward is not, however, a vital one. The best Indian artists are often content with a pittance when the work they do is religiously inspired. The modern bureaucratic machine cannot use them as artists, however lavishly it spends : it can only find a place for them as dull mechanics and discontented artisans.

Neither the building of the Victoria Memorial at Calcutta nor the building of New Delhi with a colossal expenditure has brought better opportunities or rewards for Indian artists. None have been employed in these two great projects, except in a subordinate capacity to copy the paper patterns of the European experts and to fix up sculptures and paintings made in London studios which must be totally irrelevant to Indian art and Indian life.

Elegant exercises in Indian archæology by eminent experts may serve the purpose of appealing to the *amour-propre* of Indian politicians, but they do not advance the art of building either in India or in Europe. The endowment of Chairs of Fine Art in Indian Universities, after the fashion of Oxford and Cambridge; the establishment of schools of art and architecture in which Indian students can learn the theory and practice of the fine arts, as taught in London and Paris, and the patronage of Indian artists by sympathetic Governors and high officials, do nothing to alter the bureaucratic system which is destroying root and branch the traditions of art in India. They only tend to obscure the vital issues and to create an atmosphere of make-believe which is more harmful in its influence than a policy of absolute *laissez-faire*.

If we adopted a purely Philistine attitude, declaring that our mission was to set an example of what we are proud to call plain, practical, British common sense, we should at least be consistent and straightforward. Or if we avowed that our task in India was only to protect the down-trodden pariah; to remove the barriers by which a selfish and corrupt hierarchy has prevented the intellectual and social advancement of the lower orders; to free the ryot from the bondage of the sowcar; to purify the administration and to hold the scales of justice even—we might perhaps view with a quiet conscience the continuous degradation of Indian art which we do not seriously attempt to arrest.

But this is not our attitude. We pose as apostles of higher culture, as patrons of art and letters, and exponents of a superior order of civilisation; and by so doing we have persuaded educated Indians and the aristocracy of the country, who are the principal patrons of art, to leave their artistic consciences in our keeping, to adopt the models we approve of, and to aim at the ideals at which we profess to aim.

We should not, then, introduce into Indian civic life a standard of art immeasurably inferior to its own—the contractor's art and the jerry-builder are our æsthetic importations; we should not affect to consider art as a proper moral influence for Indian jails and reformatories and shut it out of the universities; and if we argue that the indifference to Indian art of the India we have educated is a proof that it does not really interpret the Indian mind, we should at least be sure that we are better able to interpret it ourselves. You cannot know a people's mind if you do not understand their art.

We certainly do, as a rule, take a more sincere interest in Indian art than most "educated" Indians, but it is generally a purely academic and archæological interest; and it is

In a Zanana Garden. (*From an unfinished painting in the Author's Collection*).

PLATE 65

A Music Party. (*From a modern painting in the Author's Collection*).

PLATE 66

Portraits of Anglo-Indians of the Georgian period.   From drawings by a native artist in the Calcutta Art Gallery.
(*From brush-drawings in the Calcutta Art Gallery*).

PLATE 67

Illustration to the Rubàiyàt of Omar Khayyàm, by Abanindra Nath Tagore.
(*From the original in the Author's Collection, by permission of the Proprietors of the Studio, owners of the copyright*).

PLATE 68

quite natural and almost inevitable that it should be so. Many English and Anglo-Indian drawing-rooms have more or less unpractical Indian furniture, and various useless ornaments which we call Indian curiosities. At times we make spasmodic and ill-considered attempts to encourage Indian art by holding exhibitions of this class of work. These things simply show how far we are from appreciating the vital points of the question, how little we understand the Indian mind ourselves.

For this is Indian art, spurious and make-believe like our official architecture, with all the virtue, all the spirituality, all the love and worship, all that has made it great and true in the past, taken out of it. Indian art was born in the village and nurtured in the pilgrim's camp; it can never thrive in the sickly, artificial atmosphere of the European drawing-room or in a Western market-place. We have driven it from the great cities of India. It has no real part in our civic life, and its last refuge is now in the villages and towns remote from European influence. But this last refuge will always be its surest stronghold; when art in Europe gets back to the villages the real Renaissance will have begun. In the villages of India the true artistic spirit still survives, and if we and "educated" Indians would know what true Indian art is we must go there, where the heart of India beats, where the voices of her dead myriads still are heard, and learn a lesson that neither London nor Paris can teach. Some time ago I drew attention, in a monograph on the stone-carving of Bengal,[1] to some modern architectural decoration, just as beautiful in feeling and execution as the carving of a medieval Gothic Cathedral, done by Orissan sculptors, the direct descendants of those who built and sculptured the famous temple of the Sun-god, already referred to (p. 60). For the last twenty or thirty years some of them have been carving the decoration of a temple at Jaipur, the ancient capital of the province; their wages, fourpence a day, are being paid by a religious mendicant who has spent his whole life in begging for funds for this purpose.

When I suggested that wealthy Bengalis would do better in having such art as this in their houses, rather than tenth-rate commercial Italian statuary, and that Calcutta would gain in many ways if we substituted real Indian sculpture, conceived in this spirit, for foolish Gothic and classic imitations (ten or twenty times more costly), "The Statesman," one of the principal European newspapers of Calcutta, applauded the taste of educated Indians, declaring that it was highly commendable and gratifying to those who believed that the mission of Europe was to awaken Asia and lift her up to the Western level of culture.

"Until Indian art," it asserted sententiously, "has mastered the cardinal secret of simplicity; until the Indian artists have begun to understand the meaning of large effects; until abandoning mere amplification they prove capable of a conception of an organic whole, the products of native art are bound to remain in the state of arrested growth they have been all these thousands of years."

The abysmal ignorance of Indian art-history revealed in the last sentence may be pardoned, for it is not confined to the editorial columns of Anglo-Indian newspapers; but what are these "large effects," these Parnassian heights, seemingly inaccessible to ourselves, which we would fain make others climb? When we have succeeded in creating in India, either by our own exertions or through the Indian intellect, anything ethically or æsthetically as great as a medieval Gothic Cathedral we may begin to aim at something higher. But all such academic recipes, relating either to art, architecture, or general education, are just as vain and useless as the *mantras* of uncomprehended mysteries the Tibetan lama drones as he twirls his prayingwheel.

Europeans now collect Indian pictures enthusiastically and critics generally take a much more sympathetic attitude towards Indian art than they did twenty years ago; but the view that the salvation of Indian art lies only in the application of the academic nostrums of Europe still has the weight of official influence behind it. If the spirit of the

[1] Bengal Secretarial Book Depot, 1906.

present Prime Minister's eloquent appeal for the revival of English village craftsman-ship[1] were applied to administrative problems in India, there would be no reason to confine our sympathy and admiration for Indian art to the great monuments of anti-quity.   The drying up of the living springs of craftsmanship is a more grievous loss to India than the ruin of all her ancient monuments.

Change there must be in Indian art ; that is both inevitable and necessary, for there is no real life in an art which never changes.   But the change must come from the quicken-ing, not from the deadening, of the creative faculties ; from the stimulating of thought and the strenuous upholding of higher ideals, not from the substitution of one academic formula for another.

The rank materialism which is the basis of the modern Indian university system tends to produce in the Indian mind the same attitude towards art that is characteristic of the average European university man.   In this view, so contrary to all the laws of nature and all the experience of the human race, art is one of those luxuries which may be enjoyed when other intellectual and all bodily wants are satisfied ; but at the same time it is to be considered as the most easily dispensed with of all intellectual stimulants, and as having no practical bearing on the intellectual growth or spiritual life of the average human being.   It is enough for the Indian undergraduate that it counts for nothing in the university examinations, and in after-life he is quite content to accept the common formularies which regulate the prevailing fashions as representing his correct attitude towards art.

In 1905, when the reform of the Calcutta University was under discussion, a scheme for giving art design a definite place in the curriculum by the side of science, drawn up by myself and accepted by the Faculty of Arts after full discussion, was suppressed without comment by Lord Curzon's committee at Simla.   Since then, through the efforts of the late Sir Ashutosh Mukerjee, a Chair of Indian Fine Art has been created.

As regards the government schools of art, originally established to bring the fine arts of the West to the benighted East, the European directors do not now affect to despise Indian art : they profess to admire it, but attempt to justify their position as teachers by the argument that there are certain fundamental principles common to the art of all countries, which the traditional artists of India do not understand and cannot teach, and therefore the renaissance of art in India must be effected by leading Indian students to the faithful study of nature, through the paraphernalia and technique of modern European academies.

Now if Europe and Asia had both failed to produce the highest art before this academic system was evolved ; if modern universities created poets and modern ateliers created artists, there might be some logic in the argument.   But this is not the case.   Poets sometimes emerge alive from the university mill ; artists occasionally pass through academic courses of instruction without complete atrophy of their imaginative faculties. But no one can maintain that owing to this academic system modern European literature and art stand higher than they did in pre-Renaissance days.

In India, where the system has been followed, more or less efficiently, for seventy years, it has been destructive of all artistic vitality.   No modern Indian portrait-painter, led to the faithful study of nature as understood by European artists, can be put into the same class with the Mogul Court painters who followed their own traditions.   The mural paintings of Government House, Bombay,[2] the latest and technically, perhaps, the best products of the system, are a facile parody of Leighton's fresco of " The Arts of Peace " in the Victoria and Albert Museum, but they are neither Indian nor true to nature and far inferior as decorative art to the unsophisticated work of a nineteenth-century Kangra painter.   A European artist, viewing these paintings with indulgence and con-

[1] Published by the Royal Society of Arts, 1927.
[2] Illustrated in "Apollo," July, 1927.

Pl L

A Mughal Beauty. School of Shah Jahan, *c.* 1628–1658 A.D. Bharat Kala Bhavan, Banaras. This portrait, though somewhat formal, is well worth attention for its delicately modelled face, graceful figure, and the emphasis on the charm of youthful beauty. The exquisiteness of the painting is here matched only by the excellence of its technique. The lotus in the hands of the lady imparts a characteristically Indian touch.

(Courtesy, Lalit Kala Akademi, New Delhi)

descension, might find much merit in them as the work of promising Indian schoolboys, but only if he does not know or care to learn the end of the story—these clever school-boys never grow up! Therein lies the damnable defect of the whole system. Mother India may be in many ways inefficient and behind the times but in the upbringing of her own children as artists she has nothing to learn from modern Europe.

The formula of the Royal Academy curriculum from which this school of painting has its acknowledged source makes Indian ploughmen, gardeners, and basket-makers limp like antique statues and go about their work in Leightonesque poses, so that certain wall spaces in Government House may be decoratively treated. The architects of New Delhi, who as universal providers were commissioned to restore the arts of the Empire, commend these paintings and propose that the same rhythmical formula, which can easily be adjusted to all the races of mankind, as an ingenious rhymester turns out lime-ricks, shall be taught in an Imperial School of Design at Delhi by European masters who have acquired "reputations in a world-arena," so that Macaulay's ideal of education may be realised and the New Delhis of the future may be decorated, if not built, by Indians drilled in thinking imperially. This, as Dr. A. C. Benson would have said, is not art or education, but a perverse maltreatment of the ingenuous mind.

Unfortunately art and education in India are mixed up and confused with political issues. If India had no living traditions of her own, and her own culture had never risen higher than that of Africa, Australia, or Canada, the gospel of Imperialism preached by the architects of New Delhi, and the threadbare formulæ of European ateliers, might satisfy the ideals of New India by opening up careers for the literate classes hitherto almost monopolised by European experts. But a policy which starts from placing Indians on an artistic level with the uncivilised races of mankind, and refuses to utilise to the fullest extent the capacities of living Indian craftsmen ; which views complacently the drying up of the springs of Indian craftsmanship if only British craftsmanship may exhibit its superiority, does not show political wisdom or educational insight.

The recent political reforms have placed the responsibility for art administration in India in the hands of English-educated Indians, few of whom have yet shown a firmer grasp of India's artistic problems than their predecessors in office, who, if art did not happen to be their own special hobby, left the solution of them to the personal inclinations of European practitioners. New India, in matters of taste, is now split into two camps, one of which hails the propaganda of the Bombay School as the modern revelation of art to educated India, and the other which follows the lead of Dr. Abanindra Nath Tagore, the founder of the new Calcutta School of Painting.

Dr. Tagore, the artist-poet of Bengal, is not unrecognised "in the world-arena," for exhibitions of his work and of the considerable band of pupils he has gathered round him have not only established one of the most interesting social events in Calcutta, but have won high appreciation from many of the best art critics of Paris, Berlin, and London. Though well-educated in the European sense, Dr. Tagore never came within the depressing æsthetic environment of an Indian University, and very speedily gave up the European routine of technical training which was his starting-point as an artist. Having thus escaped the Scylla and Charybdis upon which so many Indian art students have been wrecked, he devoted himself to a close study of the Indian pictures which I was then collecting for the Government Art Gallery, and this collection was the guiding influence in his artistic development, though in matters of technique he has adopted a compromise between European and Indian methods.

Dr. Tagore's æsthetic outlook is not, however, narrowed down to any particular school or formula : he can fully appreciate all that is best in European art, ancient and modern, without sinking his own personality in the bog of internationalism. His art is Indian, but his own. Circumstances over which they had no control have prevented Dr. Tagore and his fellow-artists from rising to "imperial" heights as mural painters. My own efforts, as Principal of the Calcutta School of Art, were directed towards finding for his remarkable genius the widest scope in mural decoration. One of his earliest efforts was an essay in Indian *fresco buono*, Plate 69A illustrating the story of Kācha and Devājāni from the Mahābhārata. He also, on my advice, began the preparation of a series of cartoons for the decoration of the Government Art Gallery in fresco, but the scheme was dropped after my retirement, the Public Works Department not being interested in the revival of Indian art. Lord Curzon, whose interest in Indian art was only archæological, made the decoration of the Victoria Memorial an imperial reserve which Indian artists were not allowed to enter, apparently because the Victorian era did not recognise Indian sculpture and painting as fine art. The architects of New Delhi also make art only a matter of taste, of which they are the final arbiters, and exclude those who do not conform to their imperial prescription. Unless, therefore, the traditions of the old *chitra-sālas* should be revived by Indians themselves, through a sincere interest in the future of their own art, the only resource left to Indian painters is to adapt themselves to their environment by working on a diminutive scale like the Mogul painters, who likewise appealed only to an exclusive coterie of the intelligentsia.

As painters in miniature, however, the artists of the New School owe much to the lively interest and support of the European community of Calcutta, both official and non-official. The Indian Society of Oriental Art, of which Sir John Woodroffe was the leading spirit, was started in 1907 with the object of giving them encouragement, and has since become an important centre of friendly co-operation between East and West in the field of Art. Two Governors of Bengal, the late Lord Carmichael and Lord Ronaldshay, who were patrons of the Society, gave the New School the most effective official help.

Lord Ronaldshay himself, in an article printed in the "Asiatic Review,"[1] on the history and significance of this art revival in Bengal, gives details of the practical aid which the Government of Bengal afforded the school started by Dr. Tagore in 1916, with the co-operation of his gifted brother, Mr. Goganendra Nath Tagore, and his uncle, the poet. A Government grant enabled it to secure suitable accommodation for a studio and lecture hall :

"Eminent exponents of the new school were engaged as teachers, and scholarships for indigent pupils were provided. A series of lectures was planned, and the publication of an art journal under the title of 'Rūpam' (Form) arranged for. This reorganisation was explained at a gathering held at Government House on December 4th, 1919, at which recent works of a number of the artists of the new school were on view, and an address, in part descriptive and in part critical of the new movement, was given by Mr. O. C. Gangoly, himself an accomplished artist and a discerning art critic. . . . First and foremost he described the work of the school as consciously and intentionally idealistic. It was the avowed intention of its masters, he declared, to escape from 'the photographic vision and to secure an introspective outlook on things which takes one away from the material objectives of life to a rarefied atmosphere of beauty and romance.' And he went on to lay emphasis on the characteristic of the movement. Its exponents, 'instead of busying themselves with recording the superficial aspects of phenomena, have worked with a deeper motive and a profounder suggestion, seeking to wean the human mind from the obvious and the external reality of the senses, disdaining to imitate nature for its own sake, and striving to find significant forms to suggest the formless infinity which is hidden behind the physical world of forms.' They have sought, that is to say, to maintain the distinctive and essential characteristic of the art of India, namely, its extreme idealism."

In answer to the question, what is the significance attaching to the movement ? Lord Ronaldshay writes :

"It was an awakening race-consciousness expressing itself in terms of art that caused the

[1] July 1924.

B. A Sacrifice. Folio from a Ms. of *Razm-namah*, Mughal School, A.D. 1598. (*Baroda Museum*).

A. Kācha and Devāyāni. A fresco painting by Abanindra Nath Tagore. (*From the original in the Calcutta Art Gallery*).

PLATE 69

A. Portrait of an Anglo-Indian of the Georgian period.
(From a brush-drawing in the Calcutta Art Gallery).

B. The End of the Journey. Painted by Abanindra Nath Tagore.

PLATE 70

Siva-Sīmantinī.   Painted by Abanindra Nath Tagore.

PLATE 71

B. Sati. Painted by Nanda Lal Bose.

A. The Trial of the Princes. Painted by Nanda Lal Bose.

"Life of my life, Death's bitter sword
Hath severed us like a broken word :
Rent us in twain who are but one . . .
Shall the flesh survive when the soul is gone?"
—SAROJINI NAIDU

PLATE 72

brothers Tagore to sever their connection with the Government School of Art, and to turn to the cultural traditions and ideals of their own land. . . . Running like a thread through the varying forms of unrest with which India is tormented is a spirit of revolt, sometimes conscious, sometimes subsconscious, against the denationalisation of a proud and sensitive people. Many Indians have proclaimed this identity of motive behind varying manifestations of Indian nationalism. At a time when I was engaged in fighting the revolutionary movement in Bengal and in supporting the art movement which I have described, a political writer, whose sympathies were undoubtedly with the former, issued a pamphlet in which he took this matter as his theme. It was a reaction against the Westernisation of India, he declared, that was animating all patriotic Indians, and in support of his argument that this same leaven was at work in the domain of literature and art he pointed to the rise of the Tagore School. 'In Bengal,' he wrote, 'the national spirit is seeking to satisfy itself in art; and for the first time since the decline of the Moghuls a new school of national art is developing itself—the school of which Abanindra Nath Tagore is the founder and master.' "

The New School of Calcutta, therefore, though cramped in its early growth by Lord Curzon's æsthetic predilections, owes much to Lord Ronaldshay's broader views of art and statesmanship: unfortunately they were not effective in imperial concerns, nor had he the opportunity given to Lord Hardinge for removing the departmental impediments which block the main outflow of Indian artistic energy and add to Indian unrest. The direct contribution to art of the New Calcutta School has been considerable and important, but its influence on the future of Indian art will probably be still more felt indirectly, through its teaching. As an inspiring teacher, both in his own school and as Professor of Fine Arts in the Calcutta University, Dr. Tagore has had a wonderful success in re-fertilising the soil made sterile for the best part of a century by a futile academic dogma and in helping future political leaders to understand the fundamental artistic problems with which they have to deal in India.

If the New School has not yet acquired the splendid technique of the old Indian painters, it has certainly revived the spirit of Indian art, and besides invested its work with a charm of true poetry, distinctively its own. Though a protest against denationalisation it represents a happy blending of Eastern and Western thought, from the full realisation of which humanity at large has so much to gain. Mr. Kipling would persuade us that this is an unattainable consummation—a rather insular attitude which can only promote prejudice and misunderstanding.

It is on the technical side that the wrong we have done to Indian art is most apparent and least excusable. It may be difficult to provide in a state educational system, especially under Indian conditions, that intellectual and spiritual stimulus without which no real art can ever be developed. Emerson has truly said that art does not come at the call of a legislature—neither can a legislature entirely suppress it merely by neglecting to take cognisance of the artistic faculties. But nothing can excuse the crushing out of all the splendid artistry, of the technical lore and skill of hand inherited from former generations —one of the most valuable industrial assets India possesses—simply from the want of an intelligent adaptation of official machinery for making use of it.

The New School of Calcutta opens up a brighter prospect for the future, but as Professor Lethaby has said, no art that is only one-man deep is worth much. It should be a thousand men deep. Whichever school of pictorial art most accurately interprets the mind of modern India, it is politicians, rather than artists or art-teachers, who control the future of Indian art. For neither painting nor sculpture can be the great and beneficent influence in national life they ought to be when they are both cut off from the roots from which they have sprung, the craftsmanship of building. The effect is the same whether the axe used be of native or foreign make, only when we wield the axe we must not wonder that blame falls upon ourselves.

It remains to be seen whether Indian politicians, handicapped as they are by their Western ideas of art, still possess constructive as well as critical faculties. Will they follow the line of least resistance, that which seems most convenient for departmental routine and themselves, the time honoured practice of drying up the living springs of craftsmanship in controlling the artistic output of India, or will they apply themselves seriously to the problem of adapting departmental machinery to the needs and conditions of Indian life ? Will they take art as a serious study, or merely as a pleasant relaxation from the cares of office ?

Since the first publication of this book the New Calcutta School has greatly increased its numbers and has now produced three generations of artists of distinction, whose works have been illustrated in the "Modern Review" of Calcutta and in a series of fine monographs edited by Mr. O. C. Gangoly, who also edits "Rūpam," the admirable quarterly review started with Lord Ronaldshay's help, which shows the immense progress, amounting to a revolution, made in the study of æsthetics by the intelligentsia of India in the last twenty years. To these publications I must refer my readers and content myself with the illustration of a few typical works by Dr. Tagore himself and his two pupils, Mr. Nanda Lal Bose, who now directs the art work of Dr. Rabindra Nath Tagore's University at Bolpur, and Mr. Asit Kumar Haldar, Principal of the Government School of Arts and Crafts at Lucknow.

The fresco painting, Plate 69A is an early work by Dr. Tagore in which he has expressed with wonderful directness and simplicity the struggle between passion and duty which is the motive of the story. In this and in many other works of the school the fine poetic feeling and depth of expression more than compensate for obvious technical deficiencies. The story is told in the Mahābhārata thus :[1]

There was a supreme contest between the gods and *asuras* for the sovereignty of the three worlds. To control the sacrifices by which the victory would be decided, the gods chose for their priest the sage Vrihaspati ; the *asuras* appointed Sukra as theirs. Sukra knew the secret of reviving the dead, and by his wonderful science restored to life all the enemies of the gods as soon as they were slain. The gods, in despair, begged Kācha, the eldest son of Vrihaspati, to present himself to Sukra as a disciple, so that he might learn from him the mighty secret. Kācha consented and, after taking the vow of discipleship, was received by Sukra. He speedily ingratiated himself in his master's favour, and by singing, dancing, and music won the heart of his fair daughter, Devājāni.

When five hundred years of his discipleship had passed, the *asuras* discovered Kācha's intention, and finding him alone in the woods tending his preceptor's kine they slew him, hacked his body to pieces, and gave them to be devoured by wolves and jackals. Sukra, at Devājāni's entreaty, revived him by his magic, but soon afterwards Kācha was again slain by the *asuras* while roaming the forest in search of flowers for the sacrifice. This time they pounded his body into a paste and mixed it with the waters of ocean. But again he was revived by Sukra. Then the *asuras* slew him a third time and burning the body mixed the ashes with the wine Sukra drank.

Devājāni, missing her beloved Kācha, again appealed to her father ; but when Sukra exercised his power and found that Kācha was inside his own body, he cried out, "Oh, Devājāni, Kācha is within me, and there is no way for his coming out alive except by ripping open my own belly !"

Touched by Devājāni's despair Sukra adopted the only resource left to him—to impart to Kācha his great secret, under a promise that it would be used to restore himself to life as soon as the former was released by Sukra's death. Kācha, beautiful as the full moon, came out of Sukra's belly by ripping it open, and used his newly gained power for the first time in restoring his master to life.

The climax, which Dr. Tagore has taken for his subject, is when Kācha, at the expiration of his vow of discipleship, prepared to return to the abode of the gods. Devājāni,

[1] See vol. i, Roy's translation, pp. 232-40.

Krishna Meeting Radha in the Forest in Spring-time. Kangra Kalam (Garhwal School), c. 1800 A.D. National Museum, New Delhi. Grazing cattle in the forest, Krishna met Radha and unable to resist her beauty embraced her, the branches of the trees bending towards the lovers to provide a cover for them. When Nand and Yasoda (Krishna's foster-parents) appeared and cried out for Krishna, the lovers behaved as if nothing had happened—Radha with folded hands, a picture of innocence!

(Courtesy, Lalit Kala Akademi, New Delhi)

reminding him of her devotion to him, begged of him to fix his affection upon her, and to accept her hand in marriage. But Kācha, regarding their relationship as one which made marriage impossible, exhorted her thus :

"O thou of virtuous vows, do not urge me to such a sinful course ! O thou of fair eyebrows, be kind unto me ! Beautiful one, thou art dearer to me than my preceptor, but the place where thou hast resided in the holy body of Sukra hath also been my abode ! Thou art truly my sister ; therefore, O slender-waisted one, do not speak thus ! Loving one, happily have we passed the days that we have been together. There is perfect sympathy between us. I ask thy leave to return to my abode. Therefore bless me, so that my journey may be safe."

Devājāni, finding her entreaties useless, cursed Kācha, saying : "Since thou dost refuse to make me thy wife when I implore thee, O Kācha, this knowledge thou hast gained shall bear no fruit."

But Kācha replied :

"Curse me, if it please thee. I have told thee the duty of Rishis. I do not deserve thy curse, O Devājāni, but yet thou hast cursed me. Since thou hast done this from passion, not from a sense of duty, thy desire shall not be fulfilled. No Rishi's son shall ever take thy hand in marriage. Thou hast said that my knowledge shall not bear fruit. Let it be so ! *But in him it shall bear fruit to whom I shall impart it.*"

And Kācha departed to the abode of the gods.

Fitzgerald's version of the Rubaiyat of Omar Khayyam has had many illustrators, but none have been quite so successful in reproducing the delicate flavour of the poem as Dr. Tagore in his series of twelve water-colours published by the "Studio" in 1910. Plate 68 illustrates quatrain XXIX in the first edition :

"Into this Universe, and *why* not knowing,
Nor *whence*, like Water willy-nilly flowing ;
And out of it, as Wind along the Waste,
I know not *whither*, willy-nilly blowing."

The poet is shown sitting in contemplation by a river's bank, watching the dead leaves blown by the autumn wind as they are carried away by the stream. The subdued twilight tones of the artist's subtle colouring fit very well with the poet's mood, but it is hardly possible to give the finer nuances of the original painting in a reproduction.

"The End of the Journey," Plate 70B which attracted great attention when shown at the exhibition of "Les Orientalistes" in Paris, is an allegory, like the Buddhist *jātakas*, in which animals become partners with humanity in the tragedy and mystery of life. A pack-camel in the desert, worn out and abandoned by its driver, stumbles wearily on a rock and sinks to the ground in its last agony, just as the sun touching the horizon marks the close of day. The crimson glory of the sunset fills the silent sky, while the moans of the dying beast make their pitiful complaint. Dr. Tagore's exquisite feeling interprets the pathos of the scene very finely, filling the spectator with sympathy and a haunting sense of mystery. In technical accomplishment the leader of the modern school is here not far behind the best Mogul animal portrait-painters : as an artistic thinker, or poet, he rises far above them.

In Siva-Sīmantinī (Plate 71) Dr. Tagore treats Hindu mythology with the imagination and fervour of the great Chola artists. Like the Natārāja, Siva-Sīmantinī ("Siva and the Lady") combines in one person the male and female principle, and in this singularly beautiful conception of a divine incarnation of eternal youth the spiritual ideals of Hinduism have found an artistic interpreter who is modern, in the sense that he is not strictly bound by the canons of Hindu ritual, but yet truly inspired by the highest art traditions of Buddhist and Hindu India.

If circumstances had been different, Mr. Nanda Lal Bose, like his teacher, would have found wider scope for his artistic powers in mural decoration than in book illustration. His strong decorative sense is well shown in "The Trial of the Princes," Plate 72 A, one of a series of coloured illustrations for the Mahābhārata,[1] many of which are admirably adapted for fresco or tempera painting in a public or private *chitra-sāla*. The story as told in the epic is as follows :

Drona, the great master of Yoga and teacher of the Pandava Princes, wishing to test their skill in archery calls them together and, pointing to the target, an artificial bird he has placed on the top of a tree, asks Yudhishthira, the eldest, what he saw. "I see, sir, my brother, the tree and the bird," was the reply. Bidding him stand down, Drona repeated the question and received the same answer from the others until he came to Arjuna, his favourite pupil. "Tell me now, Arjuna, with bow bent, what do you see— the bird, the tree, myself, and your friends ?" "No," said Arjuna, "I see the bird only, neither yourself, nor the tree !" "Describe the bird," said Drona. "I see only a bird's head," replied Arjuna. "Then shoot," cried Drona, and the next instant the arrow hit the mark and Drona embraced Arjuna with delight as a perfect Yogi in the arts of war.

An earlier work by Mr. Nanda Lal Bose, "Sati," Plate 72 B has for its subject the tragedy of Indian wifehood. The young widow, breathing a silent prayer in her last lament, interpreted in Mrs. Sarojini Naidu's beautiful lines, prepares to throw herself upon the funeral pyre of her dead husband. Mr. Bose, like the Indian poetess, has been inspired by the tender pathos of the scene, rather than by the horror which too often accompanied it.

Mr. Asit Kumar Haldar's range of subject inclines more to the lyrical than the epic mood, but he, like many others of the school, joins the feeling of rhythmic beauty in decoration to real poetic inspiration. He may sometimes offend the academic eye in mere matters of representation, idiosyncrasies found in the work of many great masters. Dr. J. H. Cousins justly observes in his monograph[2] that "to attain to intellectual virtuosity, Mr. Haldar and his fellows would have to shut themselves out from the thrill of Ananda (joy) that appears to flicker through every line of their work."

"Rāsa Līlā," the Dance of Krishna, Plate 73, has technical weaknesses which may jar on delicate academic nerves, but it is beautifully composed and most artists, I venture to think, will join in Dr. Cousins' warm appreciation :

"Ostensibly it is a picture of a moonlight cloud moving across the sky. But superimposed on the cloud is a procession of figures in stately dance. In the centre is Shri Krishna playing on his flute, and before and after are Gopis (his girl-companions), drifting with him and with the cloud across the background of night. There is a solemn joy in every lineament of every figure—a spontaneity of chaste delight controlled by some ritual of beauty and truth, which, because it is essential, has no sense of being imposed. We feel that the song of the procession is 'wise and lovely,' as Shelley called the songs of Silenus, notwithstanding the ill-reputation of the sylvan divinity. The loveliness of Mr. Haldar's 'Rāsa Līlā' is on the face of it. . . . If an artist born in Christian tradition were to paint a picture expressing what is wrapped up in the Hebrew poet's exclamation— 'The heavens declare the glory of God and the firmament showeth His handiwork,' he would touch the significance of 'Rāsa Līlā' with this difference, that to the inner eye of the Indian artist the cloud is not an objective manifestation of a quality of the Creator, but is essentially Himself. Purusha, the Divine energy, gives out the music of his creative desire, and Nature (prakriti) in all the alluring variations of one substance moves rhythmically in response. Our artist, if he were a poet in words, as he is in colours, could not sing, as Wordsworth did, 'I wandered lonely as a cloud.' To him there is no lonely cloud, for it is the dancing feet of the Lord of Love that speed them along the sky."

[1] See "Myths of the Hindus and Buddhists," by Sister Nivedita and Ananda Coomaraswamy (Harrap).
[2] "Modern Indian Artists," vol. ii (Probsthain & Co.).

Hero and Heroine in a Pavilion. Bundi School, dated V.S. 1739/1682 A.D. Collection of Sri C. D. Gujarati, Bombay. This is one of the earliest dated paintings of this School. An inscription at the back can be interpreted to mean that it was either painted or presented by one Daudia. The hero is trying to embrace the heroine who is coyly resisting his amorous advances.

(*Courtesy, Lalit Kala Akademi, New Delhi*)

THE FUTURE OF INDIAN ART

Plate 74, "The Flight of Lakshman Sen," is a very able work by the late Mr. Surendra Nath Ganguly, whose early death cut short a most promising career. It illustrates a well-known incident in the history of Bengal. The last representative of a long line of famous Brahman kings, surprised in his palace at Nūdīah by Pathān raiders, saves himself by a staircase leading to the river, where the royal barge is waiting.

It is manifestly impossible to do full justice to the New School of Calcutta in a few selected examples by three or four of its artists, though they will suffice to show the reality and sincerity of the revival. The deeper significance of the movement lies, however, not so much in its actual accomplishment, as in the clear evidence it gives of a spiritual resurrection, of the re-awakening of the artistic soul of India from the narcotic slumber, induced by the deadly drugs of a soulless pedagogy, in which there are never dreams of beauty or visions of a fairer world.

Should we take the re-awakening as a challenge or as an inspiration to the Empire?

THE INDIAN PROCESS OF *FRESCO BUONO*

THE Indian process of fresco painting as still practised in Rajputana, the Punjab, and the United Provinces, has been lately revived in Bengal by the Calcutta School of Art. Modern fashions and modern bad taste have generally substituted insanitary European wall-papers for this most beautiful and permanent form of Indian mural decoration.

The chief difference between it and the Italian process of *fresco buono* is that the colours are united to the plaster ground by mechanical action (beating with trowel and polishing) as well as chemically, by the action of the lime. The Indian fresco is given a highly polished surface, which in the dust-laden atmosphere of India is a great advantage, as it prevents accumulations of dirt, and enables the wall to be cleaned with a dry duster or by syringing it with water.

For interior decoration the colours are absolutely permanent. The plaster is exceedingly durable, and except when saltpetre (which eventually destroys any lime plaster) rises in the walls it is not affected by a damp atmosphere. In the dry climate of Northern India it was often used for external decoration by the Moguls, and it is quite suitable for this on walls which are not fully exposed to the monsoon rains, or are protected by a verandah.

Even when saltpetre rises in the walls, owing to the absence of an effective damp course, it is more durable than common plaster, and it can easily be repaired from time to time. But in this case an upper story, to which the saltpetre does not rise, is more suitable for pictures or for elaborate decorations. For native houses, where the inmates have not adopted the European habit of wearing boots, this plaster is strong enough to be used for floors ; and formerly floors were sometimes painted in fresco, which, with its finely polished surface, possessed all the beauty of inlaid marble. The Jaipur lime, owing to its having a large percentage of alumina, makes an exceptionally strong and beautiful plaster.

THE PREPARATION OF THE LIME FOR THE GROUND

The lime must be perfectly slaked to prevent blisters appearing in the ground. It must remain under water for at least a week, though a much longer time is desirable. Then mix with the lime a quantity of powdered limestone, or fine clean sand, double in weight of the dry lime. Stir the mixture, and add water to make it the consistency of mud. Grind the mixture on an ordinary curry-stone. This plaster can be used on brick or rough stone walls. When a wooden ground is used mix the plaster with sugar, powdered *methi* (Trigonell—*Fœnum græcum*), and jute to prevent it from cracking.

THE LAYING OF THE PLASTER GROUND

The stone or brick wall must be well wetted, and while wet the prepared plaster is thinly and evenly laid over it. Drive the plaster well into the joints and crevices, and beat it all over with a long strip of wood used edgeways until it becomes slightly dry. Then wet the layer, and repeat the beating until the plaster is firm. Apply another thin coat of plaster, beating it well in the same way, until it becomes at least a quarter of an inch thick. Then level it carefully and let it dry completely. The operation lasts three or four days.

THE PREPARATION OF LIME FOR FRESCO GROUND

The lime for the final coating on which the painting is done requires very careful preparation. It must be perfectly slaked, and for this purpose the lime is sometimes kept under water for months ; a year is said

Giri Govardhan—The Lifting of Mount Govardhan, by Majnu. Kangra Kalam, late 18th century. Bharat Kala
Bhavan, Banaras. When Krishna stopped the worship of Indra, the God of Rain, the latter was annoyed and sub-
merged the countryside of Vraja under a torrent of rain. Thereupon Krishna lifted the Govardhan mountain and held
it up for seven days thus saving the cowherds, the *gopis* and the *gopas*, and their cattle. The miniature depicts the
scene when men, women and cattle are gathered under mount Govardhan which Krishna holds aloft like a mighty
umbrella.

(Courtesy, Lalit Kala Akademi, New Delhi)

to be desirabe for the very best work.   Then curds are mixed with the lime in the proportion of half a seer of curds to half a maund of dry lime.   Stir the mixture well, and let it stand under water overnight.   Next day drain off the water and strain through a piece of fine cloth.   Let it stand again under water till next day, and continue this process for at least a week.   The purity of the lime will depend upon the number of times this operation is repeated.   Care must be taken that the lime thus prepared is always kept under water ; if allowed to dry it will be useless.

THE LAYING OF THE FRESCO GROUND

Wet a portion of this plaster ground prepared as above as much as can be painted and finished in a day. If the ground is too wet it will come off with the rubbing-stone ; if insufficiently the ground will dry too quickly and the colours will not be permanent.   Then mix some of the plaster of the ground with the fine prepared fresco lime, adding water to make it the consistency of cream, and apply this mixture to the wet wall with a large brush ; rub it well over the ground with a flat stone so as to work it well into the surface.   Give two or three coats, rubbing it with the stone every time.   Then apply three or four coatings of the prepared fresco lime only, rubbing it as before with the stone.   When it is a little dry and sticky polish it with an agate polishing-stone until the surface is quite smooth and glazed ; the ground is then ready for painting. Considerable practice and dexterity are needed in this polishing process.

The process for preparing the beautiful polished white walls which were formerly common in the best houses in Madras and Calcutta, was supposed to be a lost art until I pointed out that it was identical with that used for preparing walls for fresco painting.   The walls in Government House, Calcutta, were lately renewed under Lord Curzon's orders by workmen imported from Jaipur for teaching fresco painting in the Calcutta School of Art.

THE PAINTING

The drawing, first carefully made on paper, is transferred to the prepared wall by the usual method of pricking and pouncing the outlines.   The colours are mixed with water, ground fine, and strained through a cloth. Gum is added to all the colours except black, which requires glue.   The painting must be finished in one day, while the ground is wet, as in the Italian process of *fresco buono* ; but if necessary retouching can be done the following day, provided that the painting is kept wet by covering it with wet cloths.   When the painting is finished, beat it all over very evenly with a small thick trowel until the surface is quite smooth.   Then scrape the oily liquid from the inside of a cocoa-nut, and, after heating it, apply it to the surface of the painting and rub it gently with a dry, clean cloth.   The painting must then be rubbed with a small agate polishing-stone until it acquires a surface like polished marble.   When the plaster is thoroughly dry the colours are quite permanent, and the painting can be cleaned from time to time by syringing it with water or dusting it with a dry duster.

COLOURS USED IN JAIPUR FOR REAL FRESCO

Hindustani name.	*English.*
Hazâ patthar.	Terra verte.
Pilâ patthar.	Yellow ochre.
Lâjward.	Ultramarine (lapis).
Hingûl.	Vermilion.
Sindûr.	Red lead.
Nil.	
Kajâl.	Lampblack.
Koelâ	Ivory black.
Chûnâ.	Lime.

The following colours can also be used : Raw siena, burnt siena, raw umber, burnt umber, Naples yellow, Venetian red, green oxide of chromium, cobalt blue.

THE AJANTĀ AND SĪGIRI FRESCOES

The ground on which the Ajantā paintings were executed appears to have been composed of pulverised trap, mixed with clay and cow-dung, laid on the roughish surface of the rocks to a depth varying from a quarter to half an inch. Sometimes rice-husks were added, especially on the ceilings. Over this ground was laid the *intonaco* of this smooth plaster, about the thickness of an egg-shell, upon which the painting was done (Mr. John Griffiths, "Ajantā," vol. i, p. 18).

At Sīgiri the ground was a thickness of about half an inch of tempered earth and kaolin of a reddish brown hue, strengthened with rice-husks and perhaps shreds of cocoa-nut fibre. Upon this were laid at least two coatings of white chūnā (lime), a quarter to half an inch thick (Mr. H. C. P. Bell, "Journal R.A.S., Ceylon," vol. xv, p. 114).

NOTES ON INDIAN PAINTING PROCESSES, SUPPLIED BY MR. ISHWARY PRASAD, TEACHER IN THE CALCUTTA SCHOOL OF ART

Paper for Miniature Paintings

The papers used were of three kinds: (1) called *bavsāhā*, made from crushed bamboo, (2) *tātāhā*, made from *tāt*, or jute, (3) *tulāt*, made from *tula*, or cotton.

A smooth enamelled surface was given to the paper by placing it face downwards on a polished stone and rubbing the back of it with a polisher.

Tracing Paper (Charba)

This was prepared from deer-skin. Drawings were transferred by pricking and pouncing with charcoal powder. For fine work the charcoal was made from the *arahar* plant (*Cajanus Indicus*); for ordinary work charcoal made from mango-tree twigs was used.

Brushes were made from the hair of a squirrel's tail. Worn brushes were carefully kept for fine outline work. Dr. Coomaraswamy says that in Ceylon brushes for drawing fine lines are made of the awns of *teli tana* grass (*Aristida adscensionis*), and are admirably adapted to their purpose.

The first outline was always made with Indian red (*gairika*—a red used by mendicants for colouring their cloths) used without gum. The finishing outlines were made with lampblack, prepared by burning a camphor wick in a mustard-oil lamp.

Mediums.—The mediums used with the colours were water, gum, glue, sugar, and linseed water.

Gold.—The best gold was known as Panna gold, obtained from the Panna State Gold Mines. The gold size was made by boiling fourteen ounces' weight of gum and two ounces' weight of sugar in four ounces of water; when cold it was ready for use.

The following are the technical names of the principal processes of painting:

Ābina.—Drawing a sketch of the picture with a brush dipped in water only; the paper, when dry, has a water-line impression which serves as a guide for future work (*ab*—water, *bina*—to see).

Khākā (form).—To give form to the water-line drawing with some mineral colour, Indian red being often used.

Rangamezi (colouring).

   (a) *Dagina* (marking).—The different parts of the picture, such as the face, sky, trees, dresses, etc., are marked out with various colours.

   (b) *Potna* (filling up).—The spaces thus marked out were filled up with colour-washes.

Golaī.—Gradating and softening of the colours.

Sāyā-susma (shading).

   (a) *Sāyā.*—Shading the different parts of the picture with darker tones. *Sāyā* touches are only put on the face, hands, feet, folds of the dress, and accessories such as furniture; never on the sky or on flat walls.

Lady Surprised at the Bath. Bundi School, *c.* 1775 A.D. Prince of Wales Museum of Western India, Bombay. The lady is shown throwing a robe with brocaded ends over her body as she turns her face away at the sight of the prince. The heavy shading noticeable in the face of the prince and around the lady's bust is a prominent characteristic of this group of miniatures and indicates a strong Mughal influence of the second half of the 18th century. Though lacking exquisite finesse, this painting has been done in a bold and attractive manner.

(Courtesy, Lalit Kala Akademi, New Delhi)

(b) *Susma*.—To use different colours in giving relief to an object.

Sia-kalam (ink-brush).—Finishing the whole picture with ink-lines of varying thickness and strength.

Gula-pamba (chrome yellow and Chinese white).—This was used instead of gold in painting jewellery, etc.

Sufāda.—To paint bright spots in the picture, such as the white of the eye, pearls, and jewellery, with touches of white.

Jarab.—In this process real pearls and precious stones were stuck on to the picture (see illustration, Plate 49A).

Grounds for tempera painting on cloth, wood, and walls :

Cloth.—For first-class work, boiled and liquefied *khoi* (parched paddy) mixed with gum $\frac{1}{16}$ part. For ordinary work, rice starch mixed with linseed water $\frac{1}{8}$ part , and gum $\frac{1}{20}$ part.

Wood.—Glue and sugar $\frac{1}{16}$ part, a pinch of alum and a tablespoonful of shellac, boiled together.

Walls.—Chalk and milk $\frac{1}{2}$ part, milk curd $\frac{1}{8}$, sugar $\frac{1}{16}$, and a little yellow ochre.

Dr. Waddell, in his "Lamaism in Tibet," p. 331, describes the method of preparing the ground for the sacred banners which are hung in Buddhist temples and monasteries :

"The cloth used is canvas or cotton, seldom silk. It is prepared by stretching it while damp on a wooden frame to which a margin of cloth is stitched, and its surface is then smeared with a paste of lime and flour, to which a little glue is sometimes added. On drying the surface is rubbed smooth and slightly polished by a stone, and the drawing is then outlined either by hand or with a charcoal crayon. In the more technical subjects a stencil plate is used."

AN OUTLINE OF RAJASTHANI PAINTING

By
Pramod Chandra

The regions of Rajasthan and Gujarat, closely connected culturally, hold an important place in the history of Indian painting, particularly in the Muslim period when indigenous art traditions continued to be preserved here while they almost disappeared from other parts of Northern India. The Western Indian style, the earliest records of which (apart from some wall paintings) date from the period of the Turkish invasion, conserve the decayed and disintegrated elements of the ancient tradition, even if unconsciously, from the 11th to almost the beginning of the 17th century A.D. Though the majority of the extant examples in this style come from Gujarat there is little doubt that the style was also prevalent in Rajasthan during this time. Indeed it has been suggested by some that the style may have originated in Rajasthan itself, chiefly on the basis of Lama Taranatha's statement that the School of the Ancient West founded in the 7th century A. D. was established by Sringadhara, an artist from Marudesa (modern Marwar).

There are, however, not many paintings in the Western Indian style that can be definitely ascribed to Rajasthan. One of the earliest of these is the *Savaga Padikamana Sutta Chunni* painted at the fort of Aghata (modern Aher near Udaipur) in A. D. 1260 during the reign of the Guhila Tejahsimha.[1] Another interesting document from Rajasthan in the same style is a manuscript of the *Supasanahachariyam*, illustrated and written in A.D. 1422-23 at Devakulavataka in the country of Medapata during the reign of Rana Mokala.[2] The thirty-seven illustrations of this copy are fairly elaborate, and some of them occupy the entire area of the page, which is somewhat unusual for illustrations of this style.

The Western Indian style is noted for its remarkable conservatism, remaining essentially unchanged for a period of over five hundred years, during which time it became prevalent all over India. It is only about the middle of the 16th century that we begin to observe marked changes that culminate finally in the formation of what is called the Early Rajasthani School—one of the principal glories of Indian art. These changes are best seen in a recently discovered manuscript of the *Adipurana* dated A.D. 1540 and discussed briefly by Khandalavala.[3] The characteristic protruding eye of the Western Indian style is absent, and the costumes, instead of being conventional, are contemporary, including characteristic *kulahdar* turbans and ankle length *jamahs*. One can feel a new vitality in many of the illustrations and though the older elements survive, there can be no doubt that great changes are in the offing. It is not certain whether these changes first took place in Rajasthan, for the *Adipurana* manuscript was painted at Palam near Delhi and the illustrated manuscript of the Avadhi romance *Mrigavati* (Bharat Kala Bhavan, Banaras) in a very similar style was probably done in U.P. Avadhi is a dialect restricted to the eastern U.P. and the script in which the romance is written is Kaithi, an alphabet confined to that part of the country and Bihar.

Meanwhile, by *circa* 1565 A.D. a new element was introduced in Indian painting with the establishment of the Mughal school at the Imperial court. This style patronised lavishly by the great Akbar, began to produce works of far greater magnificence than had been painted in India for at least five hundred years. The artists of the Imperial atelier worked under Persian masters, but were mostly Hindus, drawn from various parts of the empire, particularly from Gujarat and U.P. It is natural therefore to expect Mughal influence to have spread rapidly, and this is indeed what happened. The Mughal school influenced the style represented by the

---

[1] Ananda Coomaraswamy, "An Illustrated Svetambara Jaina Ms of A.D. 1260," *Eastern Art*, II (1930), pp. 237-240.

[2] Muni Punyavijaya, "Supasanahachariyam ni hastalikhita pothimana chitro," *Acharya Sri Vijayavallabhasuri Smarak Grantha*, Bombay, 1956.

[3] Karl Khandalavala, "A 'Gita Govinda' Series in the Prince of Wales Museum (in the Style of the 'Laur-Chanda' and 'Chaurapanchasika' Group)," *Prince of Wales Museum Bulletin*, No. 4, pp. 1-18.

Rāsa Līla. Painted by Asit Kumar Haldar.

PLATE 73

The flight of Lakshman Sen. Painted by Surendra Nath Ganguly.

PLATE 74

A. Painted book cover. Western Indian style, C. 13th century A.D. (*Courtesy, Muni Punyavijaya, Ahmedabad*).

B. Folio from a *Kalpasutra*. Western India style, C. 1450 A.D. (*Courtesy, Devasanopada Jnana Bhandar, Ahmedabad*).

C. Illustration from a Ms. of *Kalpasutra*. Painted at Jaunpur, A.D. 1465.

D. Illustration from a Ms. of *Kalpasutra*. Painted at Jaunpur, A.D. 1465.

PLATE 75

A.   Folio from a Ms. of *Sangrahani Sutra*, C. 1583 A.D.   (*Courtesy, Muni Punyavijaya, Ahmedabad*).

B.   Illustration from a Ms. of *Balagopala Stuti*.

PLATE 76

Adipurana of A.D. 1540 to produce a group of paintings represented by the illustrations of the *Laur-Chanda* (Punjab Museum, Simla) the *Chaurapanchasika* (collection of the late Mr. N. C. Mehta, Bombay), the *Gita Govinda* (Prince of Wales Museum of Western India, Bombay) and the *Bhagavata Purana* (Bharat Kala Bhavan, Banaras).[4] Here Mughal influence is apparent, not only in the treatment of costume but in the generally richer and more sumptuous effect of the paintings. The provenance of this group has not yet been accurately determined, though formerly they had been vaguely assigned to Rajasthan. It would not be surprising if they were actually painted in U.P., though a wider diffusion of this style, particularly in Rajasthan and Malwa, is quite possible. Not only does the *Adipurana* of A.D. 1540 from which this group has clearly developed come from Delhi, which is linguistically and culturally a part of U.P., but the *Laur-Chanda* and *Mrigavati* as mentioned previously, are poetic compositions in the Avadhi dialect which is spoken only in certain areas of eastern U.P. That U.P. had an art tradition of long standing is evident not only from the fine *Kalpasutra* done in the Western Indian style at Jaunpur in A.D. 1465 (Plate 75 C and D) during the reign of Husain Shah Sharki but also from the names of a large number of painters in Akbar's atelier, specially those belonging to Ahir and Konhar[5] castes, who came from that area. It is also significant to note that Banarsidas, a Hindi poet of the Akbar period, mentions the flourishing state of artists at Jaunpur in his memoirs entitled *Ardha-kathanaka*.[6] The date of the *Chaura-Panshasika* group on the basis of stylistic advancement over the 1540 manuscript and resemblances to certain technical features of Mughal painting should probably be somewhere in the last quarter of the 16th century A.D.

The Mughal school also travelled to Gujarat where the Western Indian style was lingering on. In the face of this new school rapid changes were effected, and the *Sangrahani Sutra* of A.D. 1583 in the collection of Muni Punyavijayaji and painted at the village named Matar in Gujarat (Plate 76A), as well as the *Uttaradhyayana Sutra* of A.D. 1591 (Museum and Picture Gallery, Baroda)[7] indicate the nature of this transformation. The protruding eye, a hallmark of Western Indian painting, disappears, the draftsmanship becomes considerably smoother though some angularity is still noticeable, the treatment of the architecture is more varied, and the men wear contemporary costumes of the Akbar period including the typical *atpati pagri*. The miniatures have none of the magnificent quality of the U.P. style but their vigorous primitive energy also bespeaks the birth of a new idiom.

However, one cannot be certain that it was only during the Akbar period that Gujarat painting took a new direction. In this connection a *pata* representing Parsvanatha with attending gods and goddesses[8] is of special interest. Though Western Indian elements such as linear draftsmanship and strong colours are present, yet the protruding eye is absent. It is also significant that the costume is not of the Akbar period at all, but conforms to the type depicted in earlier Jaina manuscripts. The figure drawing lacks the exaggeration of the Western Indian style and is instead flowing and careful. The temple architecture, the treatment of mountains, the introduction of geese patterns as dividing panels, and the decorative treatment of animals and birds, are stylistically of at least the middle of the 16th century, and there is no foreign influence of any kind discernible in the composition.

A proper search of Gujarat Bhandars should yield much more interesting materials of this nature. In any case Gujarat seems to have been a flourishing centre of this early Rajasthani style, and several newly discovered manuscripts testify to this importance. Among the finer ones is a *Sangrahani Sutra* and a manuscript of the *Uttaradhyayana*, similar to the Baroda manuscript, is in the Devasano Pada Bhandar. Hindu works were also illustrated in this Gujarati version of the early Rajasthani style, and amongst the finest is the *Bhagavata Dasamaskandha* in the Jodhpur Library[9] and over a hundred leaves illustrating the *Gita Govinda* of the early 17th century in the collection of the late Mr. N. C. Mehta.[10] Gujarat continued to produce works in this style, and amongst the better kind of work done can be mentioned the *Salibhadracharita* of the early 17th century A.D., *Sangrahani Sutra* dated A.D. 1649 and a fine Ms. of the *Balagopala Stuti* of c. 1660 (Plate 76B)

[4] Ibid.

[5] Members of the Konhar caste retain their skill in painting to the present day and continue to do the simple traditional wall paintings that are to be found on native houses. Daswanth, the great artist of Akbar's court might well have belonged to this caste (Konhars) and not to the caste of palanquin bearers (Kahars) as is commonly supposed.

[6] See Nathuram Premi (ed.), *Ardha-Kathanaka*, Bombay, 1957.

[7] Numerous illustrations of this manuscript have been reproduced in Norman Brown, *Manuscript Illustrations of the Uttaradhyayana Sutra*, New Haven, 1951, as MS JP.

[8] Moti Chandra, *Jaina Miniature Painting in Western India*, Ahmedabad, 1949, Pl. 188.

[9] Karl Khandalavala, "Leaves from Rajasthan," *Marg*, IV (No. 3), p. 17, Fig. 8.

[10] Ibid., p. 18, Fig. 10.

all in the collection of the Prince of Wales Museum of Western India.

It should be apparent thus that the period from roughly second quarter of the 16th century A.D. to c. 1610 was a time of great artistic ferment. Indian painting was undergoing rapid changes, changes which were moving more or less in one direction, namely, in the growth of a new style that is now called the Early Rajasthani School, from the fact that the great majority of paintings come from Rajasthan. The earliest known dated examples, however, do not seem to belong to that area but this may be just a matter of accident. It is only with the *Ragamala* set painted at Chawand,[11] the capital of the gallant Rana Pratap, in 1605 and now chiefly in the collection of Gopi Krishna Kanoria that we come to the first dated paintings that can be definitely assigned to a Rajasthan provenance. It is a significant fact that the powerful paintings, full of a primitive emotional quality come from Mewar which becomes the most important centre of the Early Rajasthani School and retains this position to at least 1680 when this early phase of Rajasthani painting comes to an end.

The commonest themes of this school are incidents from the life of Krishna, the *nayika bheda* of contemporary Hindi poetry, illustrations to the Hindu epics like the *Ramayana* and *Bhagavata Purana*, pictorial representations of Ragas and Raginis and the various seasons and erotic scenes. The school is essentially abstract and symbolic in nature, and Mughal influence, though important technically, is but an unfelt presence, the Early Rajasthani School preserving its idealistic and imaginative character against the realistic and naturalistic tendencies of the latter right up to the last quarter of the 17th century. In the treatment of the human figure, we notice that the faces are all in profile with large eyes, pointed nose and double chin, while the setting is architectural or natural, or very often a combination of both. The lines are vigorous and the figures they enclose, ardent and energetic. The colours, though limited, are warm and glowing and used with brilliant effect.

The Early Rajasthani School of Mewar[12] reached the peak of its development in the reign of Jagat Singh (A.D. 1628-1652) (Plate 77A) to which period belongs the magnificent illustrations of the *Bhagavata Purana* painted by Sahabdi in 1648 (Bhandarkar Oriental Research Institute, Poona). Another work illustrated by the same painter is the *Sukar Kshetra Mahatmya* dated A.D. 1655 (Sarasvati Bhavan Library, Udaipur). In the same Library is a large manuscript of seventy-seven folios, all of them illustrating the *Arsh Ramayana* painted in Chitor. The magnificent *Ramayana*, now in the collection of the Prince of Wales Museum of Western India and Sir Cowasji Jehangir, Bombay, is dated 1649. The colophon says that the manuscript made for one Acharya Jasvanta, was copied by Muni Hirananda and painted by Manohar at Udaipur. The fine *Ragamala* set in the National Museum of India,[13] the *Rasikapriya* of Kesavadas in the Bikaner Durbar, and the *Sur Sagar* in the collection of Gopi Krishna Kanoria also belong to the reign of Jagat Singh. There is a paucity of definitely dated material after him, but judging from the examples that survive it is apparent that the fine traditions of Mewar painting were continued in the reigns of Raj Singh (A.D. 1652-1680) and Jai Singh (A.D. 1680-1698). Slowly Mughal influence asserts itself and the Mewar School begins to undergo a subtle transformation, rich and pleasing at first, but leading ultimately to the banalities of the 18th century.

A charming offshoot of the Mewar School is the Early Rajasthani style of Bundi, of which few specimens are to be found. The earliest dated example known is a painting showing lovers standing in a garden dated A. D. 1692 (Prince of Wales Museum of Western India).[14] The deep indebtedness to Mewar is obvious, but the Bundi paintings possess a delicacy of lines and lyrical feeling that marks them as constituting a school apart (Plate 78B).

Some very fine paintings of the early Rajasthani school were probably produced in the region of Malwa (Plates 77B, 79A and B and 80C). The exact part played by the school of Malwa in the history of Rajasthani painting is at the present stage by no means clear. Already in the early 16th century Malwa confronts us with a new trend in the Western Indian style in the illustrations to a lovely copy of the *Kalpasutra* painted at Mandu in A.D. 1439. Persian influences are present no doubt but very very slight and can be noticed in the treatment of the horse, but the drawing of the human figure, conforming strictly to the Indian canons, and other essential features are the result of an indigenous evolution. The miniatures of the *Niamat Namah* ascribed by Archer

---

[11] A note on this interesting set has been published by Gopi Krishna Kanoria in the *Journal of the Indian Society of Oriental Art*, Vol. XIX.

[12] See Moti Chandra, *Mewar Painting in the 17th Century*, Lalit Kala Akademi, 1956, for a brief account of this school together with several splendid colour reproductions.

[13] This *Ragamala* set has been discussed by Pramod Chandra, "A *Ragamala* Set of the Mewar School in the National Museum of India," *Lalit Kala*, Nos. 3-4.

[14] For a colour reproduction see *Western Railway Annual*, 1956, p. 53.

॥वसंतरागिणी॥ सिंधेडिबिहैरीबियबहूतुपुष्पनिकंनृतलतांकुरे॥ अमुनुल
॥वासमनेगररिमनोहरोयंचवसंतरागः॥२॥

Ragini Vasanta. An illustration from a *Ragamala* series. Mewar School, *c.* 1650 A.D. National Museum, New Delhi. *Ragas* and *Raginis* are melody motifs and in the literature of Indian music each has a more or less standardized pictorial formula for depicting it in form and colour. *Ragini Vasanta* is the melody motif of spring. Here Krishna, accompanied by two musicians, is performing a dance to the accompaniment of the flute. The painting is distinguished for the brilliance of its colours. The brilliant lacquer red is used to great effect by the early Mewar artists.

(Courtesy, Lalit Kala Akademi, New Delhi)

to c. A.D. 1500[15] are but a further development of the Mandu style, treatment of the human figure being very similar, though the protruding eye to be seen in the Mandu *Kalpasutra* is missing. Archer however is of the opinion that the style of Malwa as evinced in the *Niamat Namah* is due to the Turkoman style of Persian painting current in the late 16th century at Shiraz, going so far as to state that the manuscript represents "the Turkoman style of Persian painting in the process of being adjusted to Indian requirements."[16] This is overstating the case by far, as an examination of the Mandu *Kalpasutra* will immediately demonstrate. The style represented by the *Niamat Namah* miniature appears to be the result of a natural growth from indigenous tradition already found in the early 15th century and not based on the so called Turkoman style flourishing only in the late 15th century at Shiraz, though heavily influenced by it. All the elements of the Mandu *Kalpasutra* are to be found there except in the costume where we get the trellised *Kulahdar* turban, a common feature of the group of paintings from 1540 onwards already referred to above.[17]

The next series of paintings which we can more or less definitely assign to Malwa is the *Ragamala* set distributed in various collections including those of the Bharat Kala Bhavan, Banaras, the Allahabad Museum, Allahabad, and the National Museum of India. According to the colophon, the set was painted at Narsyanga Sahar (Narsinghgarh ?) by one Madhodas in A.D. 1680.[18] On the basis of this somewhat tenuous piece of evidence, it is possible to ascribe several other paintings in the early Rajasthani style to Malwa, or at least the same provenance. Amongst the finer paintings of this style is the *Ragamala* set of 1652, now scattered but which is supposed to have an inscription with the date and the place name Nasratgarh and the set of ninety-one paintings of the *Amarusataka* in the Prince of Wales Museum.)[19]

The Malwa School is characterised by its preference for architectural setting, scrupulously flat but well patterned compositions, good draftsmanship making decorative landscape and the conscious, sophisticated use of monochrome colour patches to give relief to the figures. The men and women too are drawn with great delicacy, with slender bodies, small faces and large eyes.

It is better, from the point of view of art history, to conceive of Malwa as including portions of Southern Rajasthan and Bundelkhandi or else it would be difficult to explain the Bundelkhandi inscriptions on the *Ramayana* set (National Museum of India) done in a style which is almost indistinguishable from the Malwa style. The famous Boston *Ragamala* done in the same style as the *Ramayana* can also be assigned to the same region. The National Museum of India also has two fine sets illustrating the *Rasikapriya* of Kesavadas in the same style.

Similar to the Early Rajasthani style of Malwa but in a somewhat varied idiom is a brilliant *Ragamala* set of about the mid-17th century A.D. (Bharat Kala Bhavan, Banaras) (Plate 79 A and B). It is allied to the Malwa style but seems to belong to a somewhat different local tradition, the treatment of the human figure being bolder if somewhat sturdier, and clearly derived from the paintings of the *Rasikapriya* of Kesavadas dated A.D. 1634 (National Museum of India). The Bharat Kala Bhavan also possesses several leaves illustrating the *Ramayana*[20] almost identical in style to the 1634 Rasikapriya and possible of the same date. The group of paintings has sufficient individuality, constituting a distinct idiom.

We have no definite dated paintings to show the existence of the Early Rajasthani school in Marwar, and whatever material we have from the state shows that the painting, popular with the rulers of Jodhpur, was the Mughal style and we come across several of their portraits done in the Mughal manner. As a matter of fact, the growth of Early Rajasthani painting seems to have little to do with court patronage, the preferred style of royalty being the Imperial style of the Mughal court. It should, however, not be a matter of surprise if an Early Rajasthani school of painting related to the Mewar style was prevalent in this region as well, and paintings done in this manner, allied to Mewar but with certain local peculiarities, are to be found as isolated specimens in the museums of India.

The productions of the Rajasthani schools during the 18th century, though extremely great in quantity,

[15] W. G. Archer, *Indian Painting*, London, 1956, Colour Plate I.
[16] Archer, *Indian Painting from Rajasthan*, London, 1957, p. 19.
[17] The Prince of Wales Museum has recently acquired a very fine set of paintings illustrating the *Laur-Chanda* romance in a style reminiscent of the *Niamat Namah*. This and several other newly discovered documents will be the subject of a monograph to be published shortly.
[18] See Khandalavala, "Leaves from Rajasthan," *Marg*, IV (No .3), p. 55, Figs. 22, 25.
[19] Moti Chandra, "An Illustrated Set of the *Amarusataka*," *Prince of Wales Museum Bulletin*, 1951-52, pp. 1-63.
[20] See Rai Krishnadasa, "Bharat Kala Bhavan Ka ek mahatvapurna chitra sangraha," *Kala Nidhi*, I (No. 4), Colour Plate 3 etc.

seldom achieved the rich harmonies of the paintings of the 17th century. The local styles centred around the capitals of the various Rajput states developed idioms of their own, all of them showing a more pronounced Mughal influence than was noticeable hitherto. The work of Jaipur, Jodhpur and Bikaner artists particularly is influenced by Mughal art though not lacking a certain lyricism, and the fluent use of bright and dazzling colours. The Bundi style of the 18th century is one of the most pleasing. It owes as much to Mughal art of the late 18th century as to the Mewar School of the 17th century. The short phase of Kishangarh painting of the mid-18th century is marked by the masterpieces of the artist Nihal Chand and inspired by the poetry of Savant Singh stands apart in Rajasthani painting as the very acme of a rich and technically accomplished style of extreme sophistication.

In the 19th century, with increasing Western influence and consequent corruption of taste, the Rajasthani style enters into its phase of decline. The works turned out by the last representatives of a dying tradition lack vitality and harmony of colour. The expression is insipid and the increasing competition from cheap prints which were coming into vogue finally put an end to the last great phase of traditional Indian art.

A. A Great Feast. Illustration from a Ms. of the *Rāmāyana*. Painted at Mewar, A.D. 1649.
(*Prince of Wales Museum, Bombay*).

B. Scene from the *Rāmāyana*. Rajasthani School (Malwa), C. 1650 A.D. (*National Museum of India, New Delhi*).

PLATE 77

B. Watching the crescent moon. Bundi School, A.D. 1689.
(*Prince of Wales Museum, Bombay*).

A. Raga Malakora. Painted at Chawand, Mewar, A.D. 1605.

PLATE 78

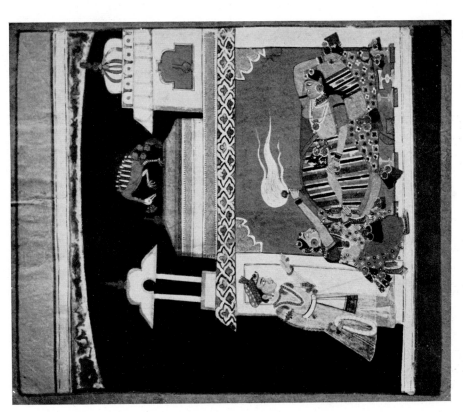

A, B.   Paintings from a Ragamala Set, Malwa (?)   C. 1650 A.D.   (*Bharat Kala Bhavan, Banaras*).

PLATE 79

A.   Women hunting.   Bikaner, mid-18th century A.D.   (*Prince of Wales Museum, Bombay*).

B.   Krishna conversing with Gopis.   Bikaner, late 17th century A.D.

C.   Woman feeding birds.   From a set of *Amarusataka*.   Malwa, mid-17th century A.D.   (*Prince of Wales Museum, Bombay*).

PLATE 80

PART II

THE IDEALS OF
INDIAN ART

PREFACE TO THE SECOND EDITION

INDIAN Art has now obtained a far wider recognition and a fuller understanding than it had when the first edition of "Ideals of Indian Art" was published. If it has not yet become a subject of general interest for the public, it is now treated more or less respectfully by our national museums : several able Indian writers have made valuable contributions to it, and European art critics, who before avoided it or gave it scant consideration, have become its appreciative exponents.

I have not, however, found it necessary to revise the passages in this book which relate to opinions current at the time when it was first published, as my readers can easily mark the differences between then and now for themselves. Except for a few necessary corrections and additional notes the text remains unaltered.

E. B. H.

November 1919

INTRODUCTION

In the present volume I have attempted to fill up some of the particulars, unavoidably omitted from my book on Indian Sculpture and Painting, which are necessary for the full appreciation of the Indian æsthetic standpoint.

Convinced as I am that the learning of the orientalist, however profound and scientific it may be, is often most misleading in æsthetic criticism, it has been always my first endeavour, in the interpretation of Indian ideals, to obtain a direct insight into the artist's meaning without relying on modern archæological conclusions and without searching for the clue which may be found in Indian literature. I started with the premise that the Buddhist divine ideal, of which the great statue of Buddha at Anuradhapura is the type, was not, as archæologists have generally assumed, a debased imitation of a Græco-Roman model, deficient in technical achievement for lack of anatomical knowledge, but an imaginative creation, purely Indian in origin, derived from the teaching of Indian Yoga philosophy which was adopted by Mahâyâna Buddhism. I would maintain that no critic who begins with this archæological prepossession is capable of appreciating the beauty of Indian sculpture and painting, or competent to interpret the intentions of Indian artists.

In the present work I bring forward evidence from Indian literature which entirely justifies my conclusions and explains more fully the origin of the Buddhist and Jain divine ideal and its derivation from the old Aryan heroic ideal as described in Indian epic poetry. The light which the Mahâbhârata throws on this point is important, for it shows the affinity of Indian æsthetic ideals with Egyptian, Cretan, and pre-Pheidian Hellenic art, a matter of the deepest interest to students of archæology.

I have also endeavoured to indicate the inspiration of Vedic thought, which still permeates the whole atmosphere of Indian life, as the originating impulse of Indian art and the influence which links together all its different historic phases, not excepting the Mogul period; but I differ entirely from the European critic whose usual attitude is to point to the Vedic and early Buddhist period as containing all that is pure and spiritual in Indian thought, and to explain the succeeding Buddhist-Hindu epoch, until the advent of Islam, as a gradual relapse into superstition and barbarism. This error is, I think, largely due to ignorance or misapprehension of Hindu artistic ideals, which also leads Western critics to disregard the paramount importance of Indian idealism, not only in Mogul art, but in the great schools of China and Japan.

I am aware that in some cases the interpretation I have given to Hindu symbolism may seem to lack the authority of Sanskrit texts; but art and literature do not always follow parallel lines, and the archæologists who have sought to interpret Indian art only by literary knowledge have often gone woefully astray. Anglo-India needs more art in its archæology and less archæology in its art.

Though in my excursions into the new world of art which India has revealed to me I have acquired an intense admiration for the great monuments of the past, my interest in Indian art is not of an academic or archæological kind. It is centred in the fact that Indian art is still a living thing with vast potentialities, of such unique value to India and all the world that it should be regarded as a great national trust which Great Britain is bound in honour and duty to guard and maintain. If to the orthodox critics my enthusiasm may seem to be excessive, I have the satisfaction of knowing that it is shared by a goodly company of my fellow artists; and the fault, if fault there be, is a venial one. Art does not die of overpraise; it cannot live or thrive in an atmosphere of contempt and depreciation. The half-hearted admirers of Indian art are those who do it most injury.

It is not a small matter, either for this country or for India, that Indian artistic ideals are so misunderstood and misinterpreted. For if a great national art affords a revelation of national thought and character more intimate, more complete and universal, than history, poetry, or romance can give us, the misapprehension or depreciation of its ideals by an alien governing race must inevitably sow intellectual antipathies, not less dangerous because they are often unconscious ones, which aggravate racial prejudices, create obstacles to that intimate social relationship without which a perfect understanding between different races is impossible, and are detrimental to good administration, especially in the vital problems of education. The mistakes engendered by such misunderstanding should be evident enough in the injury which has been done to Indian art, even in the efforts which have been made to assist it.

It would be regarded as silly and inconsequent if a critic were to complain of the sculptors of the Sphinx that they knew not how to draw or model cats and dogs. Western methods of art-teaching in India, based on the assumption that Indian artists have been always ignorant of anatomy and perspective, are not less irrelevant and uninformed.

The nation which governs India should not allow its state museums to lend themselves to the depreciation of Indian art in all its higher aspects. I am convinced that, with the spread of better knowledge, the whole consensus of artistic opinion in Europe will condemn such statements as those which appear in the official handbook to the Indian section of the Victoria and Albert Museum ; which reveal, also, the guiding principle in the whole past administration of it :

"The monstrous shapes of the Puranic deities are unsuitable for the higher forms of artistic representation ; and this is possibly why sculpture and painting are unknown, as fine arts, in India. . . . Nowhere does their figure-sculpture show the inspiration of true art. They seem to have no feeling for it. . . . How completely their figure-sculpture fails in true art is seen at once when they attempt to produce it on a natural or heroic scale ; and it is only because their ivory and stone figures of men and animals are on so minute a scale that they excite admiration."

It is easy to understand, when such ideas are given authoritative official sanction in the state collections which are designed for public enlightenment, why many sound English art-critics are full of similar prejudices, and why Indian art is generally better appreciated on the Continent than it is in this country. I hope that the selection of some of the finest examples of Indian sculpture which I have made to illustrate this book, together with those given in the previous one on the same subject, will go far to correct the false impression of Indian art which all our national collections create, and indicate the direction in which the latter may be improved.

But as the best illustrations are always poor substitutes for the originals, I hope also that they will inspire more art-students, Indian as well as European, to go and seek the truth for themselves in the places where Indian art can be properly appreciated. They will then realise fully what a mangled and distorted version of it has hitherto been presented to the Western art-world.

It is difficult to argue with those who are so steeped in Western academic prejudices as to treat all Hindu art as puerile and detestable because it has chosen the most simple and obvious forms of symbolism, such as a third eye to denote spiritual consciousness—where the classical scholar would expect a Greek nymph, or a Roman Sybil, with an explanatory label—a multiplicity of arms to denote the universal attributes of divinity, and a lion-like body in gods and heroes to express spiritual and physical strength. Such critics seem not to appreciate the fact that Hindu art was not addressed, like modern Western art, to a narrow coterie of *literati* for their pleasure and distraction. Its intention was to make the central ideas of Hindu religion and philosophy intelligible to all Hinduism, to satisfy the unlettered but not unlearned Hindu peasant as well as the intellectual Brahmin. It does not come within the province of a critic to dictate to the artist what symbols he may or may not employ—to tell him that it is true art to use x, y, and z in his æsthetic notation, but not a, b, and c ; or *vice versâ*.

In all great national art the artist invariably prefers the symbols which make the most universal appeal—those which are best understood by the people he addresses. He can only be rightly condemned if in the application of them he should offend against the universal laws of æsthetic design and rhythm. Hindu symbolism is justified because it speaks straight to the heart of Hinduism and because it is used with consummate artistic knowledge and skill.

That Hindu art was successful in its educational purpose may be inferred from the fact, known to all who have intimate acquaintance with Indian life, that the Indian peasantry, though illiterate in the Western sense, are among the most cultured of their class anywhere in the world. A very competent and independent European witness, Dr. Lefroy, Bishop of Lahore, has testified from his long personal experience to the extraordinary aptitude with which even the poorest and wholly illiterate Hindu peasant will engage in discussion of or speculation in the deepest philosophical and ethical questions. It is just because art has penetrated so deeply into national life in India that it demands the most careful and sympathetic study of every one of the governing class, whether he be artist or layman. In this respect, also, Indian art is a most valuable object-lesson to Europe ; for the rehabilitation of art, music, and the drama on a national basis is one of the great needs of Western civilisation.

Let the classical scholar by all means indulge his personal predilections privately, but those who hold Indian art up to ridicule and contempt are only condemning themselves as wholly unfit to control the policy of our state museums or to direct art-education in India.

I must render acknowledgments for assistance I have received first to my wife, whose keen artistic intuition and sound judgment have been very helpful in the analysis of the examples chosen for illustration. To Mr. F. W. Thomas, Librarian of the India Office, and Mr. Abanindro Nath Tagore, Vice-Principal of the Calcutta School of Art, I am indebted for advice and ready help in my search for literary references. I am also very grateful for the help I have received in obtaining photographs from Dr. A. K. Coomaraswamy ; the Director of the Colombo Museum ; Dr. Henderson, Superintendent of the Madras Museum ; Mr. J. de La Valette ; Mr. J. H. Marshall, C.I.E., Director-General of the Archæological Survey of India ; Mr. T. Oppermann, Director of the Glyptotek, Copenhagen ; Mr. Edgar Thurston, C.I.E.; Mr. M. Veluyathan Asari, Assistant-Superintendent, School of Arts, Madras ; Messrs. Johnston & Hoffman, of Calcutta, and Messrs. Nicholas & Co., of Madras.

March 1911.

CHAPTER I

THE ORIGIN OF INDIAN ART—THE VEDIC PERIOD

UNDOUBTEDLY the most significant fact in modern Western art is that artists, dimly conscious of the limitations which the narrow conventions of the Italian Renaissance have so long imposed upon them, have been looking for many years once more to the East for new ideas and new sources of inspiration. It is still more significant of the gulf which separates Eastern thought from Western, that in this quest British artists have not turned at once to India as the primal source from which the main current of Eastern idealism has always flowed towards Europe, but to China and Japan, which during the greatest periods of their art-history were themselves dominated by the influence of that same mighty Indian thought-stream.

The distinguished Japanese art-critic, Mr. Okakura, author of "The Ideals of the East," has rightly insisted that, in the domain of art-philosophy, all Asia is one. But if we apply Western analytical methods to the exegesis of Asiatic æsthetics, we shall never form any just or complete conception of them until we have learnt to discard all our Western academic prejudices, and realised the paramount importance of Indian philosophy and religion among the great creative forces which moulded Asiatic art.

Personally, I think that the scientific analysis of the Western art-historian is often very misleading. What art needs now, both in the East and in the West, is not analysis, but synthesis ; not a dissection of styles, methods, and principles, nor the determination of art-values by the Röntgen rays and the microscope, but a clear understanding of the great psychic currents and intellectual movements which have created the great art-schools in different epochs and different countries ; and, above all, a clearer conception of the art-philosophy upon which these schools were founded.

In this country especially, where philosophy is commonly held to have no practical bearing on life and policy, all our methods of art-teaching, since the sixteenth century, have become almost entirely empirical and unscientific in the true sense of the word. On the one hand, the puritanical sentiment of the Reformation has tended to divorce art from religion ; and, on the other hand, our universities have uprooted the idealism of the Middle Ages, and substituted for the art-philosophy of Christianity an academic formula of their own devising, the influence of which has joined with modern materialism in destroying all our great national art traditions.

Under the tyranny of this clerical and literary domination art has lost its power and influence in national education and dwindled into a special cult for a small and exclusive sect, whose dogmas are expounded by classical professors, whose places of worship are museums, picture-galleries, and exhibitions, and whose idols are the gods of pagan Greece and Rome.

It is only in the East that art still has a philosophy and still remains the great exponent of national faith and race traditions. In Indian idealism we shall find the key to the understanding, not only of all Asiatic art, but to that of the Christian art of the Middle Ages. For the original source of this idealism we must look much further back than the visible beginnings of Indian art, as we now know them from the relics of early Buddhist worship, which date from the first two centuries before Christ. We must fully understand that the motive forces which are behind all art-creation often exist in full strength long before art finds concrete, visible expression in literature and what we call the fine arts.

Archæologists dig in the ground and rummage among the ruined Buddhist *stûpas* of Gandhara, and when they find innumerable statues of the Greek and Roman pantheon placed between Corinthian pilasters, they believe that here Indian art had its main root, and that Hellenic thought first inspired the ideals of India.

Nothing can be further from the truth. Indian art reached full expression in the Indian mind many centuries before the Græco-Roman sculptors carved Buddhist images in the temples and monasteries of Gandhara. Indian art was conceived when that wonderful intuition flashed upon the Indian mind that the soul of man is eternal, and one with the Supreme Soul, the Lord and Cause of all things. It took upon itself organic expression in the Vedas and Upanishads, and though in succeeding centuries other thought-centres were formed in Persia, China, and Arabia, the creative force generated from those great philosophical conceptions has not ceased to stimulate the whole art of Asia from that time to the present day.

It is probably an unique phenomenon in the evolution of the world's art that so many centuries elapsed between the complete expression of Indian thought in the Vedas and Upanishads and the full maturity of the technic arts, as revealed in the sculptures of Elephanta, Ellora, and Bôrôbudûr, and in the best Indian Buddhist paintings from the fourth to the eighth centuries A.D., the majority of which have perished.

But when we consider the esoteric and exclusive character of early Aryan culture we shall begin to realise that what seems to be an abnormally slow development in the technic arts in Indian civilisation was deliberately willed as a part of the extraordinary precautions taken by the early Aryan immigrants in India, and their allies, to prevent what they believed to be their divinely inspired wisdom being perverted by popular superstitions.

Other races, as soon as they have perfected a written language, make haste to enshrine their most intimate thoughts within it ; but the wisdom of the Vedas and Upanishads and the national religious traditions of the Aryans were always held to be too sacred to be materialised in any form, either in the written word or in the technic arts. If the intellectual aristocracy of the Aryan tribes refrained from committing their thoughts of the Divinity to writing, and strictly observed the Mosaic law, "Thou shalt not make to thyself any graven image or likeness of anything which is in heaven or earth," it was certainly on account of the peculiar conditions in which they found themselves placed, and because they stood on a much higher spiritual plane than the races by which they were surrounded, and not from any lack of artistic genius. The proud Aryan had no missionary zeal : the fear of intellectual and spiritual contamination made him exclusive. His religion was for the chosen people, for his tribe and his family ; but, above all, for his own Self, when alone in the forest, on the hill-top, or in the privacy of an inner room in the house, his soul could commune in secret with God.

The poet-priests and chieftains who composed the Vedic hymns and expressed their communings with the Nature-spirits in such beautiful imagery, were great artists who gave to India monuments more durable than bronze ; and already in this Vedic period, centuries before Hellenic culture began to exert its influence upon Asia, India had conceived the whole philosophy of her art. It was the Vedic poets who first proclaimed the identity of the soul of man with the soul of Nature, and laid claim to direct inspiration from God. Vâc, the Divine Word, they said, took possession of the *rishis*, entered into the poet's mind, and made him one with the Universal Self.

This idea of the artist identifying himself with Nature in all her moods is really the keynote of all Asiatic art, poetry, and music. The whole theory of the sacrificial rites expounded in the Brâhmanas is based upon the assumed identity of the elements of the rite with the elements of the universe. The syllables of the Mantras recited by the priests represented the seasons ; the details of the sacrificial hearth represented the organs of the human body ; the number of the oblations represented the months of the year, and so on. The object of the sacrifices was to bring the sacrificer into direct touch with the Nature-spirits.   The *devas* themselves came down from heaven to take part in the sacrificial feast, seating themselves upon the sacred kusha grass.   "Formerly men saw them when they came to the feast ; to-day they still are present, but invisible."   On the other hand, the correct recitation of appropriate hymns transported the soul of the sacrificer to the abode of the gods, just as a boat might carry him over the sea.

From these ideas we can easily understand why the religious teachers and intellectual aristocracy of the early Aryans needed few concrete images, or symbols, to help them to realise the nature of the Divinity.   When they saw the *devas* themselves sitting at the feast, and when men could transport themselves at will to the abode of the Shining Ones, what need had they of gods of wood or stone ?   The *rishis* declared : "The vulgar look for their gods in water ; men of wider knowledge in celestial bodies ; the ignorant in wood, bricks, or stones : but the wisest men in the Universal Self."

The Vedic period in India, though it produced no immediate development in what we are accustomed to call the fine arts, must nevertheless be regarded as an age of wonderful artistic richness.   The transcendentalism of Vedic thought which could satisfy the intense reverence of the Aryan race for the beauty they felt in nature with vivid mental images of the Nature-spirits is the opposite pole to the barbaric materialism of the present day, which is the negation of all art, and very different from the narrow view of Puritanism, which makes the sense of beauty a snare of the Evil One.

Nor was the Vedic period entirely barren of art in material form.[1]   The elaborate rites of the Brâhmanas called forth the highest skill of the decorative craftsman.   In the description given in the Râmâyana of the great sacrifice prepared by Vasishtha equal honour was accorded to the skilled craftsmen,"all those who wrought in stone and wood," who made the preparations, and to the priests who performed the rites ; and the priests themselves wrought the gilded posts to which the victims were bound, and which marked out the sacrificial area :

> And now the appointed time came near
> The sacrificial posts to rear.
> They brought them, and prepared to fix
> Of Bel and Khadir six and six ;
> Six made of the Palásá-tree,
> Of Fig-tree one, apart to be ;
> Of Sheshmát and of Devadár
> One column each, the mightiest far :
> So thick the two that arms of man
> Their ample girth would fail to span
> All these with utmost care were wrought
> By hands of priests in scripture taught,
> And all with gold were gilded bright,
> To add new splendour to the rite :
> Twenty and one those stakes in all,
> Each one-and-twenty cubits tall ;
> And one-and-twenty ribbons there
> Hung on the pillars, bright and fair.

[1] No art objects that can be definitely assigned to the Vedic period have yet been discovered.   The gold repousse plaque of Prithvi found at Lauriya-Nandangarh and once thought to belong to the Vedic period is actually much later. Nevertheless the importance of the Vedas for a proper understanding of Indian art can no longer be denied.   The Buddhist art of the first three centuries before the Christian era, for example, makes use of a well developed iconographic symbolism in the exposition of what it has to say and Coomaraswamy has convincingly shown the origins of such well-known Buddhist symbols as the Dharmachakra, the earth-lotus and the Tree of Life actually to be in Vedic literature. For a brilliant exposition of this point of view see his *A New Approach to the Vedas*, London, 1933, and *Elements of Buddhist Iconography*, Cambridge, Mass., 1935.—P.C.

Firm in the earth they stood at last,
Where cunning craftsmen fixed them fast
And then unshaken each remained,
Octagonal and smoothly planed.
The ribbons over all were hung,
The flowers and scent around them flung ;
Thus decked, they cast a glory forth
Like the great saints who star the north.[1]

The carved posts were the models on which the elaborately ornamented pillars and pilasters of the later Hindu temples were designed.   The lamps of the Fire-spirit, Agni, and the libation vessels for the *amrita* of immortality, the soma juice, gave the types which are used even now in the temple services of Nepal, Travancore, and other parts of India where Hindu art-traditions are still alive.   But the visions of the Vedic seers only materialised to the wonderful sculpture and painting of the great period of Indian art, before the Muhammadan invasion—that is, from the fourth to the tenth centuries A.D.—when Vedic literature was first committed to writing.

Though the Vedic period may seem to Europeans so barren in artistic creation, it is of supreme consequence for the understanding of Indian art.   For throughout all the many and varied aspects of Indian art—Buddhist, Jain, Hindu, Sikh, and even Saracenic—there runs a golden thread of Vedic thought, binding them together in spite of all their ritualistic and dogmatic differences.   Even now, on the ghats of Benares, all Indian men, women, and children, forgetting for once sectarian and racial differences, daily join together in worship of the One God, in similar rites to those which the Aryan people used in the same spot three thousand years ago.   There we may see, if we have eyes to see, that all India is one in spirit, however diverse in race and in creed.

It is rather difficult for Europeans, bearing in mind the religious history of Europe, to understand that sectarian differences have never had quite the same significance in India as that which commonly obtains in Europe.   It would hardly occur to an Indian who is a devotee of Vishnu to believe that his neighbour, who worships Siva, is on that account a heretic and doomed to everlasting perdition.   Vishnu is to him that aspect of the One Supreme which is most favourable for himself, his family, his caste, or his race : therefore for his worldly and spiritual advantage he will concentrate his thoughts upon that aspect.   Vishnu for him becomes also Siva, Brahmâ, and Parameshwar—the Lord of All ; but he will not quarrel with his neighbour because he wishes to ascribe all the powers of the Supreme Deity to Siva, on any other aspect of the One.

Sectarian disputes, culminating in bloodshed, rapine and torture, there have been in India times enough ; but their origin has been more often connected with rights of property, political jealousies, or racial animosities than with differences of religious dogma. The description given by Chinese travellers of the fifth and seventh centuries A.D., of crowds of Indian devotees of different sects meeting together in the same place, and of Indian universities attended by scores of professors representing as many different schools of philosophy and religion is illustrative of the tolerance of Indian thought in matters of belief.   India has always taught that Truth is absolute, but there are many ways of realising it.

---

[1] R. T. H. Griffith's translation.

A. Lovers' Quarrel. Kishangarh, late 18th century A.D. (*Prince of Wales Museum, Bombay*).

B. Radha and Krishna in woodland scenery, Kangra, late 18th century A.D. (*Prince of Wales Museum, Bombay*).

PLATE 81

A, B. Seals from Mohenjodaro, C. 3000 B.C. (*Prince of Wales Museum, Bombay*).

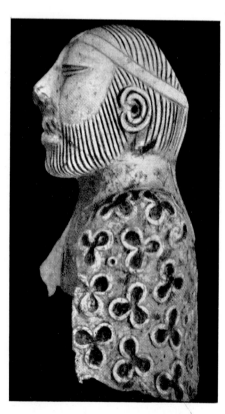

C. Seal with Unicorn and Indus Valley script from Lothal.
(*Copyright,Department of Archaeology, Government of India*).

D. Figure of bearded priest, from
Mohenjodaro.

PLATE 82

B. Yakshi from Didarganj, Patna.
(*Patna Museum*).

A. The Bharhut Rail. Inner view of the East Gateway.
(*From a photograph in the India Office Library*).

PLATE 83

A.   Avalokitēshvara.   (*From a statue at Bōrōbūdur, Indonesia*).

B.   Vishnu on Seṣha.   Ceiling slab from a temple at Aihole.   C. 7th century A.D.   (*Prince of Wales Museum, Bombay*).

PLATE 84

THE ECLECTIC, OR TRANSITION PERIOD

THE spirituality of the Vedic age was gradually obscured, for a time at least, by the complicated ritualism of the Brahman priesthood, and it was the teaching of Buddha which gave the next great impulse to the development of Indian art, widening the intellectual outlook and correlating the abstract ideas and spiritual vision of the Vedic age with human conduct and the realities of life.

But though Buddhism became the state religion and the dominant creed of the masses at this period, the term "early Buddhist art," which archæologists apply to it, does not convey a complete idea of all the influences which were then moulding Indian art. I would prefer to call it the Eclectic, or Transition period ; for it was the time when India was collecting from every quarter of Asia the different materials out of which, in later times, the perfect synthesis of Indian art was formulated, and through which the visions of the Vedic age materialised in the technic arts of the great Buddhist-Hindu epoch.[1]

This Eclectic, or Transition period is the one which has hitherto been treated by archæologists as the starting-point of Indian art : a cardinal error which is due, in the first instance, to the modern scientific method of specialisation, whereby art is treated, not as the full and complete expression of all æsthetic ideas contained in poetry, music, painting, sculpture, architecture, and the other technic arts, but as a series of disconnected compartments, each one regulated by different rules and principles. And, secondly, to neglect of the fundamental principle upon which all art-history must be based, that as art is primarily subjective and not objective, we must always seek for the origin of the great art-schools of the world, not in existing monuments and masterpieces or in the fragmentary collections of painting and sculpture in museums, but in the thoughts which created them all. The Vedic period is all-important for the historian, because, except for a very brief period of its history, the Vedic impulse is behind all Indian art.[2]

[1] The influence of Iran and West Asia on Indian art is well-known, but no detailed study of this problem in its various aspects has yet appeared. Works of art belonging to the Harappan culture owe a certain amount to ancient Mesopotamian forms and Heinrich Zimmer (*Art of Indian Asia*, New York, 1955, pp. 42-67) has traced the parallelism between India and Mesopotamia with regard to certain basic iconographic conceptions such as gods standing on their animal vehicles, "the Heaven-bird and the Earth-serpent," the close association of the serpent and saviour, etc. In the historic period beginning with the Mauryan age we also get definitely West Asian and Iranian features in Indian art. The Mauryan palace excavated at Patna follows the pillared arrangements of the Achaemenid palace at Persepolis. The lotiform bell-capital, its combination with addorsed heraldic animals, the stiff posing of the celebrated lions on the Sarnath pillar (Plate 23B), the close imitation of the Persepolitan order of capital by the Pataliputra capital in the Patna Museum to name a few, are all of ancient Oriental origins and survive up to a comparatively late period in Indian art.

As regards the *stupa* of Bharhut, which is not Asokan but belongs to the 2nd century B.C. as has been pointed out earlier, see an interesting article by C. L. Fabri, "Mesopotamia and Early Indian Art : Comparisons, *Etudes d' orientalisme*, Vol. I, Paris 1932, where the Mesopotamian influence on the *stupa* of Bharhut has sought to be estimated. A word of caution is to be uttered here, for it must be remembered that both Mesopotamian and Indian forms, instead of borrowing from each other, might be borrowing from another common source of which we may or may not have sufficient knowledge.—P.C.

[2] Since Havell wrote, the starting point of Indian art has been pushed back to the third millennium B.C. by the discovery of the Indus Valley Civilization remains, first at Harappa and Mohenjo-daro and subsequently at other sites, notably those in Saurashtra, at Rupar and finally at Lothal, near Ahmedabad in Gujarat, which has yielded important antiquities including the well-known seals (Plate 82A, B and C). For an understanding of this extremely important phase of Indian culture see John Marshall, *Mohenjo-daro and the Indus Civilization*, 2 vols., London 1931 ; E. J. H. Mackay, *Further Excavations at Mohenjo-daro*, 2 vols., Delhi, 1940. Two recent and very readable accounts are Stuart Piggott,

Except in the case of Saracenic art, it is not often realised what an important influence in the development of art, especially Asiatic, has always been the strong religious prejudice—which was as supreme in the Vedic period as it was in the Reformation in England —against the use of graven images or pictures in sacerdotal ritual.   And the art-historian is too apt to assume that, so long as painting and sculpture thus remain under the ban of religion, the fine arts are non-existent and the artistic faculties are undeveloped.   But this is by no means always the case, for thought cannot be suppressed by priestly interdict, and art will find its way notwithstanding.   It is a profound mistake to regard the Indian Aryans as an uncreative or inartistic race ; for it was Aryan philosophy, which makes all India one to-day, that synthesised all the foreign influences which every invader brought from outside and moulded them to its own ideals.

Throughout all the Vedic period the *devas* came down and sat at the feast, though they were only seen by spiritual vision, and did not reveal themselves to the vulgar.   And

Prehistoric India, Harmondsworth, 1959 and Mortimer Wheeler, *The Indus Civilization*, Cambridge, 1953. Brief accounts of the work at Rupar and Lothal are contained in Y. D. Sharma, "Past Patterns of Living as Unfolded at Rupar," *Lalit Kala*, Nos. 1- 2 and S. R. Rao, "Excavations at Lothal," *Lalit Kala*, Nos. 3-4.

Amongst the numerous antiquities unearthed, the large number of seals (Plate 82A, B, and C) carved with figures of men and animals are extremely important for an appreciation of the great contribution of the Indus civilization to art. They are small objects, on the average less than $2\frac{1}{2}$″ square, and consist of stone pieces that have been cut with a saw and finished with a knife and an abrasive.   The carving, which is a kind of sculpture in negative relief, very much as the cave temples of Western India are architecture in negative relief, was done with a small chisel and drill.   The stone was subsequently coated with an alkali and heated, this resulting in a white lustrous surface which has been commonly mistaken for steatite slip (Wheeler, *Indus Civilization*, p. 76).   A wide range of animals, real and mythical, are represented and these include the short-horned bull, the humped bull with heavy dewlap, rhinoceros, tiger, elephant and antelope.   There is also an ox-like creature with a single long horn, referred to by archaeologists as a "unicorn." The more strictly mythical animals are usually composite creatures, and one of the most interesting "has the face of a man, the trunk and tusks of an elephant, the horns of a bull, the forepart of a ram, and the hind quarters of a tiger with an erect tail," while another has a single body with six heads of different animals.   Amongst the human or divine figures represented on seals, the most interesting no doubt is the image of a god, sometimes shown with three faces, seated cross-legged in yoga posture and surrounded by various kinds of animals.   He is considered by Marshall to be the prototype of Siva Pasupati, the lord of beasts.

The style of work has received universal praise, and the artist shows a remarkable power of capturing the essence of form. "At their best," according to Wheeler, "it would be no exaggeration to describe them as little masterpieces of controlled realism, with a monumental strength in one sense out of all proportion to their size, and in another entirely related to it."   What is even more remarkable, is that even at this remote period, the basic forms that were to determine the course of Indian sculpture throughout its history had already been formulated, the mature modelling of the bull carved in the seals finding a direct echo in the Asokan bull sculptured atop the Rampurva pillar over two thousand years later.

This forestalling of the basic concepts of the Indian form is also to be seen in the marvellous torso of red sandstone from Harappa with gently protuberant belly, and reminiscent of the Lohanipur torso of the Mauryan period as well as the modelling of the colossal Yakshas of the post-Mauryan period.   The plastic qualities are so remarkably alike that several authors have doubted the early dating of the statuette.   A close study of the available evidence, however, leave no doubt as to its great antiquity.   The sculptor capable of capturing in such masterly fashion the animal forms depicted in the seals was certainly not incapable of treating the human form with the same mature ease, and the technique itself, involving separately affixed heads, and plaster inlay, recalls similar techniques in pre-historic Western Asia. "The sum of evidence, therefore, suggests that naturalistic human sculpture which even foreshadows later Indian civilization and was essentially Indian."   (Piggott, *Prehistoric India*, p. 187).   The dancing figure of grey limestone, also from Harappa, probably ithyphallic, and with separately affixed head now lost visualises another typical rendering of form in Indian art in which "facets and striations" are given emphasis rather than the ripe and smooth rendering of mass.

The bust of a bearded man with a trefoil-patterned robe (Plate 82D) which is worn over the left shoulder lacks the maturity and excellence of the Harappan torsos, but is nevertheless an important produce of the art tradition of the Indus Valley civilization.   The large eyes, which were once inlaid with shell, have compelling power, and the air of calm majesty is unmistakable.   The trefoil pattern of the robe was originally inlaid with a red paste, and socket meant to hold a metal collar, probably of gold, survive at the base of the hair.   It has been often suggested that this might be the idealised portrait of a god or a priest-king, a possibility supported by Wheeler in view of the astral symbolism with the trefoil pattern in Ancient Egypt and Mesopotamia.

The most delightful work of art from the Indus Valley, however, is not in stone but in bronze.   The Dancing Girl from Mohenjo-daro, with right hand laid on the hip, the left hand, weighed down with bangles, resting above the knee, and sensitively done head is marked by a wiry tenseness achieved by a marked attention to the human body.—P.C.

with art it is always so. We may lavish untold wealth in filling museums and galleries with the masterpieces of the world ; but to the gaping crowd the *devas*, though present, always remain unseen.

Though Buddha denied the authority of the Vedas, he was himself a Hindu of the Hindus : and it was the philosophy of the Upanishads, systematised in the philosophical schools, which eventually dominated Buddhist art and made Buddhism a world-religion. But in the first part of the Eclectic period the prevailing influence is not the idealism of Aryan thought, but the naturalism of the non-Aryan races which were converted to Buddhism.

Asoka, the Constantine of India, raised the technic arts employed by Brahmanical ritualism on to a higher intellectual plane, and made the fine arts a potent instrument in national education, and in his propaganda of the Buddhist faith, which extended to many different parts of Asia. In the Vedic age the practice of the fine arts seems never to have been a priestly vocation, and the non-Aryan tribes probably supplied Asoka with the most skilful sculptors and painters. The members of the Buddhist Sangha were often skilled artists, and wherever the Buddhist missionaries went they took with them pictures and images to assist in expounding the sacred doctrines.

In early Buddhist art, as we know it from the sculptures of Bharhut, Sânchî, and Amarâvatî, we can recognise two distinct groups of racial elements. One represents the vigorous if somewhat undeveloped indigenous Indian tradition doubtless belonging to the non-Aryan tribes, which, now released from the domination of the Brahman priesthood, took a prominent part in developing a great national religious art.

But in this group must be included an influence originating in Central and Eastern Asia doubtless brought by the tribes of the Sakas, Yuëh-chi and others which were then pouring into India over the north-west frontier. The other element, a less conspicuous one was an importation from Western Asia of the more polished and refined arts of the Persian school, then under Hellenic influence.

The *stûpa* of Bharhut, Plate 83A, with its pilgrim's procession-path enclosed by a sculptured rail, belongs to about the third century B.C.,[1] and is one of the earliest known existing examples of Indian art. It was one of the numerous monuments erected by the Buddhist Emperor Asoka, either to contain relics of Buddha or to mark the sacred places hallowed by his memory. The symbolism of the earlier sun and nature worship which survived in the Buddhist ritual is conspicuously shown in the plan of the *stûpa*,[2] with its circular rail divided by the four entrances at east, west, north, and south ; in the sculptures of the Lokapâlas—the genii defending the approaches to the earth—which flank the gateways, in the lions carved on the columns, and in the great open lotus-flowers which decorate the rail, both of which are emblems of the rising sun. The *stûpa* itself, in its hemispherical dome simulated the blue overarching vault of the heavens ; the tee, or pinnacle of stone umbrellas which crowned the summit representing the succession of higher spiritual planes leading up to Nirvana.

That Asoka made use of foreign craftsmen to assist in carrying out his colossal architectural enterprises is evident from the purely Persepolitan design of the clustered columns which flank the entrances, and from various details in the carving of the rail.[3] At the same time the sculptures bear witness to the existence, at this early period, of a characteristically Indian artistic tradition, far more virile, robust, and spontaneous than the later eclectic school of Gandhara—a fact which is almost sufficient in itself to prove the fallacy of the archæological theory regarding the predominance of Hellenic inspiration in Indian

[1] For a discussion of the date of Bharhut see foot note, p. 38.—P.C.

[2] For symbolism of the *stupa* see foot note, p. 46.—P.C.

[3] The indigenous artistic tradition in the period of Asoka is marked not by the *stupa* of Bharhut but by the magnificent image of the Didarganj Yakshi now in the Patna Museum and also the superb figure of a bull atop the Rampurva pillar and other fragmentary sculptures.—P.C.

art. Such a development as we find in Asokan art could only have been reached in the course of many centuries, but as nearly all Indian sculpture previous to the Buddhist epoch was in wood, or other impermanent materials, very few traces of its previous history have yet been discovered. Both the forms of construction and the technique of the Bharhut rail are frankly imitations of wooden prototypes.

There can be little doubt that further archæological investigations will, sooner or later, reveal some of the lost vestiges of early Indian art. Hitherto archæological excavations in India have been little more than a scraping of the superficial layers. When the sandy deserts of Rajputana and the lower strata of the alluvial deposits of the Indus and the Ganges, and other sacred rivers, are explored as scientifically and systematically as the sand of Egypt and the soil of Crete we may learn a great deal more of the indigenous Indian art which preceded the Asokan period.

In the treatment of the human form Asokan sculpture exhibits none of the idealistic tendency which is the distinguishing mark of Indian art when it became more thoroughly permeated by the philosophy of the Upanishads. The person of Buddha as a divine being was as yet excluded from plastic or pictorial representation. The Nature-spirits, such as the Lokapâlas, are treated with a naive, anthropomorphic realism, and the circular panels on the upright posts of the rail which alternate with the sun-emblems tell the story of the Buddha's pre-existences on earth in the same unaffected style of pious narration with which the legends of early Christianity are told in Western art.

The opening chapter of Indian plastic art which begins at Bharhut developed further in the Sânchî sculptures and concluded in the well-known Amarâvatî reliefs of about the third century A.D., now divided between the British, Calcutta, and Madras Museums. The latter, though marked by a higher degree of academic skill, are greatly lacking in the largeness and spontaneity of design which distinguish the sculptures of the earlier school. Much of the present misunderstanding and neglect of Indian art on the part of European critics is due to Fergusson's fatal error of judgment, followed by Sir George Birdwood, Mr. Vincent Smith, and other writers, in regarding the Amarâvatî sculptures as the culminating point of Indian sculpture. How far this is from the truth will, I think, be obvious to any artist who takes the trouble to investigate the subject for himself.

The predominant characteristic in all this early period of Indian art is a naive naturalism of an anecdotic type which runs through all Chinese art when it is not inspired by Indian idealism. Chinese influence reappears in Mogul art, but it was never more strongly felt in Indian art than it was in the time of Asoka. It is in naturalism, not in idealism, that the native, intuitive genius of the Eastern Asiatic races finds its true expression. Not until Indian philosophy and Indian religious thought penetrated into China did Chinese art take wings and soar into a higher spiritual atmosphere. But, except during those centuries when Mahâyâna Buddhism was supreme, the ideal gods of China, unlike those of India, are always of the earth, earthy. This is probably the reason why this aspect of Chinese art has always been better appreciated by Europeans than the Indian conception of divinity.

In Indian art, even in the Asokan period, a deep undercurrent of Vedic influence can be felt in the entire absence of any attempt to represent what was to a Buddhist the most sacred of all conceptions, the personality of the Blessed One himself. The numerous legends of his previous existences in the form of tree, or bird, or beast, or man; his begging-bowl, and the bodhi-tree under which he gained enlightenment, and even incidents in his earthly life as Prince Siddhartha, all come within the scope of the Asokan artists' descriptive skill; but they never ventured to portray with brush or chisel the person of Buddha, and it must have been a rude shock to pious Buddhists of the old school when, towards the end of the Transition period, the Græco-Bactrian sculptors of Gandhara, employed by the Kushan king, Kanishka, began to represent the Tathâgata as a trim, smug-faced Greek Apollo, posing in the attitude of an Indian yogi.

The importance of the Gandharan school in the evolution of Indian artistic ideals has been immensely exaggerated by writers obsessed with the idea that everything Greek must be superior to everything Indian. Gandharan art is decadent and lifeless, in so far as it is Greek or Roman ; the more it becomes Indian, the more it becomes alive. To regard the Gandharan school of sculpture as furnishing the model on which the Indian divine ideal was founded is to misapprehend entirely the philosophical basis and historical development of Indian art. Gandharan sculpture is not a starting-point but a late incident in the Eclectic or Transition period, which, excepting a few distinctive technical characteristics, left no permanent impression, and had no influence in shaping Indian ideals.[1]

---

[1] The position of the Gandharan school is discussed in greater detail in Part I, "Indian Sculpture and Painting," by the author.

CHAPTER III

THE UNIVERSITIES OF NORTHERN INDIA AND THEIR INFLUENCE ON ASIATIC ART

IT was about the beginning of the Christian era that the great universities of Northern India, in which the many schools of philosophy were combined with schools of painting and sculpture, taking the raw materials provided by the indigenous and foreign non-Aryan technical tradition, the Persepolitan tradition, and the Græco-Roman, or Gandharan tradition, and, moulding them into one, provided Asiatic art once and for ever with a philosophical basis and created the Indian divine ideal in art. This new artistic development was, in fact, the flowering of the ancient Vedic impulse, the teaching of the Upanishads systematised by the philosophical schools and applied to human life and work.

The opposition of Western materialism to the philosophy of the East always makes it difficult for Europeans to approach Indian art with anything like unprejudiced minds. The whole of modern European academic art-teaching has been based upon the unphilosophical theory that beauty is a quality which is inherent in certain aspects of matter or form, a quality first fully apprehended in the ancient world by the Greeks, and afterwards rediscovered by the artists of the Italian Renaissance.

Just as the Greeks are said to have arrived at their ideal of human and divine beauty by a process of selection between different types of men and women, so we make art a system of discrimination, or differentiation, between what we call beautiful things and ugly things. It is the common complaint of artists that modern dress and modern life are so ugly that they cannot make use of them : so art becomes an archæological cult, having no hold upon popular imagination, for it is cut off from real life and work, and its limits are artificially restricted to a narrow department of ideas into which the world of every-day life does not enter.

Indian thought takes a much wider, a more profound and comprehensive view of art. The Indian artist has the whole creation and every aspect of it for his field ; not merely a limited section of it, mapped out by academic professors. Beauty, says the Indian philosopher, is subjective, not objective. It is not inherent in form or matter ; it belongs only to spirit, and can only be apprehended by spiritual vision. There is no beauty in a tree, or flower, or in man or woman, as such. All are perfectly fitted to fulfil their part in the cosmos ; yet the beauty does not lie in the fitness itself, but in the divine idea which is impressed upon those human minds which are tuned to receive it. The more perfectly our minds are tuned to this divine harmony the more clearly do we perceive the beauty, and the more capable we become, as artists, of revealing it to others. Beauty belongs to the human mind ; there is neither ugliness nor beauty in matter alone, and for an art-student to devote himself wholly to studying form and matter with their idea of extracting beauty therefrom, is as vain as cutting open a drum to see where the sound comes from.

The true aim of the artist is not to extract beauty from nature, but to reveal the Life within life, the Noumenon within phenomenon, the Reality within unreality, and the Soul within matter. When that is revealed, beauty reveals itself. So all nature is beautiful for us, if only we can realise the Divine Idea within it. There is nothing common or unclean in what God has made, but we can only make life beautiful for ourselves by the power of the spirit that is within us. Therefore it is, as the sage Sukracharya says, that, in making images of the gods, the artist should depend upon spiritual vision only, and not upon the appearance of objects perceived by human senses.

To cultivate this faculty of spiritual vision, the powers of intuitive perception, which, until recently, have been regarded in the West as beyond the scope of educational methods, was therefore the main endeavour of the Indian artist in the golden age of Indian art and literature when Buddhism was transformed by the philosophical schools from a simple code of ethics into a world-religion ; when the immortal Hindu epics, the Râmâyana and the Mahâbhârata, were moulded into their present form ; when the poet Kalidâsa sang at the court of King Vikrama ; and when the sculptors of Elephanta and Ellora hewed out of stupendous masses of living rock their visions of the gods throned in their Himalayan paradise. And if you would inquire what this art means for us I would ask you to consider the whole art of medieval Europe, the great Gothic cathedrals, the sculpture of Chartres and Rheims, and the painting of Italy from Cimabue to Fra Angelico, and see for yourselves an art proceeding from the same inspiration and founded upon the same philosophy.

Throughout Indian art, and throughout the Christian art of the Middle Ages, we find the same central idea—that beauty is inherent in spirit, not in matter.[1] So when, at last, Indian artists of Aryan descent, in the early centuries of the Christian era, reconciled themselves to the idea of representing in material form the actual presence of the gods, they rejected the Hellenic type of gods fashioned entirely after human models, and shaped their ideal of divine form upon the ancient artistic type of an Indian hero, the superman. This was the ideal of physical perfection in human form in early Asiatic art in Egypt and in Crete ; and the symbolism it conveyed had its influence in Greek art also, until the naturalism of Praxiteles and the later schools of sculptors and painters superseded the idealism on which Hellenic art was originally based.

The Mahâbhârata tells us what this ideal of the superman was. It was the type of a mighty hunter who, in desperate conflicts with the king of beasts, had become invincible and had acquired a lion-like body, with broad chest and shoulders, long, massive arms, a thick neck, and a very slim or wasp-waist.

In the description given in the Mahâbhârata of the grand festival held in honour of Brahmâ at the Court of King Virâta it is said :

"Athletes came to witness it in thousands, like hosts of celestials to the abode of Brahmâ, or of Siva. And they were endowed with huge bodies of great prowess, like the demons called Kâlakhanyas. And, elated by their prowess and proud of their strength, they were highly honoured by the king. And their shoulders and waists and necks were like those of lions, and their bodies were very clean, and their hearts were quite at ease."[2]

Karna, the Kuru hero, is similarly described as "resembling a lion in the formation of his body. He is eight *ratnis* in stature. His arms are large, his chest is broad ; he is invincible."

One of the earliest artistic representations of this ideal is seen in the extraordinary paintings and sculptures lately unearthed by Dr. Evans in Crete. The Minoan dandies of about 3000 B.C. are here shown as actually practising tight lacing in the feminine fashion of modern Europe, pinching in their waists to a horrifying degree, apparently with the intention of making their bodies assume this ideal, lion-like form. In Egyptian sculpture and painting the same ideal type of a warrior and hunter constantly appears, though without the unpleasant deformity of Minoan art. The slim waist is also, as I have said, the characteristic of the most virile period of Greek sculpture, and even Aristophanes alludes to a wasp-waisted man as a type of physical fitness.[3]

The Mahâbhârata seems more modern in applying a similar epithet to a woman :

---

[1] Or in other words, the work of art should cater pre-eminently to the needs of the soul rather than to those of the body, though the greatest art fulfills the needs of the soul and the body at the same time. See A. K. Coomaraswamy, "Christian and Oriental Philosophy of Art," *Why Exhibit Works of Art*, London, 1943, p. 31.—P.C.

[2] P. C. Roy's translation, vol. iv, p. 28.

[3] *Plut.* 558. I am indebted to Professor A. Drachman, of Copenhagen, for this reference.

"The far-famed daughter of King Matsya, adorned with a golden necklace, ever obedient to her brother, and having a waist slender as that of a wasp."[1]   Professor Burrows gives a reference to a Japanese poem of the eighth century A.D., in which an old man is singing of the days of his youth, when his waist was "as slim as any wasp that soareth."[2]   He also refers to Professor Petrie's quotations from classical writers which seem to show that the Goths, like the Minoans, practised tight lacing.

These are instances which show how the symbolism of art or religion often takes possession of the popular mind so deeply as to reduce a whole people to a state of intellectual and physical bondage to an abstract idea.   When humanity begins to grow weary of this servitude, there is a reaction in art marked by a return to naturalistic ideals, which is not always a true artistic renaissance, though, so far as it is a protest against the undue restraint of human nature by a morbid and unhealthy ritualism, it marks a step forward in the evolution of mankind.

But in this revolt against idealism there always seems to be a tendency to fall into a worse servitude of materialism and sensual depravity.   It may be that the science of the future, psychology, will find the way to reconcile this pair of opposites, and through the middle path lead art, both in the East and West, to a grander renaissance than that of Greece or Italy.

While the lion-like body became in Indian art the symbol of physical strength, another essential quality for success in the chase—fleetness of foot—was symbolised by legs like a deer, or gazelle, a characteristic which is very prominent in the figures of the Ajanta cave-paintings and in the Amarâvatî sculptures.   Again another attribute, ascribed as a mark of noble birth to the person of Buddha—the long arms—was borrowed from the ideal of a mighty hunter or warrior.   I believe that the origin of this idea is to be found in the fact that a great length of arm connotes a long sword-thrust and spear-thrust. In primitive times the long-armed man would have an advantage both in war and in the chase, so long arms became a symbol of the survival of the fittest, an attribute of nobility.

Now let us see how the sculptors and painters, working in the great philosophical schools of Northern India, about the beginning of the Christian era, employed this very ancient ideal form[3] to express the quality of the divine nature and the power of the spirit, instead of physical strength.   At that time the original Buddhist creed had been profoundly affected by the Yoga philosophy of Patañjali, and the teaching of Nâgârjuna had created the division between the Mahâyâna and Hînayâna doctrines ; but by both schools the Buddha was no longer regarded as a human personality, or superman, but as a divine being who, through a long cycle of many previous existences on earth, and by the power of Yoga, had not only attained to perfect wisdom and thrown off the bondage of the flesh, but had won dominion over the whole universe.

Yet as this Yoga was not the terrible self-torture of the Hindu ascetic, but the Yoga of a pure and holy life, the Master could never appear to pious Buddhist eyes with shrunken flesh, swollen veins, and protruding bones—a hideous living skeleton, as sometimes portrayed in Gandharan sculpture.   Even when, in his earlier efforts to obtain enlightenment, he had practised self-mortification for six long years—"vainly trying to attain merit, performing many rules of abstinence, hard for a man to carry out,"—still, the Buddhist poet declares, "the emaciation which was produced in his body by that asceticism became positive fatness through the splendour which invested him.   Though thin, yet with his glory unimpaired, he caused gladness to other eyes, as the autumnal moon in

---

[1] "Virata-parva," sect. xxxvii. p. 90.   P. C. Roy's translation.
[2] "The Discoveries in Crete," p. 172.
[3] The ideal proportions of the human body are adhered to through the greater period of Indian art, more particularly in the Gupta age.   It survives even in the school of Western Indian painting though in a grossly exaggerated form. See note, Part I, *Indian Sculpture and Painting*, p. 69.—P.C.

B. The Trimūrti (Mahesamūrti). A colossal sculpture at Elephanta.

A. The Churning of the Ocean. Part of a relief from the temple of Angkor,
Cambodia. (From a cast in the Trocadéro, Paris).

PLATE 85

C. Brahmā.
(From the original sculpture in the Ethnographic Museum, Leyden).

B. Vishnu-Varaha-Narasimha from Kashmir,
9th century A.D.

PLATE 86

A. Vishnu. *(From a colossal statue, Indonesia).*

A. Brahmā. Ceiling slab from a temple at Aihole. C. 7th century A.D. (*Prince of Wales Museum, Bombay*).

B. Nagaraja from Nalanda, 8th century A.D.
(*Photo, J. V. Mehta*).

C. Nagaraja from Mathura, C. 3rd century A.D.
(*Mathura Museum*).

PLATE 87

Siva as Natārāja.   A bronze in the Government Museum, Madras.
(*Photo Copyright by the Department of Archaeology, Government of India*).

PLATE 88

the beginning of her bright fortnight gladdens the lotuses. Having only skin and bone remaining, with his fat, flesh, and blood entirely wasted, yet, though diminished [in body] he still shone with undiminished grandeur like the ocean."[1]

And in that supreme hour, under the bodhi-tree at Gaya, when, as his full enlightenment was accomplished, Mâra, the wicked one, fled vanquished ; "the different regions of the sky grew clear, the moon shone forth, showers of flowers fell down from the sky upon the earth, and the night gleamed like a spotless maiden"—and at last the dawn flushed in the east, and all the *devas* thronged together, and the Buddhas from worlds innumerable :

> Kings at fierce war called truce ; the sick men leaped,
> Laughing, from beds of pain ; the dying smiled,
> As though they knew that happy morn was sprung
> From fountains farther than the utmost East.[2]

Then the great Yogi was reborn, and he appeared to mortal eyes as the Victor, the Hero, the Shining One, endowed with eternal youth and strength, filling the whole world with light.

To symbolise this spiritual rebirth, Indian artists moulded their divine ideal upon the race-tradition of a mighty warrior, with supple, rounded limbs, smooth, golden-coloured skin and a lion-like body, expressing the beauty of bodily purification, when the soul is freed from the grosser attachments of earth, and the spiritual strength which every human soul might gain by the Yoga of Service, by the Yoga of Knowledge, or by the Yoga of Faith.

The Mahâbhârata, in referring to the spiritual power to be acquired by Yoga, says : "He, O King, who, devoted to the practice of austerities, betaketh himself to Brahmacharya in its entirety, and thereby purifieth his body, is truly wise ; for by this he becometh as a child, free from all evil passions, and triumpheth over death at last." But it adds also that it was through the practice of Yoga that the heavenly musicians and dancers, the Gandharvas and Apsaras, acquired the marvellous physical beauty they possessed. And so in both Hindu and Buddhist artistic canons it is laid down that the forms of gods, who also, like human beings, acquired divine powers by ascetic practices, were nevertheless not to be represented like the human ascetic with bodies emaciated by hunger and thirst, bones protruding, and swollen veins, but with smooth skin, rounded limbs, the veins and bones always concealed, the neck and shoulders massive and strong, and the waist narrow, like the body of a lion.

It was by Yoga also—by spiritual insight or intuition—rather than by observation and analysis of physical form and facts, that the sculptor or painter must attain to the highest power of artistic expression. Indian art is not concerned with the conscious striving after beauty as a thing worthy to be sought after for its own sake : its main endeavour is always directed towards the realisation of an idea, reaching through the finite to the infinite, convinced always that, through the constant effort to express the spiritual origin of all earthly beauty, the human mind will take in more and more of the perfect beauty of divinity.

The whole spirit of Indian thought is symbolised in the conception of the Buddha sitting on his lotus-throne, calm, impassive, his thoughts freed from all worldly passions and desires, and with both mind and body raised above all intellectual and physical strife ; yet filled with more than human power, derived from perfect communion with the source of all truth, all knowledge, and all strength. It is the antithesis of the Western ideal of physical energy : it is the symbol of the power of the spirit, which comes not by wrestling,

---

[1] "Buddha-karita of Ashvagosha," book xii. pp. 94-6. Translated by E. B. Cowell.
[2] "The Light of Asia," by Sir E. Arnold, p. 178, Thirty-second Edition.

nor by intellectual striving, but by the gift of God, by prayer and meditation, by Yoga, union with the Universal Soul.

The Buddhist writings are always insisting upon the power of this supreme intelligence which sees "without obscurity and without passion"; and, to quote one of the most able exponents of Indian art in modern times, Dr. A. K. Coomaraswamy :"What, after all, is the secret of Indian greatness ? Not a dogma or a book, but the great open secret that all knowledge and all truth are absolute and infinite, waiting, not to be created, but to be found ; the secret of the infinite superiority of intuition, the method of direct perception over intellect, regarded as a mere organ of discrimination."

"There is about us a storehouse of the as-yet-unknown infinite and inexhaustible; but to this wisdom the way of access is not through intellectual activity. The intuition that reaches it we call imagination, or genius. It came to Sir Isaac Newton when he saw the apple fall, and there flashed across his brain the law of gravity. It came to the Buddha as he sat through the silent nights in meditation, and hour by hour all things became apparent to him : he knew the exact circumstances of all being that had ever been in the endless and infinite worlds ; at the twentieth hour he received the divine insight by which he saw all things within the space of the infinite *sakvalas* as clearly as if they were close at hand ; then came still deeper insight, and he perceived the cause of sorrow and the path of knowledge. "He reaches at last the exhaustless source of truth." The same is true of all "revelation" ; the Veda (*S'ruti*) ; the eternal *Logos*, "breathed forth by Brahman," in whom it survives the destruction and creation of the universe, is "seen," or "heard," not made, by its human authors. . . 'The reality of such perception is witnessed by every man within himself upon rare occasions and on an infinitely smaller scale. It is at once the vision of the artist and the imagination of the natural philosopher."[1]

This conception of the Buddha reached its highest expression, in sculpture, in the magnificent statue at Anuradhapura,[2] which represents the Indian prototype of the Buddhist statues of China and Japan, as well as those of Java, though very few rise to quite the same height of spirituality. One of the exceptions is the beautiful statue of Avalokitêshvara (Plate 84A), "the Lord who looks down with pity on all men," from Bôrôbudûr, in Java, the great Buddhist temple the building of which began about the eighth century A.D. This sculpture, however, must be attributed to a later period, perhaps the tenth century. It may be compared with the equally fine Dhyâni-Buddha from the same place, illustrated in "Indian Sculpture and Painting."

According to the theogony of Mahâyâna Buddhism, the Supreme or Adi-Buddha, who corresponds to the Hindu conception of Ishvara, wished from the One to become Many, which desire is denominated Prajña, Divine Wisdom. Buddha and Prajña united were the Father and Mother of the universe. In the instant of conceiving this desire five divine beings, called the five Dhyâni-Buddhas—Vairochana, Akshobya, Ratna-sambava, Amitâbha, and Amogha-siddha—were produced. Each of these Dhyâni-Buddhas produced from himself another being, called a Dhyâni-Bodhisattva, who had each a practical part in the evolution and guardianship of the universe. The five Dhyâni-Bodhisattvas are Samanta-Bhadra ; Vajrapâni, the Buddhist Indra, distinguished by his thunderbolt, or *vajra* ; Ratnapâni ; Padmapâni, or Avalokitêshvara ; and Visvapâni.[3]

Avalokitêshvara corresponds to the Vaishnavaite conception of Vishnu as both Creator and Preserver (Plates 86A, and 103B).[4] He is adorned with similar symbolic ornaments, and on his tiara is a small figure of the Dhyâni-Buddha, Amitâbha, the Lord of Infinite Light, who, like Vishnu, is symbolised in the midday sun.

He is seated on his lotus-throne ; behind his head is an aureole shaped like the leaf of the

[1] "Aims of Indian Art," pp. 1 and 2.
[2] "Indian Sculpture and Painting," Plate 2B.
[3] Brian Hodgson, "Essays on the Languages, etc., of Nepal and Tibet," p. 42.
[4] See Marie Therese de Mallmann, *Introduction a l'etude du Avalokitesvara*, Paris, 1948.—P.C.

sacred pipal-tree.   The left hand assumes the symbolic gesture of *dharma-chakra-mudrâ* as he expounds one of the points of the divine law.   The open right hand signifies the bestowal of a gift (*varamudrâ*).   The lower limbs are released from the rigid "adamantine" pose of profound meditation assumed by Amitâbha, and the right leg, stretched out, rests in front of the throne on another lotus-flower which symbolises the universe created by the Divine Magician for his footstool.

This sculpture is distinguished by an exquisite purity of sentiment and a perfection of technique which is not excelled by any of the great works of Buddhist art in China and Japan ; but, above all, by that inspired feeling of divine grandeur and sense of high spiritual exaltation, beyond the range of human intellectuality, which animate all the best religious art of India.

It is precisely in that austere Himâlayan grandeur, in an almost indefinable sense of the sublime, where the more feminine and more realistic conceptions of China and Japan seem to belong to a lower spiritual plane than their Indian prototypes.   The divinities of the Farther East appear to dwell in an earthly paradise, a fair garden of peace planted in some quiet, sequestered valley, filled with delicately perfumed flowers, where it is always springtime.   The Indian Olympus affords no such sensuous delights : it is pinnacled among the highest Himâlayan solitudes, never trodden by human foot, often shrouded in mist and cloud, only seen sometimes from afar—as in a vision—in the rosy light of dawn, or when the last rays of the setting sun light up its furthest depths with burnished gold and show to our wondering gaze the gates of heaven.

The ritual of Mahâyâna Buddhism in Northern India, used to create in the mind of the devotee vivid mental images of the divinity invoked, throws much light on Indian religious art and the methods of the artist.   M. Foucher, in his valuable "Étude sur l'Iconographie Bouddhique de l'Inde," gives extracts from various Tantric manuscripts of the twelfth century relating to this subject.   Though, as in other religions, such formularies may become a means of self-deception and be used as a cloak for superstition and sacerdotal charlatanism, they nevertheless reflect the devotional spirit of true religious art ; they embody principles common to the whole art of Asia even in the present day, and explain the practice of Indian Yoga, as applied to æsthetics, from the earliest times.

The yogin, devotee, artist, or "magician" (in Indian thought the Creator is the Mahâ-yogi and all creative art is "magic") having purified his physical body by ablutions, and put on clean garments, repaired to a solitary place appropriate for the motive he had in his mind.   If the benign powers of nature were to be invoked, he would choose the forest shade, or the bank of a holy river ; but if the *tamasik*, or destructive powers, then he must seek a place of gloom and dread, such as a cremation ground, or cemetery.   There, seating himself on a purified spot, he invokes the hosts of Buddhas and Boddhisattvas into the space in front of him and offers them flowers and perfumes, real or imaginary.

Then he commences to recite the "Sevenfold Office"—the confession of his sins ; an expression of joyous sympathy for the merit of others ; belief in the Three Jewels of the Buddhist faith, Buddha, the Doctrine, and the Community ; a resolution to persevere in the good way ; a prayer to all the Blessed Ones that they will continue to preach the doctrine, and further consent, for the world's good, to forego for a time the right they have earned to enter into Nirvana ; and, finally, the dedication of all the merit he himself acquires to the universal welfare of humanity.

This preliminary ritual, like that which now precedes the Brahmin's daily *sandhya*, is by way of spiritual purification, to prepare the mind for the meditative exercises which follow.   He must now realise by thought the four infinite qualities, or perfect states, which are love for all, compassion for the miserable, joy in the happiness of others, and even mindedness.   The next two meditations, leading up to the final ecstasy, are on the original purity of the first principles of all things, and, as a corollary, on their emptiness or absolute non-existence.   "By the fire of the idea of emptiness," says the text, "the five elements of individual consciousness are destroyed beyond recovery." The identity of the yogin being thus completely merged with that of the divinity invoked, he has but to utter the appropriate mystic syllable which contains the "germ" of the divinity, to make the proper gesture, or *mudrâ*, and to recite the correct *mantra*, to realise his desire. The apparition of the god or goddess presents itself to his mental vision, "like a reflection in a mirror," or "as in a dream."[1]

Mutatis mutandis, this might be a description of the ecstasy of an artist monk in medieval Europe. But whereas the Western mystic seems to have allowed himself to be carried away, more or less unconsciously, by an unbalanced and uncontrolled access of emotionalism, the practice of Yoga in India, recognised as a branch of philosophy, was from the earliest times reduced to a scientific system.

Underneath the mysticism of the Indian yogin's ritual there are scientific psychological principles, fundamental to oriental idealism, the due recognition of which might greatly benefit art-education in the West. The first principle insisted upon is the influence of environment upon the temperament or mood of the artist. Next, that the faculty of artistic imagination, by which thought-forms are created, is as much susceptible to development by methodic mental practice and training as are the executive technical powers by which they become materialised in forms of art. Thirdly, the necessity for the artist to identify himself absolutely with his subject, or to merge his own consciousness in that aspect of nature which he wishes to interpret.

Shelley, in his "Ode to the West Wind," expresses perfectly the whole idea of Yoga in art :

Make me thy lyre, ev'n as the forest is.
What if my leaves are falling as its own ?
The tumult of thy mighty harmonies
Will take from both a deep autumnal tone,
Sweet though in sadness. Be thou, Spirit fierce,
My spirit ! be thou me, impetuous One !
Drive my dead thoughts over the universe
Like withered leaves to quicken a new birth ;
And by the incantation of this verse,
Scatter, as from an unextinguished hearth,
Ashes and sparks, my words among mankind !

Art thus becomes less the pursuit of beauty than an attempt to realise the life which is without and beyond by the life which is within us—life in all its fulness and mystery, which is, and was, and is to come.

It is hardly possible for a Western artist to appreciate the psychology and practice of oriental art without knowing that the practice of Yoga was combined with a most elaborate and scientific mnemonic system, by means of which the whole of Sanskrit literature was handed down from one generation to another, from the Vedic period until medieval times, without being committed to writing in any form. Probably the severely mechanical kind of mental exercise which this entailed was considered a necessary intellectual complement to the psychic training of Yoga. However this may be, the whole practice of the Indian, Chinese, and Japanese schools of painting and sculpture was based upon methods derived from this mnemonic and psychic training, as given in the Universities of Northern India ; and here the West has much to learn from the East, for the essential faculties of the artist, imagination and memory, are those which are least considered in the curriculum of modern European academies, where the paraphernalia of the studio are used to make up for the deficiencies in the mental equipment of the student.

The West, surfeited with the materialism of the Renaissance, is already slowly turning

[1] See "Etude sur l'Iconographie Bouddhique de l'Inde," par A. Foucher, Part II, Introduction, pp. 8-11.

again to the East for spiritual instruction.   The East, reawakening, is becoming conscious of the truth of her inspiration, and at the same time is learning, from contact with Western civilisation, the causes of her own decadence.

The supreme importance of the great Universities of Northern India in their influence upon the development of the whole art of Asia is not yet understood by the few English writers who have studied Chinese and Japanese art, especially by those who have never visited the East.   Mr. Laurence Binyon, in his admirable and otherwise well-informed book, "Painting in the Far East," commits himself to the following statement, which is also very typical of Anglo-Indian opinion :

"It would be natural, in lack of evidence, to suppose that India, which gave to Asia the kindling ideals and imagery of Buddhism, was the land to which we should turn for the noblest creations of art.   Yet we are confronted at once by the fact that, in creative art, India is comparatively poor."

That this should represent enlightened critical opinion in the metropolis of the Empire in the year of grace 1909 will give future historians of British India much to reflect upon. Artistic Europe has been prevented from recognising the fulness of Indian creative genius by the peculiar attitude towards Indian art taken up by the administration of the principal European Museums.   This attitude is no longer maintained on the continent of Europe ; and in Paris, Berlin, and in the Dutch Museums the student can now realise to some extent the commanding influence of Indian thought in the evolution of all the great art of Asia, an influence which has been long recognised by the best Chinese and Japanese critics.

It is not only as centres for the propaganda of the Buddhist faith, but much more as schools of Hindu philosophy, that the influence of the Indian Universities was felt in China and Japan.   Mr. Binyon refers to a Chinese artist and writer of the sixth century A.D., who published a theory of æsthetic principles "which became a classic and received universal acceptance, expressing as it did the deeply rooted instincts of the race.   In this theory it is rhythm which holds a paramount place ; not, be it observed, imitation of nature, or fidelity to nature which the general instinct of Western races make the root concern of art.   In this theory every work of art is thought of as an incarnation of the genius of rhythm, manifesting the living spirit of things with a clearer beauty and intenser power than the gross impediments of complex matter allow to be transmitted to our senses in the visible world around us.   A picture is conceived as a sort of apparition from a more real world of essential life. . . . The inner and informing spirit, not the outward semblance, is for all painters of the Asian tradition the object of art, the aim with which they wrestle."

What is this theory of æsthetic principles, with its psychic vision, or "apparition from a more real world of essential life," but the Chinese paraphrase, or adaptation to a secular *milieu*, of the Indian Buddhist religious ritual, which I have described above ?[1]

Mr. Binyon is evidently unaware that in this treatise the Chinese writer, whose thoughts were saturated with the mysticism of Mahâyâna Buddhism, is simply stating the basic principle of Indian art, a theory derived by Chinese artists from the Indian philosophical schools.   In the fifth century A.D., as Professor Hackmann remarks, commenced the great revival of Buddhism in China, and crowds of Chinese pilgrims and scholars began to flock to India, studying in the philosophical schools, where painting and sculpture were taught as a part of the Buddhist religion, and bringing back with them into China Buddhist pictures and images.   In the sixth century, when the treatise above quoted was penned, "the Patriarch of Indian Buddhism, Boddhidharma, the twenty-eighth in the list of Buddha's successors, left his native land and immigrated to China, which thenceforward became the seat of the patriarchate."[2]   This fact alone is sufficient to show how

[1] For a study of Indian and Chinese views on Art, see Ananda Coomaraswamy, "The Theory of Art in the Far East," *Transformation of Nature in Art*, Cambridge, Mass.—P.C.

[2] "Buddhism as a Religion," p. 80.   Probsthain's Oriental Series.

predominant must have been the influence of Indian thought in Chinese art and literature at that time, even though it may not be easily traced in the collections at present existing in Europe.

Europeans can better understand what that influence was if they try to realise what would have been the effect upon Italian art, supposing that in the days of the early Renaissance Rome had been converted to Buddhism by Chinese or Japanese missionaries; or, *vice-versâ*, the effect upon Chinese art if the Emperor had become Christian and the Pope and College of Cardinals had established themselves at Pekin.

It is curious that Mr. Binyon, with his rare gift of artistic insight, does not seem to perceive that, to the oriental artist, his clear recognition of the fact that India "gave to Asia the kindling ideals and imagery of Buddhism" and his denial of India's creative genius in art must seem strangely inconsistent. For, just as the whole essence of Asiatic art-creation lies in "the inner informing spirit," not in the imitation of outward semblances, so we must estimate the comparative influence of one school of Asiatic art upon another, not by mere affinities in forms of expression, or in technique, but by the extent to which the original creative thought-power in the one acted upon that of the other.

In one eloquent passage Mr. Binyon admits the influence of Indian thought in shaping the artistic ideals of China and Japan :

"The ideas of Buddhism saturate the art of China and Japan. To the Buddhist this world is transitory, vile, and miserable ; the flesh is a burden, desire an evil, personality a prison. And all through the classic art of those countries, though these conceptions have been turned to gracious and sweet uses in the life of human intercourse, and though the old Adam of humanity breaks forth from time to time in celebration of war, adventure, and the deeds of heroes, yet the Indian ideal claims everywhere its votaries, and the chosen and recurrent theme is the beauty of contemplation, not of action. Not the glory of the naked human form, to Western art the noblest and most expressive of symbols ; not the proud and conscious assertion of human personality ; but, instead of these, all thoughts that lead us out from ourselves into the universal life, hints of the infinite, whispers from secret sources—mountains, waters, mists, flowering trees, whatever tells of powers and presences mightier than ourselves : these are the themes dwelt upon, cherished, and preferred."[1]

It is just such thoughts as these which inspired the Indian sculptor and the Indian master-builder in the great epoch of Buddhist-Hindu art which was contemporary with the early schools of ideal painting in China and Japan. And though usually more austere and more severely restrained in the form of expression, the creative genius of India in sculpture and in architecture was not less great than that shown by China and Japan in the sister art. There is a reason, quite apart from æsthetics, why India has so little to show in painting compared with China and Japan. When the idea of salvation by works[2] took firm hold of the Indian mind, it became a religious duty on the part of the Indian artist and his patron to adopt the most strenuous, the most laborious, and at the same time the most enduring methods of artistic expression—for the greater the toil involved in the work the greater would be the merit won. To decorate a relic-shrine, temple, or monastery with high reliefs in stone would bring more reward in a future existence, both to the artists and craftsmen and to those who provided them with the necessities of life, than the simpler and less costly method of painting in fresco.

Thus the early wooden architecture of Buddhist India gradually gave place to lithic forms of construction, and religious fervour developed a great school of architectural sculpture by which Indian art in later times was better protected from the savagery of Mogul and other iconoclasts who have destroyed all but the last vestiges of Buddhist religious paintings.

[1] "Painting in the Far East," p. 22.
[2] See Chapter VII.

CHAPTER IV

THE DEVELOPMENT OF THE DIVINE IDEAL

IN the previous chapter I have explained the artistic ideal of the human or divine figure, expressing spiritual instead of physical strength, which Indian sculptors and painters inspired by Âryan philosophy gradually evolved out of the eclectic elements of the Transition period. It was an ideal common to all schools of religious thought—Jain, Buddhist, or Brahmanical. The Jains adapted it to their Tirthankaras, the Buddhists to their Buddhas and Bodhisattvas, and the orthodox Brahmanical sects to the divinities of their own pantheon : for, in spite of the diversity of sects, there is a common spiritual basis to all Indian art and religion. Philosophers differed as to the precise relation between Purusha and Prakriti, Soul and Matter, and religious teachers disputed over the different ways by which the soul might gain salvation ; but there were fundamentals upon which all philosophers agreed, and the end to be attained was the same to all sectarians.

Just as the great Hindu hero, Krishna, has in the Mahâbhârata a dual personality, one human and one divine, so this transcendental, lion-like ideal always retained in Indian art a symbolism of a dual character, according as it was applied to a human being or to a *deva*, a spiritual being, or Mahadeva—God. When a human being is represented, the slim-waisted, lion-like figure is the type of aristocratic birth, the mark of the Kshatriya, or warrior. In the Amarâvatî sculptures, where the transition from the Sânchî and Gandharan types to the ideal Hindu-Buddhist types is very evident, the Sâkya lords, the cousins of Prince Siddhârtha, all have this type of figure. The squat, full-bellied figures generally indicate menials and inferior races ; though, in the same artistic category, the well-fed Brahmin guru and a number of fanciful dwarfish demons were included.

When the divine being is intended a distinction is made by the nimbus round the head, the aura, surrounding the body, and sometimes the *ûrnâ*, the mark in the centre of the forehead, signifying spiritual insight. Kings and princes were also honoured by the nimbus as a symbol of their divine descent.

The aura represents the subtile, luminous envelope, by which, according to psychists, the bodies of all human beings, animals, and even trees, plants, and stones are surrounded, though to those without a developed psychic sense it is invisible. The Lalita Vistara describes how, soon as Gautama had seated himself under the bodhi-tree, a brilliant light shone from his body which illuminated, in the ten points of space, the innumerable spheres of Buddha. Aroused from their meditations by this wonderful light, the Buddhas came from every side and caused to appear all sorts of precious things, which they offered to the Bodhisattva. The gods thronged together also, and made a great rain to fall from heaven, bringing with it joy and well-being. In Buddhist pictures the aura is represented by thin, wavy lines of gold, which in Chinese are called *kao huang*—"hair-rays."[1]

Mr. E. R. Innes, in a recent number of *The Quest*,[2] has an interesting article on the aura, as it appears to the psychic, in human beings, animals, and in what are usually called "inanimate" objects. He says : "The aura of nearly all plants and wild animals is pleasant and health-giving to man. When man meets another man there is always the question of harmonising his aura to that of his companion ; for human auras are specialised." But the sensitive, "in contacting these nature-auras, experiences great refresh-

[1] Hackmann, "Buddhism as a Religion," p. 208.
[2] January 1910.

ment.   They are life-giving and soul-inspiring to his own aura ; they have the effect of sweeping it clean, or purifying it ; they tend to despecialise it, or urge it to return to a more simple or primitive mode of motion ; and this, for most men, is exceedingly bene-ficial, restful, and vitalising ; for civilised man is very liable to become too specialised . . . in the country, where man is freer and less likely to jostle up against other [human] auras, the human aura tends to expand and to reach its utmost limit."   Mr. Innes adds that perhaps this is the reason why, in all ages, those who desired to train and develop psychic capacity have been recommended to spend much time in solitude, or in quiet retreats, for here the aura expands and grows and becomes active far more easily.

The *ûrnâ*, which in Buddhist images of metal, stone, or wood was often indicated by a pearl or jewel, is the symbol of the "eye divine," and afterwards developed into the third eye of Siva.   In this form it appears also in later Buddhist images.   It is the sign of spiritual consciousness, of soul-sight as distinguished from eye-sight and intellectual perception.   It was by way of the *ûrnâ*, that the divine inspiration reached the *ushnisha*, the prominence on the Buddha's skull, regarded as the seat of the intellectual faculties.[1] The word *ûrnâ* itself, literally meaning "wool," has been a constant puzzle to Sanskrit and Pali scholars.   The explanation of it is, I believe, that the Divine Light, by means of which Gautama gained his Buddhahood, was conceived as converging towards the centre of his forehead from "the innumerable worlds" and entering his brain in flashes, like the lightning in an Indian sky, which is always drawn in Indian pictures in thin, wavy lines, never in the zigzag fashion of the "forked lightning" usually represented in European art. This practice is based on accurate observation of the lightning usually seen in Indian skies, as instantaneous photography proves.

Now a number of such wavy lines, light-flashes, or "hair-rays" converging to a single point would strikingly suggest a tuft of wool, each hair of which would symbolise a ray of cosmic light.   When Gautama at last attained to perfect enlightenment, or perfect communion with the Divine Consciousness the cosmic light he had absorbed was conceived as issuing from his brain for the enlightenment of his followers.   This mode of suggesting a mystic idea by concrete symbolism is characteristically Eastern.[2]

The tremendous power attributed to this cosmic spiritual light is illustrated in the well-known story of Kâma, the god of love, being burnt to ashes by the fire which flashed from the third eye of Siva, when, at Indra's instigation, he had dared to disturb the great god's meditation.   The comparative helplessness of intellectuality without the divine inspiration is delightfully symbolised in Hindu art by the quaint figure of Ganesha, the god of worldly wisdom, Siva's son, who is represented with an elephant's head placed on an infant's body.

The only physical action permitted in this symbolism of spiritual force is some slight movement of the hands and lower limbs, when the Buddha, or Bodhisattva, emerged from the state of profound meditation to instruct or bless his worshippers : these are the *âsanas*, the symbolic attitudes of the body, and the *mudrâs*, the gestures of the hands. In the state of profound meditation (*vajrâsana*) the legs are firmly locked together with the soles of the feet turned upwards, the hands lying in the lap, supinated one above the other, sometimes holding a vessel containing *amrita*, the nectar of immortality.   This is the pose of absolute immobility.   The first movement is one which the Buddha made at the crisis of his temptation by Mâra, when, in reply to the taunts of the Spirit of Evil, he pointed with his right hand to the earth, citing it as a witness to his attainment of Buddhahood.   This is the *bhûmi-parsâ-mudrâ*, or the earth-witness gesture.   There are various gestures having the significance of teaching, or argument, when a Buddha or

[1] For the symbolism of *urna* and *ushnisha*, see Stella Kramrisch, "Emblems of the Universal Being," *Journal of the Indian Society of Oriental Art*, III (1935), pp. 148-165.   Also see, Ananda Coomaraswamy, "The Buddha's *chuda*, hair, *ushnisha* and crown," *Journal of the Royal Asiatic Society*, 1928, pp. 815-841 ; and "*Ushnisha* and *Chhatra*," Poona Orientalist, III, (April 1938), pp. 1-19.—P.C.

[2] Mr. G. R. S. Mead suggests to me that the same symbolism may underlie the sufiism of Persia—*suf* meaning wool.

Bodhisattva is enforcing points of doctrine, or "turning the wheel of the law," emphasising them by touching or holding the fingers of the left hand with the thumb and fingers of the right. The bestowal of a blessing is indicated by the right hand being raised, with the palm turned outwards, the forearm sometimes resting on the right knee, sometimes lifted up.

The movements of the legs indicate various degrees of removal from the state of profound meditation, beginning with a slight relaxation of the rigid pose of the yogin, and ending with standing erect, a common attitude of Maitreya, the Buddhist Messiah. The symbolism of pose and gesture is brought to a fine art in the movements of Indian dancers, and this part of the subject would make an interesting study by itself; but I am not able to pursue it further at present.

In the philosophical schools the original simple conception of the Buddha's glorified personality gradually developed into that of the Dhyâni-Buddhas and Bodhisattvas. The former represent the spiritual essence, or ideal form, belonging to the Buddhas who are conceived as existing in a higher plane of abstract thought, known as *rupaloka*. Every Buddha who appears temporarily on earth to instruct humanity is a counterpart of one of these higher spiritual entities, embodied in human form. In order to provide for a head and protector of the Buddhist faith during the interval between the disappearance of one earthly Buddha and the coming of the next, the Dhyâni-Buddhas produce from themselves spiritual emanations of less potency known as Bodhisattvas, which are sometimes incarnated in human beings, *e.g.* the Dalai Lama of Tibet is said to be an incarnation of the Bodhisattva Padmapâni, or Avalokiteshvara.

When, finally, these metaphysical speculations extended to the idea of an Âdi-Buddha as the Supreme Lord and Creator of the universe, there was no essential difference except in terminology between Mahâyâna Buddhism and the orthodox Hindu pantheon.

Buddhism, as a distinct sect, disappeared from the land of its birth only because, in the general evolution of Hindu philosophy, its doctrines merged into the main current of Aryan thought, as the river Jumna is lost when it unites with the waters of the Ganges. The ethics of Buddhism became an essential part of Hindu religious teaching, and in this sense the religion of Buddha remains as potent a force in the India of to-day as it is in any other part of Asia.

We will pass on to see how this divine ideal, under the continued influence of the philosophical schools, became further modified and assumed other symbolical or allegorical forms which to academic Europe generally seem extravagant and even offensive; though in their Indian environment, even when their meaning is not fully understood, they are often profoundly impressive. The philosophic mind of India, observing the rapid working of the great forces of nature in a tropical climate, could not fail to be impressed by one fact, which is less patent to inhabitants of temperate climates. The ravages caused by frequent shock of earthquake or rush of mighty floods in the Himâlayan regions, leaving scars upon the surface of Mother Earth which in temperate latitudes would not disappear for several generations of men, under the stimulating heat of the tropical sun are healed in a few short years. Every hot season in the plains of India the scorching sun burns up the vegetation, silences the voices of nature, and makes all the land seem a dreary desert. Yet the Indian peasant knows full well that the cracking of the sun-baked soil is but one of the fertilising processes of nature, and that with the first downpour of the monsoon rains his fields will be bursting with exuberant, joyful life.

So the destructive powers which to us seem to be only malignant and ugly, fraught with evil to mankind, appear to the Indian mind as an essential part of the Divine Order, and belonging to the great Rhythm of things. Siva, the Destroyer, is also the Regenerator and the Lord of Bliss. Kâlî, the ruthless Ender of Time, who demands human victims at her sacrifices, is at the same time the kindly Mother of the Universe. The good and evil in nature both belong to God : human sickness and suffering are not, as the Greeks believed, due to the envy of the gods, but come from *avidhyâ*, an imperfect comprehension of the Divine Law.　So, whereas the Greek conception of the Divine Form confined beauty to an order of things which seemed pleasant and normal in ordinary human existence, the Indian artist makes no distinction between good and evil, as popularly understood, and, striving to show the Divine Idea in both, tells us that God's ways are not as man's ways and that the Divine Form embraces all forms.　The Divine Idea embraces both beauty and ugliness, as commonly understood, but transcends them both.

As soon as the agnosticism of Buddha's original teaching gave place to definite conceptions of the Fatherhood of God, as expounded in the "Bhagavad Gitâ," it appeared to Hindu philosophers that neither the anthropomorphic ideal of the Greeks nor the ideal of the Indian hero which the Buddhist and Jain artists had adopted was adequate to symbolise the universal attributes of the Lord and Cause of all things.　When Krishna, having bestowed upon Arjuna the gift of the "eye divine," conceded his prayer to reveal to him his Universal Form, this is how the resplendent, awful vision, never before seen by mortal man, is described by the Hindu poet :

> God ! In Thy body I see all the gods,
> And all the varied hosts of living things,
> And sovereign Brahmâ on His lotus-throne,
> And all the *rishis* and the snakes divine.
> I see Thee with unnumbered arms and breasts,
> And eyes and faces infinite in form.
> I see not either source or mean or end
> Of Thee, the Universal Form and Lord,
> Bearing Thy diadem, Thy club, and disc.
> I see Thee glowing as a mass of light
> In every region, hard to look upon,
> Bright as the blaze of burning fire and sun,
> On every side, and vast beyond all bound.
> The Undivided Thou, the highest point
> Of human thought, and seat supreme of all ;
> Eternal law's undying guardian Thou ;
> The everlasting Cause Thou seem'st to me.
> I see not Thy beginning, mean, or end ;
> Thy strength, Thy arms, are infinite alike,
> And unto Thee the sun and moon are eyes ;
> I see Thy face, that glows as sacred fire,
> And with its radiance heats the universe ;
> For all the heavenly regions and the space
> 'Twixt earth and heaven are filled by Thee alone.[1]

Even to Arjuna, though fortified with supernatural strength, this tremendous apparition seemed insupportable, and he begged of Krishna to resume his "milder, four-armed form," that which, though revealing his universal attributes, was not too awful for man to look upon.

Compared with such a conception of the universal Divine Form, the anthropomorphic gods of Greece and Rome seem puny and devoid of imagination, and I cannot help thinking that those European critics are altogether unjust and lacking in artistic insight who would judge by the ordinary conventions and canons of European art the efforts of Indian artists to express the supernatural and superhuman by forms not strictly in accordance with known physiological laws.　Art does not need to be justified by the anatomist, or the chemist, or by any other scientific specialist.　Every artistic convention is justified if it is used artistically and expresses the idea which the artist wishes to convey.　Indian

[1] The "Bhagavad-Gita," pp. 121-2, translated by John Davies.　Trübner's Oriental Series.

art is easily intelligible to those who will read it in the light of Indian religion and philosophy, which inspired both the artists and the people to whom the art was addressed. But, like all other art, it must be seen in its local environment, and in the atmosphere of the thought which created it. Nothing can be more misleading than to judge it by the isolated and generally inferior specimens which are seen in European museums, very few of which have, until recently, considered Indian sculpture and painting as worthy of serious study by Western artists.

India has always clearly recognised the limitations of artistic expression. Art is knowledge ; art is expression. Therefore art cannot supply a symbol for the Inexpressible, the Unknowable, and the Unconditioned. Though only the Qurân definitely placed a ban upon using any animate forms in art, the objection which underlies the prohibition did not originate with Islam. It is as old as the Vedas. The very word with which the Universal Self was expressed in Hindu philosophy was so holy that it was profanation for common lips to utter it. In a great Hindu temple in Southern India it is represented by Space—an empty cell. In Indian colour-symbolism it is expressed by black, the absence of colour.

The first comprehensible and expressible manifestation of the Unknowable, before creation itself, was conceived by ancient philosophers as the Egg, or Womb of the Universe, and was afterwards symbolised in India by a female form, Kâlî, as the Mother of all the Gods. I believe that the first symbols in art ever used by the teachers of Vedic philosophy were those smooth, egg-shaped stones, untouched by human craftsmen, which are placed beneath sacred trees and still worshipped throughout the length and breadth of India, though the meaning of the symbolism seems to be forgotten, except perhaps by a few intellectual Brahmins.

The stones symbolise the First Germ, the Egg of the Universe. The tree,[1] with its spreading branches and leaves, is the Universe itself : a well-known symbol of the One in many used by worshippers of Vishnu, the Preserver, in the present day. The snake which, carved in stone, is often worshipped at the same place, is a recognised symbol of reincarnation, the process by which the evolution of the soul is gained—a universal belief in India. Thus the stone, the tree, and the serpent represent the birth and evolution of the cosmos, and the passage of the soul to its goal in Nirvana ; and in this beautiful symbolism lies the root of Indan art.[2]

[1] For an exhaustive discussion of the Brahma-tree in all its aspects, see Ananda Coomaraswamy, "The Inverted Tree," *Quarterly Journal of the Mythic Society*, Vol. XXIX (October 1938), pp. 111-149.—P.C.

[2] Havell is not very clear here. What he may have in mind is the well-known imagery of the snake and its cast-off skin which symbolise the true Self of the person as distinguished from his psycho-physical personality that he discards at the moment of spiritual resurrection.

For a study of the complex symbolism of the serpent, see J. Ph. Vogel, *Indian Serpent Lore*, London, 1926. The earliest mention of *nagas* in Indian literature is in the Vedas where they are conceived as powers for evil. One of the great antagonists of Indira is the serpent Ahi who lurks in the secret depths of the waters and is responsible at the same time for constricting the flow of this life giving substance. Indra's heroic task is to slay him, releasing for the benefit of mankind what the malevolent creature had misappropriated for his own use. This important myth is the prototype of all the numerous legends of later Indian literature in which the central theme is the subjugation of the serpent-dragon who represents the powers of Darkness and Matter by the God-Hero who incarnates the principle of Light and the Spirit. Thus we have myths recounting the triumph of Buddha over Ahi, Mahavira over Samgana and Krishna over Kaliya. The rape of the Nagi by Garuda is another variant of this archetypal myth. Garuda is the traditional and implacable foe of the entire race of serpents. He is a bird roaming freely in the sky, which is the realm of the Spirit. The snakes on the other hand, are creatures of the earth, along which they creep and of which they are very much a part. There is thus a natural antagonism between the two, and the serpent, conquered by the great bird, is a natural symbol of the Spirit triumphant over Matter, or of Matter seized by the Spirit to which it is assimilated.

There is another aspect of the *nagas* as well, whereby these ambivalent creatures are considered to be powers for the good also, and worthy of being propitiated, for pleased they endow fertility and prosperity. In Buddhist lore particularly, they are represented as devotees of the Buddha and guardians of Buddhist shrines, though sometimes they achieve this beatific state only after they have been converted away from their evil ways by the influence of the Buddhist *dharma*.—P.C.

Of course it is probably the case that the use of these symbols originated with very primitive superstitions, but I think there is every reason to believe that they were appropriated and explained by Hindu religious teachers in their own way, just as the Christian churches have adopted many primitive pagan symbols in their ritual.   In the symbolism of all religions it is necessary to recognise a process of evolution following the evolution of the religion itself.   All Indian symbolism has a double meaning, one appealing to the popular mind, the other to the philosopher and religious teacher.

When Hindu religious thought had arrived at the idea that the two conditions known as Good and Evil, Life and Death, Creation and Destruction, Beauty and Ugliness, were both part of a divinely appointed order of things, it became necessary to assume a third one, a mean, to maintain the equilibrium of the cosmos between these pairs of opposites.

It is Vishnu, the Preserver, who stands between the opposing forces of good and evil and sees that right prevails in the end. "I will take care that the enemies of the gods shall not partake of the precious draught [of immortality]; that they shall share in the labour alone."

The great cosmic struggle between good and evil, or between gods and demons, is told allegorically in the Mahâbhârata and in the Puranas[1] as the churing of the waters of chaos, the primordial nature-element called the Sea of Milk.   It is a very favourite subject with Hindu sculptors and painters.

This is how the story runs :

In consequence of an offence given by Indra, the ruler of the sky, to a powerful *rishi*, who was an incarnation of Siva, all the gods lost virtue ; the three regions, earth, sky, and heaven were wholly deprived of prosperity and energy, and the enemies of the gods, the *asuras*, put forth all their strength.

Instructed by Vishnu, the gods entered into an alliance with the *asuras* in order to obtain the nectar of immortality, *amrita*.   They had been told that it must be done by churning the Sea of Milk with the holy mountain, Mandara, the abode of the gods.   Ananta, the great serpent on which Vishnu reposed (symbolising eternity) upraised the mountain with the woods thereon and the dwellers in those woods, and brought it to the Sea of Milk, the waters of which were radiant as the thin, shining clouds of autumn.   Mandara was the churning-stick ; Vishnu himself, in the form of a mighty tortoise, served as a pivot ; Ananta was the cord.   The gods and *asuras*, having poured into the sea various kinds of medicinal herbs, ranged themselves at either end of the serpent, and the churning began.

Vishnu, manifesting himself in various forms, took part with the gods.   As Krishna he had wisely stationed the gods at the tail of the serpent and the *asuras* at the head ; so that, scorched by the flames emitted from Ananta's distended hood, the demons were at a disadvantage, while the clouds driven towards his tail by the breath of his mouth, refreshed the gods with revivifying showers. "The Holder of the Mace and Discus [Vishnu] was present in other forms amongst the gods and demons, and assisted to drag the monarch of the serpent race ; and in another vast body he sat on the mountain. With one portion of his energy, unseen by gods or demons, he sustained the serpent-king; and with another infused vigour into the gods."

From the Sea of Milk thus churned by gods and demons uprose the divine cow Surabhi, the fountain of milk, first sustenance of the human race.   Then came Vârunî, the deity of wine,[2] her eyes rolling with intoxication.   Next, from the whirlpool of the deep, came the celestial Pârijâta tree, symbol of all lovely flowers and precious fruits with which the earth is blessed.   Then came the joys of dance and song, the *apsarasas*, nymphs of heaven of surprising loveliness, "endowed with beauty and with taste."   The cool-rayed moon next rose, and was seized by Mahadeva (Siva).

[1] The Vishnu Purana, translated by H. H. Wilson, p. 75.

[2] This according to Wilson's translation, but the true meaning of Varuni is "Vishnu's embodied radiance."   See "Mahânirvâna Tantra," translated by A. Avalon, p. xxxviii.

B. Ganesha. (*From a sculpture in Indonesia*).

A. Kartikeya in his War-chariot. Portion of a Kambodian relief.
(*From a cast in the Trocadéro, Paris*).

PLATE 89

B. Ganesha from Idar. 8th century A.D. (*Baroda Museum*).

PLATE 90

A. Dancing Ganesha from Halebid, Mysore. (*Photo, J. V. Mehta*).

B. Parvati. *(From a bronze in the National Museum, Copenhagen).*

A. Parvati dancing. Sculpture from the Kuruvatti Temple near Harpanahalli. *(From a photograph in the India Office Library).*

PLATE 91

C. Sudarsana Yakshi from Bharhut. Mid-2nd century B.C. (*Indian Museum, Calcutta*).

B. Chand Yakshi from Bharhut depicting "Woman and Tree" motif. Mid-2nd century B. C. (*Indian Museum, Calcutta*).

PLATE 92

A. Yakshi from Bharhut. Mid-2nd century B.C. (*Now in Bharat Kala Bhavan, Banaras*).

And then poison was engendered by the churning, which began to overspread the earth with fire and sulphureous fumes. To save creation, Siva, at Brahmâ's request, swallowed the poison and held it in his throat, whence he became thereafter blue-throated (*nila-kantha.*)

At last Dhanwantari, the divine chemist, appeared, robed in white and bearing in his hand the cup of *amrita*. Then seated on a full-blown lotus and holding a lotus in her hand, the goddess of prosperity, Lakshmi, radiant with beauty, rose from the waves. "The great sages, enraptured, hymned her with the song dedicated to her praise. Visvawasu and other heavenly quiristers sang, and Ghritâchî and other celestial nymphs danced before her. Ganga and other holy streams attended for her ablutions; and the elephants of the skies (the clouds) taking up their pure waters in vases of gold, poured them on the goddess, the queen of the universal world." Lakshmi, when bathed, attired, and adorned, threw herself upon the breast of Vishnu, and, there reclining, turned her eyes upon the deities, who were inspired with rapture by her gaze.

The *asuras*, indignant at the preference shown by the lovely goddess, snatched the *amrita* cup from the hand of Dhanwantari; but Vishnu, assuming a female form, fascinated and deluded them, and, having recovered the precious cup, gave it to the gods. The latter, revived by the ambrosial draught, quickly overcame the desperate onslaughts of the demons and drove them to the nether realms of Pâtâla : finally, with great rejoicing, the gods did homage to Vishnu, and, having restored the mountain Mandara to its former base, they left the *amrita* in the safe keeping of Indra and resumed their reign in heaven.[1]

The allegory seems to contain reminiscences of one of those terrible droughts and famines which so often desolate Asiatic countries. *Amrita*, the nectar for which the gods and demons contended, is the rain, of which Indra, the god of the sky whose *vâhan*, or vehicle, is the white elephant (the rain-cloud), is the keeper. Mandara, the churning-stick, stands for the Himâlayas, which attract the monsoon clouds and cause them to discharge their precious nectar, reviving the earth and bringing the beauteous goddess of prosperity to bless mankind. The *apsarasas* are the mists which dance in the morning sunlight.

The subject is a favourite one in Indian art, but it was never treated on so magnificent a scale or with so splendid an effect as in the bas-reliefs which adorn the colonnades of the great temple of Angkor Vat, in Kambodia, built about the twelfth century by Sûrya varman II, one of the last of the Hindu kings who ruled over the Indian colony in the Further East. The Kambodian temples rank high among the greatest architectural and artistic monuments of the world, though they are as yet little known in Europe.

A detailed description of the Angkor temple is given by Fergusson.[2] Casts of some of the bas-reliefs are in the Royal Ethnographic Museum, Berlin, and in the Trocadéro, Paris, and it is to be regretted that none of our national museums possess any reproductions of these great works. Plate 85A gives the central figure in the relief representing the churning of the ocean, the finest of the series. The grand design of the whole cannot be realised from so small a section, but it may give some idea of its imaginative power and masterful vigour.

The four-armed figure is Vishnu, "the Wielder of the Mace and Discus," who stands in front of the churning-stick—the mountain Mandara, which is pivoted on the back of the tortoise—controlling the cosmic tug-of-war. The gods and *asuras*, ranged on opposite sides, are using the body of the great serpent Ananta for the churning-rope. In another form Vishnu manifests himself on the top of the churning-stick to maintain its equilibrium. Crowds of attendant spirits are dancing in the air, joyously anticipating the triumph of Vishnu and the gods.

[1] The Vishnu Purana, translated by H. H. Wilson.
[2] "Indian Architecture," Revised Edition 1910, vol. ii., p. 380.

CHAPTER V

THE TRIMÛRTI

THE three conditions, or *gunas*—*i.e.* the opposing extremes and the equilibrating mean, represented allegorically by the gods, the *asuras*, and by Vishnu, were recognised in Hindu philosophy as attributes of the material manifestation of Ishvara, the Supreme Lord.

The famous Hymn of Creation in the Rig-Veda (x. 129) describes the universe as proceeding from the absolute Brahman, the Universal Spirit, the Unknowable, whose first manifestation when passing into a conditioned state—comparable to the passing of a human being from the state of profound sleep to a state of dreaming and then of waking —is called Ishvara. The latter in the Hindu theogony stands nearest to the Western idea of an active, personal God.

The glory of Ishvara as Purusha, or Spirit, makes manifest Prakriti, the Essence of Matter, inherent in Brahman, but until now unmanifested. Purusha, through its divine power called *sakti*, the female principle, causes Prakriti to take form. Inherent in Prakriti are three attributes, or aspects, known as the Trimûrti, which are symbolised both in Hindu and in Mahâyâna Buddhist sculpture and painting by a male three-headed divinity (Plate 85B) or separately as three divinities, Brahmâ, Vishnu, and Siva. In the theogony of Mahâyâna Buddhism the Hindu Trimûrti were identified with Buddha, Sangha, and Dharma respectively.

Each aspect of the Trimûrti is correlated to Purusha and Prakriti as follows : Brahmâ, in relation to Purusha, or Spirit, represents Being, or Truth ; as related to Prakriti, or matter, he performs the function of Creator, and represents the condition of activity, or motion. Vishnu, as related to Purusha, represents thought-power ; as related to Prakriti, he is the Preserver, representing equilibrium and rhythm. Siva, as related to Purusha, represents Bliss—the joy of creation and the perfect beatitude of Nirvana ; but in relation to Prakriti he is the Destroyer, the dissolving power—which connotes, however, the power of regeneration.[1]

This philosophic concept of the evolution of the universe is often symbolised in Hindu art by the figure of Ishvara, under the name of Nârâyana, sleeping on the waters of chaos on the serpent Sesha, or Ananta, "the Endless"—the symbol of eternity, which encircled the world in its vast coils (Plate 84B)—while Brahmâ, the Creator, appears enthroned

---

[1] The interpretation of the colossal three-headed image from Elephanta as being a composite image of Brahma, Vishnu and Siva offers several difficulties that have been discussed by various scholars. Havell himself appears to be somewhat unsure for he recognised the feminine character of the face to the left, though he seemingly got over the problem by saying that in the Elephanta sculpture, Brahma the creator was replaced by Parvati, Siva's *sakti*, also the creative aspect of Siva. J. N. Banerjea (*Development of Hindu Iconography*, Calcutta, 1956, pp. 476-477) is of the opinion that this face with "demure and downcast eyes with the finely drawn brows, the distinct pout of the lower lips, the receding chin, the jewelled curls tastefully arranged on the forehead and other features not only differentiate it from the other two faces but also characterise it as the face of a female figure." He reinforces this opinion by a reference to other mediaeval three-headed images having distinctly feminine faces and by a reference to the doctrine of the two forms of Siva, *Siva* and *ghora*. Stella Kramrisch "The Image of Mahadeva in the Cave Temple on Elephanta Island," *Ancient India*, No. 2 (July 1946), interprets the image to represent the fully manifest Siva, the central face being that of Tatpurusha-Mahadeva, the fierce face to the right that of Aghora-Bhairava, and the sensuous lovely face to the left as that of the "Beauteous God" (Vamadeva) and "also that of the Goddess Uma, who is Siva's Sakti, inseparably part of his nature." The image itself can no longer be taken to represent the Trimurti of Brahma, Vishnu and Siva, but is rather the image of Siva, the fierce face indicating him to be the Deity who ends both death and time, while the face to the left emphasizes his creative aspect which is necessarily female by nature.—P.C.

upon a mystic lotus-flower, the symbol of purity and heavenly birth, which is growing from Nârâyana's navel.

To understand this allegory it is necessary to know that the physical basis of Hindu metaphysics, upon which its artistic symbolism is founded, is centralised in the apparent movement of the sun round the earth, of which the cosmic cross was the symbol in the ancient Aryan world. The four points of the cross indicated the position of the sun at midnight, sunrise, noon, and at sunset respectively.[1]

Nârâyana sleeping, or absorbed in Yoga, on the primordial waters, is the sun from the time it disappears below the horizon until it rises again. Brahmâ, born from the lotus which grows from Nârâyana's navel, is the sunrise which causes the lotus-flowers to open. Siva, who in the struggle between the *devas* and *asuras*, or between light and darkness, claims the moon for his own, is the sun setting behind the snow-clad Himâlayan peaks, when the moon rises to adorn Mahadeva's brow. Vishnu, the principle of equilibrium, is the sun at noon, standing between Brahmâ and Siva as mediator.

The circumambulation of a shrine, the most ancient of rites and part of the ritual of Hindu worship at the present day, and the orthodox Brahmin's *sandhya*, or the prayer which he addresses to the Supreme Being at sunrise, noon, and sunset, both belong to the ancient symbolism of sun-worship.

The apparent movement of the sun from east to west was also indicated by the old-world symbol, the swastika, formed by adding four short lines of direction to the four points of the cosmic cross. According to Count D'Alviella it is the exclusive property of the Aryan race. The ascending movement of the sun naturally represented the whole principle of order and well-being in the universe, and thus the swastika became the symbols of life and of man's material prosperity. The reverse movement, indicated by the sauwastika, was the descending principle, connoting disorder and dissolution.

The philosophic debates in the orthodox Hindu schools eventually resolved the four central deities into three, by identifying Sûrya with Vishnu. Thus was evolved the idea of the Trimûrti, the three aspects of the One, which have their material manifestation in the three cosmic forces, conditions, or *gunas*.

All the innumerable gods and goddesses of the Hindu pantheon are sub-manifestations of the Trimûrti, and Sukracharya, one of the few Sanskrit writers on art whose works are at present known, classifies them as follows, according to the *gunas* which they represent :

Sattvik. "An image of God, sitting in meditation in the posture of a yogin, with hands turned, as if granting boon or blessing to his worshippers, surrounded by Indra and other gods praying and worshipping."

Rajasik. "An image seated upon a *vâhan*, or vehicle, adorned with various ornaments with hands holding weapons, as well as granting boon or blessing."

Tamasik. "A terrible armed figure fighting and destroying demons."

The imagery and symbolism with which Hindu poets and artists clothed these metaphysical ideas were generally drawn from the wonderful nature of the Himâlayan mountains and valleys. Brahmâ, from being the symbol of sunrise, developed into the per-

---

[1] One of the most ancient symbols of Hinduism is the four-headed *lingam*, many examples of which are preserved in the Indian Museum, Calcutta. The short pillar on which the heads are displayed cross-wise stands for Ishvara. The four heads are those of the four central deities of the Hindu pantheon (afterwards resolved into three—the Trimûrti), namely, Vishnu, Brahma, Surya, and Siva. Vishnu, in his dual form, Narayana-Vishnu—the one representing his yogic state, the other his active cosmical powers, eventually superseded Sûrya, whose images are often difficult to distinguish from those of Vishnu. The four points of the cosmic cross, starting from the base, thus became Narayana, Brahma, Vishnu, and Siva.

sonification of prayer, because to the sunrise all the prayers of the Aryan race had been addressed from time immemorial. It was at the end of the winding lotus-stalk growing in the cosmic waters that the lovely flower of the morning sun blossomed. AUM, MANI PADME HUM : "Hail, Lord Creator ! the Jewel is in the Lotus," was the invocation of the rising sun expressed in different formularies by all the ancient Aryan world.

As Creator, Brahmâ presided over the fertilising element, water. His *vâhan* was appropriately the imperial swan, or the lordly wild goose, which had its home in the Himâlayan lakes (Plate 87A).[1] His colour symbol was red, like the rising sun, whose rays brought life to the sleeping world, and red lotuses were the flowers which his worshippers offered to him.

The finest image of Brahmâ now extant is probably that which is now preserved in the Ethnological Museum, Leyden, Plate 86C. It is one of the great monuments of the Brahmanical period of Indian art in Java, which lasted from about 900 to 1500 A. D. The Creator is represented with four heads crowned with massive tiaras, symbolising the four quarters of the earth. Two hands clasped in front hold a phial which contains the divine nectar, the elixir of life : each of the others holds a pilgrim's water-vessel, water being regarded as the creative element. Intertwined with the water-vessel is the sacred lotus, the Creator's floral emblem. Behind the lower part of the figure, unfortunately mutilated, is Brahmâ's *vâhan*, the swan. The arms and body of the deity are ornamented with richly wrought jewellery, and over his left shoulder hangs the sacred thread, the *upavîta*, worn by Brahmins.

An awe-inspiring dignity and worshipful solemnity pervade this conception of the Grandsire of the human race, the Dyaus-pitar, Heavenly Father, Giver of Life and Receiver of all prayers. In the presence of great art like this it is mere impertinence to inquire whether such conventions as four heads and arms are permissible. In this case the end which the artist had in view is attained, and the conventions are justified thereby. The test of good art, as Rodin has said, is that the eye shall be perfectly satisfied. Here there is nothing that can be taken away, and nothing that can be added. One can only say that the artist has attained to his ideal, and that ideal is noble and sufficient. No human art is absolute and final ; it is only the *dilettante* who delights in fixing rules for it to bring it within the compass of his own understanding.

It may be granted that it is only in truly inspired art that such transcendental conceptions of the godlike can be tolerated from a purely æsthetic standpoint, but it is just the privilege of genius to break away from the limitations which bind mediocrity. Hindu art has been judged in Europe, particularly in England, not by these masterpieces of the pre-Muhammadan epoch, but by the puerile illustrations of the Hindu pantheon given by Moor and other still more prejudiced writers, or by debased modern types collected at South Kensington and elsewhere. It is as if an Indian critic were to judge the art of the Renaissance in Europe by the garden gods and goddesses now imported into India as Italian art.

Vishnu, the Preserver (Plate 86A), the second of the Trimûrti, ruled over the firmament, and his colour is the deep transparent blue, pure as crystal, of the Himâlayan sky when it has been swept by the monsoon storms. His upright, rigid, columnar pose fitly expresses his character as the Pillar of the universe ; and what could better express his sustaining, equilibrating power than his *vâhan*, Garuda, the eagle with outstretched wings, poised motionless in mid-heaven over a Himâlayan valley ?[2]

---

[1] The Sanskrit word for a swan, or goose, *hamsa*, is convertible into SA—HAM = IAM HE, *i.e.* Brahma. In poetry the flight of the swan is compared to that of the parting soul.

[2] Akbar's Hindu architects used the idea of the cosmic pillar in the Diwan-i-khas at Fatehpur-sikri, raising the imperial throne upon a column with a colossal bracketed capital which was approached from a gallery by four gangways symbolising the four quarters of the earth. A cast of it is in the Indian Section of the Victoria and Albert Museum, South Kensington.

B.   Two women from Mathura.
(*Archaeological Museum, Mathura*).

A.   A young woman pressing the Asoka-tree with
her foot.   (*From a cast in the Victoria and Albert
Museum taken from an Orissan temple*).

PLATE 93

C. A sculpture of a young woman from the Tadpatri Temple, Madras. (*From a photograph by Nicholas & Co., Madras*).

B. Yakshi from Mathura.

A. Woman with parrot cage, from Mathura. (*Photo Copyright by Department of Archaeology, Government of India*).

PLATE 94

A. Bronze statuette of Apparswami.
(*From the original in the Colombo Museum*).

B. Bronze statuette of Sundara-mūrti Swami.
(*Colombo Museum, Ceylon*)

PLATE 95

A. Ibrahim-ka-Rauza, Bijapur.

B. The Rauza of Rani Sipri, Ahmedabad.

PLATE 96

The sun which sustains the universe was his chief emblem, and perhaps the original idea of the many-armed images which represented Vishnu (Plate 103B) was to suggest the all-pervading rays of the midday sun.   His *chakra*, the Wheel of Life, which, like the Buddhist Wheel of the Law, seems to have been evolved from the swastika, symbolised not the sun itself but its apparent revolution round the earth.   It generally has the cosmic cross placed within it (Plate 86A).   The Upanishads thus explain its mystical meaning :

"As the spokes of a wheel are attached to the nave, so are all things attached to Life. This Life ought to be approached with faith and reverence, and viewed as an immensity which abides in its own glory.   That immensity extended from above, from below, from behind and from before, from the south and from the north.   It is the soul of the universe ; it is God Himself."[1]

Vishnu is also represented by the tree whose trunk is the upright limb of the cosmic cross.   It has its branches, leaves, and fruit in the starry heavens.   This is analogous to the Buddhist symbolism in which the heavenly dome is likened to an umbrella,[2] a series of umbrellas superimposed forming the "tee" placed on the top of a *stûpa* to represent the different spheres or planes through which the soul ascends to Nirvana.

The image of Vishnu in Plate 86A is another striking example of Hindu sculpture in Java which is fully equal to the finest Buddhist art at Bôrôbudûr.   The rigid uprightness of the figure is clearly intended to express Vishnu's special manifestation as the cosmic pillar, or tree, as the Preserver who keeps the balance between the contending forces of light and darkness, rather than the universal attributes which are assigned to him by the Vaishnavaite sect in modern Hinduism.

He is here represented with four arms, instead of eight, which are used to emphasise by repetition the columnar uprightness of the body.   The attributes displayed are the discus, or *chakra*, and the mace, *gadha*, on the right side ; on the left, the conch-shell, and another which is broken.[3]

The third of the Trimûrti,[4] Siva, the Destroyer, Regenerator, and Lord of Bliss, found a fitting material symbol in the snow-clad mountain-peak.   Fire was his element, at once destructive, purifying, and regenerative.   Possibly some active volcano in the Himâlayan regions may have first suggested this association ; but Siva's destructive forces would be sufficiently represented by the fury of Himâlayan storms and by the desolation caused by the frequent earthquakes which rent the mountain-sides.   Nothing could more finely symbolise the spiritual power of meditation than the serene majesty of the highest Himâlayan peaks in the morning sunlight, when Siva's "blue-throat" is seen beneath the snow-line ; or at dusk, when the crescent moon which adorns the great god's brow rises in mystic beauty over the snowy ridge.   The white ashes of the sacrificial fire and the blue throat of the flame are analogous symbols.

The cobra became Siva's especial emblem because, while its spiral coil represented the principle of cosmic evolution, or of life, the deadly poison contained in its fangs represented the principle of involution, or death ; and its habit of shedding its skin periodically was a symbol of reincarnation, or rebirth.

Siva's *vâhan* was the bull, Nandi, which carried the sacrificial wood, and also symbolised his generative force.   On the spiritual plane Nandi represents *dharma*, or the whole duty of the Hindu.   The Ganges and other sacred rivers which flowed from Himâlayan glaciers through the mountain forests, "the great god's hair," were naturally associated with the idea of spiritual purity represented by Siva himself.

---

[1] Translated by Monier Williams.

[2] For a more detailed analysis of the identical symbolism of World Tree and Umbrella, see Coomarasamy, "Ushnisha and Chhatra," *Poona Orientalist*, Vol. III (April 1958), pp. 1-99.—P.C.

[3] The mystical meaning of Vishnu's attributes are explained in detail in the description of Plate 103B., Part II, below.

[4] In the Elephanta Trimûrti, Plate 85B, Siva's *Sakti*, or female energy, Parvati takes the place of Brahma as Creatrix. See "Ancient and Med. Arch. of India," by the author, p. 163.

The philosophical concept of the Trimûrti, the three Aspects of the Supreme, correlated with the three *gunas* or conditions inherent in Prakriti, affords a common basis of belief for all Hindu sects ; but the two deities, Vishnu and Siva, gradually absorbed the special attributes of Brahmâ, who, as the chief divinity of a sect, ceased to claim many votaries for two reasons : first, because, as a symbol of prayer, he was held to be present in all worship ; secondly, because, as a symbol of creation, his special work in the cosmos was finished and he could no longer be moved by prayer. At the present time there are not more than one or two temples specially dedicated to Brahmâ in the whole of India, though his image often appears in the temples of other sects.

This process of absorption resolved orthodox Hinduism into the two main sects which exist at the present day ; the Vaishnavaites, the devotees of Vishnu, who are in a majority in Northern India ; the Saivaites, those of Siva, who are most numerous in the South. The Sauras, or worshippers of Sûrya, still remain as a distinct sect, but it is not a numerous one. The images of Sûrya are often identical with those of Vishnu.

Vishnu to the Vaishnavaites is Brahmâ, Vishnu, and Siva. In the same way Siva, to the Saivaites, represents the whole Trimûrti. This interchange of symbols between different sects often makes Indian religious ideas seem tangled and confused to Europeans. It should always be remembered, not only that any one of the Trimûrti may stand for all three, but that any Hindu deity may be regarded as a symbol or manifestation of all the powers of the One God.

Vishnu in his universal character has ten *avataras*, incarnations, or "descents," in which he manifested himself to the world. In the first, the Matsya, or fish-incarnation, he is said to have saved Manu, one of the progenitors of the human race, from a great flood. In the second, the Kurma, or tortoise-incarnation, he assisted in the churning of the ocean. The next was the Varâha, or boar-incarnation, in which Vishnu raised the earth from beneath the waters of chaos, or, according to a Puranic legend, rescued it from a demon who had dragged it beneath the sea. The Narasinha, or man-lion incarnation, was the form in which he is said to have appeared to destroy the wicked king Hiranya-kaçipu (Plate 86B). This is the subject of one of the most dramatic of the Ellora sculptures.[1] The fifth incarnation, known as the Vamana, or dwarf, refers to the "three strides of Vishnu," or the three positions of the sun at rising, at noon, and at setting. In the Puranas he is said to have assumed the form of a dwarf to recover the dominion of the earth from a demon-king, Bali.

The four historical or quasi-historical *avataras* are those of Parasu-Râma, or Râma with axe—a Brahmin who overthrew the Kshatriyas and established Brahmin supremacy in Northern India ; Râma Chandra, the hero of the Râmâyana ; Krishna, the hero of the Mahâbhârata and the inspired teacher of the Bhagavad-Gîtâ ; and Gautama Buddha, the founder of Buddhism.

The tenth and last *avatar* is that of the Hindu Messiah, Kalkin, who at the end of the present dark age, the Kâlî Yuga, is to appear riding a white horse, with a flaming sword in hand, to restore righteousness and to rule the earth.

The passage from the Bhagavad-Gîtâ quoted above[2] is one of the grandest descriptions in Hindu literature of Vishnu's universal form and attributes. In sculpture this conception of Vishnu is very finely rendered in the Mâmallapuram relief, Plate 103B. In popular Hindu art of the present day, especially in Northern India, the favourite subjects are the allegorical legends relating to Vishnu's incarnation as Krishna, his exploits as the destroyer of demons and wicked men, his sports with the *gopîs*, and the beautiful episode of Radha's devotion.

Siva, as the supreme deity of the Saivaites, is generally known as Mahadeva, the Great God. In sculpture he appears sometimes as the Great Yogi, wrapt in meditation

[1] Part I, "Indian Sculpture and Painting," Plate 13.
[2] Page 146.

like the Buddha ; sometimes in his terrific aspect as Bhairava.   One of the most inspired conceptions of Hindu art is that of Siva as the Universal Lord, or the Soul of the Universe manifesting itself in matter, in his mystic dance of creation, symbolising the perfect joy which God feels in the creation which He makes, controls, destroys, and renews at will. The Puranas record various legends which develop allegorically this fundamental concept of the cosmic rhythm.   Siva, it is said, to please his consort Parvati, performed this dance, called the Tândavan, in the presence of all the devas, to the accompaniment of the celestial drum, which, like Vishnu's conch-shell trumpet, is the symbol of vibration, the creative force.   This is the subject of the magnificent fragment from Elephanta, illustrated in Plate 108A, and of the Ellora sculpture, Plate 107B.

He is said to have also performed this dance on the prostrate body of the demon-dwarf Tripura, representing the world, the flesh, and the devil, who was sent by some envious sages to attack him.   This is the usual form in which Siva is represented in South Indian bronzes, of which the Madras Museum has two superb examples.   One of them has been illustrated in my "Indian Sculpture and Painting," Plate 19 ; the other is shown here in Plate 88.   In composition these two bronzes are almost identical, but in the latter the aura of flame surrounding the figure, and the waving locks of matted hair, symbolising the sacred rivers which flowed over Mahadeva's head, are broken away.   There is, however, a great difference in the feeling which animates the two.

In both of them Siva has four arms, instead of eight, as in the Elephanta and Ellora sculptures.   In the uppermost right hand is held a small hour-glass-shaped drum, the symbol of vibration, or the life-principle.   The corresponding left hand holds the sacred purifying fire, symbol both of the destruction of the body and of the heavenly grace which the soul may gain thereby.   In the lobe of the right ear there is a woman's ornament, in the left a man's earring : by which is expressed the nature of the Deity, combining both the male and female principle.

There is a great contrast between the elegant grace of this most delightful bronze and the vehement, overpowering energy of the Elephanta and Ellora bas-reliefs.   There is less of the divine and more of mundane feeling in its youthful, almost feminine lightness and gaiety.   We feel that the sculptor was chiefly absorbed in the effort to express the abandon of youth yielding itself wholly to the rhythm and ecstasy of the dance.   In this joyous, spontaneous mood, it is much more akin to Greek art than the trivial, decadent sculpture of Gandhara, to which many critics would attribute the source of Indian artistic inspiration.   And certainly a Pompeian or Tanagran sculptor, or their disciples of the Italian Renaissance, would be more proud to acknowledge a kindred feeling in the perfect art of this South Indian image-maker than to claim relationship with the mostly insipid and mechanical work of Kanishka's hireling stone-masons.

It is difficult at present to date these bronzes with any degree of certainty.   They are undoubtedly much later than the Mâmallapuram sculptures, and later than those of Ellora ; but they are considerably earlier than the great temple of Madura, the sculptures of which in many cases betray strong Western influence.   Târanâtha, in his brief sketch of Indian art-history, written about A.D. 1608,[1] mentions three skilful South Indian image-makers : Jaya, Parojaya, and Vijaya.   Possibly the Madras Museum bronzes may be the work of one of these artists.

The symbolism conveyed in one of the chief agents of Siva's destructive power, his son, Karttikeya, the god of war, needs no explanation.   He has for his *vâhan* the peacock, an appropriate emblem for the pride, pomp, and circumstance of war.   The superbly decorative composition showing Karttikeya in his war-chariot, flying like a whirlwind to battle, given in Plate 89A, is a portion of one of the Kambodian reliefs from a cast in the Trocadèro, Paris.

The other progeny of Siva is the dwarf, grotesque Ganesha (Plates 89B, 90A and B)

[1] See Part I, "Indian Sculpture and Painting."

who is the god of intellectuality, of worldly wisdom, Lord of the lesser divinities, protector of households, and patron of authors. The Puranas record his birth on this wise. Parvati, the wife of Siva, was having her bath in her lord's absence, and for the sake of privacy fashioned Ganesha from the turmeric paste with which she had anointed her body, and set him down at the door to keep off intruders. Siva, unexpectedly returning, found his entrance barred by the unknown doorkeeper, and in a rage cut off his head. Parvati was irate at his rashness, and would not be pacified until Siva had promised to restore Ganesha to life. The latter's head could not be found, so Siva went off into the forest and found an elephant sleeping with his head turned towards the north—the direction of his Himâlayan paradise. He thought this would serve for the head of his supposititious son, so he severed it and fitted it on to the body of Ganesha: thus fulfilling his promise, though in a rather unexpected and incongruous fashion.

The meaning of the allegory is clear. Ganesha, who is the protector of households, represents the wisdom which brings to mankind a great store of this world's goods ; the sagacity of an elephant which keeps the mind tied to earth, not the spiritual power of Siva, which can take wings and lift the soul to heaven : wherefore he is the patron deity of scribes and publishers. He was not born of the perfect union of the Soul and Matter, Purusha and Prakriti, but was fashioned from the dross of Mother Earth, and his vehicle is the mean, earth-burrowing creature, the rat. Nevertheless, he is a jovial, well-disposed deity, and always immensely popular ; and, as the intuitive intellectual power must always be joined with reason, so, by permission of the gods, Ganesha's name is always to be invoked first in sacrifices.

The same device of gentle ridicule for conveying a moral lesson is used in the story of Daksha, as told in the Puranas. In this case the moral conveyed is the inefficacy of sacrifices when directed towards selfish or unworthy objects. The explanation usually given that the story refers to sectarian disputes between the followers of Vishnu and Siva seems to me to miss the whole point of it.

Daksha is the personification of intellectual pride : his name signifies "ability," and he was said to be one of the progenitors of the human race. He had twenty-four fair daughters, who are personifications of respectability and all the domestic virtues. Among them, however, Sati, or Truth—the essence of spirituality—was passionately devoted to Siva, and, though he appeared as a ragged ascetic, besmeared in ashes and with matted hair, she chose him as her husband in preference to many other powerful and wealthy suitors.

This incensed her father, who was worldly-wise and would only pay respect to the Preserver, Vishnu, the bestower of wealth, happiness, and prosperity. Daksha had arranged for a grand horse-sacrifice, to which all the *devas*, except Siva, were invited. Sati, though uninvited, attended the feast, but, unable to bear the insults which Daksha flung at Siva and herself, she fell dead at her father's feet.[1]

Siva, then, assuming one of his terrific forms as the Destroyer, summoned all his hosts, and in a furious combat defeated and slew Daksha, though the latter was assisted by other *devas*, and carried off the body of Sati. The whole world was convulsed with the great god's grief and was threatened with dissolution, until Vishnu, with his discus, cut the body of Sati into pieces, which fell upon the earth. Siva, relieved of his burden, returned to meditation in his Himâlayan paradise.

Sati was subsequently reborn and again became Siva's bride as Umâ, or Parvati, the fair daughter of Himâlaya. At the intercession of Sati's mother Daksha was restored to life ; but, as his head could not be found, it was replaced by that of a goat. The

---

[1] According to the Bhagavat Purana, Daksha Prajapati did not perform a horse sacrifice nor was it Siva in person who destroyed the sacrifice. Angered at the insults Sati had to suffer at the hands of her father, Siva tore off a lock of hair and dashed it against the ground from which was born Virabhadra who was ordered to destroy the sacrifice, which he successfully accomplished.—P.C.

animal chosen, as in the case of Ganesha, points the moral of the story—the goat is the animal most frequently offered in Hindu sacrifices.

Like the fine sculpture of the same deity now in the Ethnographic Museum at Leyden,[1] the monumental image of Ganesha shown in Plate 89B comes from Java. Ganesha is generally treated as the Indian counterpart of the Falstaff among Chinese household gods, the round-bellied god of good luck. It would hardly occur to the Western mind that such uncompromising artistic materials as those provided by the Puranic myth— a decapitated infant's body furnished anew with the head of an elephant—could be treated otherwise than as a subject *pour rire*, a grotesque, belonging to the category of the decorative rather than the "fine" arts, according to our arbitrary and misleading modern classification.

But Indian genius has here risen above pedantic prescription and given us a really noble conception of Ganesha in a serious mood, as a personification of man's animal nature, imbued with something of the mystery of the Sphinx and a certain supernatural solemnity, carried out with magnificent strength and breadth of modelling (Plate 90B). Ganesha is a symbol of social order and stability : an apotheosis of all the qualities which man shares with the animal creation. Siva is the symbol of the soul—Âtman ; Ganesha, his son, stands for Manas, the mind.[2]

The metaphysical ideas represented by Hindu images are often symbolised more abstractly by geometric signs ; for the philosophic Hindu is often as averse to the natura- listic forms of symbolism as the most furious iconoclast of Christianity or of Islam. The laws of Manu associate the Brahmins who have charge of temple images with thieves and all sorts of disreputable persons ; and even at the present day they are, as a class, held in the greatest contempt by the learned *pandit*. It was probably Græco-Roman influence, acting upon Buddhism, which enlarged enormously the Hindu pantheon and reconciled orthodox Hindu thought to the worship of images as a spiritual aid, more especially for those who were intellectually deficient or too uncultured to understand the metaphysics of esoteric Hinduism.

In this geometric symbolism God, the Absolute or Unknowable, is represented by a point, or dot (*parm*), which is one of the Hindu sectarial marks. The symbol of God manifested in the cosmos is an equilateral triangle, the three sides of which may be taken to represent the Trimûrti. When the triangle stands on its apex it signifies expan- sion or evolution, and, like the swastika, the ascending creative force—or life. It is also the symbol of water as the creative element, and is adopted by Vaishnavaites as the symbol of Nârâyana-Vishnu. The triangle reversed, or standing on its base, signi- fies involution, or contraction, and hence fire, as the destructive element. It is one of the symbols of Siva.

The two triangles intersecting form the mystic lotus, known as King Solomon's Seal, the seat of Brahmâ, the casket which contained the Jewel of Life. It was also the symbol of the cosmic element, ether.

The spiral was another geometric symbol of evolutionary force, represented in nature by the whirling of dust-storms and waterspouts, the eddying of whirlpools, or the wreaths of evaporation in water, the curling of smoke, and in Hindu allegory by the Churning of the Cosmic Ocean. It is represented in Hindu art by the coiled, or gliding snake, the antelope's and ram's horn, the conch-shell of Vishnu and the *sri-vatsa* curl on his breast, the *salagram* stone, Nârâyana's navel, and the winding stalk of the lotus.

The mystic syllable AUM was also represented by a spiral symbol which is sculptured on one of the Elephanta reliefs.[3]

[1] See Part I, "Indian Sculpture and Painting", Plate 21A.

[2] For a traditional interpretation of Ganesha, see Hariharanand Sarasvati, "Greatness of Ganapati," *Journal of the Indian Society of Oriental Art*, VIII (1940), pp. 41-55.—P.C.

[3] See also Alberuni's "India," vol. i. p. 173. Trübner's Oriental Series.

The spiral, together with the swastika and sauwastika, and the parallel symbols of the equilateral triangles, and the three steps of Vishnu, provide the basis of innumerable intersecting patterns in Asiatic decorative art ; but this is a subject beyond the scope of my present inquiry.

Another aniconic symbol, Siva's *lingam*, which in Northern India has almost universally taken the place of quasi-anthropomorphic symbols, was in all probability originally derived from the votive *stûpa* of Buddhism. In Saivaite symbolism it represents the same ideas as those which are associated with the cosmic Tree, or Pillar, and the churning-stick of Vishnu, *i.e.* it stands for the pivot or the axis of cosmic forces, like the "poles" of the earth ; or for the pillar of the cosmic ascent, at the foot of which is the joy of creation, at the summit the bliss of Nirvana. According to a Saivaite myth both Brahmâ and Vishnu failed in their attempt to measure it : for who but Mahadeva Himself could reach to the height of the heavens or fathom the depths of hell ? Though phallic associations are undoubtedly connected with it popularly, to the cultured Hindu it is only suggestive of the philosophic concept that God is a point, formless, or that He is the One.

The ideas connected with sex symbolism in Hindu art and ritual are generally misinterpreted by those who take them out of the environment of Indian social life. In the Upanishads sexual relationship is described as one of the means of apprehending the divine nature, and throughout oriental literature it is constantly used metaphorically to express the true relationship between the human soul and God.[1]

The words of Sir M. Monier-Williams are very applicable to the whole question of sex symbolism in Indian religious art : "In India the relation between the sexes is regarded as a sacred mystery, and is never held to be suggestive of improper or indecent ideas."

H. H. Wilson also says : "Whatever may have been the origin of this form of worship in India, the notions upon which it was founded, according to the impure fancies of European writers, are not to be traced in even the Saiva Puranas."[2]

---

[1] For an excellent and brief discussion of the erotic element in Indian culture, see Mircea Eliade, *Yoga : Immortality and Freedom*, London, 1958, pp. 254-273 ; and Ananda Coomaraswamy, "Tantric Doctrine of Divine Bi-Unity," *Annals of the Bhandarkar Oriental Research Institute*, XIX (1938), pp. 173-182.—P.C.

[2] "Vishnu Purana," Preface, p. xliv.

CHAPTER VI

THE FEMININE IDEAL

HAVING seen how the male human figure in Indian art is used to symbolise the nature of Divinity, we will pass on to consider the feminine ideal. Purusha and Prakriti, Soul and Matter, are held to be inert in themselves, so each of the Trimûrti has its *sakti* or *saktis*, divine powers representing the female principle, which enable them to perform their functions in the universe. Expressed in concrete forms, the female counterpart, or wife, of Brahmâ, the Creator, is the goddess Saraswati, who symbolises learning and wisdom, and is the patroness of the fine arts. Similarly, the *sakti* of Vishnu the Preserver, is Lakshmi, or Sri, who symbolises earthly prosperity, or good fortune. The *saktis* of Siva, as the Destroyer, are Durgâ, Gâuri, and other fighting goddesses, destroyers of demons, to propitiate whom bloody sacrifices, and sometimes human victims, are offered ; but in his benign aspect the *sakti* of Siva is Umâ, or Parvati, daughter of Himâlaya, symbolising spirituality and purity (Plate 91A and B).

In Kâlî, the Ender of Time and Giver of Nirvana, the female principle is worshipped as the Mother of all the Gods. As the *sakti* of Siva in his aspect as Mahâ-kal, Time, it is Kâlî who, at the end of a cosmic cycle, destroys even her own husband and dissolves all the worlds, reducing nature and all the *devas* to their formless, unconditioned state, when Nârâyana reposes again on the primordial waters. The "Nirvana Tantram" says : "As the lightning is born from the cloud and disappears within the cloud, so Brahmâ and all other gods take birth from Kâlî and will disappear in Kâlî." Her images are always black because "as all colours, white, yellow, and others, are absorbed in black, so all the elements are in the end absorbed in Kâlî ; and as the absence of all colours is black, so Kâlî is represented black in order to teach the worshipper that the goddess is without substance and without *gunas*."

This conception of Kâlî does not, however, appear to have been prominent in the great period of Indian sculpture, when Parvati appears most frequently as Siva's consort, and the modern artistic representations of her are generally of the most puerile description.

Though intermediate between soul and matter, and except in the case of Kâlî rarely considered as having an entity apart from the male, the female principle is nevertheless regarded as the most potent force in creation, being representative of the Energy, Power, or Virtue which manifests itself throughout the universe in qualities both benign and malignant, various, elusive, and contrary as the elements of woman's nature, which an Indian legend of the creation, gracefully paraphrased by Mr. Bain, summarises thus :

In the beginning, when Twashtri [the Divine Artificer] came to the creation of woman he found that he had exhausted his materials in the making of man and that no solid elements were left. In this dilemma, after profound meditation, he did as follows. He took the rotundity of the moon and the curves of creepers, and the clinging of tendrils, and the trembling of grass, and the slenderness of the reed, and the bloom of flowers, and the lightness of leaves, and the tapering of the elephant's trunk, and the glances of deer, and the clustering of rows of bees, and the joyous gaiety of sunbeams, and the weeping of clouds, and the fickleness of the winds, and the timidity of the hare, and the vanity of the peacock, and the softness of the parrot's bosom, and the hardness of adamant, and the sweetness of honey, and the cruelty of the tiger, and the warm glow of fire, and the cold-ness of snow, and the chattering of jays, and the cooing of the *kokila*, and the hypocrisy of the crane, and the fidelity of the *chakrawaka*; and, compounding all these together, he made woman and gave her to man."[1]

In early Indian sculpture and painting, before the metaphysical idea of *sakti* began to be represented in female form, there is no super-woman. At Bharhut (Plate 92) and Sânchî both men and women are represented in a purely naturalistic manner; and at Amarâvatî, where aristocratic or divine birth in the male sex is symbolised by the super-human body, the female form still continues to be treated entirely naturalistically.

The ideal of the independent sportswoman, as the virgin goddess Diana, patroness of the chase, has no counterpart in Indian art; though as the slayer of demons, Durgâ, and as Kâlî, the Destroyer, the feminine principle in Hindu theogony is given its ferocious aspect. Hunting has always been a royal sport in India, as in all other countries, but it has never been glorified into a national cult, and the sacredness and unity of all life were principles recognised by every Indian school of religious teaching, even by those which did not distinctly forbid the killing of animals for food. Until the Muhammadan conquest, hunting was never such a favourite theme with Indian artists as it was in Assyria and ancient Iran; animals are either the object of worship themselves or they join with men, as their fellow-creatures, in worshipping at the sacred shrine the Source of all life.

When the Indian woman, from whatever impulse it might be, sought emancipation from social or domestic conventions and restraints, it was to claim equality with men in the spiritual, not the wordly life. What Mrs. Rhys Davids says of the early Buddhist sisterhood is true of Indian womanhood in general:

"To gain this free mobility, *pace* the deeper liberty, they, like their later Christian sisters, had laid down all social position, all domestic success; they had lost their world. But in exchange they had won the status of an individual in place of being adjuncts, however much admired, fostered, and sheltered they might, as such, have been. 'With shaven head, wrapt in their robe'—a dress indistinguishable, it would seem, from the swathing toga and swathed undergarments of the male *religieux*—the Sisters were free to come and go, to dive alone into the depths of the wood, or climb aloft."[2]

And Mrs. Rhys Davids's comment that, "in Buddhist hagiology there is no premium placed on the state of virginity as such,"[3] may be taken as having general application to Indian women also. The ideal of feminine purity and all the consecrations of womanhood in Indian thought are centred first in the chaste wife and mother, and next in the *religieuse*, whether she be virgin or widow. Virginity, in itself, is only a calamity which needs the solace and protection of religion. Another of the Indian legends of Creation paraphrased by Mr. Bain says that woman was made out of the reflections of man, when the latter sought companionship by looking at himself in pools of water. "The woman, as soon as she was made, began to cry, and she said, 'Alas! alas! I am, and I not.' Then said the Creator: 'Thou foolish intermediate creature, thou art a nonentity only when thou standest alone. But when thou art united to man thou art real in participation with his substance.' And thus, apart from her husband a woman is a nonentity, and a shadow without a substance; being nothing but the image of himself reflected in the mirror of illusion."[4]

The type of female beauty most common in Indian art is, therefore, that of the young matron with breasts "like a pair of golden gourds" and "hips like the swell of a river-bank." Not that Indian artists were indifferent to the charm of less mature womanhood, but social custom imposed a stigma upon the unmarried state, and physical beauty by itself is not the ideal of Indian art. Greek artists were satisfied that perfect human

---

[1] "A Digit of the Moon," pp. 13, 14.
[2] "Psalms of the Sisters," Introduction, p. xxv (Henry Frowde).
[3] *Ibid*. p. xxxiii.
[4] "In the Great God's Hair," p. 35.

The immortal Taj, Agra.
(*Photos : M. V. Vijayakar*).

PLATE 97

B. The Tower of Victory, Chittor.
(Copyright by Department of Archaeology, Government of India).

A. Colossal statue of Gomatesvara, Sravan Belgola.
(Copyright by Department of Archaeology, Government of India).

PLATE 98

B. Carved ceiling in Dilwara Temple, Mount Abū. (*Photo, A. L. Syed*).

A. Interior of Dilwara Temple, Mount Abū. (*Photo, A. L. Syed*).

PLATE 99

A. Bird's-eye view of Girnār. (*Photo, Damoder Hansraj*).

B. Pālitānā temple. (*Photo, Damoder Hansraj*).

PLATE 100

beauty, in both sexes, was in itself the type of divine beauty and all-sufficient for man's conception of divinity ; but in Indian thought divine beauty transcends all the ideals of human perfection.

Indian poets, like all others, extol the beauty of the female form (Plates 93B, 94A and B), but these physical charms are snares which disturb holy men in their devotions, spoil their sacrifices, and keep their thoughts tied to this earth. There is a fatal fascination in the beauty of the voluptuous *apsarasas*, the courtesans of the gods—

> With all the gifts of grace and youth and beauty,
> .   .   .   .   .   .yet thus fair,
> Nor god nor demon sought their wedded love—

and they are often represented in Indian sculpture. A good example is shown in Plate 93 A, a bas-relief from an Orissan temple, probably of the thirteenth or fourteenth century, in which the swelling bosom, rounded hips, and the clinging, serpentine grace of the limbs, typical of the Indian feminine ideal, are admirably rendered.

But such types, familiar as they are in Indian art, do not express the highest Indian ideal. Even Umâ, the lovely daughter of Himâlaya, could not win Siva for her husband until Kâma, the god of love, had been burnt to ashes in the fire of the Great God's eyes, and she had proved her devotion by long and trying penances. The cult of the nude female, on which all modern academic art in Europe is based, can therefore bring no inspiration to India.

It is upon spiritual beauty that the Indian artist is always insisting. Purusha, spirit, is the male principle, and the highest type of divine beauty is symbolised by the male figure, the beauty of the female divinity being considered as the reflection, or counterpart of the male form. It would be more exact to say that, in the images of Buddha and the Jain Tirthankaras, Indian artists were aiming at a divine type which combined all the physical perfections of male and female, and transcended them both. The broad shoulders and lion-like body were derived from masculine characteristics, and the rounded limbs, smooth skin without veins, the joints with the bones hardly showing, represented those of the other sex. Afterwards, when Mahâyâna Buddhism provided Buddha with a female counterpart, Indian artists made the new type of divinity conform to the original divine ideal, only adding the most prominent sexual characteristics to distinguish it from the other. Thus was created the ideal super-woman, of which the beautiful figure of Prajnâ-paramitâ[1] from Java is a type. The sexual characteristics became more prominent in Hindu female divinities, such as Parvati and Lakshmi, and in their Buddhist counterparts, the different manifestations of Târâ.

Both of the illustrations given in Plate 91A and B show the feminine divine ideal in the person of Parvati, the Earth Mother. The former, from a South Indian bronze figure of uncertain date, now in the National Museum at Copenhagen, represents her crowned as the consort of Siva ; the latter is related to the myth of Umâ's betrothal to Siva, as told in the poem of Kalidâsa, the "Kumara-sambhava." It belongs to the style of temple-sculpture known as Chalukyan, from the dynasties of that name which ruled over the provinces now known as Hyderabad, Mysore, and Dhârwâr. The style reached its greatest perfection in the eleventh and twelfth centuries, to which epoch this sculpture belongs : it is related to the early Dravidian style of Mâmallapuram in much the same way as late Decorated Gothic is related to Early English. The finest examples now remaining are perhaps the great temple at Ittagi, in Hyderabad, and those at Lakkundi and at Kuruvatti, near Harpanahalli.[2] The more famous Hoysaleshvara temple at Halebîd, though cited

[1] Part I, "Indian Sculpture and Painting," Plate 9.

[2] See Fergusson's "History of Indian Architecture," Revised Edition, 1910, vol. i. book iv. chapter i. ; and Rea's "Chalukyan Architecture."

by Fergusson as the best of its class, is as regards sculpture a decadent example, exhibiting all those faults of over-elaboration and rococo extravagance in decoration which European critics are too prone to associate with Indian art generally.

Plate 91A illustrates one of the two groups of figures placed in front and at the side of the capital of a pilaster at the east entrance of the temple at Kuruvatti. It is no less remarkable as a technical *tour de force* than for its artistic beauty, though the purist might object that the treatment of the material is more suitable for metal than for stone. The principal figure, Parvati[1] or Umâ, the daughter of Himâlaya, is dancing to the accompaniment of the pipe played with intense feeling by the boy on her left. It is not that tremendous dance of Siva, the Tândavan, with which he sets the worlds in motion and hurls them to destruction, but the gentle, swaying rhythm of the nautch which the *gopîs* danced with Krishna in the pastures of Brindâban, like the soft airs of spring which played among the trees of Himâlaya when Umâ came with the god of love to lure the Great Ascetic from his meditations :

> Bright flowers of spring, in every lovely hue,
> Around the lady's form rare beauty threw.
> Some clasped her neck like strings of purest pearls,
> Some shot their glory through her wavy curls,
> Bending her graceful head, as half oppressed
> With swelling charms even too richly blest.
> Fancy might deem that beautiful young maiden
> Some slender tree with its sweet flowers o'erladen.[2]

In this wonderfully animated and festive group, as fine in human sentiment as it is decorative in beauty, the sculptor has entered heart and soul into the spirit of Kalidâsa's verse. Very charming is the modest, half-shy expression of the beautifully poised oval head ; the robust, rich modelling of the goddess's body gives the true Indian ideal of ripe young womanhood, the full bosom, the slender waist, the swelling hips, and the tapering limbs. The joyous rhythm of the dance vibrates through the whole group like the breath of spring, in the magnificent swing of Parvati's body, like a young forest-tree swaying in the wind, in the varied curves of her richly wrought ornaments, in the fluttering tassels, and in the delightful little figures which balance the composition on either side.

The sculptor has enhanced the feeling of lightness and gaiety by converting the aureole, the symbol of divinity behind the goddess, into a flowing wreath, or scroll, which in the gracefulness of its design and perfect execution is not the least beautiful touch in this remarkable work, though the right half of it has been broken.

Most of the marks of female beauty enumerated by Indian poets, such as the navel low in the body, eyes like a lotus-petal, face like the full moon, the lines on the neck resembling those on the conch-shell, and the slender waist, were equally attributes of male beauty, and were included in the *lakshanas* or beauty-marks, prescribed for images of Buddha and the Jain Tirthankaras. Even the practice of tight lacing would seem from the evidence of the Cretan sculptures to have been originally a masculine and not feminine vanity : the purpose of it being, as I have explained, to make the male body conform to the artistic ideal of a mighty hunter.

The description of Draupadi's charms in the Mahâbhârata is a typical poetic description of Indian feminine beauty. When she came in disguise to Sudeshnâ, the wife of king Virâta, offering herself as a servant, the Queen, in astonishment, enumerates all the charms of her person, declaring that so much beauty was quite incompatible with her professed occupation :

---

[1] The image is certainly not that of Parvati, but represents a Gandhari accompanied by a musician and drummer.–P.C.
[2] "The Birth of the War-god," by Kalidasa. Translated by R. H. W. Griffith.

"You might indeed," said the Queen, "be the mistress of servants, both male and female. Your heels are not prominent, and your thighs touch each other. You have great intelligence, your navel is deep, and your words are well-chosen. And your great-toes, bosom and hips and dorsa, and toe-nails and palms of your hands are all well developed. And the palms of your hands and the soles of your feet and your face are ruddy. And your speech is sweet, even as the voice of a swan. And your hair is beautiful, your bosom shapely, and you are possessed of the highest grace; and like a Kashmerean mare, you are furnished with every auspicious mark. Your eye-lashes are beautifully bent, your lip is like the ruddy gourd. Your waist is slender and the lines of your neck are like those upon a conch-shell. And your veins are scarcely visible. Indeed your countenance is like the full moon, your eyes resemble the petals of the autumnal lotus, and your body is fragrant like the lotus itself. Surely in beauty you resemble Sri herself, whose seat is the autumnal lotus. Tell me beautiful damsel, who thou art! Thou canst never be a maid-servant. Art thou a Yakshi, a goddess, a Gandharvi, or an *Apsarâ?* Art thou the daughter of a celestial, or art thou a Nâgini? Art thou the guardian goddess of some city, a Vidyâdara, or Kinnari, or art thou Rohini herself?"

A pretty animistic conceit, which affords a favourite *motif* for Indian poets, dramatists, and artists, is that which makes the asoka-tree burst into flower when touched by the foot of a beautiful woman.[1]

It may be, as Mr. Abanindro Nath Tagore has suggested, an allegory of the reawakening of nature on the approach of spring; like the story of the marriage of Umâ and Siva, as told by Kalidâsa in the "Kumara-sambhava."

The whole of the third act of Kalidâsa's play, *Malikagnimitra*, is founded upon it. Dharini, the first Queen of Agnimitra, had been told that an asoka-tree in her palace garden was languishing. She therefore sends her beautiful handmaiden, Malika, to revive it, as she herself had sprained her ankle in falling from a swing. The King, who is deeply smitten with Malika's charms, is in the garden when she comes to fulfil the Queen's commands, and hides himself, together with a courtier, his confidant, while the preliminaries of the magic rite are being arranged. First a fellow-handmaid colours the soles of Malika's feet with lac, and skilfully draws upon them with the brush a lotus-flower in full bloom. Then she puts on her ankles a pair of *nouparas*, ornaments which are symbolic of Kâma, the god of love. Malika, taking a branch of the asoka-tree in one hand and making ear-pendants of the buds, touches the tree with her left foot.[2] The King, who is in raptures at the sight, then comes forward; but the sudden appearance of the second Queen on the scene creates an amusing but, for the King, a very disconcerting diversion, which ends this act of the play.

On the eastern gate of the Sânchî tope there is a very fine sculpture of a young woman clinging to the branches of an asoka-tree with both arms, and with the sole of her left foot pressing against the trunk. Her legs are almost completely covered with ornaments.[3] A similar subject from Gandhara is illustrated by Dr. Vogel in a recent article published in the *Bulletin de l'Ecole Française d'Extrême Orient*.[4] Plate 93A gives a more modern example from an Orissan temple.

In later South Indian sculpture a very similar *motif* is common, called by modern temple

[1] In early Indian sculpture, the woman-and-tree motif is quite clearly a representation of Yakshi dryads. They are fertility spirits of trees, whose blessings are invoked by women desirous of children. The *dohada* motif, according to Coomaraswamy (*Yakshas*, Vol. I, Washington, 1928, p. 35) "seems to be equally a form of the Yakshi-dryad theme." It is significant, he notes, in connection with Malavika's performance of the ceremony whereby the Asoka tree is made to flower by the touch of a woman's foot, that "the scene takes place besides a 'slab of rock' under the asoka tree and this shows that the tree itself was a sacred tree haunted by a spirit." *Ibid.*, p. 36.—P.C.

[2] Woman is said to have been born of the left side of Brahma, the Creator, and that seems to be the reason why the left side of her body is considered to be purer than her right side.

[3] Part I, "Indian Sculpture and Painting," Plate 25A.

[4] Juillet-Septembre, 1909.

craftsmen, "the girl with the creeper falling over her." (Plate 94 C.). A young woman, probably meant for an *apsarâ*, resting on the left leg and with the right leg crossed in front of it, stands on the back of a *makara*, the fish-emblem of the god of love.[1] The *makara* holds in its mouth the stem of a conventionalised creeper which winds in richly elaborated scrolls over the head of the figure. With one hand raised up she grasps the lower tendrils of the creeper ; the other hand rests easily upon her hip—the attitude of Malika when she ravished the heart of King Agnimitra under the asoka-tree.

It is not my intention to attempt to follow the symbology of Hinduism in all its intricate details. For understanding Indian art it is not necessary to acquire the erudition of the savant ; those who are absorbed in counting trees often miss the beauty of the wood. It is much more important to recognise principles which apply not more particularly to Indian art than to art-criticism in general.

In the explanations I have given here and elsewhere I have endeavoured to attach to Indian artistic symbols the meanings which the great Indian artists who used them intended them to convey, not that which, now or formerly, has been given to them by superstitious priests and ignorant peasants. No art can be interpreted correctly unless it is clearly understood that there is a process of evolution in the meaning of symbols, as in religious ideas. Much of the misunderstanding and depreciation of Indian culture in Europe has been due to the want of recognition of this principle.

It may be partly true, as Sir George Birdwood is always insisting, that "India has remained, to the present day, a reservation of antiquity—Chaldæan, Assyrian, and Babylonian." If local traditions and superstitions are considered, the same might be said of many parts of Christian Europe ; but one does not look to European folklore or the thoughts of the ignorant peasant to interpret the higher spiritual significance of Christianity. In the same way it is utterly misleading to interpret the great works of Indian sculpture and painting in an academic or pedantic sense totally at variance with the philosophy which inspired Indian culture in all its higher aspects, and to ascribe to symbolic forms used by Indian artists and philosophers in the fifth century A.D. meanings which may or may not have been applied to them, in other remote countries, 500 or 5,000 years before Christ.

We must attach to Christian symbols the meaning given them by Christian artists and the early Christian Fathers, not that which Hindu archæologists might be inclined to ascribe to them. Similarly, if we would understand Indian art, or any aspect of Indian culture, we must give to Siva, Ganesha, and other Indian symbols the meaning which Indian artists and authoritative Indian teachers originally gave to them, and not confuse them with the superstitions of the uncultured, or read into them their prehistoric derivations.

It is quite certain, as Count D'Alviella has so admirably explained in his book on the Migration of Symbols, that each religion preserves in its rites and symbols survivals of the whole series of former religions ; but, as he wisely observes, "it is not the vessel that is important, but the wine which we pour into it ; not the form, but the ideas which animate and transcend the form."

It is by concentrating themselves upon the forms, rather than upon the ideas which animate them, that many archæologists have gone so much astray in their interpretations of Indian art. Though Indian artists borrowed the traditional forms of Egypt, Chaldæa, Assyria, Babylonia, and Greece, it was not the ideas originally associated with those forms which gave them inspiration, but the philosophy of the Upanishads and the teachings of their spiritual leaders.

---

[1] The *makara* is a symbol of the River Goddess Ganga but Coomaraswamy, *Yakshas*, Vol. I, p. 41, agrees with Havell in interpreting the creature in the present context as an emblem of the God of Love. According to him, *Ibid.*, Vol. II, Washington, 1931, p. 47, "as a great Leviathan moving in the Waters, the *makara* is obviously a symbol of the Waters, and as will appear from its associations, more specifically of the Essence in the Waters, the principle of life." In this respect the appearance of the *makara* on the banner of Kamadeva, the God of Love, is particularly appropriate.—P.C.

CHAPTER VII

THE THREE PATHS

IN the psychology of Indian art the underlying religious ideals, which make it so closely akin to the Christian art of the Middle Ages, are contained in the doctrine of the Three Paths, the three ways leading to salvation, known as the way of works (*karma-marga*), the way of faith (*bhakti-marga*), and the way of knowledge (*gnana-marga*) ; which may be explained as the concept of the Trimûrti applied to human life and conduct.

It is hardly within the province of an artist to enter upon the archæological question as to when those ideas were first named and shaped by priests and schoolmen into definite religious concepts, or to join in the keen controversy as to how much modern Hinduism is indebted to Christian teaching. But I think it must be evident to every one with artistic insight who reads Indian art, not in Sanskrit and Pali texts, but in the great monuments which Indian artists bequeathed to posterity, that, just as the spiritual impulses which created Indian art originated in times long anterior to the sculptures of Bharhut, Sânchî, and Gandhara, so the religious ideals which underlie the doctrine of the Three Paths are of much greater antiquity than the Vaishnavaite sect of Hinduism, which now claims one of them for itself.

These ideals have been the common property of all Indian art, from the time of Asoka down to the present day. *Moksha*, spiritual freedom, has always been the goal of Indian desire, hymned with as much passionate fervour by the Buddhist *bhikku* and *bhikkuni* as by Hindu religious devotees, and striven for as keenly by the unlearned pilgrim and *sâdhu* as by the Brahmin *sannyâsi*. Islam gave the goal another name, and put forward another spiritual guide, but the goal remained the same.

The three paths to salvation distinguished three different religious temperaments, and three classifications of intellectuality, of occupation, and of social rank. The path of highest attainment, that of knowledge, was that marked out especially for the Brahmin priest or the intellectual Kshatriya : it was the shortest and most direct way to Nirvana. The path of works, or service, was for the busy man of the world, for the statesman, the artist, the merchant, the artisan, and the common labourer. The path of faith[1] had a more general application, for it was a way which was open to all classes ; all whose hearts were filled with the love of God and gave their lives to Him could find salvation in *bhakti*, though worldly pursuits might clog their feet and make the way longer and more difficult.

Bhakti comprehends all the three cardinal virtues—faith, hope, and charity. Dr. Grierson, summarising the aphorisms of Sândilya, says that "it is not knowledge, though it may be the result of knowledge. It is not worship, etc. These are merely outward acts, and *bhakti* need not necessarily be present in them. It is simply and solely an affection devoted to a person, and not belief in a system. There is a promise of immortality to him who 'abides' in Him. A wish is selfish ; affection is unselfish. It is not a 'work,' and does not depend upon an effort of the will. The fruit of 'works' is transient ; that of *bhakti* is eternal life. Works, if they are pure, are a means to *bhakti*. To be pure, they must be surrendered to Him ; *i.e.* the doer must say, 'Whatever I do, with or without my will, being all surrendered to Thee, I do it as impelled by Thee. Good actions, done for the good results which they produce in a future life, do not produce *bhakti*, but are a bondage."

Joined with this religious fervour was the intense feeling of reverence and love of nature,

[1] *Bhakti-marga.*

that which shines out first in the Vedic hymns, which illumines the great epics and all the best Indian literature. The places in which the gods loved to dwell, and auspicious for their temples, were the wooded hill-tops, the green, sequestered forest glades, and the cool mountain-ridges overlooking an endless stretch of dust-laden plain, where the weary soul could rest and sing :

Oh, free indeed ! Oh, gloriously free am I [1]

Or, as a Hindu astrologer writes :

"On sandy banks scratched by the nails of aquatic birds, and as charming to the eye and heart as the swelling hips of sportful damsels. Or near a lake azure as the clear sky, where dark lotuses are open, like so many eyes, where skipping swans form, as it were, a white umbrella, and ducks, ospreys, and cranes raise their cries. . . . Or on the seaside crowded with happily arrived splendid ships, and showing a line half dark, half white, owing to the fishes and white birds lurking in the rotang."

Or, again :

"Places where rivers flow, having curlews for their tinkling zone, singing swans for their melodious voice, the water-sheet for their cover, and carps for their belt ; regions where streams have blooming trees on the margin . . . tracts of land in the neighbourhood of woods, rivers, rocks, and cataracts ; towns with pleasure-gardens—it is in such places that the gods at all times take delight."[2]

This appreciation of nature's charm is, indeed, the feeling which inspires all art. But there is a distinction which makes the Indian outlook fundamentally different to that of the West. In Western thought man is supreme, and its whole ideal of beauty is centred in the human form. It is for man's delight that nature is so gaily dressed ; for him the sun and moon do shine, and the trees bring forth their flowers and fruit. For *his* salvation God reveals Himself. The dumb animals are his companions and friends only when they minister to his needs, sustenance and comfort ; they have no place in his heaven.

There is no parallel in Western hagiology to the touching incident in the Mahâbhârata when Yudhishthira, the sole survivor of the heroic Pândava brothers, having at last reached the Gates of Swarga, is met by Indra himself, but refuses to enter the shining car which will transport him to Paradise unless his faithful dog is allowed to accompany him : "O mighty Indra ! I will not forsake this dog of mine, even for my own salvation."

Only in rare moments of illumination has Christian Europe realised, with St. Francis, that all creation is one. It has been left to modern science to confirm what Indian philosophy taught three thousand years ago, and what Indian art has ever sought to express.

Since the days of remote antiquity when the *rishis* addressed their prayers to the Unknown God :

"He who gives breath, He who gives strength, whose command all the bright angels revere, whose shadow is immortality, whose shadow is death . . . . He who, through His might, became the sole King of the breathing and twinkling world ; who governs all this, man and beast"[3]—

this has been India's message to the world ; and this is the faith of every Indian peasant to-day.

When Râma started off to his exile in the forest, all nature joined in the entreaties of the sorrowing citizens of Ayodhya :

[1] "Psalms of the Sisters," No. XI. Translated by Mrs. Rhys Davids.

[2] "Brihat-sanghita of Varaha-mihira." Translated by Dr. Kern. *J.R.A.S.*, vol. vi. part i. pp. 72 *et seq.*, and part ii. p. 317.

[3] Rig-Veda, 121. Translated by Max Müller : "Sacred Books of the East," vol. xxxii. p. 1.

Thick darkness o'er the sun was spread ;
The cows their thirsty calves denied,
And elephants flung their food aside.

Each lowly bush, each towering tree
Would follow too for love of thee.
Bound by its roots it must remain,
But—all it can—its boughs complain,
As, when the wild wind rushes by,
It tells its love in groan and sigh.
No more through air the gay birds flit,
But, foodless, melancholy, sit
Together on a branch and call
To thee, whose kind heart feels for all.[1]

Sîtâ's first care, when the edge of the forest was reached, was to invoke the spirit of the lordly pîpal-tree :

"Hail, hail, O mighty tree ! Allow
My husband to complete his vow ;
Let us, returning, I entreat,
Kauslayá and Sumitrá meet."
Then, with her hands together placed,
Around the tree she duly paced.

It is not the ignorance and superstition of the primitive savage, but a firmly rooted belief in the doctrine of reincarnation and in the immanence of God, which makes the Indian express so reverently and worshipfully his intimate fellowship with all created things ; addressing his prayers, not to stocks and stones, but to the all-prevailing Spirit which dwells therein. Gautama himself had passed through all forms of life in his progress to Nirvana, and in the tree, worm, or insect, or in the beast of the field, there still might dwell the soul of the Buddha that is to come.

The Indian poet makes Prince Siddhartha, when finally he set out on his mission to redeem mankind, caress his good horse Kamthaka and exhort him, "like a friend, to his duty," to strive for his own good and the good of the world ; and on parting from him, when the "noblest of steeds" licked Siddhartha's feet and dropped hot tears, these were the Prince's consoling words : "Shed not tears, Kamthaka. This thy perfect equine nature has been proved—bear with it ; this thy labour will soon have its fruit."[2]

And so the Indian artist is always convinced that the *bhakti* which inspires his own work is shared by all creation. In the sculptures of Sânchî and Amarâvatî he shows the wild elephants coming to pour libations over the sacred tree under which the Buddha sat, and all the denizens of the forest join with their human fellow-creatures in adoration of the Buddha's footprints, his begging-bowl, or his relic-shrines. It is to symbolise this universal fellowship of man, the unity of all creation, that the Indian artist loves to crowd into his picture all forms of teeming life, while the Western is always insisting on plain spaces for emphasising the supremacy of man, for isolating and for preserving artistic unity. From this motive the Indian sculptor adds enrichment upon enrichment to his decorative scheme, the architect breaks up his ground-plan, divides the spires of the temples into many facets, piles pinnacle upon pinnacle, and uses every constructive feature to symbolise the universal law of the One in many.

[1] The "Ramayana," canto xlv. Griffith's translation.
[2] "The Buddha-karita of Ashvagosha," book vi. 58. Translated by E. B. Cowell.

The European critic and art-teacher, not understanding the Indian motive, and generally standing quite aloof from the Indian environment, lectures the Indian in a tone of intellectual superiority upon lack of classical simplicity and neglect of artistic "principles." The Indian, striving to learn the wisdom of the West, flounders helplessly in an intellectual element totally foreign to his spiritual instinct, and his brain merely records automatically the prescriptions of his pedantic teachers. But it is altogether unjust to attribute incoherency and want of co-ordination to Indian art in general. Nothing is more admirable in the great monuments of India than the consummate skill and imagination with which, in spite of the extraordinary wealth of detail, every part of the whole is perfectly adjusted to its place and so balanced that æsthetic unity is always perfectly preserved.

It is only when *bhakti* is lost and the whole spiritual basis of Indian art is superseded by the modern commercial instinct, when the Indian barters his birthright for a mess of pottage and manufactures by the yard for the markets of Europe, that it becomes incoherent and meretricious. And it is generally by this commercial trash that artistic Europe now judges India.

Indian art has never been surpassed in expressing, with perfect simplicity and directness, the pure devotion and self-surrender implied in *bhakti*—"Whatever I do, with or without my will, being all surrendered to Thee, I do it as impelled by Thee." It is the *motif* in the exquisite group of the mother and child before Buddha in the Ajanta cave-paintings, and in one of the most perfect of the Bôrôbudûr reliefs—that which shows the Buddha arriving on the shores of Java, having crossed the ocean on a lotus-flower to bring his message to the island. In the sky above the spirits of the air throng together joyfully, bringing their offerings and throwing flowers around him. On earth the prince and his wives prostrate themselves at his feet ; and the deer from the forest calls to her little one to join in adoration of the Lord of the deer who had once offered his life for them.[1]

As a religious cult *bhakti* finds artistic expression in modern Hindu art in subjects relating to the love of Radha for Krishna, where Krishna is the Indian Orpheus, drawing all creation to listen to the divine music of his flute, and where Radha's passionate devotion is the symbol of the soul's yearning for God.

In Southern India the religious idealism of *bhakti* is represented by a series of fine quasi-portrait statuettes now in the Colombo Museum. Plate 95A is a bronze figure of Appar-swami, a native of Southern India, who lived about the sixth century A.D. He was first a Buddhist, but afterwards became an apostle of Jainism, and his hymns in praise of Siva are still sung in South Indian temples. To testify his devotion he went about weeding the courtyards of the temples, and he is here represented with hands joined in prayer and the weeding implement resting on his left shoulder. He was a contemporary and friend of another Saivaite saint, Tiru-gnana-sambandha Swami, who was said to have been called to the worship of Siva when a child, and went about singing his praises to the accompaniment of a pair of golden cymbals.[2] There are several statuettes of this swami in the Colombo collection.

Plate 95B is from a very beautiful bronze statuette of Sundara Mûrti Swami, also in the Colombo Museum, which is attributed to the tenth or eleventh century A.D. The charming story of the saint's illumination and consecration to the service of Siva is told by Dr. Coomaraswamy in his "Selected Examples of Indian Art."[3]

These saintly legends sufficiently explain the devotional spirit by which these statuettes are animated. The spirit of *bhakti*, the simple, childlike faith which finds full and complete satisfaction of all worldly desires in the worship and service of God, is perfectly ex-

[1] Part I, "Indian Sculpture and Painting," Plate 33.
[2] See *Spolia Ceylonica*, issued by the Colombo Museum, September 1909, p. 68.
[3] Essex House Press, 1910.

A. General view of Kailāsa temple, Ellora. (*Copyright, Department of Archaeology, Government of India*).

B. Temple of Sūrya at Mudherā, Gujerat. (*Copyright, Department of Archaeology, Government of India*).

PLATE 101

B. The great bas-relief at Māmallapuram, Central part.
(*Copyright, Department of Archaeology, Government of India*).

A. The Temple of the Sun, Kanārak, Orissa.
(*Copyright, Department of Archaeology, Government of India*).

PLATE 102

A. The great bas-relief at Māmallapuram, right half. (*Copyright, Department of Archaeology, Government of India*).

B. Vishnu supporting the universe. Bas-relief at Māmallapuram.
(*Copyright, Department of Archaeology, Government of India*).

PLATE 103

A. Lakshmi arising from the Sea of Milk. Bas-relief from Māmallapuram. (*Copyright, Department of Archaeology, Government of India*).

B. Sculpture of a bull at Māmallapuram. (*Copyright, Department of Archaeology, Government of India*).

PLATE 104

pressed in the rapt face, the unstudied reverential attitude, and in the deliberate exclusion of all petty technical details which might divert attention from the all-absorbing *motif*. It is an art, with perfect control of technical methods, which from its intense sincerity and depth of religious conviction makes no parade of virtuosity; it aims straight for truth, and hits the mark with effortless ease. The personality of the artist is merged in his own creations.

This, indeed, is essentially a characteristic of all Indian religious art, which it shares with the Gothic art of Europe—that the artist seeks no reward of fame or riches. He has no biographers; his masterpieces are unsigned. He is content that his own identity shall be completely lost in his art, his name forgotten. The merit which he gains is only that which is reckoned in the great account hereafter.

Mr. Binyon, I think, wrongly infers, from the paucity of literary references to the lives and works of artists in India, that the æsthetic sense is lacking in the Indian character, that it has played an inferior part in the national life. One fact which he has overlooked is that practically the whole of that part of Indian literature, the Silpa Sastras, which is concerned with the principles and practice of art, has hitherto been completely ignored by European scholars. No one has even thought it worth while to compile a catalogue, much less to devote time to the study of it. So far as art is concerned, Indian literature is a totally unexplored field. But, even allowing that in Chinese literature æsthetic subjects are given a more important place, that by no means proves that the artistic perceptions of the Chinese races have been more developed than those of Indians. No one will say that Europeans of the present day have profounder artistic convictions, finer æsthetic sensibility, or higher accomplishments than their forefathers; yet at no period in history has European literature concerned itself so much with art as at the present time.

Art must always speak for itself; we must judge Indian art by its own achievements. In spite of centuries of vandalism and neglect, there remains enough of it to show that Indian genius has never lacked the power to express its highest religious ideals in worthy æsthetic form. True, it may be that the idea of art for art's sake did not take root in the Indian mind except in the luxurious Courts of the Mogul Emperors. That is simply an indication of the Hindu view of life as a whole, of the spirit of self-surrender always insisted upon by Indian philosophers and religious teachers—to work without attachment to the fruits of work; to realise self by resting on the One Supreme Self. This is very far from being a doctrine of æsthetic nihilism; no one who penetrates beneath the surface of Indian thought and life could take it in that sense.

Bhakti is the moving spirit in all great religious art, in the West as in the East. It is *bhakti* which lifts the art of Fra Angelico, or of Bellini, into a higher spiritual plane than that of Titian or Corregio. It is *bhakti* that we miss in nearly all the great masters of the Renaissance. Vanity, intellect, and wealth could raise another monument greater than St. Peter's at Rome; only *bhakti* could revive the glories of Bourges, Chartres, or the other great Gothic cathedrals of medieval Europe. Forced labour, money, and artistic genius might create another Dîwân-i-khâs at Delhi—another Elysium on earth for sensual desires—and perhaps another Taj Mahal. But without *bhakti* India, whether she be Hindu, Muhammadan, or Christian, can never again build shrines like those of Sânchî, Ajanta, Elephanta, or Ellora: and when *bhakti* is dead India, from being the home of the world's religions, will become the storm-centre of the East.

It is *bhakti* which now keeps Indian art alive: it is the lack of it which makes modern Western art so lifeless. The same spirit which in the days of Asoka and Kanishka brought thousands of willing craftsmen to devote their lives to the service of the Blessed One in building and adorning the *stûpas* of Bharhut, Sânchî, and Amarâvatî, that same devotion which impelled the worshippers of Siva or of Vishnu, century after century to the stupendous task of hewing out of the living rock the temples of Ellora and Elephanta, and the followers of Mahavira to carve with infinite labour, fantasy, and skill the marvellous arabesques and tracery of their temples in Western India—this *bhakti* is still a potent force in India, and if Great Britain could produce a statesman of Akbar's artistic understanding it might still be used, as Akbar used it, to consolidate the foundations of our Indian Empire. But this great spiritual force we usually ignore and condemn as superstition and barbarism. We try to exterminate it by the contra-forces of European science, European materialism, and European Philistinism.

Anglo-Indians have always ascribed the artistic triumphs of the Indian Mogul dynasty to the superior æsthetic genius of Islam; but this is a quite untrue reading of Indian art-history. They should rather be attributed to the wonderful statecraft of the freethinker Akbar in rallying round his throne all the hereditary artistic skill of Hindustan, and in building up his empire with the *bhakti* of Hinduism in much the same way as the Mikados of Japan used the national cult of Shintoism to strengthen their own dynasty. The Moguls in China, in Persia, in India, and wherever else they went, assimilated the art of the races they conquered. The art of Fatehpur-Sikri and of Jahangir's great palace at Agra is essentially Hindu art. Abul Fazl, writing with full appreciation of contemporary painting, says of the Hindus: "Their pictures surpass our conception of things. Few indeed in the whole world are found equal to them,"[1] Even in the Taj Mahal, the typical masterpiece of what we call Mogul art, many of the principal craftsmen were Hindus, or of Hindu descent; and how much Persian art owed to the frequent importation of Indian artists and craftsmen is never understood by European art-critics.

The splendid Muhammadan architecture of Bijapur (Plate 96A) derived much of its grandeur and beauty from the skilful adaptation of Hindu principles of construction and design. All the great monuments of Saracenic art in India surpass those of Arabia, Turkey, Egypt, and Spain, in the exact measure by which they were indebted to Hindu craftsmanship and inspired by Hindu idealism. The mosques of Cairo and Constantinople seem almost insignificant in design and feeble in construction compared with those of Bijapur, Delhi, Fatehpur-Sikri, and Ahmedabad (Plate 96B). The painted stucco and the geometric ingenuity of the Alhambra are cold and monotonous beside the consummate craft and imagination of the Mogul palaces in India.

And what is it in the Taj Mahal—that indefinable something always felt rather than understood by those who have tried to describe it—but the subtle inspiration of Hindu genius which animates the lifeless stones and makes one feel that it is not a cold monument of marble, but Shah Jahan's beloved, Mumtaz Mahal herself, who lingers still in all her youthful beauty upon the banks of the shining Jumna? The inspiration of the Taj came not from its Muslim builders: it was the spirit of India which came upon it and breathed into it the breath of life. (Plate 97).

Saracenic art flourished in India just so long as the Mogul emperors were wise enough to observe perfect impartiality between Musalman and Hindu. When the bigot Aurangzîb expelled all the Hindu artists and craftsmen whom his father and grandfather had attracted to the service of the state, the art of the Moguls in India was struck with a blight from which it never recovered. Even in the present day all that is most fine and precious in living Indian art is found in the art inspired by this same *bhakti* produced by the descendants of the hereditary Hindu temple architects and craftsmen whom Akbar the Great enlisted in his service to carry out all his public works, the imperial palaces, and mosques, as well as durbar halls, offices, stables, and irrigation works. The quality of

---

[1] "Ain-i-Akbari," Blochmann's translation, vol. i. p. 107. Abul Fazl's appreciation will be understood by any art-critic who has an opportunity of studying side by side a representative collection of Persian and Indian miniature paintings of the Mogul period. Those of direct Persian origin, in spite of the exquisite grace and fine technical qualities which they often have, lack the penetrative insight of the Hindu artist's work. The former might be compared with the French schools of the eighteenth century, in their daintiness and *chic*; the latter have more of the sentiment of the early Flemish schools, or of Carpaccio, with something of the profound insight of Rembrandt.

their craftsmanship is generally in no way inferior to the work of the Mogul time ; what they lack are the opportunities given them by the Moguls which we have hitherto refused to them.

Indian art can only be preserved by the survival, or revival, of the spiritual power which created it.   The spread of Western political institutions and Western religious formularies in India should not mean the sterilisation of the spirituality of which Indian art is the expression.

It is true that every age has its own special needs and its own ideals.   India may not need another Taj Mahal, or more glorious shrines than those she now possesses.   But for the *bhakti* which created these all the world has need ; and to give India's spirituality a new impetus and a wider range of activity would be the crowning achievement of British administration.

The art which we now try to propagate in India gives no spiritual impulse, and affords only the poorest mental pabulum : with its mechanical perspective, not related, like oriental perspective, and that which served the artists of Europe before the days of the Renaissance, to the laws of design, but, only empirically, to the science of optics ; with its anatomy, likewise unrelated to artistic thought ; and its "principles," which even we ourselves fail to put into practice.

Chapter VIII

THE HISTORICAL DEVELOPMENT OF INDIAN ART

The historical background of Indian art is that which is furnished by the record of India's great spiritual teachers, by the exploits of her heroes, and by the lives of her noble men and women. It may seem often to the Western critic that all Indian literature is wanting in the historic sense, just as Indian sculpture and painting are assumed to be crude and inartistic for neglect of common physiological and other scientific facts. But just as Indian art is thoroughly scientific in the Indian sense, so Indian history also fulfils adequately the purpose which Indian historians had in view.

In the great period of Hindu and Buddhist sculpture fundamental physiological truths are never disregarded, though minor anatomical details are rigorously suppressed in order to achieve the end for which the artist was striving. Though artistic facts are not always sought for within the limits of the human or animal world, yet the laws of the structure of man or beast are never ignorantly outraged. Indian artistic anatomy is a possible and consistent ideal anatomy, and Indian perspective is a possible and consistent ideal perspective. The offence, to the modern European mind, is that the science of Hindu and Buddhist art transcends the limits of modern Western science which would keep art, like itself, chained to the observation of natural effects and phenomena, as they are impressed upon the retina of the ordinary human eye.

In the same way Indian history is not all a chaos of wild and fantastic legend, without system and without sequence, though such facts as the day on which Buddha died, or the exact date of the battle of Kurukshetra, were never considered of sufficient importance to be drummed into the heads of Indian schoolboys. Indian history, like Indian philosophy and Indian art, is a part of Indian religion. The scientific basis is there : the chronological sequence is not disregarded ; but just as all Indian art aims at showing the relation between the seen and the unseen, between the material universe and the spiritual, so Indian history is much more concerned with the bearing which human events and actions have upon human conduct than with compiling a bare record of the events and actions themselves. Indian history is a spiritual guide and moral text-book for Indian people, not a scientific chronicle of passing events. Every day, in one of the innumerable worlds, a Buddha may die ; so the day of Gautama's decease matters little to us : the way he lived and the essence of his teaching are the things which are counted in the roll of the world's evolution.

Then again, Indian history, like Indian art, is ideal. The modern Western scholar is shocked at the confusion between poetry, romance, and history which is found in ancient records, both in the East and in the West—even in the Christian Bible. He assumes that the sole aim of the historian is to reveal the bare threads of the warp and weft in the loom of time, by picking out the fair flowers of the imagination, with which poetry and religion have lovingly embroidered it. But to the oriental there is a truth in idealism intrinsically more true than what we call the bare, the naked truth. Western science can never reveal the springs of human action, nor discover the spiritual bearing of human events, however minutely it may dissect and explain the organisation of matter. The "higher criticism" can never destroy the essential truths of the New Testament, nor can the searchlight of modern science diminish the truth of revelation which shines in the Buddhist and Hindu Scriptures. History is both art and science : the historian needs to be a seer and a poet to present facts in their true significance and to give to each event its relative spiritual importance. The embroidery of the great artist does not weaken the fabric which Time weaves for himself : it strengthens while it beautifies. And to those who believe in a spiritual world as even more actual and real than the phenomenal world there is as much reality in the embroidery as in the plain warp and weft with which it is interwoven. Though the foolish or unskilful embroiderer may spoil the warp, yet it is only through the imagination that we can link together the seen and the unseen, and without imagination science itself loses its vital force, and the modern scientific historian may become the falsest of guides.

There is evidence enough to show that both Eastern and Western ways of thought may lead into a morass. Art in the East may degenerate into a mechanical repetition of debased hierarchical formularies ; history, both sacred and profane, may sink into the most degraded obscurantism. And in the West, also, art may end itself in mere virtuosity, or in colour photography, machine-made sculpture, and the pianola : the historic sense may be sterilised through a foolish craze for autographs, buttons, and snuff-boxes. In the middle path, where safety lies, East and West, art and science, may go together hand in hand. Imagination must always lean upon reason : reason must ever seek a higher inspiration than its own. Siva is greater than Ganesha : yet Ganesha is always to be first invoked.

In Buddhist art the familiar story of the Great Renunciation and all the events of Gautama's life until the final attainment of Nirvana form the historical background for the expression of Indian ideals. As commentaries upon these events, the legends of his former lives, called the *jâtakas* are added to explain symbolically the process of evolution by which the soul gradually obtains liberation from its material attachments : a process perceived by Indian seers several millennial before Western science announced that all matter is instinct with life.

Through such historical facts, and fictions containing eternal verities, the Indian sculptor and painter instructed the crowds of pious pilgrims who thronged the procession-paths enclosing the innumerable relic-shrines of Buddhism, and the aisles of thousands of *chaityas*, or churches, where the members of the Sangha met for worship. As aids to meditation also, the walls and ceilings of the great Buddhist *viharas*, the monastic universities, were covered with similar historical and mythological frescoes or sculptures.

Though in the preceding chapters I have followed archæological precedent in assuming that the representation of the divine ideal in Indian art, founded upon the ideal heroic type of Aryan poetry, is first discovered in Buddhist sculpture and painting, it is by no means certain that the Indian conception of the Buddha as a divinity was not adapted from earlier anthropomorphic images worshipped by other sects.

We have seen that it was not until a comparatively late period in Buddhism that the person of the Buddha as a divinity is represented in art ; yet it is quite certain that anthropomorphic idols were worshipped in India long before the earliest Gandhara sculpture. References to such images occur in several passages in the Mahâbhârata ; *e.g.* in the Bhishma Parva[1] it is mentioned, as an omen of coming disaster, that "the idols of the Kuru king in their temples tremble and laugh, and dance and weep."

Mahavira, the twenty-fourth Tirthankara of the Jains, a contemporary of the Buddha, is commonly assumed to be the founder of Jainism ; but the Jains themselves claim for their religion a much greater antiquity, and it is possible that the earliest images of the Tirthankaras, or deified heroes, may have been the prototype followed by the Indian Buddhist image-makers.

But it was not in sculpture or in painting that the Jain creative genius asserted itself. They were magnificent builders, and, as examples of architectural design, the two towers of victory at Chittor (Plate 98B), of the ninth and fifteenth centuries A.D., are unsurpassed of their kind in the whole world, while for consummate craftsmanship and decorative

[1] "Bhishma Vadha Parva," section cxiii. Roy's translation.

beauty the vaulted roofs of shrines like that of Mount Âbû, built by a merchant prince, Vimala Sah, in A.D. 1031, equal anything to be seen in Buddhist or Hindu buildings (Plate 99A and B). Though it may not be quite true that, as Fergusson says, the Jains believed to a greater extent than other Indian sects in the efficacy of temple-building as a means of salvation, their wonderful "cities of temples" crowning the sacred hills of Pâli-tânâ and Girnâr in Gujerat have a beauty of their own which is quite unique (Plate 100A and B). The great majority of these temples are small, being the gifts of single wealthy persons, and, to quote the same authority, "they are deficient in that grandeur of proportion that marks the buildings undertaken by royal command or belonging to important organised communities." The charm of Pâlitânâ is due to its environment and the poetic feeling with which the site has been treated architecturally. The sculpture is comparatively unimportant.

The Jain figure-sculptors occasionally worked on a colossal scale in making the images of their saints, the Tirthankaras; probably the finest examples are the detached figures at Sravan Belgola (Plate 98A), Kârkala, and Yannûr, in Mysore, which range in height from thirty-five to seventy feet. These are very noble as art, quite apart from their imposing dimensions. But, as a rule, Jain figure-sculpture seems to lack the feeling and imagination of the best Buddhist and Hindu art.

The reason for this must be attributed to the character of Jain religious tenets. The sect of the Jains, like that of the Saivaites, has always preserved more of the asceticism ingrained in orthodox Brahmanical teaching than did the Buddhists, or their spiritual successors, the Vaishnavaites.[1] The Jain ideal of quietism was to be attained by the austerities of the Hindu ascetic, and the Jain saints, having reached the heaven of their desires, troubled themselves no more with any worldly affairs.

Even down to the present day, though life is regarded as the most sacred principle in nature, the Jains hold it to be the highest virtue for a man or woman to retire to some lonely consecrated spot and obtain final release from worldly cares by a process of slow starvation. At Sravan Belgola, the hill to the north of that on which the great statue of Gomata stands is full of such associations, and many inscriptions on the rocks record the passing away of devout Jain kings and queens, and others less distinguished, who thus attained Nirvana.

In Jainism there are no divine incarnations of heroes, like Krishna, who labour for the material prosperity of humanity; neither did the Jain saints or deities develop into personifications of nature's manifold aspects. The Jain sculptors and painters were therefore limited to a very narrow range of ideas: they had no rich mythology or lives of the saints, full of wonders and of human interest, to illustrate; no grand conception of nature's moods—only the fixed, immutable pose of the ascetic absorbed in contemplation. Thus Jain art, as regards painting and sculpture, deserves more than that of any other Hindu sect the reproach of poverty of invention, which is often, without any justification, laid upon Indian art in general.

The Buddhist stûpas of Bharhut, Sânchî, and Amarâvatî, with the sculptured rails which enclose their procession-paths, belong to the Transition period of Indian art, dating from about the time of Asoka, or the third century B.C., down to the third or fourth century A.D. After that time the Buddhist dynasties of Northern India succumbed to their Hindu rivals, and Buddhism itself was gradually absorbed in the general current of Hindu thought, from out of which the two great modern sects, the Vaishnavaites and Saivaites, began to emerge.

In India Buddha eventually took his place in the Hindu theogony as one of avatars of Vishnu, and the heroes of the great epics, Krishna and Râma, came forward as the most prominent figures in national art and drama. But in the meantime the artistic traditions

[1] In the fifteenth century A.D. several Jain religious teachers forbade the worship of images ("History and Literature of Jainism," by O. D. Barodia, p. 77).

of Buddhism had found congenial soil in China, from whence they spread to Korea and Japan, and in Ceylon. The disasters to the Buddhist kingdoms in Northern India had also stimulated colonial enterprise, and in the great colony of Java Indian Buddhist art flourished magnificently until the conversion of the islanders to Islam.

The splendid seven-terraced shrine of Bôrôbudûr, which has escaped Muhammadan and Christian iconoclasm, contains the most perfect series of Buddhist historical sculptures now existing. Along the pilgrims' procession-paths on five different terraces are sculptured one hundred and twenty panels illustrating events in the life of Gautama, and a similar number of scenes from the *jâtakas*.

The best sculptures of Bôrôbudûr, which belong probably to the eighth and ninth centuries A.D., reach to the highest point of Buddhist plastic art. Fergusson, in his history of Indian architecture, made the grievous mistake of assigning the zenith of Indian sculpture to the time of the later Amarâvatî reliefs, or about the third century A.D., and this cardinal error has not only led astray nearly all European writers in Indian art ever since,[1] but has formed the basis on which Indian art has been presented to the art-student by the national museums of Great Britain.

The travesty of Indian art-history which is thus put before the European public is as misleading as it would be for the museums of Tokio to exhibit Gothic art of the eleventh century as representing the zenith of medieval art in Europe, and for Japanese art-critics to write of European sculpture of the fourteenth and fifteenth centuries as unworthy of serious consideration. Not only has Indian art-history been thus horribly distorted, but the whole official system of art-education in India has been based upon a similar misconception and perversion of Indian ideals.

The art of India up to the fourth century A.D. was purely eclectic and transitional. The spirit of Indian thought was struggling to find definite artistic expression in sculpture and in painting, but the form of expression was not artistically perfected until about the seventh or eighth centuries when most of the great sculpture and painting of India was produced. From the seventh or eighth to the fourteenth century was the great period of Indian art, corresponding to the highest development of Gothic art in Europe, and it is by the achievements of this epoch, rather than by those of Mogul Hindustan, that India's place in the art-history of the world will eventually be resolved.[2]

With one important exception, the Ajanta cave-paintings,[3] practically the whole of the art of this period now existent belongs to sculpture or architectural design. This may be partly accounted for by the wholesale destruction of Indian paintings which took place under Muhammadan rule, especially in the time of Aurangzîb ; it being much easier to obliterate paintings than to destroy sculpture. But the principal reason is probably that the spirit of *bhakti*, which animated all the great art of the Buddhist-Hindu period, took more delight in sculpture than in painting on account of the greater labour and cost involved in it : from the idea that the greater the labour devoted to the service of the gods the greater would be the merit won by the devotee.

It should not be inferred from this that painting, as an art, never reached a high degree

[1] Mr. Vincent Smith in his article on Indian Archaeology in the latest edition of the *Imperial Gazetteer of India*, says that after the third century A.D. there is little Indian sculpture which is worthy to be called art !

[2] It is difficult to agree with Havell's estimation of Indian art of the mediaeval period (circa 7th-8th to 14th centuries) as the great period of Indian art. In spite of its beauty one can observe a lack of inner feeling and conventionalisation which coupled with the Islamic invasions lead to the complete disintegration of the sculptural traditions of India altogether. The orthodox view at the present day is quite different, and according to it the great promise of early Indian sculpture reached its fulfilment in the Gupta period (5th-6th centuries) after which a steady decline set in till the ancient traditions are finished off by the Muslim conquest.—P.C.

[3] Mrs. Herringham and M. de Goloubeff, with the assistance of the Indian Society of Oriental Art, Calcutta, are now engaged in making a complete artistic survey of the Ajanta paintings, for want of which I have not been able to make any detailed reference to them. It may therefore be hoped that before long the Western art-world may be enabled to appreciate fully these fragmentary but very precious remains of the great schools of Indian painting.

of perfection in India. The finest of the Ajanta paintings exhibit an amazing technical skill, a fertility of invention, and a power of expressing high religious ideals unsurpassed in any art. Although, after the time of the Buddhist supremacy, sculpture was generally preferred to painting in sacred buildings, it was the custom in every royal palace to have a *chitrasala*, or hall of painting, decorated with frescoes.[1] The art of the Mogul miniature paintings, some of which are as fine as the finest "fine art" of the West, was not entirely an importation into India from Persia, but largely a revival of the art of the Buddhist and Hindu court painters.

Nevertheless, the remains of Indian religious painting are now too fragmentary to place beside the enormous production of the great schools of China and Japan ; and the Mogul court painters, like the fine art of modern Europe, represented a distraction and amusement for cultured dilettanti rather than a great national art-tradition like that of the Far East. In the national art of Asia, China and Japan stand as supreme in their schools of painting as India does in her sculpture and architecture.

After the third or fourth century A.D., so erroneously considered as the culminating point of Indian sculpture, the Saivaites began to add a new and in some ways a unique chapter to the history of Indian art, with their great cave-temples and sculptures in stone and bronze. Like the Jains, the Saivaites were originally strict followers of the ascetic ideal : Siva being the personification of the meditative life, of that higher knowledge which is the most direct path for the soul's liberation. But, so long as the Buddhists maintained their identity as a separate sect of Hinduism their wonderful activity in artistic creation seems to have stimulated the Saivaites of Northern India to emulate the achievements of their rivals, and many of the finest Indian monuments of the pre-Muhammadan epoch—*e.g.* the temple of Elephanta and that of Kailâsa at Ellora (Plate 101A)—were dedicated to the worship of Siva.

It would, however, be quite fallacious to attempt a history of Indian art upon a rigid sectarian classification. The different currents of religious thought represented by the diverse sects of Hinduism intermingle at so many points that the only clear demarcations in Indian art-history are dynastic, racial, and provincial or local. Thus the Buddhist Mahâyâna images of Nepal often symbolise the same ideas as the Saivaite sculptures of Elephanta and Ellora ; and it is often difficult to distinguish between Mahâyâna sculptures of the eighth and ninth centuries and those of the Saivaites.

Though Siva, like Vishnu, is reputed to have manifested himself in human incarnations, the incidents of the ascetic's life do not give much scope for the exercise of the artist's descriptive power, and most of the great groups of Saivaite sculpture illustrate myths of the Hindu cosmogony connected with Siva's powers either as the Creator or the Destroyer of the Universe, or popular stories of his relations with the Earth Mother, as represented by Umâ or Parvati. But after Sankaracharya, in the eighth century A.D., overcame the Buddhist philosophers in contests of dialectical skill, and thus established the spiritual ascendancy of the Saivaite cult, the Vedic objection to anthropomorphic religious symbolism seems to have revived in Northern India ; and this, together with the influence of Muhammadan iconoclasm during Aurangzîb's long, intolerant reign, almost reduced Saivaite iconography in the north to the symbols of the *lingam* and the bull. The prohibition of image-worship on the part of Saivaite and Jain reformers at this period may have been dictated by motives of political expediency, in order to avert persecution of their faith by fanatical followers of Islam.

The splendid traditions of the Saivaite figure-sculptors were carried down to modern times by the bronze workers employed in the temples of Southern India and Ceylon. There are doubtless a great many fine Saivaite bronzes still buried underground. Many

---

[1] The custom continued until modern times, but, in the gradual extinction of all artistic culture among educated Indians, the traditional *chitrasala* has given place to collections of European pictures, generally of the most painful description.

are hidden away in temples into which Europeans are not allowed to penetrate.[1] Now that some educated Indians are beginning to take an intelligent interest in their national art we may expect that more of these treasures will be brought to light, and treated with greater artistic consideration than they are by the superstitious guardians of the temples. The degrading and vulgar modern practice of dressing up temple images with gaudy drapery, like children's dolls, reduces the status of the sculptor to that of a maker of lay figures, and accounts in some degree for the contempt with which all Indian sculpture has been regarded by Anglo-Indians.

Though Saivaism assimilated a great deal of the humanistic teaching of Gautama, the modern Vaishnavaites are more entitled to be considered the artistic heirs of Buddhism. Gautama himself, ignored by the Saivaites, is recognised as one of the incarnations of Vishnu. In the stories of Rama-Chandra and of Krishna, also incarnations of Vishnu, and of other heroes of the epics, Vaishnavaite art finds human types more closely related to the ethical ideal of Buddhism than to the ascetic ideal of the Saivaites.

But here again we must not draw such distinctions too closely : for the Râmâyana and the Mahâbhârata are as much the common property of all Hinduism as the English Bible and Shakespeare belong to all English-speaking people. The Indian epics contain a portrait-gallery of ideal types of men and women which afford to every good Hindu the highest exemplars of moral conduct, and every Hindu artist an inexhaustible mine of subject-matter.[2]

It is somewhat surprising for the student of Indian art to find that though the adventures of Râma and Sîtâ and the exploits of the Pândava heroes have such a deep hold upon popular imagination, even in the present day, and though the whole text of the great epics is regarded as holy writ, it is rarely that the subjects of important sculptures seem to have been taken directly from them in the great creative period of Indian art. The finest series of reliefs illustrating the Râmâyana are not in India but in the courtyard of a Vaishnavaite temple at Prambanam, in Java (Plates 35 and 36) : they are ascribed to about the eleventh century A.D. An incident in the Mahâbhârata is illustrated in one of the series of sculptures at Mâmallapuram, near Madras ; and the temple of Angkor Vat, in Kambodia, has reliefs on a grand scale dealing with other events of the great war ; but, with these exceptions, there is now hardly any important Indian sculpture illustrating the epics. Puranic literature supplies the subjects of practically all Hindu religious sculpture.

I think that the explanation of this is that the temples were held to be dwelling-places of the *devas*, and consequently the figures of human beings could only be appropriately represented on the exterior. Thus the principal sculptures within the sacred precincts related exclusively to the divinities who were worshipped therein, and generally to events which took place in the paradise of the gods.

From various references in Hindu dramatic writings we may conclude that the history of Râma and Sîtâ and of the Pândava heroes from whom many of the Hindu kings claimed descent were frequently illustrated in the fresco paintings of the royal *chitrasalas*, or picture-halls, which have now entirely disappeared. The epic of Indian womanhood and the Iliad of Asia seem now to be out of place in the up-to-date Indian prince's picture-gallery imported wholsesale from Europe, and the Indian aristocracy is mostly concerned in obliterating all the remaining vestiges of Indian artistic culture.

The more modern Vaishnavaite literature and art are centred in the *bhakti* cult and

[1] The treasures of bronze images in the collections of South Indian temples have gradually come to light, and form part of the large corpus of material available for study at the present day.—P.C.

[2] Nothing is more significant of the general aloofness of the Anglo-Saxon from the inner consciousness of the Indian people than the fact that, while most educated Indians are perfectly familiar with the Bible and with Shakespeare, the Mahabharata has not as yet found any definite place in English literature. In spite of the heroic but inadequate attempt of Protap Chandra Roy to render it into English, it still, for the most part, remains more inaccessible to the average Englishman than the hieroglyphics of Egypt.

in the events of Krishna's early life at Brindâban, before he became the spiritual guide and champion of the Pândavas in the great war. In some of the popular art which relates to this aspect of Vaishnavism the spiritual significance of Krishna's relations with Radha and the *gopîs* is given a grossly material interpretation. But it would be wrong to infer that the obscenities which occasionally disfigure Hindu temples are necessarily indicative of moral depravity. In the matter of sexual relationship Indian civilisation, in every stratum of society, holds up a standard of morality as high as Europe has ever done.

The splendid sun-temples of Mudherâ in Gujerat (101B) and of Kanârak, in Orissa (Plate 102A) belong to a subsection of the Vaishnava cult, still represented by the Sauras, or those who worship Vishnu in his manifestation as Sûrya-Nârâyana. The former dates from about the eleventh century, and is, even in its present ruined condition, one of the noblest monuments of Indian architecture; the latter belongs to the thirteenth century, and is distinguished by its fine sculpture, especially the two grand warhorses,[1] and the elephants, Plate 105A., which stand in front of it.

The sectarian classification of Buddhist-Hindu art, though it is useful as indicating roughly the variety of subject-matter in sculpture and painting, and to some extent the difference of architectural forms, does not imply any divergence in artistic ideals. In this respect Jain, Buddhist, Saivaite and Vaishnavaite merely represent different aspects of one idea, different streams of thought flowing in one direction in the same watershed. In the same locality and of the same date Jain or Buddhist, Saivaite or Vaishnavaite can only be distinguished from each other by the choice of symbols, and then often with difficulty.

The political supremacy of the Moguls, established by Babar in 1526, brought about a large readjustment of artistic conditions but no fundamental change in artistic ideals. The royal palace, rather than the temple or monastery, became more exclusively the centre of creative art; for the puritan sentiment of Islam, even under the free-thinker Akbar, would not concede to the highest expression of art any but material aims and a strictly secular scope. This Philistine influence reacted on the religious art of Hinduism, and no doubt stimulated, if it did not originate, the propaganda against the ritualistic use of images started by Jain and Saivaite religious teachers. From the sixteenth century the creative impulse in Hindu art began to diminish, though its technical traditions have maintained their vitality down to modern times.

In the Muhammadan Courts there was no place for the sculptor, except as a decorative craftsman; but in architecture Hindu idealism received a fresh impulse through dealing with new constructive problems, and Islam added to its prestige by the magnificence of the mosques built with the aid of Jain and Hindu temple craftsmen. Indian Saracenic architecture testifies not so much to the creative genius of the Moguls as to their capacity for assimilating the artistic culture of alien subject races. Christianity might have advanced much more rapidly in India if its leaders had not, with the puritanical intolerance of Aurangzîb, refused to allow the genius of Indian art to glorify the Christian Church, and tried to propagate the beauty of an Eastern faith with the whitewashed ugliness of Western formality.

In the reigns of Akbar, Jahangir, and Shah Jahan the court painters fulfilled the same rôle as they had done under the former Buddhist and Hindu rulers; but the Mogul Emperors laid no claim to a divine ancestry, and priestly influence was no longer supreme in the state. The dominant themes in the art of the period were therefore not religious, but the romance of love and of war, the legends of Musalman and Rajput chivalry, the pageantry of state ceremonial, and portraiture.

Owing to the presence of Persian artists at the Mogul Court, European critics have generally classified all the painting of the time under the name of Indo-Persian, assuming, as so many have done with regard to early Indian Buddhist sculpture, that the creative impulse in Indian art came always from without instead of from within. These are

[1] Part I, "Indian Sculpture and Painting," Plate 39.

illogical and inartistic assumptions. The Persian painters at Akbar's Court were neither technically nor artistically superior to the Hindus. The creative stimulus came partly from the invigorating atmosphere of Akbar's Court, and from his own magnetic personality. Hindu art had been cramped by the rigid ritualistic prescriptions imposed by the Brahmin priests, who were not artists, like many of the Buddhist monks, but a purely literary caste. The illiterate but broad-minded Akbar gave both Musalman and Hindu artists their intellectual and spiritual freedom. In adapting itself to the new social order Indian art enlarged its boundaries and renewed its former vitality, assimilating the foreign technical traditions, but always maintaining its own ideals.[1] Regarded as a whole, the Indian school of painting of the Mogul epoch is as distinct and original in artistic expression as any of the schools of Persia, China, or Japan.

With the accession of Aurangzîb the fierce iconoclasm of the first Muhammadan invaders of Hindustan was renewed, and the fine arts, including music, were placed under a fanatical priestly interdict, more detrimental to Indian art than all the asceticism of Hinduism. In modern times the influence of Western "education," with its purely commercial ideals, has been even more depressing to Indian art than the iconoclasm of Aurangzîb. Educated India under British rule, while affecting to exchange its own culture for that of the West, has remained entirely aloof from those vital movements in British art and craft which in the last half-century have derived so much impetus from the study and exploitation of oriental art. Anglo-Indian departmentalism, always slow to move in art matters, still takes refuge in British Early Victorian formularies, and the theory that India has never shown any original genius for sculpture or painting continues to produce hopeless confusion in the whole conduct of art-education. Under present circumstances it would be far better if India were allowed to work out her own artistic salvation, without interference from the State. Western methods of education have opened a rift between the artistic castes and the "educated" such as never existed in any previous time in Indian history. The remedy lies, not in making Indian artists more literate in the European sense, not in teaching them anatomy, perspective, and model-drawing, nor in manufacturing regulation pattern-books according to Anglo-Indian taste, but in making the *literati*, educators and educated, conscious of the deficiencies of their own education which render them unable to appreciate the artistic wealth lying at their doors.

For behind all this intellectual and administrative chaos there remains in India a native living tradition of art, deep-rooted in the ancient culture of Hinduism, richer and more full of strength than all the eclectic learning of the modern academies and art-guilds of Europe; only waiting for the spiritual and intellectual quickening which will renew its old creative instinct. The new impulse will come, as Emerson has said, not at the call of a legislature: it will come, as always, unannounced, and spring up between the feet of brave and earnest men.

Even now the signs of the coming renaissance are not wanting. It is impossible to believe that India will wholly succumb, body and soul, to the materialism of modern Europe; and, seeing how much both Asia and Europe owe to Indian culture, it would be foolish for politicians to regard the reassertion of Indian idealism with suspicion and distrust. It is indeed a happy augury for the spiritual and intellectual progress of humanity, and for the ultimate disappearance of those differences and prejudices which make the gulf between East and West.

[1] This ability to absorb foreign influence at the highest levels, so that what is borrowed is thoroughly assimilated and results in a new, well-integrated creation has been one of the most distinguishing characteristics of Indian art history.— P.C.

DESCRIPTION OF PLATES
102 TO 109

THE GREAT BAS-RELIEFS AT MÂMALLAPURAM, MADRAS, KNOWN AS "ARJUNA'S PENANCE"

THE great group of Hindu monuments at Mâmallapuram, consisting of monolithic temples, caves, and bas-reliefs, contains some of the finest examples of Indian sculpture now existing. They were executed under the auspices of some of the Pallava kings who had their capital at Conjeeveram (Kânchî), in the beginning of the fourth century, and gradually extended their power so that from about A.D. 625 to the middle of the eighth century they held sway over the greater part of Southern India. It is to the latter period that these sculptures belong. Many of them are said to have been executed in the reign of Mahendravarman I. (*circa* A.D. 600 to 625).[1]

The bas-reliefs, of which two illustrations are given, are carved on two huge granite boulders of about thirty feet in height and a combined length of about ninety feet.

According to popular tradition, the subject of the sculptures is that of Arjuna practising austerities in order to gain the arms of Indra, as recorded in the Vana Parva of the Mahâbhârata.[2] Though it is uncertain whether this is correct, the story is a typical one for illustrating Hindu belief in the virtue of ascetic practices for gaining extraordinary psychic powers, and it sufficiently explains the *motif* of the sculptures.

When the fateful struggle between the Pândavas and Kauravas was impending, Arjuna, on the advice of his brother Yudhisthira, set out towards Himavat to obtain the celestial weapons guarded by Indra. He was armed with Krishna's famous bow, Gandiva, with its inexhaustible quivers, and had learnt from Yudhisthira a mantra of tremendous power for controlling the forces of nature. By virtue of the spiritual power gained by ascetic practices, Arjuna sped with marvellous swiftness, and reached the sacred mountain in one day; but at the approach to Indra's paradise a celestial voice commanded him to stop.

Looking around him, he saw under a tree an emaciated ascetic with matted locks, who reproached him for disturbing his peaceful abode, and endeavoured with smooth words to persuade him to throw away his weapons. But the Pândava hero was not to be turned from his purpose, even when the ascetic threw off his disguise and revealed himself as Indra, making tempting offers if he would consent to remain and enjoy the happiness of the celestials.

"I desire not the regions of bliss," Arjuna answered, "nor the celestial peace and prosperity of the gods. Shall I desert my brothers in the forest, leaving their wrongs unavenged and the foe unvanquished, to be scorned for all ages by the whole world?"

---

[1] Vincent Smith's "Early History of India," p. 425.

[2] The subject matter of this bas-relief has been the topic of much discussion, various interpretations being suggested. Jouveau Dubreuil, Coomaraswamy and Goloubew hold to the view that the scene depicted is Bhagiratha's penance as a result of which Ganga came down from Heaven to the Earth. The entire position has been re-examined recently by T. N. Ramachandran ("Kiratarjuniyam or Arjuna's Penance in Indian Art," *Journal of the Indian Society of Oriental Art*, XVIII (1950-51) pp. 1-110). He holds to the view that the bas-relief is a representation of Arjuna's penance as related in *Kiratarjuniyam* of Bharavi, whose fame as a poet had spread far and wide when the bas-relief was carved, he being ranked with Kalidasa himself in the Aihole inscription dated A.D. 634-635 of Palakesin II of Badami. Bharavi's poem also helps one in understanding certain details of the bas-relief hitherto obscure, including the representation of the Nara-Narayana episode at the foot of the relief to the right of the river-cleft, as well as the Moon-god hovering over Siva's head. The current evidence seems to be in favour of the Arjuna identification though certain points, such as the omission of the boar-hunt, still await clarification.—P.C.

Moved by Arjuna's constancy, Indra consented to yield to him the celestial arms when Siva, the highest of all the gods, should deign to reveal himself to him.

Indra then disappeared and Arjuna prepared to devote himself to the rigid austerities of Yoga in order to obtain the desired boon from Siva. He first entered a mysterious forest full of wild beasts and fearsome monsters. The celestial drums and conches thundered above him ; thick showers of flowers fell upon the earth, and Indra's clouds darkened the sky. Reaching an auspicious spot on the banks of a foaming river, "echoing with the notes of swans, peacocks, and cranes," he laid aside his armour and weapons and began the fasting and meditation which should attract the attention of the great god, Siva. The first month he subsisted by eating fruits at intervals of three nights ; next he increased the interval of fasting to six nights ; and next to fourteen days. By the fourth month he began to exist on air alone ; standing on the tips of his toes with arms upraised. The tremendous energy produced by his mental concentration began to disturb the cosmic order, and all the great sages went in agitation to complain to Siva.

Mahadeva reassured them by saying that Arjuna's desire was not prompted by any impiety, and forthwith assuming the disguise of a hunter, he took up his bow and arrow and, followed by his consort Umâ and thousands of celestials in similar disguise, the great god descended the slopes of Himavat to test the courage of the hero. As they, approached the whole forest was illumined with heavenly light, a solemn stillness pervaded the place, the songs of birds were hushed, and the rivers ceased to flow.

Then Siva, by the power of illusion, caused a demon in the form of a wild boar to pass in front of Arjuna, who fitted a shaft to his bow to slay it, undeterred by the commanding voice of the divine hunter claiming it as his own prize. The boar fell struck at the same instant by the fiery shafts of Arjuna, and by those of Siva. An angry dispute arose between the rival hunters, ending in a terrific combat, in which Arjuna was at last struck down senseless. Soon regaining consciousness, he prostrated himself in worship at Siva's feet, who, revealing himself in his divine splendour, praised him for his valour, and promised to bestow upon him an irresistible weapon with which he should overcome all his foes.

Mahadeva, having instructed Arjuna in the use of the celestial arms, disappeared from his sight, like the setting sun in a clear sky. Arjuna, kneeling in adoration, exlaimed, "Happy indeed am I, and greatly favoured, for I have beheld and touched with my hand the three-eyed Hara, the wielder of the Pinâka, and obtained this boon! My enemies are already vanquished ! My purpose is achieved !"

Then Varuna, the god of waters, with all his attendant deities ; the river goddesses ; the Nâgas, snake-gods ; the Daityas and Sâdhyas ; came to see the mighty hero who had fought with Mahadeva himself. There came also Kuvera, the lord of wealth, seated on a splendid car ; Yama, the judge of the nether world, with mace in hand ; and Indra, too, with his Queen, mounted on the celestial elephant, Airâvata, a white umbrella over his head, looking like the moon amid fleecy clouds. They also bestowed upon Arjuna various weapons of tremendous power ; Yama, his mace ; Varuna, his noose ; Kuvera, the magic Antardhâna. Finally, taking Arjuna in his shining car, Indra bore him aloft to his heavenly city, Amarâvatî, where, with benedictions from all the *devas* he received from the hands of the Rain-god his thunderbolt and the lightnings of heaven.

At Indra's command he remained there for five years, learning from Chitrasena the divine arts of music, singing, and dancing—accomplishments which he found very useful in his subsequent adventures among his fellow-mortals.

The Mâmallapuram sculptures do not follow very closely the Mahâbhârata version of the story, but it should be remembered that there must have been many local variants of it. On the left-hand rock, the sculptures of which remain half finished, the emaciated figure, supposed to be Arjuna, is seen practising his austerities, standing on one leg with his arms raised over his head. The figure of a four-armed deity standing by him, armed

B. Nagaraja. Bas-relief from the entrance to Cave XIX at Ajanta. (*Photo, A. L. Syed*).

A. Elephant sculpture at Kanârak. (*Photo, Raj Bedi*).

PLATE 105

A. Queen Māyā and the infant Prince Siddhartha sleeping. Bas-relief at Baro, Central India.
(*From a photograph in the India Office Library*).

B. The "Linga" shrine, Elephanta. (*From a photograph in the India Office Library*).

PLATE 106

B. Śiva dancing the Tāṇḍavan, Ellora.
(Copyright, Department of Archaeology, Government of India).

PLATE 107

A. Head of a Bodhisattva from Indonesia.
(From a sculpture in the Glyptotek, Copenhagen).

A. Siva dancing the Tāndavan, Elephanta. (*Copyright, Department of Archaeology, Government of India*).

B. Roof of monolithic temple at Kalugumalai, Tinnevelly. (*From a photograph in the India Office Library*).

PLATE 108

with a huge mace and attended by dwarfs, seems to be that of Siva. Immediately below the supposed figure of Arjuna there is a small temple of Vishnu, at the base of which a number of devotees are grouped. The upper part of both rocks is covered with a great crowd of celestials, gods, and sages; the Gandharvas, the heavenly musicians with bird-like legs, and various four-footed denizens of the Hindu Olympus are hastening to watch the wonderful penance.

The right-hand rock is distinguished by the magnificent group of elephants, Indra's noble beasts, which are very realistically treated. The foremost tusker, which gives shelter to a delightful group of baby elephants stands gravely watching Arjuna, while the female impatiently waits her turn behind him.

The cleft between the rocks is skilfully used to show a Nâga and Nâgini, and other snake-deities, as coming up from the depths of ocean, drawn by the ascetic's magnetic power, to pay him homage.

NOTE.—An interesting discovery has been made lately by Prof. Jouveau-Dubreuil, that in the rainy season a miniature waterfall pours over the cleft between the two rocks. This fully explains the position of the water-deities, but the inference that the whole sculpture represents the well-known legend of the Birth of the Ganges seems hardly to be justified.

PLATE 103B

A RELIEF FROM MÂMALLAPURAM—VISHNU SUPPORTING THE UNIVERSE

PLATE 103B, a very characteristic example of the Hindu artist's treatment of Puranic allegory, is one of the most impressive and powerful of the Mâmallapuram group of sculptures.

Vishnu is here represented as the all-pervading Soul of the Universe, upholding the heavens (symbolised by the curved cornice of the Dravidian temple) with one arm, and filling space with all the attributes of his glory. Seated at his feet are four munis, or genii, the guardians of his paradise Vaikuntha, symbolising the four quarters of the earth.

Vishnu himself, in his material aspect, stands for the sun in its midday splendour, as representing the principle of all life. On the right and left are smaller figures of Brahmâ and Siva on their heavenly lotus-thrones as symbols of the sun's rising and setting. The "strides of Vishnu," or the apparent movement of the sun across the heavens, are suggested by the upraised leg and the outstretched finger of one hand which Siva is touching.

The figure with a boar's head on the right of Vishnu's head is the Varâha-avatara, or boar-incarnation, in which form Vishnu raised the earth above the Flood.

The spiritual signification of the various attributes displayed by Vishnu are thus explained in the Puranas: The Kaustubha gem which he wears in his necklace is the pure Soul of the World, undefiled and void of qualities. The chief principle of things (Pradhana) is seated on the Eternal in the Sri-vatsa mark, a curl on the breast.

The principle of consciousness (Ahamkara)[1] in its twofold division, into organs of senses and rudimentary unconscious elements, is symbolised by the famous bow Gandiva, used by Arjuna in the Great War (here held by Vishnu in his bent left arm, and by the spiral

[1] Ahamkara = the principle of individual existence, that which appropriates perceptions, and on which depends the notions, I think, I am. The three modifications of Ahamkara are (1) *Vaikarika*, (2) *Taijasa*, and (3) *Bhutadi*, corresponding to the three primordial *gunas*, or qualities—*sattvam*, *rajas*, and *tamas*. The sattvik form of consciousness produces the senses, and the tamasik the five elemental rudiments—ether, wind or air, fire or light, water, and earth. The Taijasa form of consciousness is the energic principle, causing the other two, which are inert by themselves, to act. Hence Ahamkara is described as having a "twofold division."

conch shell, the sound of which reverberates throughout the whole universe.[1] The shafts shot from the bow (*i.e.* the sun's rays) represent the faculties of action and perception.   The bright sword, wielded by the right arm, is holy wisdom, concealed at times in the scabbard of ignorance. On the right side, also, Vishnu wields his mace, which is the power of the intellect, and the discus, which is the mind, whose thoughts, like the weapon, fly swifter than the winds. (The allegorical significance of the remaining symbol, the shield held by the left arm, is not explained in the Vishnu Purana. It seems to be about to cover the descending figure whose movement symbolises the setting of the sun, and thus it may be taken to represent both the darkness of night and Mâyâ, the power of illusion, or the veil of phenomenal existence by which the Supreme Being conceals His real nature.)   His necklace is composed of the five precious gems, pearl, ruby, emerald, sapphire, and diamond, which represent the five elemental rudiments (see footnote.)

Artists of every school will recognise the splendid vigour and imaginative power with which the unknown sculptor has carved this striking composition on the face of the living granite rock. The bold generalisation of execution is quite free from the over-elaboration from which later Indian sculpture sometimes suffers. The figure of the sun-god in his midday glory, the pillar of the heavens whose glowing light pervades all space, is a grand allegorical conception worthy of a Dante or Milton. The stately uprightness of the body of the Deity, echoed by the lines of the mighty bow and sword and by the slightly varied attitudes of the four genii grouped in massive relief at the base, contrast with telling effect against the vigorous movement of the outstretched arms, forming a radiant halo behind the figure : while the ascending and descending movement of the smaller figures on the right and left balances the whole composition in lower planes of relief, which finely symbolise the gradual dawn and close of day at the sun's rising and setting. The extended movement of the left leg may easily provoke Philistine ridicule ; but the critic whose outlook is not too much narrowed by the æsthetic conventions of modern academic Europe must admit that the reverential feeling of the sculptor fully justifies the temerity which might so easily have proved disastrous to an artist of lesser power.

PLATE 104A

LAKSHMÎ, OR SRÎ, ARISING FROM THE SEA OF MILK—A RELIEF FROM MÂMALLAPURAM (CAVE XXV)

THE story of Lakshmî, or Srî, the consort, or *sakti*, of Vishnu—representing fertility and earthly prosperity—arising from the Cosmic Ocean when churned by the gods and *asuras*, is given in the text, pp. 148-9. The gracious goddess, radiant with beauty, rose from the waves, seated on a full-blown lotus-flower, attended by Ganga and other river-deities. Indra's elephants, the mighty monsoon clouds which refresh the parched plains, bring their precious waters in golden vessels, and pour them over her, the Queen of the Universe.

Like all the Mâmallapuram reliefs, the subject is treated with a freshness and directness which will appeal to European artists more than the elaborate, ritualistic formalism of some later Hindu sculpture. It is Indian art of the great Hindu epoch, strong, free, and full of creative vigour.

The old-world story lends itself to such a treatment. Like the subjects of Kalidâsa's masterpieces, *Sakuntala* and the *Meghaduta*, it strikes one of those primitive chords of human feeling on which all the great dramatists prefer to play. Lakshmî, Mother Nature,

[1] The vibration of the rudimentary elements is regarded as the material creative force. The same idea is represented by Siva's drum.

true woman and goddess most divine, is represented in the supreme moment when, rising from the waves on her lotus-throne, she gazes with undisguised rapture and wonderment upon the apparition of Vishnu in all his splendour before her. There is a fine inspiration, a touch of the eternal feminine, in her simple, spontaneous gesture, full of adoration for her divine spouse as she prepares to throw herself upon his breast. The reverential mien of the attendant river-goddesses at her side is simply and charmingly expressed ; and the colossal heads of Indra's elephants, rendered with consummate craftsmanship, make an imposing canopy for the whole group.

PLATES 104B AND 105A

SCULPTURE OF A BULL IN KRISHNA'S MANDAPAM, MÂMALLAPURAM—TWO ELEPHANTS IN FRONT OF THE SÙRYA TEMPLE AT KANÂRAK

THE grand monumental bull carved in the shrine known as Krishna's Mandapam at Mâmallapuram is one of a group illustrating the story of Krishna's exploit in lifting up the mountain Govardhana to protect Nanda and his cattle from the torrents of rain poured down by the wrath of Indra. Like the elephants in the great bas-relief known as Arjuna's penance (Plate 102B) it is frankly realistic in treatment ; yet not without the ideal feeling of classic art in its masterly generalisation of fact.

Nandi, a milk-white bull, is the name of Siva's vehicle, which is a symbol both of the deity's generative power and of *dharma*, righteousness, or the whole duty of the Hindu. The latter attribute is derived from the fact that the bull carried the wood for the sacrificial fire, and was one of the principal victims.

With this sculpture we may compare the two elephants in front of the famous sun-temple at Kanârak, in Orissa (Plate 105A), which belongs to the middle of the thirteenth century. They are companion sculptures to the magnificent horse and warrior which I have illustrated in a previous volume.[1] In such grand works as these, comparable with the finest sculptures of the West, we can find sufficient refutation of the baseless imputation so often brought against Hindu artists that they are no lovers of nature, and lack the power of truthful interpretation of it.

Because his deep religious instinct inspires the Hindu always to seek in every aspect of nature a symbol of worship and an attribute of the divine, rather than the means of intellectual distraction or idle amusement, it often seems to the Western materialist that he misses the purpose of art, and is incapable of appreciating the highest æsthetic. It would be more true to say that this is the spirit in which all the greatest works of art have been conceived, and it is just that spirit, still surviving in the East, which is needed to give a new vital impulse to art in modern Europe. There is hardly a form or symbol in Hindu art, from the gods of its pantheon to the primitive jewellery of the peasant, which has not its ultimate derivation in some aspect of nature-worship. It is true that the adoration is addressed not directly to nature, or to the symbol which expresses it, but to the all-pervading spirit which is behind it. But the feeling for beauty is everywhere revealed, even in the epithets bestowed upon the gods, and in the names of ornaments and patterns.

How "the blue-throated, moon-crested Siva" recalls the ethereal beauty of the Himâlayan peaks, with the band of transparent violet-blue just below the snow-cap ; and what poetic suggestions underlie the names of the finest Dacca muslins—"running water," "evening dew," and "woven air"!

Is there no love of nature in the reverence for all living things, great and small, which

[1] Part I, "Indian Sculpture and Painting," Plate 39.

is enjoined as a religious duty on every Hindu ? Do the people who bestow garlands on every honoured guest, who worship sacred trees, and bring flowers for their daily offerings to the gods, to whom the forest is a temple and every wooded hill-top an altar, not love trees and flowers ? If the Indian continually chooses some glorious prospect of mountain, sea, or plain as a fitting place of pilgrimage, and in passionate devotion builds or carves in the living rock a shrine for the image of Him who abides in everything—has he a lower æsthetic sense than the materialist who climbs the mountain-top to see the sunrise, and enjoy his breakfast better ?

Did the painters of Ajanta not love the nature and the teeming life of their native land which they depicted with such marvellous skill ? Had the sculptors of Ellora who transformed the rocky hill-scarp with their mystic visions of Siva's Himâlayan paradise (Plate 101A) less delight in beauty than the modern tourist with his camera, and the painter with his sketch-book ?

The book-learned Western critic starts with an *a priori* conviction that, because Buddhist and Hindu teachers have always regarded the ascetic life as the highest ideal and the shortest road to salvation, therefore there is ingrained in Indian thought generally a dislike and distrust of nature, incompatible with the aims of art, which have always warped the mind and paralysed the hand of the Indian artist, except when he was influenced by Hellenic traditions. This appears to be the view of Sir George Birdwood, who declares that "sculpture and painting, as fine arts, are unknown in India."[1] He fails to find in Indian art any examples of the "unfettered and impassioned realisation of the ideals within us, by the things without us"; and recently, in a violent denunciation of Indian sculpture in general, he characterised the Indian conception of Buddha as "a senseless similitude . . . vacuously squinting down its nose to its thumbs and knees and toes. A boiled suet pudding would serve equally well as a symbol of passionless purity and serenity of soul."[2] The illustrations I have given here and elsewhere of Hindu sculpture appear in his eyes "unshapely, unsightly, and portentous . . . for the most part mechanical bronzes and brasses and the merest Brummagem."

It is a misfortune for India that those who come forward as interpreters of her art to the West should be so constitutionally incapable of appreciating its highest ideals. It seems to me that those who refuse to recognise the intense love of nature with which Hindu thought is penetrated must miss entirely the beauty of the great Hindu poets, of Valmiki and Kalidâsa, as well as the beauty of Hindu art. For all Hindu poetry, music, and art reveal the profound insight into nature and the abiding love for it which have dominated Indian thought throughout its history. They seem, indeed, sometimes to strike notes too high and too deep for Western ears to hear; but this wider range of sense-perception is the special gift of the artist, poet, and musician.

The idea that the soul's salvation can be more speedily won by an ascetic life is, after all, no peculiarity of Hinduism, and the ascetic ideal had no more power to repress the free development of the fine arts in India than the monasticism of the Middle Ages had in Europe. Those who pursued that ideal in daily life were only the smallest fraction of the whole population; generally those whom misfortune, or some great loss or grief, had driven to seek consolation in retirement from the world. The respect with which they were treated did not prevent others from enjoying the amenities of life in full. Just as in medieval Europe the religious impulse which dominated the masses sought active expression in artistic works, in the building and adornment of innumerable temples, monasteries, rest-houses for pilgrims, bathing tanks, etc., to which they contributed, some by gifts of kind or money, some by their labour, some by dedicating their lives to the temple service. The extraordinary productiveness of Hindu art in its great creative period is sufficient in itself to prove a deep devotion to the study of nature, for creative

[1] "Industrial Arts of India" (Handbook of the Victoria and Albert Museum), part i. p. 125.
[2] *Journal of the Royal Society of Arts*, February 1910.

art can no more proceed from distrust or hatred of nature than music can proceed from an abhorrence of sound.

All art which is not purely eclectic and academic represents the attempt to probe into nature's secrets and relate them to human life and work. Thus all art which is vital and creative is as closely related to the study of nature as all true science and philosophy must always be.

"Puranic" art, or Indian Gothic, which Sir George Birdwood condemns wholesale, is Hindu science and philosophy allegorically interpreted by the great masters of India, in exactly the same way as the great musicians of modern Europe have used popular folk-music as the basis of musical drama. Puranic art is the idiomatic art of India, which hardly became truly Indian until it became Puranic. If it seems strange to Western minds, we should always remember that it was an art language perfectly intelligible to the people to whom it was addressed. It is the complete expression of the Indian conscious-ness at the height of its greatest intellectual, literary, and artistic activity ; and for any critic to affect to despise it is simply to exhibit his incapacity for approaching Indian art from the Indian point of view.

It is within the province of a critic to ridicule the work of an individual, of a clique, or of a school ; but it is presumption to condemn whole centuries of creative art—cen-turies which are mighty landmarks in the history of a great civilisation. The art of indi-viduals or of cliques may be perverse, but the art of a whole people cannot be wrong. It is a revelation of themselves—a part of the process of their spiritual evolution, and it cannot be wise for the nation which rules India to allow Indian art to be either ignored or misrepresented in its public museums.

According to Sir George Birdwood and most other Anglo-Indian writers, it was first the Greeks and afterwards the Muhammadans who infused into the Indian mind that love of nature which is necessary for the development of "fine art"—a most extraordinary misreading of Indian art-history. There is no phase of Indian art less free and spon-taneous than the decadent work of the Gandhara sculptors, and no Hindu canon was ever so blighting in its effect on the higher development of art, or so significant of a dis-trust and hatred of nature, as the ascetic law of Islam which forbade the representation of any living creature. Not until the rigour of that law was relaxed, when Islam became inspired by the nature-loving traditions of China and Hindustan, did Saracenic art rise to greatness. Both Greeks and Hindus were lovers of beauty. The former loved it for its own sake—for the refinement and abundance of joy which it brings into life ; the latter for the intimation it gives of a higher life than this—for life, to the Hindu artist, had a more profound significance than it had to the Greek. The sculptors who carved the great bull at Mâmallapuram and the elephants at Kanârak were as perfect masters of their art as the Greeks. Both the realism of such works as these and the idealism of the sublime Buddha at Anuradhapura, of the four-armed Siva of the Madras Museum (Plate 88), or of the four-headed Brahmâ at Leyden (Plate 86 C), proceed from a reverent and profound study of nature, and neither the one nor the other could have been achieved without it.

PLATE 105B

BAS-RELIEF FROM THE ENTRANCE TO CAVE XIX AT AJANTA

STUDENTS of Indian art are accustomed to think of the Ajanta caves as representing the great epoch of Buddhist painting, but they also furnish some of the most perfect examples of Indian sculpture and architectural design. Among them it would be difficult to find anything to surpass this exquisite sculptured group by the entrance of the most splendid of the chaitya-halls, known as No. XIX.

A Nâgâraja is sitting in the pose known as that of kingly ease, his head canopied by a great seven-headed cobra. His Queen, with a single cobra over her head and holding a lotus-flower in her left hand, is seated by his side ; a female attendant stands on his right. The King and Queen are draped in diaphanous garments, the ends of which fall over the roughly hewn seat. Very little is known of these Nâgâ people, serpent-worshippers converted to Buddhism, who figure so frequently in the paintings and sculptures of Ajanta, Amarâvatî, and elsewhere. They adopted the hooded serpent for their tribal ensign. Nâgâ dynasties, says Fergusson, ruled in various parts of Central India and Rajputana from the seventh century B.C. till at least the fourth century A.D. There were also mythical Nâgâ folk, half-human and half-serpentine in form, who dwelt in the depths of rivers, lakes, and seas, and inhabited Pâtâla, the regions below the earth. They were skilled in all magical arts, and their women were of surpassing loveliness. Many are the legends of their love for mortals, and how they lured them to their wondrous palaces beneath the waters glittering with crystal and gems.

Something of this feeling of mystery is reflected in this Ajanta sculpture, and something of the devotional spirit of Francesca's or Fra Angelico's paintings. The three figures are dominated by an overpowering sense of other-worldliness which fills body and soul and lifts them out of themselves. They might perhaps be listening in rapt attention to the chanting of the monks within the chaitya-hall, seeming to them like echoes of a celestial choir. Or perhaps the sound of many waters coming from the ravine strikes their ears like the voice of the Master whose teaching brought into their lives the fulness of divine content.

There is the same quality and the same degree of technical achievement in this sculpture as in the painting of the mother and child before Buddha in cave XVII. The genius of the artist is felt through the perfect revelation of his subconscious self rather than by the display of his scientific knowledge, the subjective expression dominating objective realities. In the one case the painter uses a sweeping brush-drawn line so intense and full of vitality that it needs only the slightest complement of colour and tone to perfect the æsthetic creation. Similarly, the sculptor, in concentrating himself upon the spiritual feeling of the subject, uses the boldest effects of chiaroscuro, and reduces all lines and modulations of surface to their simplest forms, so that no superfluous details distract the eye from the essential points of movement and expression. This does not imply any neglect of technical resources, but rather that supreme power of synthesis which is characteristic of all great art. Both the Indian painter and the sculptor lavish infinite care and skill upon necessary enrichments, such as the jewelled tiara and ornaments, just as the Indian singer will subtly accentuate a phrase with his grace-notes and quartertones.

The masterly treatment of the cobra's hood is a striking feature in this sculpture.

PLATE 106A

QUEEN MÂYÂ AND THE INFANT PRINCE SIDDHARTHA SLEEPING

THIS very remarkable piece of Buddhist sculpture is from the Baro temple in Central India, known as the Gadarmalka-Mandi. The temple itself was a medieval structure of about the eleventh century, but it was destroyed and rebuilt a century or two later. The date of the sculpture cannot, however, be determined with any certainty from the age of the building : it probably belonged to a much earlier Buddhist temple or monastery.

In dramatic feeling and wonderfully dignified treatment of his subject this Indian sculptor anticipated the style of the great Florentine masters. There is a grand harmony and repose in the gently undulating lines of Queen Mâyâ, sleeping with her infant pillowed by her side. The beatitude to which she was to attain in the Tusita heavens, seven days after her child's birth, already fills her soul ; a presentiment of the blessing and consolation which the Tathâgata was to bring to a suffering world, and of the infinite peace of Nirvana which would end the long cycle of his earthly lives. The rhythmic swell of a calm sea seems to be suggested in the wavy edge of the carpet in which the mother and child are resting.

The four female attendants standing alert by the Queen's side express perfectly in their attitudes their watchful attention and sense of high responsibility for the great trust committed to their charge. The very expressive figure of the other one who supports with tender solicitude her royal mistress's head rounds off the composition and strikes, as it were, the final chord with a deep note of human feeling.

PLATE 107A

HEAD OF A BODHISATTVA FROM JAVA

THE original of this plate is preserved in the Glyptotek at Copenhagen ; it was brought there from Java, probably from Bôrôbudûr.

Indian Art in Java has a character of its own which distinguishes it from that of the continent from whence it came. There runs through both the same strain of deep serenity, but in the divine ideal of Java we lose the austere feeling which characterises the Hindu sculpture of Elephanta and Mâmallapuram. There is more of human contentment and joy in Indo-Javanese art, an expression of that feeling of peaceful security which the Indian colonists enjoyed in their happy island home, after the centuries of storm and struggle which their forefathers had experienced on the mainland.

This is a head which, for its masterly generalisation of form and line might superficially be labelled Greek, but it is penetrated by a deep religious conviction totally different to that which inspired Hellenic ideals. We can feel that the sculptor in his generalisation was not content with formulating a type of physical perfection. He only used the formal beauty to reveal, as in a mirror, the pure soul of the Bodhisattva ; the release from the bondage of intellectual and physical strife ; the exaltation of the spirit that is purified from the dross of worldly desires; the penetration of a mind that sees through the veil of its earthly environment.

It is a face which incarnates the stillness of the depths of ocean; the serenity of an azure, cloudless sky; a beatitude beyond mortal ken. Yet in all its aloofness from human passion there is still some reflection of that divine compassion for struggling humanity which inspired the life and teaching of Sakya Muni.

PLATE 106B

THE "LINGA" SHRINE OF THE GREAT TEMPLE OF ELEPHANTA, BOMBAY

THE inner shrine, or *garbha*, of the great rock-cut temple of Elephanta contains the *lingam*, Siva's emblem, symbolising the reproductive powers of nature. The shrine itself, approximately cubical in form, symbolises the earth. It has four entrances, facing east, west, north, and south, each of which is guarded by two colossal figures, now badly mutilated, representing the protecting genii of the four cardinal and intermediate points. These majestic figures, each about fifteen feet in height, are among the finest sculptures at Elephanta. Equally noble in design are the massive columns which support the huge weights of the superincumbent rock. Their gourd-shaped capitals are similar to the so-called *amâlika* which crowns the curved spire of Hindu temples, and is probably derived from the fruit of the lotus-flower. The latter, as Count D'Alviella remarks,[1] symbolises less the sun itself than the solar matrix, the mysterious sanctuary into which the sun retires every evening, there to acquire fresh life.

PLATES 107B AND 108A

SIVA NÂTARÂJA, OR NATÊSA, LORD OF DANCERS

THE magnificent fragment from Elephanta shown in Plate 108A is the prototype of the South Indian bronzes of Siva as Nâtarâja, illustrated in Chapter V (Plate 88). Even in its present mutilated condition it is an embodiment of titanic power, a majestic conception of the Deity who for His pleasure sets the worlds innumerable in motion. Though the rock itself seems to vibrate with the rhythmic movement of the dance, the noble head bears the same look of serene calm and dispassion which illuminates the face of the Buddha. It belongs to the most virile period of Hindu sculpture, *i.e.* from the sixth to the eighth centuries, and in technical achievement marks its highest development. Like all the Elephanta sculptures, it was mutilated by Portuguese buccaneers in the sixteenth century, and has suffered much from subsequent neglect and vandalism.

The sculpture of the same subject from the Ravanaka-kai Cave at Ellora, Plate 107B, must belong to a somewhat later date. It is more florid in style and less accomplished in technique, though not less strong and expressive in its movement; and fortunately it has suffered less from mutilation than its great Elephanta prototype.

One of the charges which unsympathetic and uninformed critics frequently bring against Indian art is its want of originality in the unvarying repetition of traditional types. It is true that Indian artists, like the great masters of the West, always expressed themselves in the forms and conventions of artistic tradition—the art-language of the race. But it only shows ignorance of the subject to assert that they have always lacked creative power. In the great period of Indian sculpture, before the Muhammadan invasion, which is just that with which most European critics are least acquainted, it is only necessary to compare the different artistic developments which belong to different localities and different times to recognise that, in the treatment of traditional subjects, the individuality of the Indian artist always strongly asserts itself.

It will be obvious, in the case of these two typical examples of the same subject, only slightly varied in general lines and disposition of masses, how individual each one is in artistic expression, and how much they explain the religious atmosphere of the schools to which they belong.

The Elephanta sculpture reflects the lofty idealism and intellectuality of the Upanishads. At Ellora we feel more of the spirit of medieval priestcraft, with all its ritualistic pageantry and superstitious emotionalism. It shows us the corrupt state of Hinduism at the time when the great reformer Sankaracharya began his mission. Here Siva, with the hissing cobra as a girdle, and the grim skeleton of Death lurking behind him, is only the terrible Destroyer rejoicing in the dissolution of the worlds.

[1] "Migration of Symbols," p. 28.

A. Temple of Rājarāni at Bhuvaneshwar, part of the western facade.
(From a photograph in the India Office Library).

B. Pillar in the Siva Temple, Vellore.
(Photo, E. S. Mahalingam).

PLATE 109

UPPER PART OF ROCK-CUT TEMPLE AT KALUGUMALAI, TINNEVELLY DISTRICT—TEMPLE OF RÂJARÂNÎ (CIRCA A. D. 1000) AT BHUVANESHWAR, PURÎ: PART OF THE WESTERN FAÇADE

THE latest of the series of Dravidian rock-cut temples is in the extreme south of Madras, in the Tinnevelly district, at Kalugumalai. It has been dated by Fergusson at about the tenth or eleventh century, but from the style of the sculpture I am inclined to think this is a century too late. From an architectural point of view he rightly observes that, had it been finished, it would have been one of the most perfect gems of the style. From the sculptor's point of view no such qualifications need be made : the fact that it is unfinished rather adds to its interest.

Though the design is strictly architectural in form, it belongs technically entirely to the plastic or glyptic form of art, and the human figure plays as important a part in it as it does in many masterpieces of Renaissance monumental sculpture. Very few critics will refuse to admit the extraordinary technical skill displayed in planning out and carving a complex form of such dimensions from a ridge of granite rock. There are some, however, who would deny the existence of any scientific or intellectual basis in Eastern art. A writer in *The Edinburgh Review*, in an article on "Eastern Art and Western Critics,"[1] asserts that "every kind of manifestation, scientific, political, literary, of order, discipline, and coherence will be looked for in Eastern life in vain"—his impressions of Eastern life being derived from three years passed among the Tamil coolies and Cingalese villagers of Ceylon. "It would be easy to show," he affirms, "that Western civilisation, Western knowledge and science and thought and literature, and also Western politics and government and methods of colonising and ruling—in short, the Western influence in all its effects—has been of a distinctly intellectual and rational quality, and has been closely identified with the establishment of order, discipline, coherence—in a word, with the vindication in all things of the principle of form" : his thesis being that the intellectual West has, in the domain of art, spoken in terms of form, the emotional East in terms of colour.

The distinction he draws is a wholly imaginary one. Even in pictorial art the Oriental has always relied upon line rather than upon colour, as a means of self-expression ; and line, if it expresses anything, expresses form. Colour was always used by the great artists of the East as a subordinate instrument, to accentuate and develop the forms which the line expressed.

Again, Indian art, in its greatest achievements, is more concerned with sculpture and architecture than with painting. How, then, does this colour-theory apply to it, more than to Greek sculpture and architecture ?

It is, in fact, difficult to draw a hard-and-fast distinction between Western and Eastern art, because there have been periods in which the West has gone over to the East, and *vice-versâ*. But, in the true Eastern ideal, form is used merely as a vehicle for self-realisation. The West, more idolatrous than the East, often regards the realisation of form as the end of art.

The idea of Indian art as a nebulous, chaotic mass of glowing colour, charged with emotion, may give a sufficiently clear indication of the critic's Eastern impressions, but his sweeping generalisations will be astonishing to any one who has realised how deeply all Indian life and culture, even to the lowest strata, have been permeated by the teachings of the philosophical schools. It was the work of the great universities of Northern India to co-ordinate the artistic traditions of the heterogeneous racial elements which composed Indian society at that time, to rationalise them and use them for the

[1] No. 344, October 1910.

interpretation of the esoteric teachings of philosophy and religion.   The men who created Indian art were not, as the Western academic critic assumes, of an inferior intellectual calibre to the poets, philosophers, and religious teachers; for art was not then, as it is now, a specialised study divorced from religion and ignored by the universities. It was an integral part of national life and thought.   To assert that Indian art has failed to interpret Indian thought is a contradiction in terms : for no art can live for more than twenty centuries which fails to express the intellectuality of a people.   But there are evidently still some critics who, like Macaulay, refuse to admit the intelligence of Eastern races: who, because Indian art seems to them obscure, will deny that it satisfactorily expresses what its creators intended.

It is a common view of Indian art to regard it as undisciplined, incoherent, and without any intellectual foundation; an assumption only proceeding from our profound ignorance of all aspects of Indian culture, of its history and scientific principles.

We still cling foolishly and arrogantly to the belief that, by totally ignoring the living traditions of Indian art, and by teaching Indian students anatomy, perspective, "model drawing," and the orders of classic architecture, we are fulfilling our intellectual mission in the East; and this we do in sublime ignorance of the fact that Indian art has its scientific principles and laws of form as clear, precise, and intelligent as the æsthetic formularies of Greece, or as the grammar and syntax of its classical language, Sanskrit.

The assumed antagonism between the root principles of Hellenic art and Indian comes, to a large extent, from our modern empirical methods of applying them.   It is open to question how far our admiration for Greek art is based upon a deep intuitive sympathy for the highest æsthetic qualities which the Greeks themselves admired and strove to realise, and how far it is influenced by inherited tendencies towards Puritanical plainness and whitewash, by academic prepossessions of the mind inculcated by generations of classical schoolmasters, and by pride in the belief that the mechanism of the Greek æsthetic is known to us and can be applied by ourselves with such facility as modern European art and architecture indicate.

It is easy to imagine what an uproar there would be if some mischievous sprite with a magic wand were suddenly to restore the Elgin marbles in the British Museum to their pristine condition, give to the classical statues which originally had it the final coat of coloured wax (which to the Greeks represented an art higher than that of the sculptor), and added to the model of the Parthenon all the richness of its painted decoration which it had in the days of Pericles.   How classical scholars and critics would blaspheme and denounce the emotional barbarians who dared to desecrate the purity and intellectuality of the art of Hellas with an oriental paint-pot!   Their classical ideal would be lowered to the level of an Indian pagoda! Certainly it is the limitations, rather than the merits, of Greek art, its simplicity rather than its nobility and refinement, which make it appeal so strongly to the man in the street, the building contractor, and the amateur artist or architect.   And it is equally certain that, while very few Western critics have gained their knowledge of Indian art at first hand, the recognised exponents of it, unconscious of their own limitations, have been its chief detractors.

The Greeks themselves, I have no doubt, would have scoffed at academic distinctions between "fine" art and "decorative" : they would have given unstinted praise to the sculpture at Kalugumalai, and recognised in the Sun-temple at Mudherâ, in Gujerat, an art not less perfect than their own.   Nor would they have denied the intellectuality in the decorative scheme in Plate 109A from the Râjarânî temple at Bhuvaneshwar, in Orissa. What their comments would be on the "classical" art which we substitute for Indian in Calcutta public buildings may well be imagined.

If Greece, at the time of her greatest artistic development, had established a permanent empire in India, and all the wealth of Indian nature, with its infinite suggestions, had been revealed to her mind; if Vedic culture had been added to the philosophy of Pythagoras and Plato; I cannot conceive that Indian art would have taken a very different course to that which it actually followed. It is impossible to believe that Greek æsthetic thought would not in such a case have responded to the influence of its environment, as art in its very nature must do; that her architecture would not then have reflected something of the wild grandeur of the tropical forest, as well as the trim beauty of the olive and cypress grove ; and that, with a wider experience of life, the sculpture of her pantheon would not have acquired a more profound metaphysic than that represented by the gods and goddesses of the Parthenon.

After all, invidious comparisons between different schools of artistic thought are altogether unprofitable.   It is futile to discuss whether the lily be more beautiful than the rose; and if intellectuality were the only quality in art, the most perfect æsthetic might be found in a correct solution to a problem in compound proportion. The real issue, which my critics persistently evade or try to confuse, is not an academic one—whether from an intellectual standpoint Indian art should or should not seem great in Western eyes— but a practical and vital one, whether, because we think our own art finer, we are justified in exterminating that which belongs to Indian civilisation.   Does a good gardener, because he loves the lilies best, uproot all the roses ?   In India we propagate the weeds, and let the roses die.

The absorbing interest of Indian art, to all artists in the West, must always lie not so much in the magnificence of its ancient monuments as in the fact that such exquisite art as that of the Râjarânî temple, unapproached by any Western architectural sculpture of modern times, represents a living tradition still practised by large numbers of Indian craftsmen.   If there were any sound artistic or scientific principles in our educational methods, India would need no schools to stimulate such a grand tradition into new life : or even if we would leave things alone, and not pretend to teach, Indian art would still be better off.

The folly of the present departmental system is that, with such a tradition still alive, with numbers of such master craftsmen still obtainable, we allow Indian revenues to be spent in producing mechanical imitations of Gothic or Renaissance sculpture at ten or twenty times the cost of good Indian art ; and this, forsooth, because some Western doctrinaires believe that Indian sculpture is not "fine" !

PLATE 109B

A CARVED PILLAR INSIDE THE SIVA TEMPLE (KALYANA MANDAPA) VELLORE, MADRAS

THIS is a superb example of Dravidian architectural sculpture attributed to the middle of the fourteenth century.   Essentially Gothic in feeling, it will bear comparison with the best work of the cathedral craftsmen of medieval Europe.   Dravidian art reflects the wild luxuriance and mysterious beauty of those dense jungles of Southern India, haunted by *rakshasas* and fearsome beasts, through which Râma and his faithful monkey allies forced their way to rescue Sîtâ from her prison in the stronghold of the demon-king, Ravana.

In the wonderful pillared halls attached to the temples of Southern India is concentrated, as it were, the essence of the beauty of a tropical forest, perfectly ordered to fulfil architectonic and æsthetic purposes.   No one who has not seen them can have any conception of their great beauty and perfect art.

It is, of course, a defect inherent in the quality of art such as this, that in its romantic imaginativeness and the energy of its creative power it has a tendency to become sometimes incoherent, and to lose the sense of co-ordination and æsthetic unity.   But this is only to say that all art in its decadence converts its own merit into an offence, just as a beautiful body from which life has departed begins to putrefy.   One might just as well blame Nature herself, and say that her tropical moods cannot inspire great art, as charge Indian sculpture generally with incoherency.

It is only because Indian sculpture is solely judged in England from the few fragments promiscuously thrown together at South Kensington and the British Museum that a keen and cultured art critic like Mr. Roger Fry can write of the difficulties of an approach to the understanding of Indian art as follows: "It is rather the curious incoherence —for to us it appears such—of Indian sculpture, its want of any large co-ordination, of any sense of relative scale.   In its choice of relief and of the scale of ornament it appears without any principle.   It is like a rococo style deprived of the lightness and elegance which alone make that style tolerable.   Such a treatment implies for our minds a fundamental conflict between the notion and its expression; for these heavily ornate reliefs —one cannot but have in mind the Amarâvatî sculptures of the British Museum—are intended apparently to convey notions of grave religious import, and such ideas are for us inevitably connected with a certain type of line, with a certain austerity in the treatment of a design, with large unperturbed surfaces or great and clearly united sequences of plane."[1]

Such criticism may be perfectly just as applied to the particular instance cited ; the error lies in taking the Amarâvatî sculptures as typical of the best Indian art.   Even in this case it is necessary to remember that these reliefs were originally painted, and the total effect of them, *in situ*, in the brilliant Indian sunshine, can hardly be judged in their present position on the staircase of the British Museum.

[1] *Quarterly Review*, January 1910.

INDEX

PART I : INDIAN SCULPTURE AND PAINTING

Ajantā, paintings at, 11, 33, 68-72, 74, 91
Akbar's painters, 72, 81-83, 84, 87
Akbar-nāma, 82, 89
Akota, 35
Amarāvatī sculptures, 33, 38, 42-45
Ankhor Vat, 47, 56
Anuradhapura, Buddha figure at, 11
Asoka, 33, 35, 38-9, 40, 41
Aurangzīb, 86, 92, 93

Bagh, paintings at, 11, 74, 81
Baldwin, Mr. Stanley, 32, 102
Bāz Bahādur, 92
Bhagavad Gītā, 21-22
Bhārhut, sculptures at, 36, 38, 40-41
Bichitr, 88, 91
Binyon, Mr. Laurence, 6, 71
Birdwood, Sir G., 5
Bitpalo, 35
Bodhisattvas, images of, 14, 58
Bombay School, 102
Boole, George, 27
Borobudur, 11, 12, 46-54, 58
Buddha, image of, 14, 15, 42, 59; painting of, 71-72

Calcutta School, 103-109
Calligraphy, 87
Cambodia, 47, 56
Chidambaram temple, 21, 29
Chinese painting, 79
Chitra-salas, 65, 80, 89, 104
Cousins, Dr. J. H., 108
Craftsmen, 77-78
Curzon, Lord, 104, 105

Dance of Siva, 16, 27-30, 74
Dārā Shikoh, 85, 89
Delhi, New, 65, 99, 103
Devapāla, 35
Dey, Mr. Mukul Chandra, 70
Dharma, 17
Dharmapāla, image of, 22
Dhiman, 35
Dhyānas, 16
Dhyanī-Buddha, 12
Durgā, image of, 18, 23

Education, Indian, 99
Elephanta sculptures, 24
Ellora sculptures, 23-25

Fazl, Abul, 81-82, 87
Fergusson, James, 40, 41
Foucher, M., 14, 72
Fresco buono, 72, *appendix*

Gandhāran art, 8, 11, 12, 14-15, 45, 57
Ganesha, images of, 29-30
Gangoly, Mr. O. C., 31, 106
Ganguly, Mr. Surendra Nath, 109
Ghiberti gates, 49, 50
Ghose, Mr. Asit, 76
Ghulām, 88
Goloubeff, M. Victor, 71, 72
Gothic art, 7, 78
Griffiths, Mr. J., 70

Haldar, Mr. Asit Kumar, 74, 108
Hashim, Mir, 89
Himalayas, 8, 11, 47
Hindu painters, 91-96, 98

Impressionism, Indian, 92

Jahāngīr, 83-85, 89
Jain school, 69, 70
Java, sculpture in, 17, 23, 30, 58
Jouveau-Dubreuil, Professor, 72, 73

Kailāsa, Mt., 8, 10, 11, 12, 28, 46 47; temple, 23; of the human body, 28
Kālī, 18, 75
Kanārak, temple at, 32, 60
Kangra school of painting, 74
Kashmir school of painting, 35
Kramrisch, Dr., 76
Kutb Shah, Sultan Muhammad, portrait of, 89

Lakhanas, 16
Lecoq, Dr. von, 68

Mahābhārata, 8, 10, 11, 33
Mahā-kundali, 27-28
Mānasarovara, Lake, 8
Manjusri, image of, 18, 23
Manohar, 91
Mansur, Ustād, 90-91
Mantra, 16
Marshall, Sir John, 32, 72
Mogul paintings, 77-91
Mohenjo-Daro, 58
Murad, Prince, 88

Nādānta dance, 27-29
Nākhon Vat, 56
Nālanda University, 44-45
Natārāja, 14, 18, 27-29, 31
Nivedita, Sister, 21

Orissan school of sculpture, 60; modern, 32, 101

Padmapāni, image of, 12
Pala schools, 35, 69
"Pat" drawings, 76
Peshawar, stupa at, 11
Prajñāpāramitā, image of, 17
Prambānam sculptures, 55-56

Qudsi, Muhammad Jam, portrait of, 88

Rāgas, 16
Rajasthani painting, 114-118
Ramāyana, 33
Realism in art, 6, 10, 94-95
Rembrandt, 85
Rodin, Auguste, 29
Ronaldshay, Lord, 104, 105, 106
Ruskin, 6, 8, 61

Sānchī sculptures, 41-42
Sankarāchārya, 21, 97
Sarasvati, 16
Sarnath, 58
Shah Jahān, 85, 89
Shāktas, 18

Shakti, 16
Shapur of Khurasan, 80-81
Sigiri paintings, 11, 73-74
Sittannavāsal paintings, 72-73
Siva, images of, 14, 17, 18, 21, 27-29
Siva-Sīmantinī, 107
Smith, Dr. Vincent, 72
Sringadhara, 35
Sudarsana-Chakra, 12
Sukrāchārya, 20, 57
Swastika dance, 29
Symbolism of colour, 75-76

Tagore, Dr. Abanindra Nath, 32, 72, 96, 103-107
Taine, H., 5, 6
Tāj Mahall, 99, 100
Tāla, 16
Tārā, image of, 17
Tāranath, history of, 32-34, 35
Tibetan painting, 75
Triangle, symbolism of, 12, 13, 16
Trimurti, image of, 17

Universities, Indian, 44-45, 99, 102

Vajrapāni, image of, 14
Vishnu, 12, 18, 24-25

Western Indian painting, 69-70
Woodroffe, Sir John, 18, 27

Yantras, 10, 12-13, 16, 18, 27, 34
Yazdani, Mr. G., 71
Yoga, 7, 8, 10, 27-28, 29, 109-110
Yogi, The Divine, 8, 10, 11, 12, 16, 46

PART II : THE IDEALS OF INDIAN ART

Abu, Mount, 174
Adi-Buddha, 138, 145
Agni, 128
Ahamkara, 185
Airavata, the elephant, 184
Ajanta paintings, 136, 168, 175, 190
Ajanta, sculptures at, 189-190
Akbar, 170, 178-179
Amalika, the, 192
Amaravatī sculptures, 131, 132, 136, 143, 167, 196
Amrita, 128, 149
Angelico, Fra, 135
Angkor, temple at, 149, 177
Animals in Indian art, 160
Anuradhapura, statue at, 138, 189
Apparswami, statuette of, 168
Apsarasas, 148, 149
Arjuna, 146, 183-185
Art, aim of Indian, 134, 137, 140, 168
Art, living Indian, 170, 171, 179, 195
Art-philosophy, 125, 134-135
Art, Puranic, 189
Art, Saracenic, 130, 170, 189
Art-teaching, 134, 140, 171, 195
Aryan antipathy to idols, 126, 129
Aryan philosophy, 130
Asanas, 144
Asoka, 131
Asokan sculpture, 132
Asuras, 148, 149, 186
Aura, 143-144
Aurangzîb, 170, 175, 176, 178, 179
Avataras of Vishnu, 154, 185
Avidhya, 145

Bain, Mr., 159, 160
Beauty in nature and art, 134-135
"Bhagavad-Gita," 146
Bhakti-marga, 165
Bharhut, *stupa* of. 131, 160
Binyon, Mr. Laurence, 141-142, 169

Birdwood, Sir George, 132, 164, 188-189
Bodhisattvas, 138, 145
Borobudur sculptures, 168, 175
Brahma, 150, 151, 152, 154, 159
Brahmanas, ritual of the, 126, 127
Buddha, attributes of, 136
Buddha, enlightenment of, 136, 137
Buddhism in China, 141-142

Chakra of Visnu, 153
Chalukyan architecture, 161
Chartres, sculpture at, 135
Chinese art, 132, 138, 139, 141, 176
Chitrasalas, 176, 177
Chitrasena, 184
Chittor, towers of victory at, 173
Churning of the Ocean, 148-149
Cimabue, 135
Cobra, emblem of Siva, 153
Conch-shell of Vishnu, 153, 157, 186
Coomaraswamy, Dr., 138
Creation, Hymn of, 150
Creation, legend of, 159, 160
Cretan art, 135
Critics, Western, 193-195
Cross, the cosmic, 151, 153

Daksha, 156
D'Alviella, Count G., 164, 192
Davids, Mrs. Rhys, 160
Dhanwantari, 149
Dharma, 187
Dhyani-Bodhisattvas, 138, 145
Dhyani-Buddhas, 138, 145
Divine form, 150
Divine Ideal in woman, 161
Divine Ideal, the Indian, 134-137, 143-149
Draupadi, 162, 163
Durga, 159

Eclectic period, 129-133
Egg of the Universe, 147
Egyptian art, 135
Elephanta sculptures, 153, 191-192
Ellora sculptures, 153, 192

Fazl, Abul, 170
Feminine beauty, 160
Fry, Mr. Roger, 196

Gadha, or mace of Vishnu, 153, 186
Gandhara sculpture, 29, 131, 132, 133, 155, 189
Gandharvas, the, 185
Gandiva, Arjuna's bow, 185
Ganesha, 144, 155, 157
Geometric symbolism, 157
Gods, dwelling-places of the, 166
Grierson, Dr., 165
Gunas, 150, 151, 154, 185

Hellenic art, 194-195
Hellenic ideal, 135
Hînayana doctrine, 136
History, Indian, 172-179
Hymn of Creation, 150

Ideal, the Divine, 134-137, 143-149, 161 ; in woman, 161
Ideal, the physical, 135-136
Images, classification of, 151
Images, prohibition of, 174, 176
Indra, 148, 149, 183, 184
Innes, Mr. E. R., 143
Intuition, 126, 138
Ishvara, 150
Ittagi, temple at, 161

Jains, the, 143, 173-174
Japanese art, 139
Jatakas, the, 173, 175
Java, Indian art in, 152, 153, 191

Kali, 145, 147, 159
Kailasa temple at Ellora, 188
Kalidasa, 135, 161, 162, 163, 186
Kalugumalai, temple at, 193
Kama, 144
Kamthaka, the horse, 167
Kanarak, elephants at, 187
Kao-huang, 143
Karna, 135
Karttikeya, 155
Kauravas, the, 183
Keynote of Asiatic art, 126
Krishna, 143, 146, 148, 168, 178
Kuruvatti, temple at, 161, 162
Kuvera, 184

Lakkundi, temple at, 97
Lakshanas, or beauty marks, 162
Lakshmi, 149, 161, 186
Lalita Vistara, the, 143
Lingam, the, 158, 191
Lokapalas, the, 131, 132

Mahabharata, the, 135, 137, 143, 148
    162, 173, 177
Mahayana doctrine, 136
Mahayana ritual, 139-140
Maha-yogi, 139
Mahendravarman I., 183
Maitreya, 145
Makara, 164
Mamallapuram sculptures, 154, 177
    183-189
Mandara, 148, 149
Manu, laws of, 157
Mara, 137
Marks of beauty, 162, 163
Maya, Queen, 190, 191
Minoan art, 135
Mnemonic system, 140
Mogul art, 170-171, 178-179, 189
Moksha, 165
Mudhera, temple at, 178, 194
Mudras, 139-140, 144

Nagarjuna, 136
Nagas, the, 184, 185, 190
Nandi, Siva's bull, 187
Narayana, 150, 151
Narayana-Vishnu, 150
Nataraja, 155, 189, 192
Nature, Indian love of, 165-166,
    187-189

Okakura, Mr., 125
Origin of Indian art, 125-128
Outlook upon nature, 166-167

Painting, Hindu, 170
Paintings at Ajanta, 136, 168, 175,
    190
Palitana, temples at, 174
Pandavas, the, 166, 183
Parijata tree, 148
Parm symbol, 157
Parvati, 156, 159, 161-162
Patañjali, 136
Paths, the Three, 165-171
Persepolitan art, 131
Pillar of the Universe, 152, 153
Prajna, 138, 161
Prakriti, 67, 143, 150
Puranic Art, 189
Puritanism in art, 126, 127
Purusha, 66, 77, 143, 150, 154

Quran, the, 147

Radha, 168
Rajarani, temple of, 194, 195
Rajasik images, 151
Rakshasas, 195
Rama, exile of, 166
Ramayana, the, 127, 177
Reincarnation, belief in, 167
Rheims, sculpture at, 135
Rig-veda, the, 150, 166

Saivaites, the, 176-177
Sakas, the, 131
Sakti, 150, 159, 186
Salvation by works, 142
Sanchî, sculptures at, 131, 132, 160,
    163, 167
Sandhya, 139, 151
Sandilya, aphorisms of, 165
Sankaracharya, 176
Saracenic art, 130
Saraswati, 159
Sati, 153
Sattvik images, 151
Sauwastika, the, 151
Sea of Milk, 148
Sectarian disputes, 128
Sesha, the serpent, 150
Sevenfold Office, the, 139
Sex symbolism, 157, 158
Shelley and Yoga, 140
Siddhartha, Prince, 143, 167, 190, 191
Silpa Sastras, 169
Siva, 146, 150, 151, 153, 154,, 155,
    157, 183,-185, 192
Siva and Daksha, 156
Smith, Mr. Vincent, 132, 175
Spirals, symbolism of, 157
Sri-vatsa, mark of Vishnu, 185
Stupa, symbolism of the, 131, 158

Subjectivity of art, 129, 134
Sukracharya, 134
Sundara Murti Swami, statuette
    of, 168
Sun-worship, 131, 178
Superman, the Indian, 135-136
Surabhi, 148
Surya, 151
Swastika, the, 151, 153
Symbolism, evolution of, 147, 148

Taj Mahal, the, 169, 170
Tamasik images, 151
Tandavan, Sîva's dance, 155, 162
Tara, 161
Taranatha, 155
Tre, symbolism of the, 131, 153
Tree, the cosmic, 153
Triangles, symbolism of, 157
Trimurti, the, 150-158
Tripura, 155
Tusita Heavens, 191
Twashtri, 159

Uma, 156, 159
Unity of creation, 166, 167
Unity of Indian thought, 128
Universities, Indian, 134-142, 193
Upavita, 152
Ûrna, 143, 144

Vac, the Divine Word, 126
Vahan, 151, 152
Vaishnavaites, the, 174, 177
Varaha incarnation, 185
Varuna, 184
Varunî, 148
Vasistha, sacrifice of, 127
Vedas, sacredness of the, 126
Vedic influence in Indian art, 129, 132
Vedic period, 125-128
Vellore, carved pillar at, 195-196
Vishnu, 128, 147, 148, 150, 153, 157,
    185-186
Vishnu, attributes of, 185-186
Vishnu, incarnations of, 154, 185
Vishnu, three steps of, 154, 158, 185

Waist, narrow, 135
Woman, the Indian, 91-93, 159-160

Yama, 184
Yoga, austerities of, 183-184
Yoga, Indian art and, 136-140
Yoga philosophy, 136, 137
Yudhisthira, 166, 183
Yueh,-chi, the, 131